The Margins of
City Life

ENGLISH CHANNEL

PAS-
DE-CALAIS

NORD

SOMME

AISNE

ARDENNES

MOSELLE

BAS
RHIN

Ingouville
Le Havre

SEINE-
INFÉRIEURE

OISE

Reims

MEUSE

MEURTHE

MANCHE   CALVADOS

EURE

Paris

SEINE-
ET-MARNE

MARNE

ORNE

SEINE-
ET-OISE

AUBE

VOSGES

FINISTÈRE   CÔTES-DU-
NORD

EURE-
ET-LOIR

HAUTE
MARNE

HAUT
RHIN

ILLE-ET-
VILAINE

MAYENNE

SARTHE

LOIR-ET-
CHER

LOIRET

YONNE

HAUTE
SAONE

MORBIHAN

MAINE-
ET-LOIRE

INDRE-
ET-LOIRE

CHER

NIÈVRE

CÔTE-D'OR

DOUBS

LOIRE-
INFÉRIEURE

VENDÉE

DEUX-
SEVRES

Châtellerault

INDRE

ALLIER

SAÔNE-
ET-LOIRE

JURA

La Roche-sur-Yon

Poitiers

VIENNE

Mâcon
AIN

HAUTE
SAVOIE
(1860)

ATLANTIC
OCEAN

CHARENTE-
INFÉRIEURE

HAUTE
VIENNE

CREUSE

PUY-DE-
DOME

RHÔNE

Lyon

SAVOIE
(1860)

CHARENTE

CORREZE

LOIRE

ISÈRE

DORDOGNE

CANTAL

HAUTE
LOIRE

GIRONDE

Bordeaux

LOT-ET-
GARONNE

LOT

ARDECHE

DROME

HAUTES
ALPES

LOZÈRE

BASSES
ALPES

LOT-ET-
GARONNE

LANDES

AVEYRON

GARD

VAUCLUSE

TARN-ET-
GARONNE

TARN

Nîmes

VAR

ALPES-
MARITIMES
(1860)

GERS

HAUTE
GARONNE

HERAULT

Marseille

BASSES
PYRENEES

AUDE

BOUCHES-
DU-RHÔNE

ARIEGE

Perpignan

Mediterranean
Sea

CORSE

HAUTES
PYRENEES

PYRENEES
ORIENTALES

Rhine R.

Seine R.

Garonne R.

Loire R.

Rhône R.

**FRANCE IN THE
NINETEENTH CENTURY**

The
MARGINS
of
CITY LIFE

Explorations on the French Urban Frontier, 1815–1851

John M. Merriman

New York   Oxford
Oxford University Press
1991

Oxford University Press

Oxford   New York   Toronto
Delhi   Bombay   Calcutta   Madras   Karachi
Petaling Jaya   Singapore   Hong Kong   Tokyo
Nairobi   Dar es Salaam   Cape Town
Melbourne   Aukland

and associated companies in
Berlin   Ibadan

Library of Congress Cataloging-in-Publication Data

Merriman, John M.
The margins of city life : explorations on the French urban
frontier, 1815–1851 / John M. Merriman.
p. cm. Includes bibliographical references.
ISBN 0–19–506438–0
1. Suburbs—France—History—19th century.
2. Marginality, Social—France—History—19th century.
3. Neighborhood—France—History—19th century.
4. Suburban life—France—History—19th century.   I. Title.
HT352.F8M47   1991   307.74′0944—dc20   90–34841

Frontispiece: France in the nineteenth century, with principal cities
and towns discussed in the text.

1 3 5 7 9 8 6 4 2

Printed in the United States of America
on acid-free paper

For Carol

Preface

Earlier research on the city of Limoges helped focus my attention on the role of the faubourgs in the emergence of workers as contenders for political power. I do not know exactly when I first became interested in the edge of the city. My experiences with the world of French *banlieues* were limited. When I was doing research for my dissertation, I was fortunate enough to have friends living in Le Perreux-sur-Marne in the eastern suburbs of Paris. Living in Paris and spending a good deal of time in Limoges, Guéret, and Tulle, I did not know much about the capital's suburbs or those of any other French city. But I had been struck by the ways in which French, indeed European, suburbs differed so fundamentally from American suburbs. The suburbs of Paris seemed not only vast—vaster by far than the city of light itself—but unfamiliar and vaguely threatening from what I had heard about them, at least from affluent Parisians.

While working in the Limousin, I returned to Paris on weekends and stayed in Le Perreux. One night, eating and drinking with a friend in town, I gave up, for the sake of another glass of wine or two, the last métro to the place de la Nation and the connection for the métro express (RER), and, finally, a bus from Nogent-sur-Marne. That left me at the old bar Le Petit Pont—no longer recognizable, having been completely rebuilt—near the Seine at about two in the morning without any way to get home. I walked to Nation, a manageable trek, but then was faced with getting from there to Le Perreux; furthermore, having deprived myself of public transportation, I didn't even know where Le Perreux was. I hitchhiked, getting a ride beyond Vincennes. Nor did my benefactors know how to find Le Perreux. After several communes had flashed by, they deposited me near where we thought it might be. Although there were lots of houses about, it seemed like the middle of nowhere. I began to walk, hoping to find a reassuring sign.

After a while I came upon a green and white bus parked on a wide street. The bus was evidently out of service; in those days no buses ran at night in the suburbs, or even in Paris itself. But inside the bus was a bus driver, in uniform and cap, sitting in the driver's seat, reading. I still do not know why he was there—perhaps a family problem. In any case, he seemed perfectly content to be reading. I walked up to the driver's window and asked him if the bus was in service. He replied, logically enough and a little scornfully, "Of course not!" Then I asked him if he could tell me how to get to Le Perreux. It was a good distance, he said, and pointed me in the right direction. I then set off along the right road, running. About five minutes later, hearing a horn beep, I looked back to see a bus—the same bus—looming just behind me. "Montez, chef," said the driver. He then asked where I was going in Le Perreux and drove me there, having to back up to make the turn in the right direction on the boulevard d'Alsace-Lorraine. He took me right to the door. I didn't know how to thank him and, perhaps a little deadened by bad wine, hesitantly began to take a bus ticket out of my pocket as if to cancel it. The driver laughed. A ticket wasn't necessary. I thanked him. He drove off, probably to continue reading somewhere. As in most of France, the suburbs had proved very welcoming indeed.

As geographic marginalization—the relegation to the periphery of unwanted activities and people—is a salient theme of this book, it seems appropriate, though somewhat sad, to report that during the years I have been working in departmental archives, they, too, have been peripheralized. Arguably one of the reasons that quaint old buildings in the center of town have been abandoned has been to provide more storage space for ever expanding archival holdings, more tables and seats for *chercheurs,* and even parking places to accommodate a larger clientele, particularly local people and tourists undertaking genealogies. Unfortunately many of the newly built departmental archives are structures of questionable taste, completely *privé d'âme*—without soul or character—like the one on an upper floor of a modern tower near the station in Alençon. At a time when those embracing the popularity of techniques borrowed from literary criticism seek to marginalize—or at least relegate to the bin of the old-fashioned—research into the lives of real people in space and time, physical access to French archives has in some places become more difficult.

During the last ten years or so, while studying French cities in the first half of the nineteenth century, I noted that the Archives Départementales of Haute-Vienne moved from its convenient and cozy locale in the center of Limoges to the outskirts of town, near the university. The Archives Départementales of the Pyrénées-Orientales had already moved outside Perpignan, near the rather pleasant housing development of the Moulin-à-Vent. As the archives still close for two hours at lunchtime—a quaint but vanishing tradition I happen to like—those without a car must take the bus into town to find something to eat. Other departmental archives now relegated to the periphery include the Nord, one of the first to be placed relatively far from town, though not an unpleasant bus ride from the center of Lille; Deux-Sèvres, now a stiff walk up the hill from Niort; Hérault, a bus ride from Montpellier; Bas-Corse on the bleak, distant outskirts of Ajaccio; Sarthe, so far from the center of Le Mans and difficult to find as to give the impression of being cleverly hidden; Doubs, a sizable trip from Besançon, with access through a parking lot at the Mammouth supermarket; Calvados, equally far from Caen, near virtually nothing except the isolated university and the freeway; and that *grand champion* of inconvenience, the Archives Départementales of the Haute-Marne in the commune of Choigne beyond Chaumont, beyond a garbage dump, not even near a bus. Genealogists usually have cars, yet some older people and most students do not. And so on.

Still, at least some centrally located, charming, even relatively intimate archives remain, such as those in Nîmes, Poitiers, and Rodez; Dijon, where Mozart once gave a concert in the elegant room now serving as the *salle de lecture;* in the Palais des Papes at Avignon (but surrounded by the increasingly greedy commercialization of tourism); Auch, less than a tempting block away from André Daguin's restaurant, the Hôtel de France; the tiny reading room of the archives of the Alpes-de-Haute-Provence in Digne; the modest facilities of the Creuse in Guéret; Eure-et-Loire, in the shadow of the cathedral of Chartres, on the street named after the memorable Cardinal Pie; the Indre-et-Loire archives in the quarter of Tours depicted by Balzac; the hopelessly crowded but livable archives of the Maine-et-Loire in Angers; the Isère archives in Grenoble, which serve as something of a *club du troisième âge* in the afternoon; the magnificent Grande Ecurie adjacent to the château de Versailles, home of the Archives Départementales des Yvelines; the Dordogne archives in Périgueux; and the Lozère archives in Mende. Other *déménagements* and *travaux* are recently completed or under way in Clermont-Ferrand, La Rochelle, Saint-Brieuc, and many other places since I have worked there. Even greater convenience for the user, in some ways, does not make up for the lost charm and intimacy of the old archives. At least the documents themselves are still there, if sometimes relegated to the periphery of urban life.[1]

I am grateful to the following friends, who read parts of the manuscript, engaged me in discussion, or made bibliographic suggestions: Christopher Johnson, Robert Herbert, Steven Kaplan, Peter McPhee, Alan Forrest, Susan Kent, Keith Luria, Michael Burns, Patrick Geary, Elinor Accampo, Robert Schulman, Peter Sahlins, Johan Åhr, Susanna Barrows, Judy Coffin, Josef Konvitz, and Joby Margadant. The manuscript particularly benefited from Ted W. Margadant's close, thoughtful reading. Charles Tilly, as usual, helped the author keep the forest in mind as well as the trees. Peter Gay, colleague and friend, listened to much of the book over countless lunches and read the manuscript with care. Many thanks in general to other friends at Yale: Roberto González-Echevarría, Jonathan Spence, Ivo Banac, Richard Brodhead, Peter Brooks, John Blum, Robin Winks, Piotr Wandycz, David Montgomery, William Parker, James Scott, Victoria Johnson, David Marshall, David Weir, David Brion Davis, Jeffrey Burds, George Priest, Jessica Johnson, and, last but hardly least, Larue Brion; and in France to Jeanne and John Innes, Edward Rohrbach, Richard Van Ham, Jean-Claude Petilon, Roger Chartier, Michelle Perrot, Patrice Bourdelais, Jean-Luc Pinol, and especially Yves and Colette Lequin and Maurice and Marie-Claude Garden.

The early stage of my research for this book was funded by a Guggenheim Memorial Fellowship. Subsequent research was facilitated by a full leave of absence graciously made possible by the late former president of Yale, A. Bartlett Giamatti, who has left so many friends behind. I also want to acknowledge summer research funds provided by the Whitney Griswold Fund and the Yale Center on International and Area Studies. Many thanks again to Oxford University

Press: to Nancy Lane, friend and editor; to Henry Krawitz and David Roll for looking after the manuscript; and to Clifford Browder for his skillful copyediting. Laura and Christopher Merriman, who were both born well after I began work on this book, have brought me much joy. So, too, has Carol Merriman. This book is dedicated to her, in appreciation for her love and insight as well as patience.

Balazuc, France   J.M.
December 1989

Contents

The Margins of
City Life

1

The Urban Frontier

In Verdun, on June 20, 1826, six prostitutes, "somewhat drunk," staged their own version of an ecclesiastical jubilee. They held their small procession along the rue des Ramparts de la Porte Saint-Victor, between the lower and upper sections of the strategically important town Vauban had fortified in the seventeenth century with walls that all too arbitrarily marked the end of the countryside's vineyards. One of the prostitutes led the way, using a plain stick for a bishop's staff, while another followed, lifting the back of her friend's long dress above the dust of the town's periphery as if it were a clerical robe of silk. Each carried a broomstick in lieu of a candle. They sang "unintelligibly" to the tune of a church hymn or canticle. They told each person they met that "they were participating in the jubilee." Their first "station" was not of the cross but a cabaret on the rue Saint-Victor, from which they were quickly expelled. They tried to get others "from the same class" to join in but managed only to attract a following of six children, "as they were in a quiet little place" before the police arrested them. They ultimately received six months in prison and a fine of three hundred francs—a stiff sentence but one in tune with the times under the recently crowned Charles X.[1]

Our only source for this minor incident is a police report tucked away in the Departmental Archives of the Meuse in Bar-le-Duc. The report provides no indication of what the prostitutes said either before or at the time of their arrest. We do not hear their side of the story. Outraged indignation seeps through the document, one highly biased against the women, who stood accused of sacrilegious behavior. This account is typical of reports reflecting official fear of the "disorder" that people who were considered "marginal" represented. "Marginal" is used here in both a social and geographic sense: on or beyond the fringe of bourgeois society, and at or beyond the frontiers of its urban world.

There are several ways to read this particular incident. First, it could describe social reality; the prostitutes *were* troublesome, vexing, disorderly, even dangerous to public order in the France of Charles X. Second, the event, however minor, could be taken to symbolize the bourgeois fear of ordinary people, in this case those situated at the edge of the city; the periphery itself, as I will argue, increasingly became identified with those fears. Third, it could be interpreted as an incident of solidarity and deliberate resistance articulated by the supposedly inarticulate, a mockery of hierarchy and authority at a time when the Restoration government was, if not besieged, at least challenged by liberal political opposition

3

and by ordinary people as well. Fourth, it could be taken as a justification by the state, on behalf of the upper classes, for extending police control into the outskirts of France's cities and towns to check the supposed disorganization of plebeian life.

This minor drama can serve as the basis for a more complex and nuanced understanding of the relationship between center and periphery.[2] The prostitutes entered the gate from the outskirts of Verdun, where they probably lived and sometimes worked. In Verdun, among other places, prostitutes—at least the lowest or most desperate sort—counted among *les marginaux,* or marginal people; some of them were identified with the geographic boundaries of urban life, the faubourgs and nascent suburbs (*banlieues*[3]) of France's growing cities and towns. The joyful though ill-fated procession in Verdun was indeed something of a symbolic, carnivalesque conquest of the fortified town launched from the outside, the ambiguous no-man's-land between city and country. They had taken refuge in that no-man's-land after being repeatedly expelled by the police, having worn out their welcome in one of the brothels that served the garrison, where they passed on venereal diseases. The *clandestines,* working alone, also took refuge in the outskirts at night; some set up shop beyond, but still within the shadow of the ramparts. These prostitutes were probably *faubouriennes* in a town without faubourgs; because Verdun was fortified, one could not build immediately beyond the gates. Yet their presence at the edge of the fortress town would more than likely have been temporary, even if they had not been arrested and incarcerated by the authorities, who found nothing amusing or even pathetic about their jubilee. Their short stays at the frontiers of urban life, also contributed to their image of marginality (*la vie en marge, la vie marginale*).

Marginality has thus taken on a resounding meaning, "equally loaded with a social sense and inscribed in social polarity."[4] This term is to be understood in the sense of "uncertain," or "bad reputation," beyond the control of the law both normatively and in fact, refusing to submit to the control of the authorities. Bernard Vincent has described the evolution of the word *marginal* in French from an adjective to a noun, "after a stage when we became aware that individuals could be marginal with regard to a center that is constituted by society as a whole." He considers two recent examples: participants in the events of May 1968 in France were assumed to be "people no doubt marginal, without home or work," while in the early 1970s a work of literature was described as an "Occitan text, under-ground, marginal, refusing assimilation." Vincent argues that the marginal person is someone "who voluntarily takes leave of society or he whom the world of production rejects to the frontiers." The "excluded" (*exclu*) or "outcast," on the other hand, "is deliberately condemned by law or by the dominant culture. Marginality is a transitory state, ephemeral, while exclusion is durable, indeed in certain cases definitive."[5]

In the words of Bronislaw Geremek, historian of marginal Parisians in the fourteenth and fifteenth centuries, "the milieu of urban misery is the zone of contact where marginal people brushed up against society."[6] Preindustrial societies were characterized by a high degree of geographic mobility, both collective and individual. Some portion of it was regulated by institutional controls (for example, religious pilgrimages or artisans going on the *tour de France* to perfect their skills). Such organized and monitored "collective wandering" was not considered dangerous: "[I]t was [geographic] mobility that was uncontrolled or individual that worried and threatened traditional societies."[7] Vagabonds were—and still are—people defined as *sans domicile fixe,* without permanent residence, "living everywhere."

For example, colporteurs—hawkers and peddlers—were by definition rootless men on the move, suspected and feared by urban elites. At the very least, they stood accused as outsiders who damaged the local economy by taking business away from someone everyone knew. They were suspected of peddling stolen goods that they themselves had perhaps taken, stuffing them quickly into their heavy leather bags. Since their survival depended upon selling merchandise, colporteurs could, it was thought, be easily tempted by other, less savory work. In the early 1840s, a well-known study of French popular culture put it this way: "[I]f need be, the colporteur will become a smuggler, messenger, even a spy, if necessary, during time of civil war and other troubles."[8] Indeed, colporteurs were blamed and persecuted for the diffusion of democratic socialist propaganda during the Second Republic.[9] Tighter legislation and passport requirements facilitated but could not guarantee arrest. Lacking property, rootless by nature and occupation, a purveyor of rumor and bad news, shiftless and devious as well, the colporteur could not be trusted. He knew every trail, path, road, and short cut, each back door.[10]

Geography mobility itself was suspect, even frightening. Adolphe Thiers, one of the more frightened observers, and agressively so, put it this way: "A man has all his moral value, according to us, only in the middle of his fellow citizens, in the city where he has always lived under the eyes of these citizens, watched, judged, and appreciated by them . . . but in general the displaced person, whom we call a vagabond, no longer has his moral value."[11]

Long before the time of Thiers, elites had ceased differentiating between the "peaceful vagabond" and the "redoubtable vagabond."[12] In the sixteenth and seventeenth centuries, the medieval image of the poor as the "living image of Christ" waned, as beggars and vagabonds "found themselves assigned a place on the margin." In the words of Roger Chartier, if elites did not create beggars and other poor, "they introduced criteria of marginality to designate them."[13] Prostitutes, lepers, and beggars were the classic marginal people of medieval Paris, their roles so well-defined that they were almost institutionalized.[14] By the nineteenth century only the lepers had disappeared.

The concept of marginality has a geographic as well as social meaning—"rich significations in vocabulary linked to place."[15] Says Geremek: "Infamy and social marginality are also linked to space . . . generally speaking, misery and crime go together in urban space, beyond the center of town, toward the faubourgs," the dumping ground for "physical and moral rubbish."[16] As Antoine Bailly puts it, "marginality, like centrality, encompasses simultaneously a social state and a geographic position."[17] In terms of the growth of cities, spatial marginality suggests the urban frontier, the city's advancing border.[18]

Geographers and sociologists who discuss spatial marginality therefore emphasize the dichotomy between center and peripheral spaces.[19] Center represents the primary impulse of urbanization—capital—and thus the economic and political power of social elites. The periphery becomes that space at the edge of the city where the power of government, capital, and urban elites is unevenly felt and resisted: the gray suburbs, the shantytown, the *bidonville, la zone,* "suburbs, home of small houses, small gardens, small dreams, and meager ambitions."[20]

Social marginality was and is not, of course, confined to the edge of urban life. In the urban world, as it presently exists in the United States—with elite suburbs built on the impulsion of flight from the deteriorating, dilapidated, and dangerous urban core—the relationship between center and periphery offers a dramatic contrast with the European experience. Nor is the periphery necessarily just the realm of the excluded. France too had its privileged residences on the edge of urban life, of which Versailles and Saint-Germain-en-Laye are just two examples. The industrial town of Mulhouse had a small southern faubourg of elite residences; by 1900 the faubourg du Miroir was one of that city's most elegant quarters. Yet the perimeter of urban life in France was closely associated with elements of social marginality—relatively recent arrival to the city, lack of skills, uncertainties of employment, and vulnerability to economic crises.[21] Coupled with this was the image of transience and the presence of people considered more likely to have committed crimes. This was the world of "professional strangers."

We move from Restoration Verdun to the *haute ville* or upper town—the working-class faubourgs—of the ecclesiastical, commercial, and industrial center of Reims in 1834. That year, several strikes of spinners occurred. Frequent and well-attended meetings took place almost every day in the open spaces outside the city walls, such as the woods beyond the faubourg Fléchambault and the porte Dieu-Lumière. Soldiers and the national guard moved in to disperse them and police prevented workers from marching through the streets with a banner defying their employers' attempt to reduce their wages. Hand-spinners and mechanized spinners for the first time joined forces, singing a song denouncing their bosses to the tune of the "Marseillaise."[22]

Four years later, the workers of the upper town marched down into the elegant center of Reims after rumors spread that a priest from the Bordeaux region, a missionary preparing to plant a giant cross, had insulted the memory of Napoleon. Thousands of workers came down from the faubourgs and set upon the church of Saint-Jacques. The national guard, drawn from the elite quarters below, could not prevent the crowd from storming the sacristy and smashing its furniture.[23] During the July Monarchy the workers of the faubourgs were pitted against the center of the city in other such incidents.

In 1840, a year of economic crisis, bands of workers met beyond the northern ramparts near a cemetery during a brief strike, and returned to town carrying a black flag. After being prevented from damaging several factories, they managed to affix the flag to the statue of Louis XV in the center of the place Royale.[24] Four years later, workers gathered at the place Saint-Nicaise to demand jobs. As republican songs echoed in the streets, they scrawled posters threatening arson and insurrection—acts revealing not only the social crisis of unemployment and deprivation but also the workers' resentment toward the *beaux quartiers*. The sense of periphery attacking the city was again present.[25] It was also present, as we shall see, in the mobilization of the workers of Reims after the revolution of 1848 and throughout the Second Republic.[26] The mobilization of the upper town in defense of the Republic ended after the Eighteenth Brumaire of Louis Napoléon Bonaparte, on December 2, 1851, with a demonstration in the upper town—a failed attempt to bring about an insurrection, followed by arrests and court-martials. The center—state and municipality—had defeated the outskirts, but the battle was less one-sided than the brief and ill-fated incursion of a small group of the prostitutes of Verdun into town. The workers of the upper town of Reims were determined and organized.

1848 was a year of revolution in the agro-town (*agro-ville*) of Perpignan in Roussillon, or French Catalonia, highlighting the contrast and conflict between the French culture of the government and Perpignan's urban elite on the one hand, and the peripheral or marginal Catalan culture of ordinary people on the other. On Sunday, June 4, the national guard company from the *quartier* of Saint-Mathieu went into the countryside for a banquet. Many, if not most, were *brassiers* (day laborers who worked in the fields) or had other occupations that took them almost every day into the countryside. The rural character of the quarter had earned it the title of "faubourg," although it lay within the fortifications, beyond which the army forbade settlement. The bitter enemies of the brassiers were the "peasants" of the quarter of Saint-Jacques, who remained intransigent royalists. The February Revolution had increased conflict between Perpignan's two plebeian, agricultural, Catalan, warring quarters.

Upon the return of the national guard company to Perpignan, the police arrested one of them for firing his pistol in the air in celebration. The men from Saint-Mathieu then attacked the "forces of order," freeing their friend. More trouble followed. Rumors spread that the reds of Saint-Mathieu had hidden arms and munitions in their quarter. The next day a patrol of two hundred troops and guardsmen was attacked by "workers from the parish of Saint-Mathieu" armed with swords and pistols, wearing red caps, and shouting in Catalan at the entrance to their quarter. During the Second Republic, Saint-Mathieu remained the bastion of the left in the capital of Roussillon, after many of the bourgeois radicals of the fancy quarters had given up commitment and hope. Their bitter enemies, the men of Saint-Jacques, for the most part remained staunch royalists.[27] The marginal population of Saint-Mathieu, culturally peripheral, challenged the center above all for power. As Chartier writes, "marginality is indeed as much an ideological as a socioeconomic phenomenon," cultural as well as political.[28]

The prostitutes of Verdun, the textile workers of Reims's upper town, and the peasants of the faubourg Saint-Mathieu in Perpignan preoccupied the police during the first half of the nineteenth century. The threat that the prostitutes seemed to pose to bourgeois society was slim indeed, a "moral" danger defined somewhat hypocritically by the upper classes, since bourgeois clients helped sustain the cash economy of prostitution. The workers of Reims and the rural day laborers of Saint-Mathieu in Perpignan were taken more seriously, by the centralized repressive apparatus of the state because of the threat they increasingly posed, in succession, to the July Monarchy and the conservative Republic initiated by the revolution of 1848.

This in itself might seem surprising. After all, the weight of contemporary literature about the evils and dangers of evolving urban life emphasized the disorderliness, indeed danger, of the central city. It follows that the "professional-ization" of policing—including its centralization, bureaucratization, routinization of specialized activities, and the expansion of the political function of the police—is seen as primarily concerned with urban growth and concomitant social problems and fears associated with the central city. The police were increasingly, and perhaps primarily, concerned with the emergence of ordinary people as organized contenders for political power. Like the police, historians need to consider not only the center of the city, but also its fringe.

For elites, the urban frontier—faubourg and suburb—represented an urban future that was in many ways anything but reassuring. An essential part of that urban future included workers gathered on the edge of the city, where life was cheap. What made them seem more and more threatening was not the criminality feared by urban elites, but the workers' organized bid for political power. This bid came from the periphery, not only socially, but also spatially and culturally. Shortly after Louis-Philippe became the first—and last—Orleanist king of the French, his official Chabrol warned him, in the wake of the insurrection by the Lyons silk workers in 1831: "Your prefects of police are allowing the capital to be blocked by a hundred factories. Sire, this is the cord that will strangle us one day."[29] The "dangerous classes," the "new barbarians," were gathered on the edge of the capital, and of other cities as well. The result of this awareness, indeed fear, was an expansion not only of police activities but of the reach of the police into the outskirts of French towns and cities, and ultimately, in the case of large cities, the imposition of order, the conquest through incorporation of suburbs seen as threatening.

The "marginal" and the "excluded" are almost by definition propertyless, geographically mobile, and without trade, at least without a *métier* for which there is demand.[30] Outsiders, they reflect Victor Turner's contrast between structure and antistructure; they are "liminal *personae*" or "threshold people."[31] For Turner, "[s]ociety . . . is a process in which any living, relatively well-bonded human group alternates between fixed and—to borrow a term from our Japanese friends—'floating worlds.'"[32] These "floating worlds" are inhabited by many people weakly integrated or unintegrated into the economic, social, political, and cultural life of the city. The periphery, home to the marginal, including those of "lowermost status, and structural outsiderhood,"[33] may also be seen to represent something of a free and open space, a subculture with its own argot, delinquent in resisting not only laws but cultural traditions, defiantly *contre-pouvoir*.[34] Turner calls this world of "communitas, or social anti-structure (since it is a 'bond uniting . . . people over and above any formal social bonds,'") one that can be marked by an "egalitarian 'sentiment for humanity,' indeed one that can even come to represent, on behalf of the poor, humanity itself."[35]

Faubourg and suburb retained their seemingly contradictory images—somewhat agricultural, somewhat industrial, somewhat urban, somewhat rural—contributing to a hodgepodge of activities and appearances. The periphery lent a feeling of uneasiness, a certain sadness, captured by Baudelaire, musing over his own vicarious role as modernist poet as well as *"flâneur,* apache, dandy and ragpicker,'' in his poem ''The Seven Old Men'' from *Les fleurs du mal:*

> One morning, while along the melancholy street
> The houses, which the fog did greater height impart,
> Were like unto the wharves of rivers in full spate,
> And while, stage-setting like unto the actor's heart,
>
> A dirty yellow fog came in from ev'ry side,
> Tensing my shaken nerves to play a hero's part
> Debating with my soul, already sorely tried,
> I followed the faubourg shaken by heavy cart.[36]

It was on the fringe of agglomerated urban life that city and country met in that uncertain and awkward embrace. The images and realities of urban and rural life coexisted as often as they clashed: ''There are no landscapes more composite than those of the suburb where city and country come together . . . sometimes it is an abrupt break, but often enough it is a progressive transition never fixed, always changing.''[37] Industry and agriculture coexisted, even in the same families and sometimes in the same persons. This too may have made the periphery seem more confusing, if not more uncertain, even threatening. Robert Herbert, Paul Tucker, and T. J. Clark have shown how the Impressionists, particularly Claude Monet, wrestled with the changing landscape on the edge of Paris in the last decades of the nineteenth century.[38] The bourgeoisie, particularly the petty bourgeoisie,[39] of the capital went out as Sunday conquerors, a veritable shock troop of pleasure seekers. They stormed Argenteuil, where the ''countryside was being made part of the city.'' Here, on the outskirts, the demarcation between urban and rural gradually faded, as industrialization wrought ragged changes in the landscape, represented by chimneys belching smoke. Vincent van Gogh's *The Outskirts of Paris* and Jean-François Raffaëlli's *Sunday Walkers,* analyzed by Clark, capture some of these tensions, as well as the ''vulgar figures''—as a British critic called them—painted by Manet at Argenteuil.[40]

Cultural marginality is a related phenomenon. It too has a significant spatial component that must be explored. The Jewish ghettos of the Middle Ages and afterward have left in France—Pézenas comes immediately to mind—telling architectural ensembles and street names (the rue des Juifs). Indeed, Jews may have been the quintessential urban ''marginal people,'' residing in the center while being socially, politically, and culturally peripheral. Enfranchised by the French Revolution, many took advantage of their changed legal status and the end of the Napoleonic wars to migrate from village to town and city, and from city to city. Yet it was not only in Alsatian cities that they often faced discrimination and hatred; some Jewish communities remained isolated, even in the midst of the bustle of the changing urban world.[41]

The Catalans of Perpignan, including the people of Saint-Mathieu, living in the shadow of the Pyrenees 550 miles from Paris but only 30 from Spain, provide another example we shall explore more fully later. With nineteenth-century urbanization, whether tied to large-scale industrialization or not, the residual rural component of French cities seemed out of place, marginal to a changing urban world. For some, it seemed strange to visit agro-towns where urban and agricultural life greatly overlapped. In these towns, neighborhoods particularly tied to agricultural production seemed like urban villages. Indeed, they were. Urbanization did not simply overwhelm the rural dimension of French urban life in the way that the rue du Chemin Vert on the edge of nineteenth-century Paris found itself well within surroundings decidedly less rustic than its beautifully archaic name. Many peasants and agricultural laborers, like protoindustrial homeworkers, remained an essential part of the urban experience, however much perceived as marginal by the nineteenth-century bourgeoisie. Along with the industrial workers of the periphery, marginal socially and geographically—the feared barbarians at the gate[42]—the "rural" population of the *agro-villes,* and of other towns as well, seemed to be on the margins of urban civilization. The parishes or quarters of Saint-Mathieu and Saint-Jacques provide an example not only of the spatial concomitants of cultural marginality but of the importance of neighborhood solidarities as well. In Perpignan, during the Second Republic, these neighborhoods, arguably the most radical, led the way.

As the examples cited above suggest, nineteenth-century painting can lead us to another, more familiar kind of cultural marginality. Marilyn Brown argues that the gypsy, or *bohémien,* had emerged over the centuries as arguably the most salient symbol of the "excluded," propertyless, mobile individual, living everywhere but nowhere—*errant*—and eternally suspected of pilfering. By the 1830s, the term "gypsy" had taken on "a secondary connotation of a life of vagrancy or social disorder." The *bohémien* came to represent "real or permanent social dissidence." Karl Marx's memorable description in *The Eighteenth Brumaire of Louis Napoleon Bonaparte* was thus filled with irony; he referred to the Bonapartist entourage of hangers-on in on the coup d'état as "vagabonds, discharged soldiers, escaped galley slaves . . . beggars—in short, the whole indefinite, disintegrated mass, thrown hither and thither, which the French term *la bohème.*" Of course, from the point of view of Louis Napoleon's government and admirers, the image of *la bohème* seemed more appropriate to those who opposed the destruction of the Second Republic. The gypsy seemed to lurk menacingly on the edge of the city. The number of gypsies outside the gates of Paris had been swollen by the political upheavals in Central Europe. One of the first decrees following the coup d'état of December 2, 1851, ordered the deportation of all gypsies to Cayenne, or at least outside France, though there was not the slightest bit of evidence linking them to resistance on behalf of the democratic and social Republic. In 1871—*l'année terrible*—bands of gypsies were seen gathered outside the walls of the capital, and were noted again a few years later by, among others, Emile Zola.[43]

Vagabonds, *saltimbanques,* jugglers, poachers, tramps, the rootless poor, sometimes traveling in families, the proverbial Wandering Jew of Gustave Courbet, even *flâneurs* who "wander not imperatively, out of necessity, but dawdlingly, out of choice or indecision; not out of social duty, but out of a dandylike attitude of philosophical superiority," became, to a lesser or greater extent, identified with the dangerous classes. During the early 1830s, Alexandre-Gabriel Decamps, among others, produced lithographs and paintings, represented in the Salon of 1831, "of Savoyards, beggars, and *saltimbanques* as direct studies of gypsies of industry, the vagabonds of the faubourgs and suburbs beyond the Butte Montmartre."[44]

Another meaning of "gypsy" or "bohemian" emerged in response to the continued fascination of artists with, and their increased exposure to, the image of the ultimate outsider, a meaning "filled with mulitple significations . . . in the works of numerous artists the visual sign of gypsies and related wanderers became rich in potential metaphor." Charles Dickens observed from across the Channel that "the Parisian bohemians of today are a tribe of unfortunate artists of all kinds—poets, painters, musicians, and dramatists—who haunt obscure cafés in all parts of Paris, but more especially in the Quartier Latin." In 1850 Gustave Courbet confessed: "In our oh-so-civilized society it is necessary for me to lead the life of a savage. . . . To that end, I have just set out on the great, independent, vagabond life of the gypsy." In the 1880s Vincent van Gogh, among others, had appropriated the metaphor of the gypsy or bohemian as a self-referential metaphor for the artistic avant-garde.[45] Appropriately, Montmartre, having in 1860 lost through incorporation its former administrative independence but not yet all of its rural character or physical and social remoteness from bourgeois Paris, became a center for *la nouvelle bohème*.[46]

Raffaëlli was among those artists searching the outskirts of Paris for subjects. He associated the ragpicker (*chiffonnier*), as illustrated by his *Butte of the Ragpickers* (1889),[47] with "an idea of liberty, of savage independence, naïvely or mistakenly, he claimed, 'these men have no masters.' " Indeed, the ragpicker was sometimes feared because of his knowledge of the intimate geography of Paris. For Raffaëlli the ragpickers and tramps of Asnières, where the artist, himself something of an outsider in the world of art,[48] took up residence in 1878, are "emblems of the artist's progressive notion of 'characterism,' that is, of free individualism, more than socially integrated representations of class." The ragpicker became, through his fierce independence and bohemian ways, the *chiffonnier-philosophe*. Charles-Joseph Traviès's depiction of "the celebrated ragpicker-philosopher Liard . . . contributed to the myth of the heroic and solitary ragpicker, an independent individual elevated by noble sentiments above the squalor of his class."[49] Charles Baudelaire's "The Wine of Ragpickers" offered an only slightly less romantic view:

> Often at night beneath a street-lamp's reddish glow,
> With rattling glass and a flame-a-flicker in the snow,
> Within an old faubourg, a dirty grimy maze
> Where stark humanity must spend its restless days,
>
> One sees a ragman on his way, with nodding head,
> Stumbling and tripping just as he were poet bred,
> Who, never paying heed unto surrounding eyes,
> Pours out his very heart in glorious rhapsodies.

He preaches sermons wise and dictates laws sublime,
Gives unto victims ease, and punishment to crime,
And, underneath the sky like a suspended throne,
Grows drunk with splendors that he makes for all his own.[50]

In or rather on Montmartre, "bohemian individualism" enjoyed a relatively free and open space. The artists and writers of Montmartre, including the Symbolists, rebelled against conventional cultural dictates. They found solidarity in the cafés and cabarets on the hill, which, although it had long since lost its image of a rural village, still offered relative isolation. An Austrian visitor described it in 1898: "The Butte, the real Montmartre, seems at first view to be one-half country village and one-half provincial town . . . one would believe himself more than two hundred miles from the metropolis."[51] Artists and writers whose cultural rebellion rendered them sympathetic to anarchism made Montmartre their own, and were only half joking when they planned to create a free city. Virtually all anarchist newspapers and reviews were published there, discreetly (or sometimes indiscreetly) applauding the explosions of bombs in the *beaux quartiers* below. Not surprisingly, the anarchists of the century's last decade drew a disporportionate share of their support from the proletarian eastern and northern faubourgs of Paris. The faubourg, after all, "stood for work," with its own argot, the vernacular of labor.[52]

As recent work on medieval Paris suggests, faubourg and *banlieue* were hardly new spaces.[53] These *extra muros* settlements had characterized the ancien régime. Landless labor—whether employed, underemployed, or unemployed, whether hoping for urban work, rural work, or any work at all—camped like the highly mobile army of proletarians they were, beyond the gates of the city. The growth of faubourgs and suburbs followed the arrival of unskilled, but not necessarily industrial, labor. The periphery, even if only woods, fields, and scattered settlements not yet called "faubourgs" (which term suggested at least some urban organization), often lodged the poorest of the poor of Lyon, Marseille, and other urban centers. In Nîmes, France's Belfast, the precocious growth of industrial faubourgs in the middle decades of the eighteenth century provided the spatial organization for the religious war between Protestant and Catholic quarters during the Revolution and throughout much of the first half of the nineteenth century. Montauban, an important textile town during the ancien régime, had the well-developed industrial faubourgs of Sapiac, Le Moustier, and, above all, Villebourbon, "vast entanglements of huts where, in the middle of small vegetable gardens, teeming families of children, half workers, half peasants, crowd together and mingle." These were "neighborhoods without hygiene, overpopulated and foul-smelling," particularly the faubourg of Villebourbon, the work of whose dyers lent a pungent odor to the neighborhood, across the Tarn from the elegant red tiles of the place Nationale—though it was not called that in those days—and the aristocratic residences of the center.[54]

However, the growth of faubourgs and suburbs particularly characterized nineteenth-century urban development. Mulhouse provides an obvious example, with its *cités ouvrières* constructed on its northern edge near mills and factories.

Some of this growth was fueled by the locus of industrial work in and around cities: manufacturers took advantage of the availability of land and cheaper costs beyond the *octroi,* the customs barrier where taxes on goods brought into each town of over five thousand people were collected, as in and around the *ville-faubourg* Saint-Etienne, Lille and its burgeoning faubourgs/suburbs turned conurbation, the northern faubourgs of Limoges,[55] and communities across the Vienne from the center of Châtellerault. Well before 1850, industrial workers living and working on the city's edge contributed to the commonly held association between the urbanization of the periphery and large-scale industry. The development of faubourg and suburb was closely, but not exclusively, tied to large-scale indus-trialization, a relentless though—in France—gradual process, that ultimately gen-erated a ''mass marginalization''[56] during the nineteenth century.[57] Capitalists searched for open and cheaper land on which to build factories and warehouses near thoroughfares, railways, canals, and rivers. Extending their control of economic life to the urban outskirts, bosses and their foremen attempted to impose industrial discipline on a recalcitrant work force.[58] The search for raw materials and cheaper labor eventually extended beyond the city to colonies, and finally to independent Third-World nations.[59]

The faubourgs came to house some of the poorest of the poor. Faubourg and suburb were places of residence for generally unskilled laborers, recently arrived and/or unable to afford the higher prices of the center. Generally speaking, the farther away from the urban center one went, the less expensive land became; essential commodities too became cheaper, a fact to be accounted for in no small measure by the placement of the *octroi* on the formal limits of the city. Employed, underemployed, and unemployed laborers settled beyond the *octroi,* drawn by the possibilities of work there. The location of faubourgs could be determined by physical features, as for example the presence of valleys (the Bièvre and Chev-reuse south of Paris, or above all the Seine) which served as routes of transporta-tion to and from the city. The *auberges* and rural *guinguettes* that lined the main roads in and out of cities and towns were the seeds of development for the settlements, faubourgs, bourgs, and suburbs that followed.

The dichotomy between center and periphery in the first half of the nineteenth century has left many interesting archival traces. In 1838 we find the poor *femme* Dussus condemned to six months in prison ''for absconding with and strangling domestic animals.'' She declared, in her defense, that she did not commit a theft in taking cats that had the bad fortune to be wandering on the public way when she came by with her large bag. Misery had forced her ''to carry out this Saint Bartholomew's Day of cats.'' She got by because of her modest, awful business, selling their skins and flesh, ''of which the wretched cooks of the faubourgs and the suburbs make excellent stews.''[60]

The social differentiation between center and periphery could also be seen in much smaller places, as for example in the tiny departmental capital of Auch, where, ''since the sixteenth century, four to five hundred people of the lowest class teem in the faubourgs of Barry, Saint-Pierre, and especially in the quarter of Treille.'' During grain shortages and bitterly cold winters, such as that of 1831–32, they suffered more than anyone.[61] And in Verdun, which was without true faubourgs at that time, "the peripheral neighborhoods near the ramparts lodge the modest classes, workers, or simply day laborers and indigents, to which are added poor farmers and farmhands."[62]

Changing Images of Fear

Rapid urban growth, at least by French standards, during the first half of the nineteenth century generated contemporary literature expressing fears of the consequences of urbanization. In 1840 Antoine-Honoré Frégier, a bureau head in the headquarters of the Paris police, published a book in Belgium that won a prize from the Academy of Moral and Political Sciences. His work *Des Classes dangereuses de la population dans les grandes villes et des moyens de les rendre meilleures* postulated a direct relationship between urban growth and criminality. Frégier described Paris as characterized by "the vicious and delinquent agglomerations which agitate the metropolises and in the substantial cities of countries other than France."[63]

Frégier's association of the "dangerous" with the "laboring" classes reflected much of contemporary bourgeois opinion. In two succeeding studies with similar preoccupations, the use of the word "agglomeration"—which Frégier had used to designate gatherings of criminal types—came to represent the city itself. French census takers had defined as "urban" any "agglomeration" of 1,500, and then, as of 1841, 2,000 people in a nucleated settlement. But it was not with small urban areas that these critics of France's developing urban world were primarily concerned. The term "agglomeration" took on frightening significance.

In 1867 the economist M. A. Legoyt lamented the migration of so many rural people to Europe's burgeoning cities, whether they were pushed from the land by its increasing subdivision or *morcellement,* or attracted by industrial and service work, or by the ease with which they could reach the city thanks to the railroad, or by urban charitable institutions. In *Du progrès des agglomérations urbaines et de l'émigration rurale en Europe et particulièrement en France,* he postulated that increased criminality and political disruptions were the result of rapid urbanization: "There exists in urban agglomerations a sort of exceptional moral temperature. Thoughts and feelings are particularly intense there and become excited to the level of passion." Legoyt recited the litany of what he took to be the horrors of urban life: drunkenness, bad health, illegitimate births, and debts. Legoyt admired, despite himself, the progress and glory of Paris, but his principal concern was to suggest how the movement to the cities might be slowed down and some of the purported virtues of rural life retained.[64] In 1871, a Doctor Sarrasin of Douai found a sympathetic audience attending the International Congress of Hygiene when he asserted that "human agglomerations sometimes become veritable foyers of sources of infection." The history of nineteenth-century French cities has even been described as a "phobia of contact."[65]

Thirty years later, Paul Meuriot's study of *Des agglomérations urbaines dans l'Europe contemporaine* offered what has since become known as the "uprooting hypothesis."

It is incontestable that political morals are more changeable in the great urban centers of population . . . one can even say that in all times the urban masses have always had a more tumultuous character than anyone else. First, in any human agglomeration, passions always ferment more; furthermore, the population of great cities is renewed more quickly, and tradition has less of an effect on the new elements. In reality, the general political tendency of urban and rural populations responds to the two eternal instincts of the human soul—that of desire and that of conservation.[66]

He reminded his readers that Rousseau himself had condemned the concentration of people, and pointed out that, while alcoholism and suicide were not inevitable in cities, they were more likely to occur there. So too was "the development of political equality . . . [which is] almost everywhere in the great states, a consequence of the development of urban agglomerations." To Meuriot, stern representative of "the bourgeois century," this did not seem a good thing.[67]

The moralist Louis-René Villermé's description of working-class cities, published in 1840, had evoked the horror of physical deprivation and linked it to moral deprivation.[68] Eugène Buret, a journalist, had published *De la misère des classes laborieuses en Angleterre et en France* in the same year, offering a more charitable view of those suffering in France's largest cities. In cities, "misery increases with the population . . . the more numerous the armies, the bloodier the battles . . . the hospitals of the largest towns are like the ambulances that march behind great armies." Buret pointed to increasing class antagonisms in French cities, and to the growing physical separation of people of wealth from those of poverty, the latter being frequently piled up on the edge of the city, marginal in both complementary ways. Cities nurtured crime as naturally as they bred disease.[69]

In France, the most persuasive and well-known espousal of the "uprooting hypothesis" in this century has undoubtedly been that of Louis Chevalier, who relies upon the observations of contemporary novelists and social reformers to describe life in Paris in his *Laboring Classes and Dangerous Classes in Paris during the First Half of the Nineteenth Century*.[70] For Chevalier, Eugène Sue and Honoré de Balzac only confirmed what the techniques of social science could demonstrate: two races confronted each other, biologically different and unequal before the harsh tests of disease and mortality. The uprooted poor, arriving in great numbers, torn free from their rural roots, were feared by the bourgeoisie as the "dangerous and laboring classes."[71] Who could have been more dangerous than Balzac's evil and clever Vautrin, lurking on the edge of seedy respectability in the Vauquer rooming house near the Panthéon? For Balzac, as for the bourgeois of his city and his era, the dangerous, criminal classes were a fact of urban life, though in his novels actual bourgeois encounters with that class were relatively rare. Sue's serialized novel *Les Mystères de Paris,* published in 1842–43, captured the imagination, and the fear, of the middle classes with its sensationalized descriptions of the *menu peuple* of the capital.

Like Sue, Victor Hugo was sympathetic to the misery of the urban poor, and went into exile after the coup d'état of 1851, when he took their side against Louis

Napoleon Bonaparte. He described Paris as "a maelstrom in which everything is lost; and everything disappears in this whirlpool of the world as in the whirlpool of the sea."[72] For Hugo too, Paris generated misery, malaise, crime. For Chevalier, by implication, political uprisings and revolutions were spawned by the pervasive mood of aonmie. Unsettled and unsettling desperation and social disorganization inevitably followed the surge of migrants to Paris, the size of which almost doubled during the July Monarchy alone.

Chevalier's methodology and his conclusions have been frequently criticized.[73] The spate of studies of the various "crowds" in the revolutions of 1830 and 1848, as well as in other uprisings during the period, has demonstrated that, despite bourgeois perceptions, those who rebelled were not the uprooted, "dangerous" classes or the poorest workers, the *marginaux* of organized society, but artisans defending their way of life against large-scale economic changes over which they no longer had any control.[74] Trade solidarities and organizations led them to the barricades. In any case, one student of the period has concluded that the "dangerous" classes represented a minority of industrial workers.[75]

It is important to note that fear of the faubourg also took its place within contemporary literature denouncing urbanization as inevitably bringing about social uprooting. The faubourgs and edge of the city—the world of the "professional stranger"[76]—loom frighteningly to Chevalier as well, as he paints a terrifying picture of the links between deprivation and crime. "By a simple kind of predetermination," he writes, [Sue's] *Les Mystères de Paris* begins in the center of Paris, in the Cité, on the rue aux Fèves, and ends at the barrière Saint-Jacques. . . . No place could be more suitable for assembling in a final appearance—but merely by chance—all the characters in the novel at one of the crucial moments of their lives and for bringing together in the narrowest possible space all the mob's violence and all its delights, from carnival masquerades to the thrills of execution."[77]

The gates of the city (*barrières*) were part of the violent world of the novelists' Paris—and of Chevalier's, as we shall see in a subsequent chapter. In *Les Misérables* the *barrières* represented anything but a triumphant entry into the City of Light; rather, they imbued "the solitary stretches near the faubourgs with something of the distress and dreary foreboding" of what might occur. It was there that the *compagnons* fought it out, and "above all, crimes [took place] among the migrant workers, who lay in wait for, robbed, and murdered each other." Poverty and criminality went hand in hand to the *barrière*. The guillotine was moved to the barrière Saint-Jacques, near the desolate landscape of Montfaucon, "which summed up more thoroughly than any other setting the past and present horrors of the city." The faubourg Saint-Jacques, a dumping ground for garbage and even corpses in the eighteenth century, retained its identity as the refuge of the pitifully poor, the unwanted, the unemployed, including ill prostitutes and others no longer even able to afford the *garnis,* or rooming houses, of the center. It became, appropriately enough for those who viewed the fringe of urban life with disdain, the site of some public executions.[78]

The physical space of the faubourg takes on for Chevalier a great significance: "Hugo does not use '*faubourien de Paris*' to mean the inhabitant of the faubourgs, or even of the faubourg Saint-Antoine, the faubourg par excellence, but to designate part of the capital's working-class population."[79] The faubourg took on a specific meaning for many contemporaries. Chevalier quotes Hugo: "The Parisian race, we say again, is found most truly in the faubourg; there it is pure-blooded, there we find the real physiognomy, there the people work and suffer; and toil and suffering are the two faces of man." He offers a word of warning to those who would be reassured by the small size of the average Parisian, wracked by want: "Take care. . . . If the hour strikes, this man of the faubourg will grow big, this small man will arise and look terri[fying] and from this poor narrow chest a breath will swell strong enough to unfold the Alps themselves."[80] It thus became possible to refer to "precocious, sick flesh of the faubourgs."[81]

Frégier too treated the faubourg with a special concern: the tax-free wine known appropriately as *vin de la barrière* was consumed; worse, "there are women who do not hesitate to follow their husbands to the *barrière* with their children, who are old enough to work. . . . Afterward they start their way home half-drunk and act more drunk than they are, so that everyone may notice that they have drunk quite a bit. Sometimes the children follow their parents' example." Beyond the *barrière,* "a worker displayed his enjoyment of that wine full of pride and defiance as the only enjoyment granted to him."[82]

Unhealthy, disagreeable industries were expelled from city and town and settled on the outskirts—moves first ordered by monarchs and then by prefects, later with the encouragement of hygiene councils. Tanneries, glue factories, and the production of other products from dead animals such as "animal charcoal," as well as chemical factories, gas factories, and even madhouses were often relegated toward the outside, out of sight, smell, and mind for urban elites. In 1834 the mayor of Montaud, one of the booming industrial suburbs of Saint-Etienne, complained that an entrepreneur under contract with the latter municipality was dumping mud—something of a euphemism—in the smaller peripheral commune. Furthermore, the unfortunate souls responsible for getting rid of old horses were not putting them out to pasture, but rather leading them at night "to different points of this commune, the closest [to Saint-Etienne], and then killing them in the meadows, fields, or most often along the paths where they flay them for their skins, leaving behind them, if not all, at least the greatest part of the beasts, which are then devoured by the dogs of the vicinity." In 1852 the municipality of Saint-Etienne decided to construct a slaughterhouse in the commune of Outre-Furan, the municipal council of which angrily responded: "We are very astonished to see the town of Saint-Etienne, which has at its disposition so many more appropriate locations, choose the most beautiful and utilized promenade in the region for the location of this disgusting and noxious establishment." This futile protest was, as it turned out, one of the last independent actions taken by Outre-Furan, which was soon incorporated unwillingly into the commune of Saint-Etienne.[83]

During the ancien régime, Saint-Marcel was the "sick faubourg" of Paris, with its piles of rotting corpses, animal and human. Among the living, Raffaëlli's ragpickers chose it as a favorite place of residence. During the first half of the nineteenth century, the ragpickers of the capital were divided between the central quarters and the faubourgs. But at the end of the 1840s, and particularly with the rebuilding of Paris during the next two decades, the ragpickers left "bourgeois Paris" for the fringe; a contemporary observed in 1894: "The ragman is now a country person, if indeed Saint-Ouen, Pantin, or Clichy can give one the least idea of a green meadow." The *cités* of ragpickers in the Parisian suburbs were themselves "only in fact a particular form of a precarious habitat which developed on the periphery at the end of the century." One of the most "marginal" of traditional occupations itself became more and more physically marginalized, expelled from Paris by regulations and rising prices, pushed to the outside.[84]

In Paris too, particularly during the Second Empire, hospices and hospitals were expelled to the perimeters of urban life. The hospice for incurably ill men was moved from the faubourg Saint-Martin to the barracks of Popincourt and finally to Ivry, beyond the city limits. Two hospices for incurably ill women were likewise moved to the outskirts, and a third simply closed. One of the former was the hospice of Sainte-Perrine, which, although not far from the edge of town, happened to be near the Champs-Elysées, already a favored promenade and site for *cafés-concert*. Jeanne Gaillard concludes that, in step with the reconstruction of the Hôtel-Dieu on the Cité, officials sought "the relegation outside the town of all those whom age or infirmity had rendered useless to the smooth running of the city. The new town was par excellence the abode of able-bodied men and women, the residence of those of an age and size to work."[85] Other examples, which abound, include the Hospice de Josaphat, where more than one hundred foundlings and incurably ill indigents were cared for in Lèves, outside of Chartres, and the asylum placed in the faubourg Saint-Sever, across the Seine from Rouen. These people were to some extent the descendants of medieval lepers, marginalized, removed to the fringe.

Public execution too was in some towns relegated to the faubourgs. In Paris during the July Monarchy, the prefect of the Seine ordered the guillotine moved from the place de l'Hôtel de Ville to the nearest gate of the city.[86] In Bordeaux in 1823, the residents living on or near the place d'Aquitaine petitioned to have the site of public executions moved to the peripheral place Mériadec. The former square was one of Bordeaux's most handsome, "inhabited by a community of respectable folk." They occasionally awoke to the sound of hammers and nails building the scaffold of execution. "One cannot hide from the fact how this terrible spectacle is painful for visitors," the residents wrote, "but it is even more so for the people who live here." On the occasion of a visit by the Duchesse d'Angoulême, the driver of her carriage took a wrong turn: "Barely had the executioner finished dispatching the three condemned men, hardly had the earth received their blood, when the carriage of Madame, driven by someone unaware of what had occurred, came upon the site in horror." Perhaps even worse, the houses of the residents had declined in value. The place Mériadec was in a sparsely inhabited quarter bounded by marshland. The minister of justice was not sympathetic: public executions had a purpose beyond punishment—to make the crowds fear the revenge of God and society against the wicked. Furthermore, moving the place of execution farther out would only increase the anguish of the criminal by prolonging the trek from the prison.[87]

In Alençon, also in 1823, the mayor ordered that executions no longer be carried out at the centrally located place du Vieux Palais, but rather at the place du Marché aux Bestiaux on the edge of town. Here, it should be noted, the argument was less that executions were unsightly, but rather that the square was too small to accommodate the throngs that arrived for such festive occasions. More people could then witness and be deeply impressed and frightened by justice being carried out. In any case, the reflex—to move it to the periphery—was the same, and was opposed by the people of the faubourg. In 1843 the leading merchants and lace manufacturers of Le Puy were among the many people who signed a petition asking the prefect to order that the place of public execution be moved from the centrally located place du Martouret to the open spaces of the periphery. Executions in Le Puy always attracted huge throngs—in March of that year an estimated twenty thousand people, far more than the population of the town, watching from roofs, windows, or anywhere they could. Such spectacles, they argued, disrupted the normal flow of traffic and commerce.[88] In Poitiers, Guéret, and other places the sites of executions were also moved away from the center during the July Monarchy. Some more rustic charm vanished from the environs of city and town.

During the nineteenth century, the term "faubourg" lost much of its neutral, descriptive sense to take on a perjorative, even threatening, meaning. *Faubourg* comes from the Roman *foris burgus* or *furis burgum* (1478)—from *de furis,* outside, and *burgus,* bourg, that is "that which is outside the bourg," just beyond the city walls—by way of old French *fursborc* or *furborc* (late twelfth century) or *furbours* (1260),[89] as seen in the Picard *forbourg* or *forbou* and the Burgundian *faubor.*[90] But the etymology of "faubourg" is sometimes given as the medieval Latin *falsus burgus* or *faux bourg,* "false city." This alternative etymology is particularly appropriate as a secondary etymology.[91] It is this developing disparaging use of the term "faubourg" that concerns us, as examples chosen for dictionary descriptions make clear. The sixth edition of the *Dictionnaire de l'Académie française:* "Faubourg. The part of a town that is beyond its gates and wall . . . name given, abusively, to the quarters of a town that were formally only faubourgs."[92] The definition of faubourg came to include "by extension, the working-class population of the faubourgs," as the " 'sulfuring' faubourg, the name that the Parisian people give facetiously to the quarter of Saint-Marceau, by double allusion to the numerous factories making sulfuric matches there before the invention of chemical matches, and to the wretchedness of the inhabitants of this quarter."[93] For the *Grand Robert,* "faubourg" refers to the working-class population of a town and its faubourgs. Thus Balzac describes a *faubourien* as "a simple worker, one of the joyous residents of the faubourgs . . . a gay fellow."[94] Maupassant, drawn on by the *Grand Larousse* for an example of "inhabited space on the periphery of a large city," chooses Rouen's dreary Saint-Sever, "the faubourg of manufactures, pointing its thousand smoking chimneys toward the heavens." Or an example from Anatole France: "flowers are rare in this faubourg soiled by the soot of factories."[95] Raymond Abellios's description is even less flattering: "The faubourg of Minimes was really a faubourg, by this I mean one of those hybrid places where one finds oneself exiled from town without being welcomed by the country; this explains a mentality that is complex and properly *faubourienne,* in which the sense of rejection is accompanied by a state of excessive watchfulness and aggressiveness born of marginal situations.''[96]

As an adjective, *faubourien/ienne* becomes even more pejorative, describing habits and language. It became insulting to say someone had ''faubourg-like manners,''[97] or spoke a ''faubourg-like language,'' or had been unable or unwilling to overcome a ''very faubourg accent.''[98] The examples by the *Grand Robert* includes ''vulgarity of the faubourg'' and ''an exchange of faubourg-like pleasantries.'' Jules Romains complains of the ''base pronunciations of the faubourg, of which I have a horror.''[99] Bescherelle's *Nouveau Dictionnaire national* (1887) selected the following as examples: ''Plunged completely into the feelings of the moment, no thought of the future ever entered the mind of a *faubourien.* He is indifferent to duties, love for one's family, all that joins and links other men; he exists only to amuse himself'' (St. Prosper); ''Those who have still not arrived at wisdom, but are lodged in the faubourgs'' (Malherbe). Drawing on Bescherelle, the *Grand Larousse* (1973) defines *faubourien* as ''pejorative. That which relates to the plebeian faubourg and its inhabitants. 'Under the parasol waiting for us was the little laundress in her Sunday best. I was surprised; she was truly nice, although pale, and gracious, although with an allure that was somewhat *faubourienne*' (Maupassant)''; it also cites: ''It was the voice of a well-educated man, without the trace of an accent of the faubourgs'' (Jules Romains).[100] Again the *Grand Robert,* choosing an example of a *banlieusard,* or resident of the suburbs: ''He is ashamed of himself, ashamed of never rising, in his liaisons, above the employee, the secretary, the little suburban woman.''[101]

The assumed revolutionary tradition and potential of the faubourgs passed from bourgeois fears to dictionary definition. The Littré (1863) offered, as an example of the use as ''faubourg'' ''to raise up the faubourgs.'' The *Complément du dictionnaire de l'Académie française* (1862) stated: ''The faubourgs (hist.) mean, absolutely, the populace of Paris, especially in the history of our Revolution. To arm, raise up the faubourgs . . . particularly the faubourg Saint-Antoine and the faubourg Saint-Marceau. It is employed in speaking of popular uprisings.'' The *Trésor de la langue française* (1980) provides four examples, the first of which, from a history written in 1870, suggests the dichotomy between center and periphery: ''He [Bonaparte] armed the residents of the faubourgs immediately, thinking that they would have an old score to settle with the gentlemen of the Lepelletier section and its vicinity.'' The second example: ''in speaking of a physical trait, of comportment; generally implying an unfavorable impression,'' as ''his faubourg-like verve, his vocabulary of a thug.'' Third: ''The workers of the factory passed by . . . with silk caps on their faubourg heads, mean and corrupt.'' And, finally, the image of criminality: '' 'You won't take me,' he cried, 'dirty bourgeois!' In uttering this exclamation of the faubourgs with a dreadful irony . . . he fell into the arms of the guards, seized by convulsions that stopped almost immediately. He was dead.''

The ''peripheral people'' of French urban life are worth knowing about because social historians are concerned with the experience of ordinary people as they try to make sense of the dynamics of economic and social change and the vicissitudes of political power. Faubourgs and suburbs were familiar ground for prostitutes, among other symbols of marginality. But they are uncharted terrain for historians, whose interests in the relations between cities and their peripheries have skipped from a preoccupation with the relations between town and country during the ancien régime to the emergent *banlieues* of the Second Empire and Third Republic.[102] During both periods, towns and cities appear as predators, reaching octopus-like tentacles of capital and coercion into the countryside. Under the ancien régime, the urban world established its hegemony through the purchase of land by urban noble and bourgeois alike, or by binding rural industry to the city through networks of capital. The Second Empire pulled the urbanizing near suburbs into the all-powerful city by expanding the *octroi,* and thus the reach of the state taxing apparatus (*le fisc*), the structure and collection of indirect taxes that weighed upon the poor and generated popular resistance.

Yet we know little about the physical margins of French urban life during the first half of the nineteenth century, a period crucial to the development of urban society in France, and even less about the solidarities and organization emerging in the "floating worlds" of the periphery. The working-class faubourg, long identified with the second half of the nineteenth century, or with our own, must be squarely placed in the context of economic change and urban growth during the first half of the so-called "bourgeois century," even before and as railway and streetcar lines slowly stretched from Paris and other large cities. The increasing role of large-scale industrialization and relatively rapid growth differentiate the faubourg of the first half of nineteenth century from that of the ancien régime.

Space itself is a dimension—indeed, in some ways a dynamic—of economic, social, and political change. David Harvey has argued that "there has been a strong and almost overwhelming predisposition to give time and history priority over space and geography."[103] To understand the city, one must explore its frontier. Pierre Ayçoberry, the French historian of Cologne, puts it this way: "The story of suburbs is precisely that of urbanization, in the strongest sense of the term, of a process by which semiurban space is covered, not only by factories and lodgings but also by a network of relations, and produces a complex society, subordinate but also complementary to the mother-city."[104] It was on the frontier of city life that the economic, social, and political processes created by urbanization and the spatial contradictions they engendered were often most dramatically reflected. The periphery was where the process of urbanization was most dramatically occurring, where the city was becoming itself, regenerated and expanded. For urban dwellers, the uncontrolled growth of faubourgs represented the uncertain, even somewhat anxiety-provoking future of town and city. This process greatly impressed Victor Hugo:

> A city like Paris is in perpetual growth. In it, there is a perpetual vegetation of carpentry and stone. . . . You are gone for two months; upon your return, everything is changed. . . . Where will this growth of Paris stop? Who can say? Paris has already lept past five fortified walls. Now they are talking of building a sixth. Before another century, it will have exceeded that one, then it will go

beyond another. Each year, each day, each hour, by a sort of slow and relentless
infiltration, the city spills over into its faubourgs and the faubourgs become the
city, and the fields become the faubourgs![105]

There was, and is, another way of looking at the "floating worlds" of the periphery. It was a source and locus of economic vitality, beginning in towns like
Nîmes in the eighteenth century. Mary Douglas's discussion of "primitive
religions" in her study of concepts of pollution and taboos suggests another view
of the potential of the marginal, of the periphery:

> Granted that disorder spoils pattern: it also provides the materials of pattern.
> Order implies restriction; from all possible materials, a limited selection has been
> made and from all possible relations a limited set has been used. So disorder by
> implication is unlimited, no pattern had been realized in it, but its potential for
> patterning is indefinite. That is why, though we seek to create order, we do not
> simply condemn disorder. We recognize that is destructive to existing patterns;
> also that it has potentiality. It symbolizes both danger and power.[106]

For Turner, describing preindustrial societies, "communitas itself soon de-
velops a structure, in which free relationships between individuals become
converted into norm-governed relationships between social personae."[107] This
type of "open" or marginal society "often draws upon poverty for its repertoire of
symbols, particularly for its symbols of social relationship." This applies nicely to
the prostitutes of Verdun, who, using broomsticks for candles, mocked the
religious jubilee celebrated by the town's elites in the cathedral.

Borrowing from Arnold van Gennep, Turner might define the condition of
these particular "threshold people" to be "liminality."[108] The angry response of
the administrators and magistrates of Verdun echoes Douglas's contention that the
"physical crossing of the social barrier is treated as a dangerous pollution,"
although Douglas is considering primitive societies.[109] Unlike the mystical or
religious powers sometimes attributed to or assumed by people on the margins in
"primitive" societies and in medieval and early modern Europe—for example,
millenarian movements—the "powers of the weak" on the rugged frontier of
urban life became "dangerous" through consciousness and organization.[110] We
will thus have even more reason to return to Perpignan's neighborhoods of
"peasants" and to the *haute ville* of Reims.

We will distinguish marginal people—*les marginaux,* in whose ranks urban
elites would include the *brassiers* of Perpignan and the woolen workers of the
faubourgs of Reims—from outcasts or *les exclus,*[111] represented by the prostitutes
of Verdun. Yet government officials and bourgeois tended, like Chevalier, to
consider both groups part of the "dangerous classes."[112]

"Marginal" thus takes on an ironic meaning as well. The collective identity of
les marginaux is crucial.[113] Steven Kaplan has suggested that the "false workers"
(*faux ouvriers*) of the faubourg Saint-Antoine in the eighteenth century, in the
tradition of medieval workers without masters,[114] formed a fairly organized
counterculture, a kind of "negative integration," as suggested by the work of
Victor Turner cited earlier, accentuated by a feeling of rejection by the authorities
and elites of city and town.[115] They had both the feeling of not belonging, and that

of defiantly belonging to someone else. For solidarities of neighborhood and of class were the other side of marginality, however much confused with it by the French state and urban elites.

David Garrioch suggests that the faubourgs of eighteenth-century Paris were less well policed than the city itself, and that "less police presence in turn meant that greater community self-regulation was necessary and possible. It is no coincidence that all the examples of *charivaris* [noisy mock serenades, the "rough music" provided by banging on pots and pans, directed at people accused of violating communal norms or traditions] . . . came from the *faubourgs.*" He contends that, with its own special legal status and traditions of work, the faubourg Saint-Antoine "was economically and socially the most homogeneous of the quarters of eighteenth-century Paris." He shows how the internal topography of the faubourg Saint-Antoine, and other faubourgs as well, helped shape a sense of communal solidarity, reflected by less frequent abandonment of babies. Long, parallel streets taking the same direction, and smaller houses more dispersed than those of the center city, without secondary buildings behind, accentuated the social role of the street. These factors "contributed to the unity of the *faubourg* by giving all its inhabitants, to some degree, a shared physical space, although this was significant only as long as the population remained small enough for people to know each other."[116]

During the first half of the nineteenth century the residents of the faubourgs, even those without the strong ties of work experience and organization of the cabinetmakers of the faubourg Saint-Antoine, emerged as contenders for political power, as the Saint-Antoine workers had during the Revolution. The faubourgs and open spaces around town and city provided places for workers to gather to discuss demands to be made of their masters; from there they marched to other shops, calling on more workers to join them, then often returned to the periphery to plan their next demands or course of action. Faubourgs and open spaces around the city played a part in the maturation of strikes, during the July Monarchy, as workers met beyond the prying eyes of prefect and police. To urban elites, this made the periphery even more threatening, more dangerous, particularly as spatial marginality exaggerated the extent of social differentiation between the workers and the bourgeois of the center.[117] For within the faubourgs, social solidarities developed, and were expressed and reaffirmed by festivals, songs, strikes, and political movements.

The State and Urban Order

Studies as diverse as those by the early French geographers and Eugen Weber's considerably more recent study of the "modernization" of France, *Peasants into Frenchmen,* have complemented the traditional view of the city as a predator. France's humanistic geographers (as they are sometimes called), writing at the turn of the century, wanted to study the impact of environment on people. André Demangeon and followers of his like Paul Arbois and Jacques Levainville considered the relations of city and country to be a veritable war between urban civilization and those geographic and geophysical impediments believed to stand

in the way of its development. They described how human ingenuity and persistence overcame natural impediments such as hills and the lack of natural
resources for industrial development, and how towns such as Clermont-Ferrand,
Grenoble, and Rouen came to prosper economically only after struggle. The
humanistic geographers also left out politics completely.[118]

Weber's view of the relations between city and country is similar, to the extent
that he sees them in the context of a struggle between progress and "backward-
ness," modernity and archaism. To Weber, the city and its culture conquered the
savage, superstitious, autarkic world of the peasant sometime between 1880
and 1914, so that Frenchmen could all go off to war patriotically singing the
"Marseillaise" in acceptable French, feeling themselves French. Dramatically
improved transportation and communication, mass education directed from Paris,
and military conscription combined to stamp out those colorful "mad beliefs" of
the countryside and thus "modernize" France. In this way peasants, Weber
argues, became Frenchmen.[119]

The relationship between city and country is considerably more complicated
than that, as critics of Weber's provocative and entertaining book have demonstrated. Weber's description of rural France overlooks the vast complexity of rural
social structure. It also ignores the complexity of city and town, particularly, as we
shall see in Chapter 2, the strong remaining rural component of nineteenth-century
French urban life. The question of timing, too, is fundamental. Elements of his
"modernization" theory, which still retains influence among those seeking to
understand the past (and which assumes at its worst that the only purpose of history
is to uncover a few selected threads to the present), work for some French departments.[120] Elsewhere, for example in the Loire valley, these changes occurred
much earlier, at the beginning of the century, or before, or not until after World
War I, or may have yet to take place. Weber's interpretation cannot account for the
massive politicization of country people in parts of France during the Second
Republic.[121]

Yet there is something to this model of conquest that the humanistic geographers and Weber have postulated, when one considers the way in which urban
elites and the state viewed, feared, and ultimately acted to control the relatively
unpoliced, wide-open zones to the fringe of urban life. The physical characteristics
of the faubourg and outskirts of the city often mirrored the economic structure of
the mother city and at the same time helped determine their relationship. So also
did the unequal relationship between the centralized, powerful French state and its
urban minions. For the French state not only perpetuated the uncertain margins of
the urban periphery, but intensified the arbitrary division between city and country
represented by ramparts and other fortifications. Decisions taken by the powerful
could influence the evolution of faubourgs, the most obvious case being Louis
XIV's decision to build his palace west of Paris in Versailles.[122] Finally, the
decisions taken beginning in the late 1830s and 1840s on the routes that railroads
would take greatly spurred the development of the suburbs, even by mid-century.
By 1841 Corbeil, thirty kilometers southeast of Paris, was only an hour from the
capital by any of eight trains a day.

The relationship between center and periphery is defined by relations of domination and subordination. The state and municipal police try to impose their will on the outskirts of urban life, expanding the "bounded territory" of authority.[123] Government seeks to prevent smugglers from operating in the vicinity of the *octroi*. It seeks to impose order by demanding that inns and rooming houses keep records of all lodgers. It tries to keep an eye on the wide-open rural taverns, or *guinguettes,* beyond town walls. It searches for draft dodgers in time of war. In short, government seeks to impose both normative and spatial order.[124] The absorption of surrounding communes has usually been associated with the Second Empire and with the desire of municipalities to enhance their tax revenues.[125] Yet fear of the fringe must also be considered. Police action thus becomes the "faithful echo of the tested fear of marginal people . . . the organization of space, making it appear disciplinary and coercive, becomes again a means of control and of the social panopticon."[126]

Increasingly, organized workers seemed a far greater threat to the economic, social, and political order than the "dangerous classes." No one was more aware of this than the police. By the Second Empire, as Jeanne Gaillard has written, "[t]he fear of the faubourgs replaced the fear of the sick quarters of the center."[127] The *marginaux* gradually emerged as contenders for political power. Like the Limousins, Cantalous, and Vosgiens who formed the urban villages in Paris, the "marginal" person represented an urban experience far more stable than that predicted by the various uprooting hypotheses considering the social effects of migration, and thus of social and physical marginality.[128] Above all, the political threat posed by newly organized workers, more than the threat of the criminal "dangerous classes" identified with the center, lay behind what was an ever more efficiently organized and effective policing during the first half of the nineteenth century. State and municipality—and most af all, the political police—tried to impose order on the changing urban landscape. Thus "order" appeared on the edge of chaos in two ways: first, the victories, however partial, of the center and its police over the uncertain edge; second, the building of social and political movements by the marginal, for whom a collective identity or consciousness replaced the loose group solidarity characteristic of a "society of uprooting (*déracinement*)."[129]

The revolution of 1848 made the threat even more concrete, and the massive police repression that followed the June Days, and that was finely honed by Louis Napoleon Bonaparte in the name of "social order," included an almost frantic extension of police authority into the suburbs. One of the orchestrators of repression was Georges Haussmann. Born and educated in Paris, the functionary had been dismissed after the revolution of 1848 because of his loyal service to the July Monarchy as subprefect of the arrondissement of Blaye in the Gironde. Reinstated as prefect of the Var, a radical department, in January 1849, he was then transferred to the Yonne, another Montagnard stronghold, in May 1850. Days after his promotion to the prefecture of the Gironde in Bordeaux, in late November 1851, Louis Napoleon Bonaparte effected his coup d'état. Haussmann was now a rising star. Two years later he was named imperial prefect of the Seine.

David Harvey considers the rebuilding of Paris during the Second Empire in terms of the role of capital in the urbanization of social and spatial relations. For

Harvey, capitalism engendered "a dramatic transformation in the sense of urban space as the democracy of money increasingly came to dominate the land market in the nineteenth century." In an analysis strikingly similar to that of the humanistic geographers, Harvey describes the edge of the city as representing uneven development, "the barrier to be overcome" by capital, while providing housing and work for the burgeoning proletariat of the Paris region, including those recently expelled from the center by urban rebuilding and high prices. According to this interpretation, during the Second Empire the suburbs acted as something of a safety valve, however potentially explosive, for the grand scheme to reorganize the center, following the logic of capital and the imperatives of power. More than ever, Paris in 1870 was two cities. One Paris had wide boulevards "lit by gas lights, dazzling shop window displays, and cafés open to the street (an innovation of the Second Empire) . . . corridors of homage to the power of money and commodities, play spaces for the bourgeoisie,"[130] with its arcades of iron and glass housing luxury shops, and their even more aggressive offspring, the department stores.[131] The other Paris was much darker, particularly its virtually unlighted outskirts, densely populated, and feared.

Most people would agree that the authoritarian Second Empire was a turning point in the history of French urbanism. Napoleon III and Haussmann, whom Richard Cobb has dubbed "the Alsatian Attila," wanted above all to "improve the capacity for the circulation of goods and people within the city's confines." One result was the continued flow of heavy, light, and particularly "dirty" industry toward the outside. Dramatically increased social segregation was another, represented by the famous east-west dichotomy, with the residents of the bourgeois neighborhoods of the west reassured by enhanced isolation from ordinary people: "The chronic slum of the center, which affected mainly new immigrants and the old, was now matched by the suburbanization of family poverty affecting the young." The incorporated suburbs became "an educational wasteland" of little religious attachment.[132]

Boulevards had plowed through some old working-class neighborhoods, among them that of the rue Transnonain on the edge of the Marais, a street identified in the collective memory with the massacre of workers by the bourgeois national guard in 1834. Haussmann pulled no punches in his *Mémoires,* specifically associating the street with the insurgency.[133]

French cities, avaricious predators hungry for land, cheap labor, and taxes, thus also sought security. Harvey argues that Haussmann's "concern for the totality of the urban space was best represented by his fierce struggle, successful in 1860, to annex the suburbs where unruly development threatened the rational evolution of a spatial order within the agglomeration that was Paris." The incorporation of the near suburbs of Paris follows the relentless logic of capitalism.[134] It was not by coincidence that the peripheral communes of the near suburbs of Paris were annexed as of January 1, 1860.[135] Montmartre, Belleville, Vaugirard, and Grenelle, rapidly growing yet retaining much of their rural character, were among the twelve communes pulled into Paris as state and city extended the *octroi.* They formed part of newly reorganized arrondissements that have lasted to this day.

Daumier lithograph: "Now we're Parisians!" (Bibliothèque Nationale)

A Daumier lithograph (see illus.) shows two slightly bewildered peasants, residents of the former suburbs, exclaiming, "Just think! Now we're Parisians!" Villagers of the suburbs became Parisians, like it or not, and most apparently did not. The annexed zones became known popularly as "the faubourgs."[136] The outward expansion of Paris toward the periphery continued beyond the new limits of the capital. La Guillotière, Vaise, and the notorious Croix-Rousse had already been attached to Lyon while still under martial law in 1852. "Reclassification" became, along with net migration and excess births over deaths, a factor contributing to urban growth. Cities were centers of coercion, as well as of capital.

A contemporary observed in 1863: "The transformation of Paris, having forcibly removed the working population from the center toward the extremities, has made two cities of the capital—one rich, one poor. . . . The deprived classes form an immense cordon around the well-off." In 1870 another declared, "The flood of poverty rose in Belleville, while the river of luxury flowed at full crest in the new quarters of Paris."[137] Harvey quotes a journalist's description of Belleville, marked by "the deepest depths of poverty and of hatred, where ferments of envy, of sloth and anger, bubble without cease." The last resistance of the Paris Commune was battered down in the northeastern corner of Paris, including the heights of Belleville.[138]

In the wake of the massacre of twenty-five thousand people in the repression that followed the Commune, the Third Republic sought to "moralize" the peripheral population with voluntary associations sponsored by social elites and the clergy, and the construction of new churches in the faubourgs and industrial suburbs. The construction of the bizarre church of Sacré-Coeur on the Butte Montmartre best represents the concern of the conservative republic with a symbolic "conquest" of the fearful fringe and, particularly, its "commanding heights" where the uprising had begun.[139]

A recent study of Bobigny, in the internal northern *banlieue* of Paris, argues that it was not until the interwar years, after Communist successes in legislative and municipal elections in 1924–25, that the myth of the red belt and "a sudden crystallization of the social sphere of suburban space" developed.[140] In the red belt that grew up around Paris, Bretons "who came from hungry Brittany without much of a political consciousness began turning toward the left—toward social-ism," even before World War I.[141] Michelle Perrot has placed "the birth of the suburbs" just after the turn of the century, before the red belt of Paris emerged as the periphery's dominant political image, closely associated with the Communist party.[142] Yet well before, during the July Monarchy and in the wake of the revolution of 1848, the faubourgs and suburbs became part of the image and reality of that challenge. One cannot understand the Paris Commune and the fear it engendered for decades within the upper classes, which contributed to the apocalyptic image of the May 1 parades of workers as a dress rehearsal for revolution, without considering the bourgeois fear of the heights of Montmartre and Belleville. In Austria and Italy, among other places, the working-class suburbs were closely identified with the socialist challenge for power after World War I—for example, the famous *Rotgürtel,* the red belt or ring around Vienna.[143]

The conquering impulse of state and city had already, before the Second Empire, begun to reach out to pull periphery settlements, faubourgs, and com-munes into their official orbit. Some of these communities had already received a modicum of dignity, which they may or may not have wanted, by being referred to as "suburbs." The reason for such administrative absorption often had little or nothing to do with increased tax revenue, or the desire to provide municipal services to poor communes that could not afford them. It had much to do with a desire to control people like the prostitutes of Verdun, identifed with the "dan-gerous and laboring classes."[144]

Bernard Vincent has written that "marginality is a mirror." Attitudes toward the marginal "reveal both the consensus and the preoccupations of society as a whole."[145] For Roger Chartier, "it is often in discovering its margins or opposites and in trying to subdue, by acts of language, that which worries it that an established society best reveals its malaises, fissures, and phantasms."[146] Michael Foucault's contention that social elites seek to purify and consolidate social order through the creation or at least recognition of the "other"—for example, the "mad"—complements the spatial concomitants of center and periphery.[147] Elites sharpened and consolidated their own domination. After rejecting the "floating worlds" that they arguably helped create, they reached out to conquer the margins of city life. Ordinary people often resisted. This study is not only about the assumed disorganization and marginality, physical, social, and cultural, associated with the edge of urban life; it is also about solidarities of class and neighborhood—in short, about organization, about building a sense of belonging out of that of rejection, of not belonging.

Such an undertaking has presented major challenges of sources and documentation. Life beyond the barriers of urban space also meant life beyond close police surveillance, so reporting is sketchy. We need, as André Vant puts it, "to describe marginality in its locations, comportments, rhythms. . . . We must understand the time and space of the unemployed, poachers, vagabonds, prostitutes . . . to the extent that each marginal person or group has its own territory as each territory has its marginal people."[148] To describe, evoke, and analyze the marginal people of peripheral spaces is no easy task. Indeed, as Charles Tilly once put it, "Bitter hard it is to write the history of remainders."[149]

In subsequent chapters we will consider the period from the return of the Bourbon monarchy to the coup d'état of Louis Napoleon Bonaparte in December 1851. We begin with an overview of the development of faubourgs in France during the first half of the century. Chapter 2 emphasizes "that awkward embrace" between city and country not only in the faubourg but also in the persistence of an urban agricultural population. In addition, it considers how the troubled relationship between state and city affected the urban periphery, and presents an overview of the role of industry in the development of the faubourg. Chapter 3 considers the question of the "fearsome faubourgs," when and how the physical margins of urban life came to be so suspect. The urban periphery, the leading edge of urbanization and the future of the city, challenged government officials, urban elites, and the police. If, during the Restoration, the uncertainty of the city outskirts seemed fearsome, during the July Monarchy and, above all, after the revolution of 1848, faubourg and *banlieue* took on a more concrete image, that of increasingly organized workers contending for power.

Chapter 4 presents the theme of center and periphery, contrasting three towns in the conservative West. The nobility and clergy still dominated the administrative and ecclesiastical town of Poitiers, a town of nobles, clerics, functionaries, and landlords with no concentration of industry and small, insignificant faubourgs, but, like every other town, with specific spatial identities. Thirty-two kilometers away, Châtellerault offers an example of the classic nineteenth-century French commercial and industrial town, albeit of modest proportions. It drew its vitality from its faubourg Châteauneuf, the locus of industry. During the Second Republic, it was the workers from that faubourg who mounted a political challenge to the elite of Châtellerault. Here the political outcome, reflecting different patterns of economic development and urban settlement, was quite unlike that of administrative Poitiers, its stuffy aristocratic and clerical neighbor. Finally, we move on to what was France's newest town. The urban settlement that begun as La Roche-sur-Yon, became the town of Napoléon, then Bourbon-Vendée, and then Napoléon again, before becoming once again La Roche-sur-Yon, was as close to a true urban frontier as one could find in France. La-Roche-sur-Yon was a faubourg without a town. It became anything but a Vendean Shangri-la. For some time it barely existed but for the fact that the state, with Cartesian logic, had made it a departmental capital, yet it deserves a detailed albeit somewhat whimsical look nonetheless. For if Louis Chevalier is right about the impact of urbanization, La Roche-sur-Yon should have been the most dangerous city in France.

In chapter 5, we return to Perpignan, whose marginal Catalan people have already been briefly introduced. Perpignan provides a splendid example of the spatial dimensions and identity of cultural marginality. As the police discovered, there was nothing disorganized about the *paysans*—not really peasants, but an agricultural population of *brassiers* or day laborers, gardeners, and a smattering of small property owners—most of whom lived in two neighborhoods with identical cultural traditions but markedly opposite political identities and rival social solidarities. We will follow these peripheral people through the political awakening that pushed Perpignan to the left, a transformation inexplicable without an understanding of the solidarities of the two neighborhoods. The French police tried to impose their order upon ordinary people in Perpignan. Here too the political threat posed by the left increased the reach of the police and intensified the war of the state against Catalan structure.

In chapter 6 Nîmes offers a complementary but intriguingly different case. Its precocious faubourgs, well established by the middle of the eighteenth century, formed the basis for political mobilization and bitter rivalry between Catholics and Protestants. Here too, neighborhood solidarities were crucial to political life. Here too, the mobilization of ordinary people challenged the police, but not the kind of criminality described by Chevalier. Despite a level of urban violence perhaps unmatched in France, organization, not disorganization, was the experience of the people of the city's faubourgs and the bane of the police. Protestants and Catholics became, in turn, marginalized by the shifting fortunes of French political elites during the first half of the century.

We then turn to Reims in chapter 7. Despite its long tradition as an ecclesiastical center—the site of coronations since the time of Clovis—large-scale industrialization made Reims one of France's fastest growing cities. The workers of the vast faubourgs of Fléchambault and Cérès struggled against the woolens manufacturers' domination of political power after the February revolution of 1848. In doing so, they frightened the bourgeoisie of the center city, the state, and the police that served them both. Did the feeling or self-identification of marginality, of not belonging to the center, contribute to the formation of a new collective consciousness of belonging that seems to have been shared by the workers of the upper town of Reims? Did this feeling of exclusion help shape the sense of belonging—a negative integration—that generated a working-class challenge to the center for political power?

Finally, in chapter 8 we return to the relationship between state, city, and periphery to discuss the conquest of faubourgs and suburbs, as the police reached out to impose order on the urban frontier. We will find examples in the suburbs of Paris and in the troubled relationship between the port of Le Havre and its seemingly turbulent suburb, Ingouville, situated beyond and above the city gates, as if poised to attack—like the silkworkers of Lyons in 1831 and 1834—the *beaux quartiers* below.

2

City and Country:
That Awkward Embrace

Town and country, city and state, industry and agriculture, bourgeois and proletarian, settled resident, prosperous or not, and uncertain newcomer, met and at
the same time created the faubourg and suburb. The faubourg was by definition a
space of uncertainty, ambivalence, and marginality, the periphery in every sense,
but at the same time the urban future. Here again is Victor Hugo in *Les Misérables:*

> To wander in a kind of reverie, to take a stroll as they call it, is a good way for a
> philosopher to spend his time; particularly in that kind of bastard countryside,
> somewhat ugly but bizarre, made up of two different natures, which surrounds
> certain great cities, notably Paris. To observe the *banlieue* is to observe an
> amphibian. End of trees, beginning of roofs, end of grass, beginning of paving
> stones, end of ploughed fields, beginning of shops, the end of the beaten track, the
> beginning of the passions, the end of the murmur of things divine, the beginning
> of the noise of humankind—all of this holds an extraordinary interest. And thus,
> in these unattractive places, forever marked by the passer-by with the epithet *sad,*
> the promenades, apparently aimless, of the dreamer.[1]

To understand the urban periphery in France during the first half of the
nineteenth century, we must first explore three things: the relationship between
state and city as reflected in town walls, particularly military fortifications; the
persistence of rural life on the edge of city and town, and within it; and finally, the
place of industry in the emergence of the nineteenth-century faubourg.

The State, Ramparts, and Faubourgs

The physical shape of faubourgs depended to some extent upon whether town
walls or ramparts remained. During the first half of the century, many towns were
freed of their walls, although not as rapidly as their populations desired.[2] The state
thus played a central role in establishing the physical and social perimeters of the
periphery and of the inhabitants who came to be considered marginal. Since the
ramparts of Paris had been ordered down by Louis XIV in the 1680s, a wall of
surprisingly modest dimensions had been constructed shortly before the Revolution, to facilitate the collection of the *octroi* taxes ("le mur murant Paris rend Paris
murmurant," went a popular lament).

Elsewhere, particularly in the case of cities and towns of no particular strategic significance, the walls—or at least most of them—had come down for good. This was true of big cities like Rouen, the fortifications of which had disappeared in the 1780s, and smaller towns like Figeac, Tarbes, Guéret, Mende, Dreux, and Agen. In the modest industrial town of Saint-Claude in the Jura, only vestiges of the ramparts survived, although its faubourg, surrounded by orchards and gardens, remained hemmed in by the left bank of the Bienne river and the mountains.[3] Parts of the walls survived in Orléans during the July Monarchy, but the old moats had been transformed into gardens or had helped form exterior boulevards. In 1795 a member of the municipality of Chartres had proposed that his town be "de-gothicized" and aired out by the destruction of its fortifications. During the July Monarchy an exterior boulevard was built following the path of the old ramparts; the last gates, with the exception of the porte Guillaume, preserved as a historical monument, fell between 1832 and 1847. The people of the textile town of Vire in Normandy, grateful that most of the town walls had at last fallen, were embarrassed that some remnants of the ramparts remained. The latter seemed too much vestiges of the past, not modern.[4]

The ramparts that remained reinforced the complicated, ambivalent attitude of garrison towns toward the military presence. The walls helped cut down on smuggling, the bane of tax officials and municipal budgets, but a boon to ordinary people trying to make ends meet. Indirect taxation remained the basis of French taxes. The *octroi* was collected at the edge of French cities with a population over five thousand until World War II. Tax offices were often attached to or near the gates themselves, an example of which may be seen in the porte Saint-Martin in Paris today (or in Chaumont, Cahors, and other places where splendid examples of small *octroi* offices and posts remain). In cities and towns that had been freed from ramparts and fortifications, the *octroi* provided a less imposing physical barrier between city and country, so that smuggling or cheating on the entry tax was easier.[5] In response to urban growth and the need to facilitate collection, the *octroi* was simply pushed farther out, extending the circumference of the city into the periphery, beyond which new settlements developed.

Military fortifications constrained urban growth where the army established building-free zones that extended beyond the ramparts themselves. Although not all garrison towns had thick walls, it was in France's fortified towns (*villes fortes*) that they were most resented, preventing the natural development of faubourgs. Garrisons brought hard-drinking soldiers, eager contenders for the affection and favors of local women, and boisterous and sometimes violent clients of the prostitution houses. Yet there was another side to the military presence. Merchants drew upon an expanded clientele, and municipal budgets increased modestly from additional provisions passing through the *octroi*. The municipal council of Auch had this in mind when, in 1819, it implored the army to send a regiment not out of fear of invasion from Spain, but "to revive commerce and industry and provide an outlet for essential goods."[6]

Garrisons were decidedly a mixed blessing, but urban dwellers had other reasons to resent the ramparts that remained. They impeded building and traffic. The walled circumference of Grenoble was expanded to incorporate the southern faubourg; beginning in 1840, this ultimately doubled the land within the ramparts. But the work proceeded slowly, at least partially, because an economic crisis prevented the expansion of the new quarters as rapidly as had been hoped. And because the municipality and the state had come to no agreement as to what would happen to the old walls, they stood until the mid-1850s, further blocking the development of the anticipated new neighborhoods.[7]

In fortified towns, where the army limited or forbade building within one hundred meters of the walls, so that a besieging enemy could not make use of structures outside the ramparts, there were few or no faubourgs. If faubourgs did exist, they could be reached only after passing through the open spaces dictated by the military engineers. This was the case with most of the towns fortified by Vauban in the seventeenth century. Sedan remained "locked in its old walls." Verdun suffered even then at the hands of an army—its own—"captive in a tight corset of ramparts."[8] A history of Nantes published by two bitter legitimists, supporters of the deposed Bourbon Monarchy, in 1836 complained of the "uselessness" of their city's fortifications.[9] Townspeople bitterly resented the limitations and regulations established by army engineers. In Perpignan, as we shall see, the municipality was at loggerheads with the army shortly before the revolution of 1830, because the military engineers forbade building in the zone of the fortifications. It was the same in Quesnoy in the Nord, another of Vauban's towns.

Caen, with a population of 41,310 in 1836, was outgrowing its walled center. Six faubourgs had developed: Vaucelles, south of the Orne, near which an eleventh-century church had been converted into a gas factory; Calix, named after a fountain, which led to Hérouville to the east along the old road to Rouen; Vaugueux, north of the upper town and east of the château, where one could drink at the Auberge de la Giraffe; Saint-Julien, northwest of the château; Abbé, the site of the prison at Beaulieu on the route west to Cherbourg; and finally, Saint-Ouen (sometimes called Bretagne), which led to Granville and followed the canal d'Adam. The faubourgs grew to include about a third of the houses of Caen. Here many migrants, particularly those from rural Calvados and the Manche, contributed to the city's modest growth from about 36,000 under the Empire to 45,000 in 1851. Not surprisingly, the faubourgs of Vaugueux and Vaucelles suffered a disproportionate number of deaths during the cholera epidemic of 1832. The old Norman city bitterly resented the zone that the army controlled beyond the ramparts and in 1835 asked that its château be "declassified" as a military fortification.[10]

In the Pas-de-Calais, Montreuil had fought the same battle, complaining that buildings within the military zone could not be kept up; the departmental general council wrote that army regulations were interfering with the development of local commerce and industry.[11] Ramparts also limited the physical expansion of the port city of Toulon, one of the fastest growing cities in France during the first half of the century (increasing from 28,000 in 1831 to 45,000 in just fifteen years). The result was that migrants and temporary residents piled into the overcrowded central city or lived in the faubourgs that developed beyond the military zone. Between 1820 and 1840, the peripheral communes of Saint-Jean-du-Var and Le-Pont-du-Las reached several thousand in population; residents remained cut off from Toulon by the imposing ramparts at night, and were subject to delays at the gates during the day. Not surprisingly, the leftist Ledru-Rollin was a popular candidate in these working-class faubourgs in the 1848 presidential elections.[12]

The walls of Cambrai, another of Vauban's masterpieces of military defense along the northern frontier, also limited the development of that town. They separated the commercial center from the sizable zone outside the ramparts where "the habitat disperses along the footpaths and village roads [and] activities remain rural. Relations between the two are not always easy." The municipality neglected the *extra muros* inhabitants, such as those of the faubourg Notre-Dame. The prefect had to force the council to allocate money to repair the paths outside the ramparts.[13]

Far to the south, encircled by fortifications and an exterior moat, Narbonne had virtually no faubourgs in the 1820s. On the route to Perpignan a small settlement included two *guinguettes,* several tile works, and a delapidated aqueduct. At the time of the municipal census of 1820, there were only fourteen households on the route to Saint-Pons; in 1851 there were still only eighty-nine. Narbonne remained a large bourg imprisoned in its ramparts, which imposed a quite arbitrary barrier between countryside and city. Three of its gates were closed at night; that the fourth was open encouraged speculation on the land around it. The fortifications enhanced resentment against the tax on drink, culminating in serious riots in 1831. Yet despite the fact that the Narbonnais denounced the walls as impractical, no changes could be made until the army agreed to remove the town from the list of "places of war." Louis-Philippe allocated funds to rebuild the walls where they had been weakened. Only in 1865 did the army consent to "declassify" Narbonne, and even then the town got rid of its ramparts only at great expense, having to purchase them from the state for 500,000 francs so they could be knocked down. Narbonne's faubourgs then developed rapidly.[14]

The population of Chaumont, a fortress town in the East, "suffocated in the tight wall of fortifications." Designated a *place de guerre* in 1821, with fresh memory of the allied invasion of 1814 and the peace treaty signed there that year, Chaumont was delighted to be demoted to the rank of a military post in 1842. The municipality subsequently petitioned that the town lose its military classification entirely, then in 1848 took advantage of the administrative chaos to demolish the fortifications, a process completed within a few years. The residents of Chaumont, enjoying the infusion of fresh air, watched as new boulevards followed the traces of the old walls, and buildings took shape where peripheral gardens had once stood.[15]

There were of course towns of very modest growth that did not push against the ramparts. La Rochelle, still surrounded by walls (with the remarkable towers of the Chain, Liberty, and the Lantern facing the sea), in 1844 had seven gates but only one faubourg, Tassin, which had been burned several times during the wars of religion. Besides the military engineers and the lack of industry, the infertility of the salt marshes around La Rochelle was to blame. The population of the seventeenth-century city increased very slowly, reaching only 14,857 in 1841, and this largely because its climate and location attracted retired people. La Rochelle would have been little more than an overgrown fishing village, had it not remained the largest commercial port between Nantes and Bordeaux. With but one modest faubourg, the once proud fortified port that had defied siege for so long hardly seemed like a nineteenth-century city.[16]

Faubourg, Country, and City

City and country met in the faubourgs. In Carcassonne, where agricultural day laborers and gardeners lived in the poor peripheral quarters of the lower town, they were gradually pushed by higher prices up into the picturesque but impoverished Cité.[17] Here and elsewhere, the half-rural, half-urban character of the faubourg persisted, called by "its picturesque or common names," or simply "path" (*chemin*), or nothing at all. Low houses with straw roofs still characterized many faubourgs, defiantly stressing the rural side of the equation. So did its residents' lack of variety in clothing, which remained rural in style, constrained by function, habit, and poverty, as on the outskirts of La Rochelle.[18]

So too, some faubourg dwellers retained superstitious beliefs characteristic of the countryside. In 1833, at a time when many fortune-tellers were about, a "grotesquely dressed" woman entered several houses on the outskirts of Issoudun and gravely informed the woman of the house that "her husband or her father or her mother is dead, burning in the flames of hell," or that "her spouse will die at a certain time or that her child will be cut up into pieces." Whether or not her victims agreed to have their fortune told, for fifteen centimes, they were informed of the terrors that lay ahead or had already begun. She willingly proposed a way "to avoid such unhappiness. It will not occur, if you give me money to have Masses said." Not just any Masses would do, but one said by the Pope himself, with whom she was in constant touch. For this, two francs was the charge. One franc could get a suffering soul out of Purgatory. Sufficiently frightened, the women sometimes gave her their prized possessions—perhaps some bread, oil, eggs, or a little money. The prophetess of doom, Patra Thérèse, who claimed to be a "musician" from the Loiret traveling with her husband and three children, found gullible victims even on the edge of relatively cosmopolitan Issoudun.[19]

The omnipresence of vineyards, as along the valley of the Seine or from Ivry to Juvisy east of Paris, also lent a rural image to the urban periphery. So did the country houses scattered throughout the hinterland of most cities and towns, some of which, overwhelmed later in the century by urban growth, remained as memorials to an earlier period, surrounded by considerably more modest structures, like a group of ugly ducklings huddled around an elegant mother duck. The rural character of the *guinguettes* and *bouchons,* or modest cabarets, went beyond their cheaper prices, as seen in their sloping roofs, often of straw, their stables, and their hard-drinking clientele drawn from several worlds. Each time the Paris wall and its *octroi,* or those of other cities as well, had been extended, the *guinguettes* had taken up farther out. The heights of Ménilmontant, with a population of about eight hundred in the 1820s, had become a "gathering place for the people of the faubourgs." The *Guide résumé du voyageur aux environs de Paris,* published in 1826, carefully listed what the author considered the most attractive *auberges* and *guinguettes.* During the Restoration, the environs of Paris attracted promenaders and revelers fleeing toward the open spaces of the countryside, as for example Romainville—''The Parisians go there in droves—it is famous for its woods, which have a charming effect''—and Sceaux, offering ''public promenades of the best taste.'' Parisians still went to Longchamps during Holy Week as under the ancien régime, to ''hear beautiful voices sing the mysteries,'' but the liturgical attraction was secondary at best. The abbey of Longchamps no longer existed. Holy Week now served as ''a profane diversion during the most sacred time of the year.''[20]

The pervasive influence of agriculture and rural life within nineteenth-century French cities and towns is often forgotten. The agricultural preoccupations of the urban periphery not only persisted in most places but were accentuated in many with the development of garden or truck farming in response to the demands of the increased urban population. If the stomach of Paris was Les Halles, the long arms and deft fingers of the capital reached ever more persistently and efficiently into the periphery to find food. Faubourgs and suburbs could, like the towns they led to and from, contribute to urban growth without industry.

On the other side of the Loire from Orléans, itself sometimes already described as a faubourg of Paris, the faubourg of Saint-Marceau stretched along the route to Toulouse. Its population had reached two thousand—enough, had it been a separate commune, to have been considered an urban area. It housed truck farmers producing for the Orléans market and led to country houses owned by wealthy Orléanais, who did not have far to go to reach the countryside. Saint-Marceau served as a cord that pulled the bourg of Olivet, on the other side of the Loiret, into the grudging status of a suburb of Orléans, as Olivet was described in 1837, when it had a population of 3,352. Nearby, the village of Sandillon had swelled to three or four thousand, mostly market gardeners, day laborers, vine dressers, and iron workers. A hand-drawn map of a military survey shows that the faubourg of Saint-Marceau had almost reached Olivet by 1837. Industry, the modest role of which was rapidly declining in Orléans, had virtually nothing to do with the growth of the city's major faubourg and suburb.[21]

The faubourgs of the stately *ville parlementaire* of Rennes provide another example. These faubourgs grew without really losing their ancien régime character.[22] By 1822 there were so many settlements along the route to Lorient that everything between Rennes and the village of Mordelles was considered to be part of the faubourg; ''everything reflected daily relations'' between the two. The largest of the faubourgs of Rennes, the faubourg de Paris, still ''seems like a village'' in 1847, although it had already been necessary to widen the road running through it. The faubourg straggled down the hill upon which stood the abbey of Saint-Méline, toward the hamlet of Saint-Méen. An officer surveying the faubourg described the first houses upon leaving the city as ''pretty, gracious,'' like much of Rennes, which had been rebuilt in the wake of the terrible fire of 1720. Farther out, the houses gradually diminished in size ''as one approaches the countryside. Finally you find only farms and thatched cottages'' of a single floor with open yards, modest stables, bales of straw propped up against tree trunks, and ''nauseating dunghills'' in the mud. ''Villages, hamlets, faubourgs of the towns, isolated dwellings in the countryside, everything is on this model," stated the survey of 1858, indicating that virtually nothing had changed. Finally, one reached Saint-Méen, where a convent had been transformed into an *hospice des aliénés.* The nearby faubourg Saint-Hélier, on the left bank of the Vilaine, offered a contrast: the houses farther out were more solid in construction, including elegant country houses and even châteaux several kilometers from the old noble city. That faubourg, however, was also populated with poorer residents; each day three hundred meals were distributed to the poor.[23]

Because these faubourgs, and many others on the outskirts of French cities, were not industrial, did not mean that conditions of life were necessarily any better. Most of the inhabitants of the faubourgs, after all, lived there because they lacked resources to live in Rennes itself. Many had to walk into town to work as day laborers or domestics. The houses of the faubourgs, though usually smaller than those of the center, were not necessarily any more spacious or clean. The carpenters complained in 1848 that they were "very poorly lodged in the houses of the faubourgs . . . piled on top of each other, breathing foul and fetid air."[24]

The faubourgs of many towns thus retained an essentially agricultural population. Agro-towns characteristic of the Mediterranean coast and of Alsace, above all, reflected the close relationship between town and country, not only serving as market centers for agricultural production, but housing a sizable agricultural population whose interests and work lay in the hinterland.[25] In fortified agro-towns like the Mediterranean towns of Toulon, Perpignan, Narbonne, and Béziers, "peasants"—small property owners, gardeners, and *brassiers,* the land-less laborers who worked the surrounding fields and, increasingly, vineyards—lived within the ramparts in quarters so rural in character that they were referred to as "faubourgs." It was more than metaphor. In 1851—the year of the census, as well as of Louis Napoleon's coup d'état, unpopular in Narbonne and much of the Aude—more of a third (37%) of the active population of the city was in the agricultural sector. The rural character of parts of the "large bourg" of Narbonne was readily apparent in many of the *ilôts,* or "small islands" of residence.[26]

The rural side of faubourgs reflected the mixed character of many cities themselves in the first half of the nineteenth century. It was more than just the meeting of rural and urban life on the edge of the city: rural life had long been inserted into the texture of urban life.[27] In many ways Chartres, despite its towering cathedral and imposing seminary (where the future Cardinal Pie learned his unfailing orthodoxy; see chapter 4), remained a somewhat overgrown bourg. Its population reached 13,800 about the time that the revolution of 1830 reduced the influence of its clergy, and stood at only 18,000 in 1850. This agricultural population was as common inside the city as outside: 300 vine dressers lived within the communal limits, particularly in Bourgneuf and in the faubourg Saint-Jean; many *cultivateurs* too resided in the faubourgs, especially in the Grand Faubourg beyond the place des Epars. A spate of municipal decrees, such as that regulating the raising of pigeons and forbidding marching batallions of geese ("who run every day through the streets and squares of this town; their droppings cause great filth and a horrible stench"), seemed more appropriate to a small bourg than an administrative, ecclesiastical, and commercial center.

As Chartres slowly grew, the place des Epars, which had been on the periphery, took on ever increasing importance in the life of the town. It linked the faubourgs to the center, and served as a point of departure for coaches. New buildings settled around the square, described in 1831 as "modern and in good taste," including the Hôtel du Grand Monarch, still there today. The stone houses of the wealthy Chartrains contrasted sharply with the medieval wooden houses of the lower town. The last four gates of Chartres were dismantled during the July Monarchy. Although the *octroi* barriers remained, the disappearance of the gates and remaining parts of the wall facilitated entry into Chartres, as well as the development of a new neighborhood around the boulevard Saint-Michel.[28]

The markets of Chartres still determined its life and prosperity. In the early 1830s, on some days seven thousand sacks of grain changed hands. The markets were "regulated to the last detail," overseen by "sworn and responsible" men and served by paid measurers and weighers and their clerks. Chartres's best-known *corporation* ran the grain market. The *leveuses de cul-de-sac*—sixty-seven members in 1831—were divided into fifteen small associations, or *corporations,* including Les Baudouines, Les Mulottes, and Les Luttonnes. They kept track of the sacks of grain, noted the going price, loaded the sacks to be measured, and sold them on behalf of their owners, who returned to claim their money from the women at the end of the market. The association was collectively responsible for any errors made by one of its members.

Men of wealth in Chartres who made money from the grainfields of La Beauce invested it as rapidly as possible in the surrounding countryside.[29] Some 12 percent of the population lived from rents from the countryside, most within thirty kilometers; they may have owned 40 percent of the land of the region. Even by its forms of sociability, Chartres seemed part of the rural world: "The bourgeois of Chartres takes walks around his town as the farmer tours his fields on Sunday." The putting out of textile work, such as vests and wool socks, into the countryside from thirty-five to forty merchant capitalists also helped affirm the intersection of rural and urban life in Chartres.[30]

Even cities and towns less integrated with the world of agriculture than Chartres followed the rhythm of the countryside. Verdun, where we began, offers another good example. Here too, the ritual opening and closing of the gates represented an artificial separation of "the countryside and a city still completely penetrated by rural life." In 1842, 90 percent of the goods that passed through the *octroi* of Verdun were farm products. In 1825 there were thirty-nine cowsheds and pigsties within the walls; entire streets constituted "village streets inserted into the urban fabric." This rural nature contributed, it was thought at the time of the 1832 cholera epidemic, to health hazards, its "urban structure favoring the accumulation and confusion of activities and agricultural waste products (dunghills, etc.)." In contrast to the relatively modern technology available to the garrison, Verdun lacked sidewalks until the 1840s. Townspeople complained. Vineyards covered the nearby hills, producing a wine of such mediocrity that the phylloxera epidemic of the 1870s may have seemed to some an act of mercy. During the July Monarchy complaints surfaced about the slaughter and roasting of a pig in the middle of the street. The *Journal de la Meuse* insisted that "the economic reality gives a better idea of the image of the city. . . . [Agricultural life] strongly penetrates the city. Is Verdun a rural town? In any case, one vigorously engaged in the agricultural economy.'' The countryside ran headlong into the ramparts, as if stopped dead in its tracks from reaching its natural goal, an illusion belied by the nature of Verdun.[31]

Sixty-five miles to the southeast, market gardeners and vine dressers still resided in Nancy, and even more in its developing suburbs.[32] In Sedan two large faubourgs, Cassine and Ménil, formed the lower town (*ville basse*), and another, Le Fonds de Givonne, was separated from Sedan by fortifications. Sedan's faubourgs reached into the countryside, toward villages that gradually became faubourgs themselves. One of these was Torcy, across the Meuse, populated (1,835 inhabitants in 1840) by ''half-worker, half-peasant weavers.''[33]

The population of Albi, too was ''still very close to the rural world . . . natural rhythms impose themselves on everything, the rhythms of the seasons and of day and night were more significant than today.'' During the Restoration a mayor complained about pigs wandering through the streets unattended and offered a small reward to anyone who captured one of the cranky beasts and took it to the hospice, where it was not to be healed but eaten. Auch ''still retains the allure of an overgrown bourg, with gardens, orchards, and meadows coming right up to the first houses'' of the outskirts, with manors close to the town. Farmers and agricultural laborers lived in town as well as on its outskirts; were it not for the *octroi,* it would have been almost impossible to know where the town began.[34] Producers living in Angers provided 10 percent of the town's cereal and 95 percent of the potatoes. More than one hundred varieties of fruits and vegetables were produced on the periphery of the agricultural town. The development of the many lucrative nurseries on the edge of the city closely followed ''the triumph of rural investment'' in Angers. It seemed most appropriate that the visit of the widely traveled Duchesse d'Angoulême in 1823 should serve as the pretext for the baptism of a new kind of autumn pear. Agriculture still employed 23 percent of the working population of the town at midcentury.[35]

In Dijon, where about 1,800 of the town's population of 22,300 lived in the faubourgs in 1850, the lives of the inhabitants of the latter were ''organically tied to the economy of the soil.'' There too, ''the countryside penetrates the town: gardens and enclosed fields are found in great number around the convents, behind respectable houses, among the old fortifications.''[36] The rhythms of commerce in the capital of Burgundy were those of ''a semirural life'' centering on its three large fairs. Farm laborers, gardeners, and vine dressers who worked outside the walls made up a small but solid agricultural population (3.5%) in 1836. Most lived in the parishes of Saint-Pierre and Saint-Philibert, on the periphery of Dijon, yet within the walls, or in the faubourg Saint-Nicolas. The exodus of wealthy Dijonnais leaving for country houses was ''one of the most respected rites'' of the July Monarchy.[37] Even in Le Mans, where tensions between city and country— exacerbated by the Revolution, when the city had been besieged by its royalist hinterland—the farming population of the faubourgs were a common sight.[38] In the faubourg Saint-Jacques in Nantes, separated from the port city by the Loire, straw roofs could be seen in 1827.[39] ''A population of gardeners and wine growers

(6%), day laborers (6.2%) and even farmhands'' resided in the faubourgs of Blois, the commerce of which depended on marketing the agricultural produce of the surrounding region.[40]

The geography of hilltop towns like Poitiers and Angoulême seemed to accentuate the considerable rural character of the faubourgs that lay below. Laon, capped by its Gothic masterpiece, the cathedral, consists of two hills joined by a passage 160 meters wide. Its six faubourgs, each formed by the arrival of the principal roads to the *chef-lieu* of the Aisne, lay on the plain 120 meters below, at the level of the Ardon river. The porte de Soissons today reminds one of the imposing climb that wagons and pedestrians faced as they approached the *octroi*. Although physically separated from ''the mountain'' of Laon, the villages of Saint-Marcel, La Neuville, Vaux, Ardon, Semilly, and L'Avilly remained largely agricultural faubourgs.[41]

Just as it is simplistic to imagine that France's ''countryside'' somehow represented a single ''peasant'' culture where rural people worked their own land or someone else's, so too is it an error to think that there was but one ''urban'' culture that ultimately reached out to conquer the countryside in the name of ''modernization.''[42] The ebb and flow between city and country included merchant capitalists who brought raw materials to villages, hamlets, and isolated farms where cottage industry and agriculture coexisted, as for example the rural embroiderers of Lorraine, many thousands of whom were still producing in the last decades of the nineteenth century. Agro-towns provide the most obvious example of the impingement of rural life on the urban world, particularly along the Mediterranean and in Alsace. But, more than this, several salient aspects of rural life had survived even within the formal limits of French cities and towns. There was nothing marginal about these agricultural folk who happened to live in cities and towns. They were an intrinsic part of French urban life during the first half of the nineteenth century, and beyond.

The Faubourg and Industry

In the nineteenth century the growth of faubourgs was most closely tied to large-scale industrialization. The periphery offered open space; land that became less expensive the farther out one went from the center; and proximity to routes, rivers, canals, and, beginning in the July Monarchy, railroads to haul in raw materials and take away manufactured goods. The location of most railroad stations on the edge of town reinforced this trend and created new quarters, as in Saint-Etienne and Perpignan.

The larger workshops, factories, and warehouses of the urban outskirts attracted an under- or unemployed proletariat that settled on the periphery, taking advantage of lower costs and, for many, proximity to work in Paris, if they were lucky enough to find a job. The peripheralization of certain unhealthy trades like tanning, as we have noted, contributed to the association of the city's outskirts with both industrial work and marginality. Faubourgs that were largely of a single trade, such as the silk weavers' Croix-Rousse in Lyon and the cabinetmakers' faubourg Saint-Antoine in Paris, relatively close to the quais of the Seine in eastern

Paris, became rarer. They gave way to more heterogeneous industrial faubourgs or suburbs such as Belleville and Saint-Denis on the edge of Paris, or La Guillotière across the Rhône from Lyon. Eighty miles south of Lyon, on the outskirts of Montélimar, before the bridge across the Rhône to the Ardèche, the hamlet of Montélimar-les-Travailleurs attests to this spatial evolution.

In 1822, junior officers began undertaking military surveys (*reconnaissances militaires*) of the outskirts of Paris, its faubourgs, and the villages surrounding the capital.[43] They and subsequent officers offered firsthand testimony, and in many cases documented statistically the ongoing transformation of the Parisian periphery. The population of the environs of Paris grew rapidly. Garden farming became more lucrative in response to the booming Paris market. However, officers reported, and sometimes seemed surprised by the fact, that industrial concentration was altering the dominant rural character of many of the surrounding communes. The *Guide résumé du voyageur aux environs de Paris* (in 1826) also expressed considerable interest in the changing landscape, noting with pleasure that the hamlet of Alfort offered visitors not only a "great concourse of visitors in good weather" but also a "splendid hydraulic machine."[44] Paris was and is not France, but the industrialization of its environs reflected a process occurring on the fringe of many French cities and towns. This process was well under way at the time of the annexation of its near suburbs in 1860.[45]

A walk out through the gates of Paris, beyond the wall more than three meters high, was thus an exploration into the capital's future. Several settlements around the city still consisted almost entirely of country houses or permanent residences of Parisian bourgeois, such as Saint-Mandé to the east ("almost all bourgeois, no peasants, few tradesmen"). Auteuil, which, with a population of 1,100, had once counted La Fontaine, Molière, and Condorcet among its residents, at least for the good season.[46] Visitors eagerly sought the idyllic pleasures of the Seine and the Marne and the greenery and woods of the outskirts. But despite the remaining rural landscape and colorful taverns and other drinking spots where people on both sides of the customs barriers gathered, the trip was increasingly not a pretty sight. These officers discovered the margins of urban life.

Many prosperous farmers remained in the communes surrounding the great capital that provided their prosperity. They contrasted with less sedentary workers forced to sell their labor, when they could, for pitifully low wages. The latter lacked enough to eat, worked too hard, and aged prematurely. The proletarian image of the faubourg gradually became that of the full-fledged suburb. The parts of Ivry that lay between its center and the fortifications (and which, after 1860, would join the thirteenth arrondissement) had become "particularly desolate, bringing together a poor population" in need of assistance.[47]

North of Paris, Le Bourget in 1825 had 45 houses, 407 people, 1,500 sheep, and no workshops or factories of any kind, and Pantin was "a handsome enough village along the road to Meaux." The fertile plain of Saint-Denis, that commune of 1,400 later to be most identified with the suburban proletariat, produced a variety of vegetables. On the edge of Paris, La Chapelle was known for its commerce in drink, most of which was consumed there by "the poor people" of Paris.[48]

To the east of the capital, Vincennes and particularly Montreuil were renowned for delectable vegetables and fruits. Of Montreuil's population of about 3,200 in 1825, 2,400 were farmers of some kind, producing some 40,000 francs worth of fruit each year. In Fontenay there were few people not involved in raising wheat, rye, barley, or vegetables for the urban octopus. One hundred and fifty artisans lived in Nogent-sur-Marne, but its many *maisons de campagne* and 800 *cultivateurs* reflected its lingering rural image. In 1836 its thousand full-time inhabitants still included peasants who "know how to take advantage of the smallest plots of land." With a good number of country houses scattered among the vineyards, it looked more like a town "than many towns of the provinces."[49] The hamlets on the route de Bondy from Vincennes to Rosny likewise almost all produced fruit and vegetables for Paris, bringing the inhabitants "prosperity and even a certain relative luxury."[50] Most of the 1,900 inhabitants of Vitry, "a place of nurseries, vineyards, and arable land," worked the soil.[51] To the south, Fresnes shipped grain to Paris, while Sceaux, already a sizable market town of 1,700 people, specialized in small-scale farming amid country houses for Parisian tables.[52]

To the west, Neuilly lay beyond the unfinished Arc de Triomphe. Although far from being the most chic of suburbs, it was already a sizable settlement in 1822; it had 430 houses, a population of "fixed" residents of 2,900, and 3,400 classified as "mobile." There was little farming or gardening in Neuilly; although there was a gas factory, laundering the clothes of Parisians was the most prevalent economic activity.

The western environs of Paris, including Passy, Auteuil, and Boulogne, produced great quantities of wine. From these communes too, laundresses made the trek to the capital, some in wagons, some on foot, to pick up laundry to wash in the Seine.[53] On the left bank, agricultural Asnières, with a population of about four hundred, sold food and wine to Paris, as did adjoining Besons. Argenteuil, eight kilometers away, was covered with vineyards that had the reputation for producing the best wine in the region (in contrast to "Suresnes wine," of such bitter taste that the expression came to mean any awful wine).[54] Argenteuil's well-aligned, paved streets gave it the look of a small town, but one still close enough to nature to attract Monet. The wall that had once protected the town had been taken down, its path now covered with gardens and a boulevard planted with trees. By 1833 some 3,500 of its 4,727 people depended on the production of wine for their livelihood; vineyards occupied 70 percent of its arable land. Colombes too, with 1,600 people, had many vineyards and gardens.[55]

In place of these Restoration images of gentle, bucolic, agricultural villages serving and profiting from the voracious urban market there emerged another reality, an explosion of industry. Courbevoie's well-built houses and gardens may have lent it an "enchanting aspect," at least to the officer carrying out a military survey—in 1822 two-thirds of the families worked the land—but he also mentioned several manufactures, including a distillery for eau-de-vie made from grain and potatoes, and a linen factory. Ivry to the southeast of Paris was already a sizable settlement of 1,359 people. Workers there spun wool and produced bottles, roof tiles, and construction stone. A sign of the times, there were no fewer than sixty-three cabarets and *auberges* in Ivry, a few within the shadow of the château of the Duchesse d'Orléans. In 1822 some of the buildings of the estate of a member of the Chamber of Deputies housed "improved workshops" for spinning textile production.[56] Vaugirard, with about four thousand inhabitants in 1826, had earned the affection of soldiers and workers for its taverns. Nearby, workers spun cotton and produced chemical products in the shadow of the capital.[57]

The northeastern heights of Belleville had long been known for their quarries, which challenged vineyards for space. The commune's industrial future was already apparent, with five factories and many workers among its relatively poor population of 5,000. In 1826 the *Guide résumé du voyageur* gave high marks to Belleville's "taverns, where the working class goes to drink and dance."[58] The village of Saint-Ouen boasted a factory turning out laminated lead and a small cotton-spinning operation. Thirty wet nurses produced milk for the babies of well-off Parisians, and farmers sold asparagus to the markets of the capital. The "mobile population" of 697, including outsiders, domestics, and workers passing through, already outnumbered its "fixed" population of 608, in addition to those occupying country houses during the summer.

La Villette's working-class population likewise rose rapidly. The proximity of Paris was also felt in a different way. The almost daily trips to Paris of residents who worked or sold fresh produce there had, in the opinion of one visitor, given the suburban residents "this air of suspicion and sometimes even insolence."[59] The concentration of such "mobile inhabitants" or professional strangers—workers passing through, or who camped outside the walls by night and looked for work by day in Paris—already had begun to frighten the affluent residents of the capital. Refineries, shops producing chemical acid and faïence, and a factory making ammonium salt on the chemin d'Asnières had begun to corrupt the "good air" of Choisy. Charenton had a "handsome, vast iron fondery," owned by an Englishman. Clichy had become a town of 5,000, including 800 merchants and tradesmen, 550 who worked the land, 1,000 artisans, and 10 factories making, among other things, cartons, glue, and lead.[60]

In the larger settlements of the southwest, vine dressers mixed with workers returning from the capital. Two thousand day laborers lived in Saint-Cloud alone, some of whom worked for farmers in the region, others finding occasional industrial employment inside the *octroi*. Most people living near the Bièvre river found work in the countryside; some toiled in a mechanized linen factory. Sèvres had even more industrial laborers, what with several shops producing ladders and spinning cotton, as well as the Royal Porcelain Factory.[61]

That was in 1822. Fifteen years later, military surveys reflected the decided tilt of the balance toward industrial work. "Veritable agglomerations surg[ed] even at the gates of old Paris."[62] The population of the suburbs had increased even more rapidly than the capital itself, at a rate greater in the first than in the second half of the century. That of nine communes south of the Orge river, on the southern border of the department of the Seine, had doubled between 1801 and 1836.[63] Between 1800 and 1851 the capital's population grew by 92 percent, and its surrounding communes by 339 percent, so that the latter's population rose from 15 to 35 percent of that of Paris. The red belt was born. As the cost of living in the overcrowded capital rose (for example, the average rent went up from 89 to 111 francs between 1817 and 1829), the periphery continued to attract the poor. The suburban population had three times the number of indigents per capita, with the communes of the periphery having five times less the material resources to cope with their desperate poverty.[64]

The near northern and northeastern suburbs, Les Batignolles, Montmartre, La Chapelle, La Villette, and Belleville, grew particularly rapidly. Together accounting for 40 percent of the total suburban population in 1831, they constituted 55 percent of it in 1856, four years before their annexation. Recently completed canals facilitated the industrialization of the near suburbs.[65] Some villages could now have been considered urban areas. Nogent-sur-Marne had almost 2,000 inhabitants by midcentury, Argenteuil had over 4,000, Montrouge almost 6,000, Créteil 1,700, Pantin 2,400, Sèvres 4,000 (by 1837), and Boulogne well over 5,000. Montreuil had grown to the point that in 1843 an officer wrote that it could be taken for "a pretty provincial town."[66] No longer a large village, Issy presented "rather the appearance of a town," the residence of many shoemakers and locksmiths, among others, employed in Paris shops.[67]

During the 1830s and 1840s the development of industry continued unabated on the edge of Paris—an "America open to pioneers," in the words of Jeanne Gaillard.[68] Speculators eagerly bought up land, particularly along the Seine. The chemical, leather, and textile industries helped fuel the growth of the suburbs. Demand for the stones from the quarries in the environs was boosted not only by the rapid growth of Paris but also by the construction of the controversial forts well outside the walls. Some workshops moved from artisanal quarters of the capital like the Marais to beyond the *octroi* in search of cheaper costs and more space, and were joined by manufactures of many sizes hoping to make their fortune there.

More than any others, the northern suburbs continued their industrialization, aided by easier access to water transportation, the developed commercial land routes to the north, and a greater reservoir of available labor. Closer to the *octroi*, La Villette had achieved the status of being "in some ways sort of a faubourg" of the capital, a single street 1,000 meters long on which lived 1,580 people (350 households).[69] Many residents cultivated cabbages, artichokes, potatoes, and beets for the rich markets of Paris; nearby lived plaster workers and others dependent upon the capital for work. Manufacturers produced soap, candles, sugar, and perfumes, among other items, getting supplies by the Ourcq canal. Beyond the city walls, they were exempt from the *octroi*. In 1844 some of the forty-one industrial establishments in La Villette, including metallurgical and chemical industries, could not only be seen but smelled. The commune also benefited, in a manner of speaking, from "unhealthy or incommodious industries expelled from Paris," including chemical factories. Warehouses dotted the urbanizing landscape. La Villette's population, which stood at 1,666 in 1800, soared after 1846, reaching 30,287 in 1856. It was overwhelmingly working-class in composition, as its density per hectare increased from 38.1 to 58.3. In a single generation, a village where Parisians of the Empire and Restoration had enjoyed leisurely promenades along the canal and basin to rustic taverns, had become a town with a population almost twenty times that of 1800. In 1860 it was pulled by administrative fiat into the surging metropolis.[70] In the meantime gardens, foliage, and fields continued to recede with the inevitability of a balding man's hairline.

The railroads that had begun with two competing lines to Versailles on opposite sides of the Seine (the right bank line carried 321,588 passengers in 1841 alone) had destroyed the best vineyards, those most exposed to the sun. Suresnes became known more for its printed cloth, employing two to three thousand workers preparing cloth bought from Reims and Roubaix, than for its bad wine. It also produced enough tiles and bricks to fill sixteen large boats a year. A gas factory stood just beyond the walls at Courcelles. Saint-Denis, with about a thousand inhabitants living on two main streets forming a cross and on muddy side streets that went off in almost random direction, still had an agricultural population farming its plain, and a number of vineyards, but there were now more factories and mills.[71] A large factory stood among the rural houses and gardens of Le Bourget.[72]

The suburbs of Paris not only grew, they proletarianized. Wealthy property owners and other notable residents formed half the electors during the July Monarchy; they were more often than not appointed as mayors of their communes. But the changing character of those peripheral communes in many cases left the walled property of the people of means isolated in an increasingly urban, plebeian setting. Other signs all reflected the transformation of the periphery. Châteaux disappeared, including those of Clamart, Plessis, Issy, and Fontenay. A notary purchased Saint-Frambourg in Gentilly, had it demolished and the trees cut down, then subdivided the property into lots that he sold. Large estates in Gentilly and Ivry were divided up. Some of the fabled forests of the Ile-de-France fell before the expansion of industry and population on the periphery of Paris. Most houses were now covered with tile or wood; straw roofs became rare in the vicinity.[73]

Gentilly's population doubled between 1801 and 1836, reaching 9,450 inhabitants. It became the second largest town in the department of the Seine, with an *octroi* established in 1826. Its population included the owners of 237 shops and their clerks, 140 wine merchants selling to Paris, farmers, and over a thousand workers and their families, employees of the Gobelins manufacture of Paris, leather dressers, wool washers and cleaners employed by the industries utilizing the turgid waters of the Bièvre river, and the inmates of Bicêtre. At midcentury Ivry-sur-Seine had as many workers—over a thousand—as it had residents at the beginning of the century, thanks to its quais and industrial development. Charenton had a "permanent" population of 1,002 in 1841, but a floating population of more than twice that number because of the quarry workers.[74]

Because there was no tax on produce unloaded at Puteaux, many of the principal wholesale merchants of the capital chose to have their warehouses there. Puteaux had had but two factories in 1827; fifteen years later there were fifteen, convincing one visiting officer that in twenty or thirty years the town might become another Saint-Etienne. Many peasants held on to their land, which appreciated in value. Some cultivated roses for rose water sold in Parisian pharmacies.

But all was not roses in Puteaux and the other industrializing suburbs. Only a few communes—and within these, a small percentage of the population—prospered. There seemed to be more people in Puteaux every day, including a floating population of workers seeking to sell their poorly paid services. This posed new problems. The officer making a military survey in 1842 insisted that "the government should seek to assure tranquillity and order, which one day could be broken by movements of workers," as occurred in large industrial centers. He recommended that the army build a barracks so that Puteaux might have a permanent garrison.[75]

The "civilization" that the military observers identified with the capital had indeed brought several noticeable benefits, not the least of which was an increasing level of literacy by the end of the July Monarchy. There were few children who could not at least read. Yet they stood accused of having the "loose morals" associated with the City of Light.[76] The fast life of Paris, where many of them worked, and the omnipresent *guinguettes* beyond the walls of the capital presented a moral challenge many failed to overcome: "Young men have seen Paris, and trips there excite in them desires and passions which do not generally serve to inspire the taste for work and for virtue."[77] The increasing and, for many, almost daily contact with the great capital was transforming life in the environs. Romainville now boasted a "modern church." But, "brought up at the gates of Paris, its inhabitants faithfully copy the capital's civilization and morals."[78] This did not always seem to be a good thing, at least to outside observers. In the opinion of another military man, the people of Maisons Alfort spent a week's earnings in a single day; the women were "indolent and lazy, coquettish and sacrificing everything to their pleasures," and then asking for charity in the winter when they had no money.[79] Some of the people of the communes surrounding the capital were not only "inhospitable" (though it is easy to understand why they might not be particularly friendly and chatty, when confronted with a man in uniform asking questions) but even "dishonest." The taste for luxury so worshiped in the capital had made an impact in the suburbs. Women had stopped wearing the costumes of their villages and tried to look like Parisians, even when they could not afford to do so.[80]

Communes had virtually no relations with one another (when they did, it was often unpleasant, as in the long-standing and angry dispute between Vincennes and Montreuil over water). But they were being overwhelmed by the growth and influence of the capital. Better roads beginning about 1820 and the railroad, the effects of which were apparent by the early 1840s, vastly improved transportation (however expensive) to Paris and between some suburbs.[81] Patois had almost completely disappeared in the environs, reported one survey; there were no longer even special words to designate objects of daily use: "it is astonishing to hear a language so free of patois and local words." The residents of the suburbs could be identified only by their somewhat slower pronunciation, particularly the end of words.[82]

Then there was the problem of drink. The closer one came to the gates of the capital, the more taverns one encountered, particularly beyond the barrière d'Enfer, near Montparnasse and the chausseé de Maine, and in Montrouge, which emerged as a Mecca for drinkers. These were far more popular centers of leisure than the small theaters of the suburban communes that depended upon visiting Parisians for their clientele.[83] Beyond the gates of Paris at the place du Trône (briefly the place du Trône-Renversé during the Revolution), drinking establishments vied for the business of arriving travelers and reveling Parisians. Not only did the image of "the drunken commoner" begin to emerge, it developed a recurrent geographic locus on the edge of the city, where the poor people went to drink, have fun, and mock their social superiors.[84] The suburbs found themselves blamed for the activities of boisterous and sometimes drunken Parisians.

The periphery of provincial cities replicated on a smaller scale the transforming faubourgs and suburbs of the capital. Faubourg and industry were also closely linked in the rapidly growing suburbs of France's second city during the first half of the nineteenth century, even more so thereafter.[85] On the periphery of Lyon, garden farming for the insatiable urban market developed rapidly, the most productive land being that closest to the city and its suburbs. Each dawn when the gates of Lyon were opened, lines of wagons waited their turn to be waved through after paying their tax.[86] By 1825, "the nascent and prodigious growth of the industrial population since the beginning of the Restoration could be seen in the villages surrounding the great city."[87] Lyon itself experienced only a moderate rate of growth, from 150,800 in 1836 to 177,000 in 1851, just before its suburbs were annexed in March 1852. The development of the faubourgs and surrounding communes largely accounted for the significant growth of the region. By midcentury, Lyon had "a ring of 100,000 suburbanites who surround the city of rivers. The newly arrived pile on top of one another in these faubourgs, attracted by lower rents and a more modest cost of living not increased by the taxes of Lyon's customs barrier."[88]

The Croix-Rousse was arguably the most famous and feared industrial suburb in France. Perched on its hill, its apartments with high ceilings accommodated almost two thousand looms, most of them the large new Jacquard model; the narrow passageways—the *traboules*—kept the silk dry during transport, stretching down the steep incline toward the elegant quarters below.[89] The Croix-Rousse was "uniquely populated by silk workers. From sunrise to sunset, one only hears the monotonous, regular sound of the machine striking the cloth . . . this is an immense beehive."[90] With the memory of two recent insurrections in mind, the officer carrying out a military survey in 1841 described its inhabitants as "energetic," which he attributed to the healthier air they breathed by virtue of being above the city (in fact, the poor health conditions of the Croix-Rousse were already notorious). But he went on: "morals are coarse and it is easy to see why. Situated near a large and completely corrupt city, populated by people whose pecunious situation puts them into the lowest class of society . . . the Croix-Rousse is nothing more than the depository of a large and miserable population. Civilization there is barely advanced." The population of this "new town," as the surveying soldier put it inaccurately in 1841, swelled prodigiously from 6,000 in 1806 to 28,700 in 1851, with the arrival of immigrants from, among other regions, the Bas Dauphiné. Unlike almost all other faubourgs, some of its black buildings reached eight stories high, and the Croix-Rousse plateau had some wide streets.[91]

Across the Rhône, during the Restoration the faubourg of La Guillotière had become a bourg of 13,000 inhabitants (1828) with wide, paved boulevards. It remained a center of agricultural and silk production, overland and river transportation, horse trading and other commerce. But La Guillotière had already begun to attract noxious industries unwanted in Lyon, such as soapmaking and the production of sulfuric acid. In contrast to the Croix-Rousse, it became the logical locus of the newer industries of the Lyon region, particularly metallurgy.[92] The population of La Guillotière, "the physiognomy of which is completely different" from that of Lyon itself, increased sixfold during the first half of the century, from 7,000 in 1806 to 41,500 in 1851, which would have put it among the thirty largest cities in France. La Guillotière already represented the future of the large-scale industrial suburbs, "without any monument worth anything except for several ugly churches, around a completely undistinguished town hall . . . distinguished from an enormous village only by large sheds and dispersed workshops, marked here and there by high smokestacks of red brick that could withstand the river's torrents."[93] It too developed its own periphery, including Villeurbanne and its infamous hamlet of Charpennes, to which we shall have occasion to return. The ironworks of Oullins and a blast furnace in La Mulatière in Sainte-Foy also attested to the implantation of large-scale industry on the edge of Lyon.[94]

The faubourg of Vaise, a growing river port and intersection of several routes, became a center of metallurgy, steamboat construction, tanning, and dyeing. Reached by the narrow faubourg de Vaise, fifty *auberges* and cabarets on the other side of the *barrière* awaited travelers coming from both directions, at least those undaunted by the nearby glue factories. Vaise became a separate commune in 1838. Its population quadrupled from 2,200 at the fall of Napoleon to 8,800 at the time of his nephew's coup d'état, shortly before it was incorporated into Lyon in 1852. Whereas half its territory had been occupied by market gardens in 1825, almost all was now covered with factories, houses, or cafés.[95]

By midcentury, then, Lyon was surrounded by largely industrial suburbs with over a hundred thousand residents and an undeterminable temporary or transient population. Most migrants to Lyon and its immediate region settled in the faubourgs turned suburbs.[96]

A strenuous walk in the hilly surroundings of Rouen demonstrated that, if faubourgs were traditionally the place where city and countryside met in an awkward embrace, the city and its industries had wrestled the countryside to the ground. Since the fortifications of Normandy's largest city had disappeared between 1780 and 1790, there was little—not even the imposing hills—to block the expansion of the faubourgs, most notably after 1830.[97] During the first half of the century, some of France's most fertile land was absorbed into Rouen's industrial faubourgs.

Normandy's capital appeared in 1824 as three different towns. There was the old town, "an enormous mass of very high houses, most built of wood," tightly packed around the cathedral and the place du Marché, where Joan of Arc had been burned at the stake in the fifteenth century, and running down to the Seine. "Locked within its confining walls," the people of Rouen were forced to live wherever space could be found. In 1824 an officer was unimpressed by "very narrow streets that give the town a disagreeable aspect." To see the sky in some places, one had to go to the boulevards. Beyond them lay the second town, which pleased visitors with its wide thoroughfares with sidewalks and trees on both sides, the trees having been planted in 1770 by the intendant de Crosne. The regular form of the streets impressed the officer, as did the "modern buildings," which contrasted dramatically with the old quarters. Here there were still open spaces and gardens and, even more noticeably, building sites: each year some were filled by "handsome residences and pretty houses, which spread along the row assigned to them."

The third Rouen was that of the periphery. Across the Seine, the faubourg of Sotteville gradually became a full-fledged industrial town. In 1824 an officer wrote: "The faubourgs of a town as large and as confined as Rouen should stretch far into the distance; indeed, they spread out to the surrounding hills, into the valleys and the slopes that adjoin them." The houses of the faubourgs had gardens, and the farther away from Rouen one went, the more large gardens there were. In the faubourgs, industry and agriculture coexisted. Buildings were either factories or workshops, or belonged to gardeners. Apple trees stood here and there, a sure sign of Normandy.

Darnétal, once exclusively an agricultural community serving the needs of Rouen, had become "in some ways one of Rouen's faubourgs." There the expansion of industry had been accompanied by a marked decline in farming. The manufacture of cotton created the faubourgs of Rouen. The lives of rural workers were also transformed: "The most evident consequence of the industrial agglomeration has been the transformation of the independent country worker who was both spinner and weaver into an urban worker narrowly specialized in one small part of the production process." The survey of 1824 reported that in the commune of 5,000, one found "only factories and workers' houses." Caudebec, thirty-six kilometers up the Seine, was also considered something of a faubourg of Rouen.[98]

Industrialization transformed Lille's faubourgs. In 1833 the faubourg des Moulins, still part of the commune of Wazemmes, had 300 grain mills. The hedges of the faubourg Saint-Maurice attracted Lillois in search of fresh air and greenery. Every Sunday evening "the long procession of strollers loaded down with flowers and fruits hurry toward the gates of Lille, which close at 10 P.M." But by 1848 much of this had changed. The faubourgs rapidly lost their rural character. It was not only the working-class quarters of Lille, the particularly notorious Saint-Saveur, where several thousand people lived in what amounted to caves, that attracted the attention of reformers. A doctor wrote: "Shouldn't the people who fill these neighborhoods generate as much interest as horses whose straw is changed every day?" The faubourg de la Barre and the faubourg Saint-André grew up around workshops for the construction of small boats and barges. Lille's faubourgs marched into the small, essentially agricultural communes that lay outside the city. New buildings seemed to pop up every day in Wazemmes during the 1840s. The town was almost inseparable from Lille's three largest faubourgs by 1846, though part of it had already been joined to Lille in the early 1830s (and today is well within the limits of the city proper). By the end of the July Monarchy, Wazemmes had ten thousand inhabitants. The simple village of Fives had become an industrial center. Roubaix and Tourcoing grew from villages into imposing industrial centers in their own right, giving France its first conurbation.[99]

The houses of Esquermes—just beyond Lille to the southwest, near which the owner of a château in Canteleu had recently built a textile factory—were almost all of recent brick construction, of one story, and covered with tiles, as if manufactured in a factory. Five kilometers from Lille, the residents of the "agreeable village" of Loos, crossed by the Haute Deile river, made linen, spun cotton, or worked in a quarry. The inmates of the prison, housed in an old abbey, produced cheap textiles. On the right bank of the Deule stood a factory producing sulfuric acid. The wealthy lived in large brick houses; the poor occupied small, squat houses with only a ground floor that were almost indistinguishable from many poor farmhouses, except that straw roofs had been banned as a fire hazard. Farther out, there were still some houses made of earth that "inspire disgust and sadness," so low that one could easily touch the roof. Virtually every village in the vicinity had a *brasserie,* sometimes two, producing beer for local consumption. To the southwest, Haubourdin, dotted with country houses owned by Lillois, had become an industrial town during the July Monarchy, generating enough travel to and from Lille that an onmibus made the trip of seven kilometers every half hour.[100]

In Nantes, workers lived in every quarter during the July Monarchy; vertical social segregation within buildings remained the rule, with workers living in mansards and attics. But poor spinners, weavers, hatmakers, and fishermen were concentrated beyond the center in one of the most miserable neighborhoods, on the island and in the filthy neighborhoods of the left bank of the Loire. By the 1820s, although the houses of the faubourg Saint-Jacques across the river were generally covered with tiles, "those of the poorest people are covered with straw." The embellishment of old Nantes made the contrast between center and faubourg even more apparent.[101]

In Le Mans, a commercial, republican town surrounded by a monarchist hinterland, the industrializing faubourgs grew much more rapidly than the central neighborhoods. These villages crouched on the edge of Le Mans and its recently embellished bourgeois quarters, such as Greffier and the avenue de Paris (Billée), and the modestly improved workers' neighborhoods of the central quarters. Sainte-Croix, which had a foundry, increased from about 700 in 1821 to 2,000 in 1846; Pontlieue, from 1,300 to 3,400 over roughly the same period. The miserable conditions of the weavers in the humid, filthy lower town along the Sarthe were duplicated on the right bank of the Sarthe in Saint-Gilles and Saint-Jean-de-la-Chèvrerie. The first machine in France that could spin hemp was located in a factory in the faubourg d'Alençon. Mechanization ruined the hand production centered in the traditional working-class quarters along the river, pushing industrialization into the faubourgs. Textile workers increasingly settled in the commune of Saint-Pavin-des-Champs, living in houses tailored to their work, with steps leading to a cellar, and little more.[102]

In Dijon too, not even a modest center of manufacturing, the growth of the faubourgs was tied to industry, however small in scale. Those of Ouche and Raine were transformed slowly by their proximity to the canal; the faubourgs of Saint-Pierre and Saint-Nicolas also lost their rural character. The faubourg Guillaume developed so rapidly around the new railroad station in the late July Monarchy that it never had a rural character. "The calm rustic streets of the faubourgs" were described as "modernizing woefully, plunged into banality, tumult, and unsightliness." Archaic, evocative, and charming local names—des Ormeaux, de Belle-Croix, des Coquins, des Capucins—were replaced by "any names whatsoever," banal, anonymous, like the image of the faubourg itself.[103]

In Angers, a marked contrast emerged between the larger industries of the eastern periphery and the "multiplicity of small workshops dispersed in the urban fabric, working especially for the local market, run by bosses proud of the small scale, employing at the most several dozen people." Life in the faubourgs was different; the workers of the small shops could "in no way understand the conditions of work in the factories of thousands of their comrades in the faubourgs."[104] In Vienne, where the utopian socialist Etienne Cabet had many followers among the artisans, the officer carrying out a survey in 1835 was so intrigued by the large iron foundery in the faubourg de Grenoble that he provided a detailed description of it.[105] In the underpopulated, rural Landes, the only concentration of workers was found in Saint-Esprit, a faubourg of Bayonne across the Adour river in the department of the Basses-Pyrénées.[106] In the Haut-Rhin, Colmar was rapidly supplanted by Mulhouse as the center of economic, social, and political life, even though it retained its administrative and judicial role as *chef-lieu* and seat of the royal court. But here too, working-class life "was relegated" from the center's winding streets (noted as entirely paved and clean, as they would be in Alsace) to the outskirts. The entrepreneurs Schlumberger and Herzog opened a factory that stood five floors high in 1828, and the Haussmann brothers established factories in the faubourg de Rouffach to the west of Colmar, extending to the canal and commune of Logelbach. More than one thousand textile and metallurgical workers lived in the immediate vicinity of these factories; the population of Logelbach itself rose from 819 in 1830 to 2,755 in 1859. Thus a "veritable street of factories" developed beyond the canal. To the east, the smaller faubourg de Brisach also developed rapidly, from 694 in 1830 to over 5,000 early in the Second Empire. The faubourgs made possible Colmar's increase from about 15,000 in 1825 to 20,000 twenty years later, a significant rate of growth, although far behind that of its rival, Mulhouse.[107]

A similar transformation could be seen in Montluçon on the left bank of the Cher. An industrial faubourg grew rapidly after the Restoration, when vine dressers were the second most common occupation after day laborers. The number of inhabitants rose from about 5,000 in 1836 to 15,000 twenty years later. The quarters on the left bank, with but 1 percent of Montluçon's inhabitants in 1825, housed 30 percent in 1856. This growth followed the settlement of industrial workers and day laborers east of the route de Tours along the canal de Berry (1840). From the left bank, steam and smoke from the coal-burning furnaces of the iron and glass manufactures signaled a new economy and a new town, both centered in the faubourg across the river from old Montluçon, dominated by its château. This development left a striking contrast between the old city populated by property owners of aristocratic pretension, shopkeepers, artisans, and officials, and the town across the river. The residents of the latter exhibited markedly different demographic behavior, tied to the changing occupational structure of Montluçon. They married earlier and had higher rates of fertility, but also of mortality. Maintaining close ties to their villages, the migrants' patterns of sociability, including the sacrifice of numerous rabbits and pigs to Baal at the traditional cookouts (*grillades*), reflected the close links of the migrants to the rural world. But they were now also rooted squarely in industrial life.[108]

There were few towns in France whose growth was totally dependent upon industrial growth. Paris, Lyon, Rouen, and Lille were the four most significant industrial cities. All had been important commercial, administrative, and military towns long before becoming centers of large-scale industrial production. There were a few smaller centers of industrial production that had grown up so quickly that they might be called *villes-faubourgs,* faubourgs with little of an urban core, such as Montceau-les-Mines and La Grande Combe.[109] Decazeville, a hamlet whose mines transformed it into a company town, was so recent in origin that it was named after a political figure—its founder—who was still very much alive.[110]

Le Creusot was another, its spatial organization dictated by the factory built by Eugène Schneider after his arrival there in 1836. Streets and squares were placed with reference to their location vis-à-vis the château of the nineteenth-century *seigneurs* of industry. Schneider provided the infrastructure of a town. He donated the land for a church, so that Mass no longer had to be said in a store (although the new church waited ten years for a bell tower), as well as a school installed in an old workshop, company lodgings for the workers—appropriately called barracks— and a town hall. Although about a quarter of the Schneider workers continued to live outside of town, the population of Le Creusot jumped from 1,300 in 1826 to 6,300 in 1846, then soared to 13,000 in 1855.[111]

The *Ville-Faubourg:* Saint-Etienne

In 1820 Saint-Etienne was a town of relatively little significance, without an imposing set of traditions or a rich collective memory, and without important commercial, administrative, or political functions. France's Manchester grew so rapidly, filling the valley of the Furan river, that in many ways it seemed to be a *ville-faubourg*. With the frenetic energy of the sorcerer's apprentice, it quickly swept beyond the old town.

"Almost everywhere," exuded a visitor in 1846, "one encounters different types of factories, especially the coal mines, with their smoking obelisks, and ovens that spread into the distance a thick, black smoke which destroys the vegetation and turns everything a shade of black." The cloud of smoke at the level of the surrounding hills made it difficult to see the houses. Already there were complaints about "deleterious emanations harmful to health and vegetation." At night the mines and factories still "present a truly surprising spectacle, infernal to those who are seeing it for the first time."[112] Yet anyone arriving in Saint-Etienne during the day might have had the impression that no one lived there, as the streets seemed deserted. Virtually everyone was at work indoors, in factories, workshops, or at home. Noon or toward dusk were the best times to observe "the Stéphanois and his demeanor . . . at the hour when workers leave the workshops to go take their meal, an immense throng hurries through the squares and streets, and the town presents the most lively and curious view."[113]

There had been some industry in Saint-Etienne for centuries. Since at least the thirteenth century it had been a regional center for the manufacture of tools and hardware (*quincaillerie*) and armaments, drawing iron from the nearby mines. With a license granted by François I and a subsequent monopoly on the supply of guns for the royal armies, its arms manufacturers filled their coffers. The town suffered less than did others in the Forez during the religious wars—according to one interpretation, because both sides needed its "population of workers."[114] By the beginning of the seventeenth century, the region's mines and forges were known in much of Europe. Yet the small town of Montbrison, not Saint-Etienne, became the capital of the department in 1795, and the prefecture in 1800, by virtue of its more central location and the presence of lawyers, notaries, and other professions that normally serve an administrative center.[115]

During the Restoration, artisanal ribbon and braidmaking, introduced as early as the sixteenth century, emerged as the most important industry, outdistancing armaments and hardware. By 1846 there were 10,000 looms in the arrondissement (including about 800 Jacquard looms, which had saved the industry from being ruined by Swiss competition), turning out 440,000 kilograms of silk each year. In 1840 the ribbon industry employed 12,500 men, 18,000 women, and 2,000 children.[116] The town seemed on its way to becoming at least "a town of the second order."[117]

The diversity of industry made Saint-Etienne's future seem bright. The metallurgical industry, with the exception of its armament branch, was of relatively recent origin. The first steel mill began early in the Restoration. The Jackson company, begun in 1820 at Le Soleil by Englishmen, became the country's largest producer of iron and steel by 1847. In 1846 the arms manufacture turned out 30,000 to 40,000 guns a year, employing about 1,200 workers. Saint-Etienne turned out more rifles than the other four factories in France combined. Yet the manufacture of guns, too, retained essential aspects of traditional production: artisanal and homework production remained important in the industry. Most of those working for the arms manufacture were homeworkers living in Montaud.[118]

France's first train hauled its first load of coal from near Saint-Etienne to Andrézieux on the Loire in 1827. The railway solved the problem of the Loire's lack of navigability during part of the year. The results were quickly apparent as the mines dramatically increased production. The giant Compagnie Générale des Mines de la Loire, created in 1844, soon owned five-sixths of the coal extracted in the region. The mining companies, the metallurgical industry, and the miners were at its mercy. The company increased shifts from fourteen to fifteen hours and reduced wages. Most safety precautions were thrown to the winds as the Compagnie tried to extract every ounce of coal from the mines for as little cost as possible. Miners were old before they had a chance to be young; most did not live past thirty-eight or forty, many dying of disease or from accidents. Many had little choice but to stay on. With a vast reservoir of labor in the region, they could be easily replaced.[119]

Signs of industrial concentration were everywhere apparent in and around Saint-Etienne. A railway constructed at great cost pulled by a giant steel cable stretched across the hills of the industrial village of Terrenoire. There were four blast furnaces and twenty-four other forges and factories in the immediate vicinity. Other factories and workshops produced tiles, glass, bricks, and plaster. The mines of La Ricamarie, the filemaking town of Le Chambon Feugerolles, the diversified metallurgical production of Firminy to the southwest, the ribbonmaking center of Saint-Chamond, and the mines and heavy industry of Rive-de-Gier transformed the two valleys that ran to the northeast toward Lyon from the plain around Saint-Etienne.[120]

Saint-Etienne's population grew from 13,000 in 1790 to 19,000 in 1820. It then almost doubled in six years, reaching 37,000 in 1826, then 41,500 in 1836, 48,500 in 1841, and about 56,000 in 1851.[121] Saint-Etienne had quickly become one of France's ten largest cities.[122] Migrants, many with personal histories of small-scale or cottage industrial work, poured into the region. Ribbonmaking and filemaking remained largely artisanal, but semi- and unskilled work proliferated.[123]

The town expanded from its earlier limits roughly between the place Marengo (place Jean Jaurès) and the place du Peuple, north and south along its main axis along the Furan (now Furans) river, the direction of growth being determined by the valley in which the plain lay.[124] The growth of its main street was something like that of a boom town in the early days of the American West. By 1846 it stretched six kilometers in length. Another major street cut across, running 1,760 meters east to west, so that the two formed a cross. Streets parallel and perpendicular began to fill the plain. In 1856, two of every three houses had been built since 1817.[125]

The new town overwhelmed the old, with which it offered an almost astonishing contrast. South of the point where the two major arteries crossed, new and old Saint-Etienne met. There was little left of the old town. Of the ancient, undistinguished château, built at the end of the tenth century by the counts of Forez, barely enough remained to provide a modest police guardhouse. Near the church, built in the fifteenth and sixteenth centuries, when the town had about 200 houses, stood a small tangle of "narrow, somber, winding streets, always humid and dirty, lined with low houses badly built without order or taste," a few of medieval origin. In 1819, when Saint-Etienne had but one fountain, almost all the streets of the center were less than twenty-four feet in width. It seemed somewhat appropriate that the municipal council was relegated to meeting in a room only nine feet by twelve.[126] Rare were new houses such as those with symmetrical façades on the rue Saint-Louis (rue Gambetta) and the place Monsieur (place de l'Hôtel de Ville), described as "tall and perfectly regular in appearance, the result of excellent architecture." Characteristic of "anarchic" growth, most of the buildings of recent construction had been hurredly pieced together; sometimes leaning against the rocks of the hills, they had three or four stories, and courtyards leading to still more houses—a maze of poor, unhealthy residences.[127]

The metallurgical workers still lived in the old town during the Restoration.[128] The neighborhoods around the hôtel de ville were "animated by the coming and going of ribbonworkers, bringing in their work and receiving more to do."[129] The networks of capital that controlled life in the city were still based in the old town; the parish of Saint-Charles remained the center of commerce. As Saint-Etienne rapidly filled the plain, social structure took on a horizontal dimension, while maintaining something of the old vertical hierarchy. The latter was represented by the old nucleus "of the vast and luxurious apartments of the manufacturers, from the first floor of buildings to the small rooms and garrets housing single spoolers, folders, or warpers." During the July Monarchy the ribbonworkers began to settle to the northwest toward Montaud, which tripled in population, or toward the Crêt du Roch and the hill of Sainte-Barbe. In the Restoration, Outre-Furan had already begun to absorb much of the new population, more than doubling in size.[130]

The municipality of Saint-Etienne struggled to keep up with the prodigious development of the town, asserting in 1818: "in our town, everything must still be created. . . . Inheriting a town where everything was in disorder and simply thrown together at the beginning of the nineteenth century, the municipal government celebrated everywhere they could the cult of the straight line, beginning with the great north-south artery and all the rectangular streets that were built or prolonged to accompany it."[131] Lacking adequate resources, officials struggled to keep up with the growth of the city. Despite a growing population—and therefore tax revenue from the *octroi*—it was difficult to borrow money for essential projects. Accomplishments were modest: the completion of the town hall, construction of a barracks, beginning work in 1828 on sewers, and the building of a new prison in which prisoners in all cells could hear Mass said from a central point.[132]

Even in the eighteenth century, one visitor complained that "all the houses seem to have been built on the same model: seeing one by walking through its interior, is to have seen the entire town. All the streets are, with one exception, out of harmony."[133] Nor did the new Saint-Etienne necessarily leave visitors with a good impression. The town hall, completed in 1835 after fifteen years of interrupted construction, was as tasteless as it was inadequate to the needs of the growing city; Flora Tristan described it as "hideous, nothing more than a large pile of rocks."[134] A visitor complained of the revolting filth of "everything outside, that is to say, the streets, courtyards, and staircases," leaving little out. He went on, "could brooms be that expensive here? Is water so rare and help so hard to find that it is impossible to free the streets, sidewalks, and courtyards from even a part of the sickening mud that covers them?"[135] Even after the advent of gas lighting in 1839, Saint-Etienne seemed perpetually in the dark of night, except for the glow of the blast furnaces. Sidewalks rescued pedestrians from the mud and other disagreeable substances only in the wealthy neighborhoods. A surveying officer remarked that he found not a single "public edifice of interest," although he commended the "sturdy" construction of the new town hall.[136]

Thus emerged what one historian calls the "inferiority complex" of a city without allure. It lacked the infrastructure of the very large city, which seemed to be the fate of a town "which has been swollen out of proportion and whose image of 'urban vegetation' prevails."[137] Stendhal gloomily evoked the unhappy fate of a friend forced to spend six months in Saint-Etienne, France's Coketown. A Lyonnais journalist denigrated the region as "the most unpoetic place on the earth," and Saint-Etienne as "only a pile of horribly blackened houses inhabited by wretched and hideously filthy families," which could not have helped the city's self-confidence.[138] It had grown so rapidly that one officer undertaking a survey observed: "In our day, it is rare to encounter a town of some importance which does not have its own history. Saint-Etienne, a manufacturing town par excellence, is unfortunately in this small number." His search of the municipal library could not turn up a single book describing the city's past.[139]

All this would have been terribly sad, one visitor admitted, "were it not for the activity of the people" of Saint-Etienne, the houses of which had already become black from furnaces and chimneys. Black, the color of coal, which in the seventeenth century had symbolized activity, by virtue of its identification with fire, now emerged as the classic and lasting description of the Stéphanois region, the "black country."[140] Some visitors were intrigued by the newness of the city in a country of very old towns, as well as by the variety and productivity of its industries. The wide streets stretching into the distance in the new neighborhoods impressed them. Some of the new stone houses that lined them reached six floors. The municipality was unwilling and unable to limit the city's growth, but insisted that new buildings follow the regular grid pattern, the kind of planning that pleased visitors.

The faubourg-city represented the exciting economic potential of the urban periphery, the industrial future of France. In the 1840s the region's industrial base seemed so solid and secure that all crises were believed to be short-term. A mineralogist determined that the coal mines would continue to produce wealth until approximately 1970. Industrialization and proletarianization had transformed the entire Stéphanois region. The rural industries that had spread throughout the mountains in the previous century had blossomed. "In each village some people are involved in production; the thatched cottages have become workshops, the products of which nourish the factories of Saint-Etienne," reported one officer in 1826. By midcentury even the smaller communes had lost their rural image.[141] The vast majority of the agricultural population abandoned the soil in favor of industrial work; deserted, the fields—many of which had produced crops only every other year—turned to yellow, then black. In 1850 no local statistics or printed information on the region's agriculture was available; what could be found dated from the end of the previous century.[142] The farmers remaining in Montaud and Outre-Furan protested in vain against the fumes and smells emitted by the industrial establishments in their communes.[143] The only way to escape from large-scale industry was to go, as many Stéphanois did, to Mont Pilat, 1,400 meters in elevation, southeast of the city, from which the Rhône valley and the Alps could be seen on a clear day, or to Saint-Galmier, eleven miles away, the source of Badoit mineral water.

Saint-Etienne seemed to exude an almost volcanic energy. The Furan river fit popular images of the Stéphanois: "short but terrifying [twenty-one miles in length], hardly pleasing to the eye, it crosses no picturesque site, the shade on no tree embellishes its sad banks, one rarely hears the sweet murmur of waves coming in cascades, its waters are imprisoned by a multitude of canals from which they sadly pass from factory to factory to have their repulsive forces squandered." The Furan was barely more than a filthy stream into which butchers and tanners casually tossed animal parts, and into which other industries, and residents as well, emptied their waste. Mercifully, it had already been covered over in places, but it was particularly noxious during the summer, when little water flowed to keep the muck moving.[144]

The Furan's function was not to please the eye but to provide for industry. Its waters were fine for metallurgy and silk dyeing. But the diminutive river could explode in a frenzy, as in 1826 and 1837. The worst flood was that of July 12, 1849. After a day of bright sunshine, clouds suddenly covered the sun, and torrential rains began. The Furan ''swelled in the blink of an eye,'' flooding Saint-Etienne. ''No obstacle could stop or even slacken its impetuous charge. It knocked over and carried off everything in its way. In a single instant, prosperous stores and elegant cafés . . . were flooded.'' The houses of the poor in the valley of Rochetaille were swept away, as were entire factories, leaving ''ruins, debris, broken furniture, laundry scattered about, workers bowed by the weight of their fate.''[145]

The Furan fit the image of Saint-Etienne in another way as well. Like the river, the workers were sometimes described as docile.[146] They seemed religious, calm, superstitious.[147] If they were considered dangerous, it was only because of the proximity of Lyons. Many migrants originated in the Haute-Loire, well known as a region of fervent religiosity; Flora Tristan had complained of the ''crosses, Christs, saints, relics, and all the tinsel of Catholicism.'' In 1828 Jules Janin described ''this people who at first glance seem so ferocious and wild'' as ''exceedingly calm and sweet. Disorders are not as frequent as one would imagine, given the multitude of inhabitants. . . . If they occasionally go beyond the boundaries of subordination and dependence, they quickly return to normal.''[148] The next year the municipal council asserted that ''the mass of the population is quiet and laborious; there is no risk of insurrection or popular uprising.''[149]

In November 1830, the Duc d'Orléans came to visit Saint-Etienne. The sub-prefect welcomed him to ''the classic land of industry . . . this region . . . arms our warriors and clothes our ladies. This population, so varied in its work, suffers from the slowness of commerce, but it suffers without murmur, full of hope for the future of our beautiful country.''[150] In 1837, three years after the second and more memorable of the insurrections of the Lyon silk workers, an officer compared the workers of Saint-Etienne to those of France's second city. Limited agitation, now including strikes, could still be blamed on contagion from Lyon, but had subsided. The Stéphanois workers were not dangerous. If at first glance the concentration of workers appeared dangerous to public order, the power of the manufacturers was such that any movement by the workers seemed, for the moment, improbable. One of the few public buildings constructed by the hard-pressed municipality was a barracks, so that Saint-Etienne would have a perma-nent garrison. Given the rapid concentration of workers in and around the burgeoning faubourg-city, danger might lurk in the future.[151]

The industrial faubourg, then, emerged as arguably the most representative symbol of the relatively rapid urbanization that took place in France during the first half of the nineteenth century. The locus of industrial production on the urban periphery was not the only cause of the growth of faubourgs, as we have seen, and a proletarian population on the edge of city and town had characterized the eighteenth century as well. Even so, the increasing association of the periphery with social marginality was closely tied to bourgeois fears of an industrial proletariat. Faubourg and suburb emerged as a frightening specter, even more terrifying if they served as the locus for working-class organization and militancy.

3

Marginal People, Peripheral Spaces, Fearsome Faubourgs

Workers are outside political life, outside the city. They are the barbarians of modern society. They should enter this society, but only be admitted to it after passing through the novitiate of owning property.

Journal des débats, April 18, 1832

Louis Chevalier's "dangerous and laboring classes," in his classic restatement of the uprooting hypothesis that equates rapid urban growth with chronic disorder bubbling to erupt in revolution, or at least in purse snatching, resided for the most part, as we saw in chapter 1, in central Paris. Arguing "the imprint of crime on the whole urban landscape," Chevalier also, it will be recalled, emphasizes a fear of criminality that focuses on the edge of the city. "At the old gates and on the outer boulevards," he writes, near the *barrières,* "until the railroads were built, highwaymen carried on the traditions of the ancien régime and, as the lower classes drank and danced nearby, forgathered in the shadows with criminals of a new type spawned by the recent outward sprawl of the city."[1] Hugo, for one, identified the "expression of the aggregate of Paris criminality in the *barrières* surrounding the city," principally those of the southeast, including the boulevard and *barrière* of Saint-Jacques and the gates or *barrières* of Italie, Croulebarbe, Oursine, the aptly named Enfer, and the "sick" faubourg Saint-Marcel. Here infection, illness, and death seemed more rampant than anywhere else in and around Paris. This was "a disinherited zone of tanners, skin dressers, curriers and ragpickers . . . 'very like a fifth- or sixth-class town, a district entirely apart from the other districts of the capital.'" Hugo's Jean Valjean "did not enter Paris by one of the *barrières,* but he went there at once . . . the characters in *Les Misérables,* try as they may to move into other districts, fall back to this *barrière* as if weighted toward it by a species of gravity."[2] Public executions took place at the barrière Saint-Jacques until 1870.[3]

"You barely surmise the existence of another half of Paris," proclaims a young man of means in 1806 in *Voyage aux faubourgs Saint-Marcel et Saint-Jacques par deux habitants de la Chaussée-d'Antin.* "Do you feel up to embarking upon a journey through the dirty, smoky streets of the faubourgs? Personally, I adore contrasts, and methinks 'twill be a pleasure to observe the manners and customs of an almost savage tribe."[4] Here workers settled grudges with determination and violence, asking for and receiving no quarter. "If you want to know about the temper of the workers of the faubourg Saint-Antoine," Chevalier quotes a contemporary writing in 1854, "you must study them on Monday, for that is their holiday. You must enter the taverns on the place du Trône with them and watch how they settle their scores."[5] In 1826 the *Guide résumé du voyageur aux environs de Paris* observed that, more often than not, one had to go beyond Saint-Antoine to locate the workers of that faubourg in Saint-Mandé.[6]

Chevalier argues that the differences between the savage periphery and the center, as described by the residents of the chaussée d'Antin in 1806, had virtually disappeared thirty years later. Waves of impoverished migrants made all of the unequal equal, so to speak. Early in the 1830s, the faubourgs Saint-Jacques, Saint-Marcel, and Saint-Antoine remained, with the Cité and the quarter of the Hôtel de Ville, at the top of the list of "disfavored" districts of Paris marked by high mortality rates (the famous "inequality before death" at the time of the cholera epidemic in 1832) and by wrenching poverty. During the Restoration and the July Monarchy, the government provided services to the elegant quarters of the center, while ignoring the poorer neighborhoods of the northern and eastern sections, "a voluntary social choice, certainly, but also one dictated in part by difficulties of a technical order" because of the altitude of Belleville, Ménilmontant, and other proletarian districts.[7] Hugo described the "circumference" of the center: "It was not the country . . . it was not the town . . . the place where a plain makes its junction with a town is always imprinted with a species of penetrating melancholy." Balzac too, Chevalier notes, was anxious about the ongoing changes in the peripheral landscape: "For here it is no longer Paris; and here it is still Paris."[8]

The association of the faubourgs of Paris with poverty, immorality, and vice goes back a long way. Despite the difficulties of accurately establishing the social geography of poverty, it is known that in the fourteenth and fifteenth centuries the "northern fringe, along the ramparts" was suspect; "generally speaking . . . wealth was allocated concentrically; the periphery seemed poorer, while the center, the nucleus, groups bourgeois of means."[9] In her evocation of social life and policing in eighteenth-century Paris, Arlette Farge cites contemporary elite complaints about "the men, women, and children of the faubourgs and the environs."[10]

The writer Louis-Sébastien Mercier, in his *Tableau de Paris* (1781–88), wrote with some exaggeration that "there is more money in a single house of the faubourg Saint-Honoré than in all the faubourg Saint-Marcel, or all Saint-Marceau taken together." He described its inhabitants, like Chevalier long afterward, as a race apart: "ruined men, misanthropes, alchemists, madmen, people of independent means but limited horizons, and also a few studious wise men . . . who prefer to live totally unknown and separated from the noisy quarters full of entertainments." He was quick to add: "If one visits that district, it is only out of curiosity. There you find a people who have nothing in common with the well-to-do Parisian along the Seine. . . . It is the inhabitants of the faubourg who on Sundays fill Vaugirard and its numerous cabarets . . . they drink enough for eight days. The people of this faubourg are the meanest, the most inflammatory, and more quarrelsome and mutinous than those of the other quarters.'' The police, he insisted, were afraid of men like the infamous laborers (*gagne-deniers*) and other toughs who worked in the Halles, returning at night to their domain. In 1739 the police of Paris had reason to be concerned about, for example, the riotous assemblies in the faubourg St-Antoine consisting of an infinite number of workers, common laborers, and individuals without any occupation or trade, who publicly insult merchants of the faubourg by singing in front of their doors and shops songs in which the merchants are referred to or even named.''[11]

The peripheral faubourg had emerged as a central figure in the discourse of fear and rebellion before the Revolution. Steven Kaplan's study of the ''false workers (*faux ouvriers*)'' of the ''Faux Bourg'' of Saint-Antoine in Paris during the eighteenth century offers an excellent case in point of what we mean here by the ''floating worlds'' of the periphery. In that faubourg lived the ''usurpers,'' workers ''without skill,'' working ''without limit or discipline,'' living in the neighborhood beyond the Bastille that became identified with revolutionary disorder. Their ''illegal'' work and lower wage demands challenged the monopoly of the recognized *corporations*. There, benefiting from the size and complexity of the neighborhood and from the complicity of those who profited from their work or shared their status as outsiders, these ''false workers'' created ''a world of parallel work, outside the communities of craft, perceived of as socially illicit, political seditious, morally corrupt, and technically incapable.'' In the opinion of those who tried to control and impose order on them, they were little more than vagabonds who, ''looking in the faubourg for shelter first and then a job,'' successfully resisted various campaigns by the *corporations* and the state to break their defiance. ''Even the extent of the faubourg'' seemed alarming, ''sort of an interminable frontier, infinitely extendable, which 'seems to rise up against Paris to destroy, in the end, the city itself.' ''[12]

In the world of the faubourg ''everyone was not equal, far from it; but no one was *a priori* excluded for lack of title.'' Small wonder that demands for improved policing of the faubourg Saint-Antoine were heard: ''To search without warning, inspect without restrictions, check the quality of the work and of the worker. This was the equivalent of the town's reconquest of the faubourg, of its quasi-incorporation, and the end of its extraterritoriality.'' This, as always, proved an impossible task. The Bastille notwithstanding, no ''iron curtain'' could prevent the entry either of faubourg-produced goods into Paris or of Parisian workers into the wide-open world of the faubourg Saint-Antoine. Turgot's famous edict of 1776, then, seemed to the enemies of the faubourg to represent nothing less than ''the rehabilitation and the triumph of the 'false workers.' ''[13] Unless the edict was withdrawn, argued the guild of buttonmakers, ''all Paris will become the faubourg Saint-Antoine.'' Kaplan depicts the imagined consequences of ''the privileged locus of libertinage and disorder, exempt from corporate inspection, where false workers conspired against their masters and the public. Paris would lose its very integrity: it would literally become a *faux*-bourg, a false city—unsound, artificial, perfidious—gorged with *faux*-ouvriers producing false goods and services.'' Turgot had, after all, specifically cited the faubourg Saint-Antoine in the February edict as living proof that workers in an environment of economic freedom " 'work no less well' than those in a corporate ambience.' ' [14]

Part of the fear of the faubourg Saint-Antoine during the eighteenth century, particularly in its last decades, was that "riot breaks out more quickly in the faubourg than in the town itself." [15] The events of the Revolution, beginning with the storming of the Bastille and the decapitation of its commander, Delaunay, certainly seemed to confirm that. An indictment of the Revolution published in 1817 was also an indictment of the faubourg Saint-Antoine:

> At the beginning of our political troubles, where did the rebels go to find support? Not inside town, where the workers of various trades, organized then into guilds and thus accustomed to dependence and order, act with more moderation and wisdom. It was to the faubourgs, where the guilds did not exist, home of the multitude of undisciplined proletarians, deluded authors of all of these disorders and crimes. We have not forgotten the part played by the Faubourg Saint-Antoine in the most deplorable excesses of the Revolution. [16]

Beyond the faubourgs, the edge of the city threatened in a different way. Past Aubenas on the road to Alès lay the hamlet called Prends-toi-garde, suggesting that all was not always well even on the outskirts of only the third largest town in the Ardèche. Richard Cobb evokes travelers' fears of criminals lurking in the woods around Paris under the ancien régime and during the Revolution. Rivals in romance and other kinds of enemies dueled in the woods of the Bois de Boulogne, beyond surveillance. Robbers working alone, in pairs, or in bands, including the infamous bandits (*chauffeurs*) who stuck their victims feet into fire until they came up with cash, took advantage of the absence of effective policing. They descended on passersby and then easily vanished into the forests. [17] In 1774 the municipality (*conseil de ville*) of Nîmes had decided unanimously to demolish the walls of the city. An account of this decision is revealing: "The demolition of the ramparts appeared as sort of an exorcism of the quasi-visceral fear of the 'outside,' of the outsider, which is one of the essential characteristics of the towns of the ancien régime." [18] The *Guide résumé du voyageur aux environs de Paris* (1826) described the "unfortunate notoriety" of the forest of Bondy. In 1808 a band of thieves had terrified passersby; renowned as violent troubadours, they celebrated their successes with couplets, "some of which were not bad." [19]

In the nineteenth century fear came to dominate bourgeois discourse: prostitutes, beggars, criminals, and other outcasts became at least partially identified with the edge of cities. But not only "outsiders" provoked uncertainty and anxiety. Workers, who seemed now almost "dangerous" by definition, were increasingly identified with the periphery of the city, being "outside of the city" and "outside of property." Faubourg and suburb seemed beyond the law, beyond policing, even beyond understanding. Workers referred to the new exterior boulevards of Paris as "the shores of the New World." [20] Prostitutes may have been common sights in the "consumer society" of the central city, but "the worst" sort, down and out, often took refuge on the periphery. There they might avoid the degrading weekly or monthly checkups for venereal disease. Near the end of her own wretched life and of Zola's novel *L'Assommoir,* Gervaise prostitutes herself on the outer boulevards, where life was notoriously cheap. [21]

Even the small town of Sedan, with a population of only 12,600 in 1822, provides an example of the identification of the periphery with vice. A textile town with 67 cloth manufacturers, proud of its elegant buildings and fortifications, Sedan had four faubourgs; Rivage, Mesnil, Cassine, and Le Fond de Givonne. In 1825, 250 of the town's 932 houses lay outside the ramparts, lodging virtually all the gardeners and day laborers of Sedan. Located near quarries, Le Fond de Givonne was the home of "a sizable working-class population concentrated within the walls and in the faubourgs." A besieging enemy would have to conquer the faubourg before laying seige to Sedan itself. Beyond Vauban's massive ramparts, vice, particularly prostitution, seemed rampant. The "village" of Le Fond de Givonne had a population of 1,223 in 1838. Workers and soldiers flocked to such cafés as the Charrue d'Or at the porte de Balan, and the Six Fesses—run by three sisters—in the faubourg Mesnil. Sedan seemed a refuge for young girls who found work in the textile workshops and elsewhere. A surveying officer found that "morals there are somewhat loose in the lower classes," including the young girls "who have left home to give themselves over to debauchery." They found shelter in Sedan, "where they continue to lead scandalous lives despite the efforts of the police." Hoping to "moralize" the periphery, the Church constructed Saint-Etienne du Fond de Givonne, completed in 1849.[22]

Most towns had their "amorous woods" on the outskirts, usually beyond the *octroi,* where lovers, long-term and momentary, could avoid the prying eyes of neighbors, friends, and worst of all, spouses, as well as the police, whose jurisdiction stopped at the *octroi.* The Bois de Boulogne outside Paris was already as famous as a refuge for lovers as it was for duels and robberies.[23] In the woods beyond Limoges, complained one official, "passersby and children behold the most scandalous things."[24] In tiny Guingamp, subprefecture in the religious Côtes-du-Nord, there were "a great number of prostitutes" in 1819. They were not to be found in prostitution houses in town, where none were permitted; "several isolated houses in the suburbs or in the faubourg sheltered the prostitutes who come there from time to time to meet with a number of disreputable sorts."[25]

Examples abound of the association of the periphery with the "worst" kind of random prostitution. In the early 1820s, outside of Vesoul in eastern France, entrepreneurs had constructed three rough sheds or shanties of earth and branches along the road to Besançon. The mayors of the virtually unpoliced communes of Navenne and Echenoz, on whose territory the shanties stood, seemed unconcerned about the problems that they and a nearby tavern posed for public order. The shanty in Navenne was near the old mission cross, a mere 800 meters from Vesoul, but beyond the jurisdiction of Vesoul's police. Two other such primitive structures stood 200 to 300 meters farther along the road. All three had become "dens of debauchery where our young men, peasants from the vicinity, soldiers, and indelicate travelers come to find prostitutes, waste their time, and lose their health and money." It was there the prostitutes evicted from Vesoul during the day took refuge at night; they hid and, like the peasants in daytime, worked in the vineyards and fields. Thieves and other disreputable types also hung out on the periphery. The proprietors of these "disgusting places"—Catherine Millot, the widow Moriot, and Joseph Mathieu—were "canaille, capable of anything." The mayor of Vesoul wanted the huts and their sponsors forced away, or into town where they could be taxed and watched—the last thing the owners and their clients wanted.[26]

Likewise, beyond the reach of the police of Bernay, a subprefecture of the Eure, the cabaret A l'Enseigne du Cheval Noir had become "the meeting place for all the suspicious people of the region," as well as, if the gendarmerie is to be believed, a point of exchange for stolen property (and for "the worst sort of remarks about the king"). Two prostitutes, Marie-Madeleine Chertix and Catherine Corbelly, who had spent time in jail in Bernay after a previous conviction, worked there. Not far away on the edge of Evreux, at about the same time, Marie Houlette habitually solicited "soldiers and other men ready to share her immorality" near the old cemetery of Saint-Denis.[27]

If in 1824 the seven brothels of Lille seemed unruly and difficult to police, the prostitution of the environs of the burgeoning textile city was even more difficult to control. The mayor tolerated brothels because of the size of his growing city and its large garrison. Controlled prostitution seemed something of a safety valve "in order to avoid even greater disorders." Several of the establishments were on or near the commercial rue du Bois Saint-Etienne, close enough to the police station that surveillance seems to have been relatively frequent and repression swift, when the limits of toleration had been passed. Several dozen residents of the quarter petitioned the municipality to close down brothels on their street, complaining about carousing at night. A police patrol investigating in the middle of the night "heard noise coming from the said house; there was dancing and singing, and everyone there appeared to be drunk." The petitioners did not question the right of the houses to exist; they suggested that the police "relegate these places to a site far away from the center of town." This proposed solution was the urban reflex in action, deflecting accepted yet unwanted activities to the periphery, out of sight if not out of mind.[28]

The authorities never succeeded in completely pushing prostitution to the outskirts, and until the 1840s they did not try all that hard. Jean Ojardia ran one of the brothels in central Lille. In June 1848 he complained that, after twenty years of running a proper house on the rue de la Nef, a cul-de-sac near the Grande Place, in 1846 he had been forced by the municipality "to transfer our establishment to the neighborhoods away from the town itself." He closed his place but had been unable to rent it for other purposes. It remained empty and so, he pleaded, did his pockets. Claiming to be unable to pay his property taxes, Ojardia enclosed a statement from his former neighbors on the street, attesting to his good conduct and morality, but received no official response. In 1846 the central police commissioner proudly reported that no brothels remained in the central city. Most of the action now seemed to be on the edge of town.

Some of the prostitutes chased from Lille took refuge in Haubourdin; there anyone looking could find "debauchery" at the cabaret Le Bon Pêcheur, or at La Clef des Champs, run by Josephine Scran, a domestic looking for better things (instead, she contracted syphilis). In the 1840s Lille seemed deluged by women from the surrounding communes working on their own as prostitutes until caught and sent home. Eighteen-year-old Rosalie Melchior, known as Josset(te), born on April 27, 1824, was probably sadly typical. Raised in a Paris hospice, before the age of twelve she had been placed in a boarding institution in the countryside near Valenciennes and had come to Lille, she insisted, hoping to find employment as a domestic. Her *livret* indicated that she had lived briefly in Onnaing, Beuvrages, Anzin, and Saint-Saulve, among other stops. Josset had begun to sell herself and was expelled from Lille on November 11, 1842. She returned the following day, dodged the police until the 15th, and upon a second arrest, announced that she had contracted a venereal disease, which the doctors of the dispensary confirmed. But the municipality was unwilling to care for her. Here we lose track of her, but may imagine things did not go well.

Another such woman was Sylvie Descamps, "suffering from venereal disease, now in Lille without shelter, in absolute destitution." She had been a prostitute in Wazemmes for eight months and, since being evicted from that commune, "had constantly wandered without being able to stay anywhere because of her degree of illness." No municipality wanted to pay for her medical treatment, although she and her friends had infected a good number of soldiers. The police of Lille watched the prostitutes who worked there, but complained that the authorities in burgeoning Roubaix and, most notoriously, in wide-open Wazemmes ignored the problem. Venereal disease increased markedly.[29]

Drink also had a direct association with the urban periphery. Cabarets, taverns, and particularly *guinguettes,* by definition outside the city walls, lured clients with their cheaper prices. The *guinguettes* beyond the Paris *octroi* were particularly renowned for good times in the eighteenth century, offering "the freedom of the countryside," including gardens for dancing.[30] The names Montparnasse and, above all, Gaieté evoke today the old world of pleasure of the capital's fringe. In the first decades of the nineteenth century, the communes of the urban periphery lay beyond the jurisdiction of the municipal police, and gendarmerie patrols were relatively infrequent. In Strasbourg, with 628 licensed places to drink at midcentury, 45 were beyond the eastern walls, 21 to the west, and 34 toward the north, a figure that did not include the notorious "hot spots" of the commune of Robertsau.[31]

The development of the arsenal of Toulon, which accounted for much of that port's population growth of 66 percent between 1831 and 1846, pushed the development of its faubourgs beyond the military zone of the fortifications. Workers from Provence and Italy gave Toulon's "other" city the appearance of "a Turkish faubourg . . . one has the impression that already at the beginning of the nineteenth century, the arsenal of Toulon was a place where the uprooted and the isolated came to seek their fortune." Toulon's elite, safely ensconced within the ramparts, eyed the workers of the periphery with suspicion. On Sundays and holidays an imposing number of cabarets attracted plebeian revelers to the outskirts. Drinking, an essential element of popular (as well as upper-class) sociability, embellished bourgeois perceptions of the plebeian, dangerous by virtue of class and habits. In Maurice Agulhon's words, "The tavern is sort of a public country house . . . the collective abode of the poor with no place of their own." Outside Toulon, white walls and plentiful, cheap drink drew ordinary people, while drawing anxious glances from those hurredly traveling to country houses.[32]

Lyon's faubourg of La Guillotière on the left bank of the Rhône seemed to enjoy its unsavory reputation. On Sundays and holidays as many as thirty thousand people crossed the Rhône bridges to amuse themselves in Brotteaux, a northern district of La Guillotière, with its many *guinguettes*, theaters, and other kinds of entertainment. It was far more than a single police commissioner attached to La Guillotière could handle, even assisted by the gendarmerie. Worse, the "mob of vagabonds who infest Lyon and its suburbs" retreated to La Guillotière, where they found "a quantity of crooks of all ages" enjoying themselves in the open fields, playing *boules* and other less salutary games.[33]

La Guillotière's myriad cafés, cabarets, and dance halls thrived. La Guillotière remained a no-man's-land of raucous charivaris and other pleasures including, it seemed, promiscuity. All of which was facilitated by the absence of lighting: the residents of the faubourgs, permanent or temporary, were often described as "profiting from darkness," as in the case of the angry crowd that surrounded and "mistreated" a policeman who had bravely tried to disperse an unruly charivari reverberating in front of the house of a newlywed couple, a widower and his young bride. Gendarmes and troops rushed to the scene but found it deserted—"not even a cat to clarify the facts"—neither then nor when "witnesses" were called, all of whom insisted they had seen and heard absolutely nothing.[34]

In the 1820s, reported thefts in the region increased with the rise in suburban population across the Rhône. There were other kinds of "disorders" as well. The journeymen of various crafts, wearing the symbol of their *compagnonnage*, drank, sang loudly, taunted, and fought in the wide-open space of Brotteaux. Police and gendarmes tried to prevent anyone crossing the bridge from Lyon from wearing flowers, ribbons, or any other "symbol of identification" in their buttonhole, a restriction not applied to "bourgeois returning peacefully with their families from a walk."[35]

The hamlet of Charpennes in the commune of Villeurbanne beyond La Guillotière had the reputation of being the worst of the worst. Renowned for inexpensive drink, Charpennes was the refuge of "all the evil-minded whose proximity and mobility threaten the security of Lyon and its faubourg . . . outsiders of a very suspicious kind, such as peddlers, loaders, haulers, traveling musicians, quack doctors, tumblers, and jugglers."[36] Police "visits" in September 1825 turned up no crimes or infractions, only those people "normally found in the immense confusion of men and women of the lowest classes, those with turbulent and dissolute customs, and who do not feel satisfied unless they have drunk too much and settled several arguments in their own way." Charpennes was also the preferred place of combat for journeymen. Its cafés, overflowing with workers and prostitutes as well as wine, "revolt people of sensibilities with licentious conversations, the most indecent songs, and acts even more indecent, as well as innumerable brawls and assaults."[37]

The *auberge* of Saint-Nicolas was particularly infamous, the hangout of "a great number of prostitutes in the company of their madames, workers, cat-burglars, and laborers, most of them married and imposing deprivations on their families because of their wild and disgusting expenses."[38] The prefect of the Rhône takes us upstairs.

I learned that men and women were sitting around a table in a separate upper room, and that, during the meal, they said indecent things and sang songs no less obscene. At dessert, everyone undressed completely. Paired off in couples, they proceeded to simulate the ceremony of marriage. One of them, dressed in certain derisive garments kept in a closet, "married" a couple in a parody of the religious ceremony of the Church. After he pronounced a ridiculous sermon, the couple then went into an adjacent room to consummate their "marriage." Afterward they returned to wipe each other off. These ceremonies, as shocking as they are sacrilegious, continued as many times as there were couples to be joined in this scandalous manner.[39]

Even if the story had been wildly exaggerated by the time it reached the prefect, *something* was going on at the *auberge* of Saint-Nicolas that shocked Restoration prissiness, and that might have outraged less fastidious regimes. The original source of this particular story had to be considered, if not suspect, at least sadly biased. A wife, left with her children by her husband, had learned that the most likely place to find him, day or night, was that particular *auberge*. There she came upon a *mauvaise surprise,* which she indignantly related to the police. Her story may not have been typical, but it did not help the reputation of the *auberge,* Charpennes, or the environs of Lyon.

Far to the north, the cafés of the faubourg du Canal drew revelers to the outskirts of Dunkerque.[40] One of the most notorious faubourgs of Troyes, many of the houses of which still had straw roofs during the July Monarchy, was the commune of Saint-Martin-ès-Vignes, beyond the old walls northwest of the city, its population consisting largely of day laborers. It included the faubourg de Preize, whose cabarets welcomed the workers of Troyes. In 1831 many unemployed workers gathered there each morning with impunity; some sang "seditious songs." An illegal grain trade went on in the Auberge de la Belle Hôtesse and in other less elegantly named inns and cabarets in the faubourg Saint-Savine, again just beyond the town limits. It was the same in La-Chapelle-Saint-Luc, and in the home of a *limonadier* at the end of the faubourg Saint-Martin, in 1831 as in 1829, the revolution of 1830 having here made no difference at all.[41]

In 1843 the faubourgs of Troyes came alive with crime, particularly at night.[42] People were attacked on the tree-lined malls of Preize and Madeleine. Vagabonds hung around the neighborhood of Le Mail (Mall), and in October a man jumped out of bushes and hit a passerby with a "massive blow of his fist," while another stroller was attacked with a stick. The mayors of Troyes and the suburban communes asked for the establishment of a guardpost at the theater, halfway between the promenades of Preize and La Madeleine. A large theft had taken place the previous year; now the mayor of Troyes asked for a second permanent post at night and increased surveillance in the lower town, all the way to the *barrière* and the faubourg Saint-Jacques. When a guardpost was established nearby, and the newfangled gas lighting was hurriedly put into place, problems of security moved even farther away from town. Several attacks and a single reported theft would hardly constitute a crime wave in this day and age, but they necessarily made those wanting to stroll on the outer *promenades* of Troyes anxious enough.[43]

During the hard times of 1847, with the textile industry virtually shut down, by

August the number of desperately poor and hungry people—about six thousand—
was far beyond the capacity of the Bureau de Bienfaisance and the efforts of a well-
meaning group who loaned money for the purchase of cheaper grain in Le Havre
and Marseille. A crowd of five thousand, some singing the "Marseillaise,"
pillaged the shops of bakers (one of whom was jailed, presumably for hoarding or
cheating on prices) and some mills outside town. The crowd dispersed just before
gendarmes and troops arrived in the faubourg de Preize and the commune of Saint-
Martin. The incident, which underlined the role of the periphery in social conflict
in Troyes, helps explain the violent explosion in the city that followed the
revolution of 1848.[44]

In the Puy-de-Dôme, the battle of center and periphery was being waged
between Clermont and its small neighbor and rival, the commune of Montferrand,
which had less than one thousand inhabitants. As Clermont slowly grew, Montferrand had become, quite unwillingly, its faubourg. Montferrand was administered
by one of Clermont's deputy mayors. People in Clermont resented the cocky
independence of Montferrand and, even more, the fact that the latter's lively
sociability went beyond the limits of the law, particularly after its *commissariat*
had been eliminated to save money in 1832. Its *guinguettes* stayed open long into
the night; its woods were swarming with prostitutes. In the no-man's-land
between, *cafetiers ambulants* sold wine at low prices, some of it to "malefactors"
who gathered there.[45]

In Montferrand people had long resented its arrogant, condescending neighbor. Like the Goncourt brothers, they may have poked fun at its "cathedral of
charcoal burners" and other monumental structures built from the "awful rock of
the region, the slated rock of Volvic which resembles the stones of a dungeon,"
and its "windows and doors bordered with black that reminded one of receiving a
death announcement in the mail."[46] Clermont's apparent joylessness and grim,
authoritarian-looking architecture—someone in the eighteenth century once called
the town "an ugly painting in a magnificent frame"—contrasted with the festive
air of wide-open Montferrand, which thus attracted certain boisterous Cler-
montois. The deputy mayor in charge of Montferrand had even insulted his
charges by referring to the bourg as a "ball and chain dragged by Clermont." On
two occasions the municipality of Montferrand declared its desire to be completely
independent, presenting maps to show that the two uneven partners had always
been separate. Clermont retorted that Montferrand's complete independence
would only make it more difficult to control.[47]

Most people in Montferrand wanted theirs to be a separate commune; they
resented having to ride or walk on the muddy road to Clermont to register births,
marriages, and deaths. They also sensed that the open space between the two
would be filled up, to their detriment, by cemeteries, slaughterhouses, gas
factories, and other "unhealthy or incommodious establishments" that the people
of Clermont would eagerly foist off on them. Montferrand was becoming
Clermont's dumping ground. In 1848 some residents petitioned that Clermont and
Montferrand be officially separated: "For a great many years, Clermont has been
embellished with monuments, public squares, sidewalks; its streets have been
widened and straightened; its commerce has developed with speed." Montfer-

rand, on the other hand, had been "entirely forsaken; its streets are badly paved, poorly lighted, and left uncleaned; its public buildings have been sold off or destroyed . . . and its commerce, once so flourishing, has completely disappeared." When Clermont finally received gas lighting in 1848, well after such lesser lights as Moulins, Aurillac, and even Mende, Monferrand was excluded.

The leading taxpayers of Clermont now had another reason to be against separation, fearing lest their town lose population and perhaps also the academy and railroad—and therefore status—that had been promised to the struggling capital of Auvergne. They feared the competition of a rival market, and that their gauche neighbor might fall into the hands of "people of uncertain enlightenment" and "of very little influence." In July 1850 the arrondissement council opposed separation, while the departmental general council supported it. In 1861 Clermont and Montferrand officially became, for better or for worse, Clermont-Ferrand.[48]

Disputes between center and periphery could be violent. Some of the fighting on the outskirts of towns and cities pitted residents of the faubourgs against men and boys from the more central quarters, at least where the faubourg population had been there long enough to develop sufficient solidarity. In 1823 the men of the hillside town of Rochemaure on the Ardèche side of the Rhône battled their antagonists from the faubourg and hamlet of Les Fontaniers, who had taken down their maypole. This quarrel, in which one person was badly hurt, had political overtones: Rochemaure was enthusiastically royalist, their opponents decidedly not. Each side had organized a farandole dance, offending the other.[49] In 1817 the young men of two rival quarters in Béziers carried their quarrel from the cabaret to the no-man's-land beyond the porte des Carmes. The arrival of the national guard was greeted with a hail of rocks. Rocks met bullets, and a man from one of the warring quarters, Saint-Jacques, died as he staggered home. Saint-Jacques was the peripheral quarter of peasants; its rival was a neighborhood of the "town," although its residents too were principally peasants.[50]

Another example comes from the small Catalan town of Collioure, barely large enough to count as urban, though the third largest town in the Pyrénées-Orientales. On a Sunday in June, "several habitants of the town and of the faubourg of Collioure" began to fight, including men and women of various ages. They brawled at the Hermitage of Consolation, high on the mountain slope overlooking Collioure, one of France's most beautiful towns. The Hermitage, treasured site of a fisherman's chapel, was (and is) a popular site for eating, drinking, and dancing on Sundays and holidays. The incident led to a much more serious encounter far below in Collioure involving some three hundred or more people five days later, on the no-man's-land formed by the territory adjacent to the fortified château, which separated the town from its hated faubourg. "An equal fury seemed to motivate each combatant. Men fought, while the women and children provided them with weapons," rocks above all. An official's attempt to intervene was ignored, that of gendarmes "violently resisted," their commander being hit and his clothes torn. A detachment of troops was required before order could be restored. There was nothing political about this particular Restoration battle, though there could easily have been; it reflected the bitter rivalry of town and faubourg, a long, seething hatred possibly exacerbated by competition between the two in the region's active smuggling industry.[51]

Likewise, much of the fighting in Chartres took place in the faubourg de Bonneval or that of Saint-Maurice, where public gardens attracted both townspeople and soldiers in search of drink and fun. Many confrontations started like the one in August 1826, when a woman refused to dance with a soldier. One insult led to others. Young workers and other people of the villages outside town had to be restrained from attacking the garrison. It was on the edge of Chartres in the "faubourg" of Saint-Chéron that eighty people prevented tax officials from taking inventory of the wine harvest. Twelve hundred meters from Chartres, the village of Lèves had a tradition of occasional turbulence. In 1826 its festival ended in a brawl. The commune rose as one against the bishop of Chartres in 1833, when its popular priest, who had been the first to run up the tricolor in July 1830, was put under interdiction by his superior and then replaced. His loyal parishioners then defiantly proclaimed allegiance to the dissident Eglise Catholique Française, the influence of which undoubtedly had brought about their priest's dismissal. They carried the body of a recently deceased villager to their old friend for burial, against the wishes of his family. They then—particularly the women—attempted to prevent the arrival of the new curé, ringing the tocsin, shouting insults, and singing republican songs. They built barricades around their church, put a cap—perhaps a Phrygian cap—on the head of the terrified new priest, and forced him to raise a stick with tricolor ribbons above his head while repeating "Down with the Church!" The crowd then stormed the bishop's palace in Chartres and pillaged it; when the national guard arrived, it retreated home, beating up the deputy mayor when he stood against them.[52]

Brawling on the urban edge was one thing, murder another. Le Puy was known as "the holy city," its religious *cité* being dedicated to the Virgin Mary; the romanesque cathedral of Notre-Dame du Puy, of somber stone and Byzantine influence, towered over the red-tiled roofs of the modest town below. In 1860 the giant statue of Notre-Dame-de-France was placed on the Rocher Corneille, so that today, with the eleventh-century chapel of Saint-Michel-d'Aiguilhe, Le Puy's trinity of religious monuments appears as something of an oddly shaped clerical fork encased by the surrounding hills. But if Le Puy itself had traditionally offered shelter to pilgrims going to Saint-Jacques-de-Compostelle and served as a respite for other travelers to the Vivarais and Provence, the outskirts and small faubourgs of Le Puy were anything but reassuring.

For Le Puy, as for most other cities, police reports are sketchy for the *monarchie censitaire*. But scattered evidence suggests that, even in the rural and fervently religious Velay, the environs of the town were, if not dangerous, at least unsettling. A peddler died on the edge of town in March 1817, attacked by two men from the Ardèche whom the victim had managed to describe after being stoned and stabbed.[53] At around 9 P.M. one night in August 1821—when it would still have been reasonably light—a gardener living in the faubourg Saint-Jean, a scene of recent brawls, was found stabbed to death. His field, where he had been found alongside a haystack, was not far from town, behind the cemetery of Carmes. Two of the three men arrested, including Moulon, known as Sheep's

Tail, lived in the same faubourg. They had eaten with their victim in a café what turned out to be his last supper, then escorted him back up the hill to his small plot of land and killed him.[54]

The unfortunate gardener was not the only one to die violently on the outskirts of Le Puy. In 1829 Baptiste Glaisi, *cultivateur*, left a cabaret on the route de Paris, run by Bon, called the Hermit—a lovely rustic image—to head home. He did not get very far. Three men attacked him at La Descente des Estrilles, stealing his twenty-one francs and hurling the poor man against the rocks. He escaped by throwing himself over a fence into a vineyard. Discovered by good samaritans who carried him to the Auberge Barthenay, in the faubourg de Breuil, Glaisi died several days later.[55]

The outskirts of Le Puy were far more dangerous than the town itself, where the police and other officials could be found, and where there was at least the light of the oil lanterns. Brawls were common enough, as town and country people fought each other and among themselves. Murders, however, were rare and not quickly forgotten. Both town and country people must have thought twice upon realizing that dusk was falling and they had some distance yet to travel. Three years later, in 1832, there were rumors that "strangers" were hidden in the adjacent commune of Polignac, near the medieval château of that fanatically royalist family whose scion two years earlier had helped bring about the revolution that overthrew the Bourbons. Systematic searches by the gendarmes revealed only a great number of beggars living there, as well as invalids, very old people, and some women and children, all from the locality, too poor to afford to live in town or evicted by the police.[56] In 1833 there were complaints that "the thefts taking place for some time in the vineyards that surround Le Puy seem to be increasing every day, without even one of these audacious rascals being brought to justice."[57]

After the early nightfall on December 27, 1843, at about 9:15 two cattle merchants returning to Le Puy from the market at Allègre heard one shot, a scream, and another shot coming from the cabaret Ma Campagne on the edge of Le Puy, followed by silence. The cabaret, the site of frequent boisterous drinking and occasional brawls, was located on the road from Paris, in the neighboring village of Espaly. As the men approached Ma Campagne, they smelled the strong odor of gunpowder; soon the cabaret was in flames. By the time firemen arrived—without water, since there was none available nearby—it was too late to do anything except discover the charred remains of the cabaretier, Pierre Chanal, and his domestic, the widow Giraud (thirty-six) on what had been the third floor. There was stupor and fear in and around Le Puy, although it was soon discovered that the murderer was one André Gros, a printer, thirty-two. Gros was the lover of Chanal's estranged wife (who had left with their child five weeks earlier, as "M. Chanal did not live on good terms with his wife"—quite an understatement). He learned, presumably from Mme Gros, that the innkeeper had just received six hundred francs in cash. The firemen, poking through the ruins, found only two five-franc pieces.

The gruesome nature of the murder was unsettling enough, but even more so the fact that there had been a series of robberies at night "at the gates of town," and several attempted thefts "even in the center of the *cité*." The suspect was arrested with his lover, and his brother Augustin too, an accomplice. Gros escaped from Le Puy's jail within a week, hid for about a year in the wilds of the mountainous canton of Saint-Julien-Chapteuil to the east, and escaped, it was thought, across the Swiss border to Geneva.[58]

Even the residents of the Haute-Loire's small subprefecture of Yssingeaux, briefly under the command of Georges Haussmann during the July Monarchy, had reason to take extra care while approaching or leaving town. With the advent of winter in 1836, a number of robberies occurred at nightfall outside town. Each time the perpetrators managed to escape or fade back into the countryside, leaving little doubt that they were being assisted and protected by local people who selected the victims and may have also stood guard during the crimes. Finally someone responded to the appeals of the police. Based upon this information, three people were arrested at the market in Yssingeaux, though after a violent struggle and only with the help of people at the market, while a fourth was sought and presumably caught. Local authorities voiced the usual complaints about the inadequacy of forces at their disposal: Yssingeaux had no garrison, no national guard, and only a single undermanned and overworked brigade of gendarmerie to cope with, among other things, the turbulent population of Saint-Julien-Chapteuil, long feared in Yssingeaux.[59]

Two years later, in 1838, there were many thefts in the region of Yssingeaux, and a few violent crimes. On November 17 a minor crime wave took place on the outskirts of the small subprefecture: three armed robberies at almost exactly the same time, all within a shout of town. While gendarmes were arresting three thieves in the faubourg de Villeneuve, a holdup occurred on the road to Le Puy, and another on the route to Retournac. Who was terrorizing the people of Yssingeaux? Four members of the notorious Riou family, including Pierre, nicknamed Chantemesse, were denounced by the deputy mayor of Saint-Jeures, ten kilometers away, as having committed one of the robberies on the route from Le Puy. They were arrested in a cabaret after a struggle. Other arrests followed, including J. Pérard, called Canard (Duck), of Yssingeaux. After a total of eleven arrests in eight days—all from town, except for the Riou family—the crime wave on the outskirts of Yssingeaux was over, at least temporarily. But anxiety about the surrounding area, particularly at nightfall, must have remained, even though surveillance by the gendarmerie and the police increased in the vicinity.[60]

In December 1844 the brutal murder of three people—an aged café owner and his two domestics on the edge of Blois, with the owner of an adjacent building critically injured—sent shivers throughout much of France.[61] For weeks, anyone passing through or returning home to the faubourgs, particularly in Blois or anywhere in the valley of the Loire, and in other cities as well, must have jumped at the shadows of trees moving in the wind. Yet the very fact that the minister of the interior sent a circular to every department describing the murders does suggest how rare such events were, even in the faubourgs.

At least two killers had entered the building through the café. Little was known about the murderers, except that the three victims had been dispatched with a *burin*, a pick used to pierce rock. Stone breakers fell under suspicion. The café stood near the construction site for the railway to Tours. Here we can observe three components of the changing nature of fear of the periphery. First, large-scale industrialization—the railway as an often terrifying symbol of a new age that in some ways seemed out of control: the frightening crash, symbolic and real, in Zola's *La Bête humaine*. Second, the "dangerous classes" attracted by such work—often skilled or semiskilled, but by definition nomadic, requiring such attention that during the Second Republic special police commissioners were named to oversee the policing of the construction sites (the origin of the special police commissioners—*commissaires spéciaux*—attached to the railway stations in the Third Republic). As the tracks drove far into the countryside, the work areas offered a strange juxtaposition of modern industrialization in a rural context, without the intermediary of rural industry. Third, the plebeian carbaret—for the bourgeoisie, a symbol of uncontrolled disorder, particularly when located beyond the *octroi*.[62]

There had always been rumors of brigands coming to rob and loot, although these focused more on marginal workers than rural people. In 1820 a band of thirty-nine thieves terrorized Auvergne, led by a certain Bruno, whose strong Provençal accent made people believe he was from near Avignon (indeed, some of the members were known to be from Provence). The mayor of Clermont suggested that the police spend the night outside town, so as to watch the isolated houses and sheds from which the band was expected to operate.[63] In June 1822 a rumor spread in Bar-le-Duc and other towns in the Meuse that "brigands were hidden in the woods, and that they had mistreated several inhabitants, and had asked for the names of the richest people in Vaucouleurs, whose houses were insured." As this rumor coincided with a wave of arson in northern and western France, it could not be taken lightly; a good number of people removed the insurance emblem from the outside of their house. The rumor stemmed from the presence of a family of ten Alsatians traveling through and begging in the arrondissement of Commercy. Arrested by gendarmes as they slept in the woods, they were returned to the Bas-Rhin, despite the fact that their passports were in order.[64] In 1844 thefts increased in the vicinity of Bourg-en-Bresse. This was particularly alarming, coming just after the atrocious murders outside Blois described earlier. There had been rumors of a band of gypsies in the woods the previous year. Brigades of gendarmes arrested six people—three in the act of thieving, and three vagabonds for good measure.[65] Increasingly, one found reports like that of the mayor of Nantes in 1822, who complained that the *guinguettes* of the proletarian Ville-en-Bois across the river always seemed packed with undesirables: "Conspirators could easily find there the means of bringing together and finding adherents among the working class and the sailors." There was some talk of uniting the troublesome peripheral commune with Nantes. This was the last thing in the world he wanted; the only advantage would be fiscal. It was best, he reasoned, "to remove as far as possible from this city this source of every kind of corruption."[66]

The *octrois,* which defined the edge of town, were a privileged site of disorder, particularly during hard times. During the first half of the nineteenth century, the tax barriers and their adjacent offices were *points chauds* of protest. When grain prices soared during the winter of 1816–17, it was the "nightly gatherings in the faubourgs of this town" that frightened property owners.[67] The young men of Issoire (Puy-de-Dôme) were divided into three clubs: "each of them, according to an old tradition, led by musicians, marched through the different neighborhoods of town, making this tour of the town several times a day" on certain occasions. During another period of protest against the high cost of living, in September 1831 the members of the town associations joined the young men of the faubourgs in rare harmony. Their songs quickly changed to angry shouts of "A bas les rats!"— the tax employees of the *octroi*.[68]

In Angoulême in 1814, it was above all in the faubourgs that "agitation" against indirect taxes led people to burn the registers. The faubourg L'Houmeau was the most populous and plebeian; six roads crossed where it began. It was separated from the hilltop town by ramparts six to ten meters in height, but also by the steep incline that confronted the mighty and the humble (and those, like Balzac, who lay somewhere in between: he had his hair cut near the somber neoclassical Palais de Justice). In 1820 the population of the faubourg L'Houmeau stood at 6,064, one-third that of Angoulême. The faubourg was thus more of an adjoining bourg stretching along the Charente, with its own commercial elite, a few enriched by the salt trade, and a little industry. (During the Restoration it also had, bizarrely enough, a small naval school, until it was transferred—reasonably enough—to the seacoast.) More than this, it was here that the "most ardent"— that is, liberal—opponents of the government lived, and greeted their deputies with enthusiastic serenades. As he considered the problems of policing in Angoulême, the prefect had to admit that the faubourg presented the most problems.[69]

In Belley (Ain) in 1823, the people of the faubourg Saint-Martin, "all of whom work the land," resisted paying the tax on drink at the *octroi*. As Belley was an "open" or unwalled town, they brought their harvests in as they pleased, and then awaited with trepidation the "visit" from the taxman sent to carry out an inventory. After one poor harvest, when wine was worth only twice the tax paid on it, they resisted in the name of justice (indeed, one of their leaders was known as "the prosecutor"), claiming that the *octroi* employees used a measure that magnified the amount of wine being brought into town.[70]

Many of the disturbances that followed the revolution of 1830 pitted angry residents of the faubourgs against *octroi* officials, gendarmes, and sometimes soldiers. Believing that the fall of the Bourbons marked the end of the *octroi* tax, particularly on drink, the residents took out their frustrations on the barriers, tax employees, and the most attractive target of all, the tax registers. A serious incident in Orléans serves as an example. When officials returned to the *octroi* in the first days of September 1830, the residents of the faubourgs destroyed the tax offices at the barrier of the faubourg de Paris and of the faubourg Bannier, hurled stones at a baker (another unpopular occupation) who happened by, and burned the tax registers. The crowd responded to the appearance of the national guard by destroying houses adjacent to the *octroi*, whose residents they believed were carrying on an illegal traffic in grain. The guardsmen ran to defend the house of a grain merchant who lived in the same faubourg. According to the chief magistrate of the Orléans court, the people of the faubourgs had been "excited" by "men from other parts of town and by unknowns''—a common, usually groundless, accusation. The residents of the faubourgs needed no prodding to hate the *octroi,* which had been extended farther out to include them within its fiscal net, and, in the wide-open period immediately following the July Revolution, to act in their own interest.[71] To the south, "fifty vine dressers and people of the faubourgs" of Châteauroux marched to the town hall two years later, singing the "Marseillaise" and shouting the time-honored slogan of "Down with the rats!"[72]

The attack upon the *octroi* remained, at least until midcentury, the most typical of protests by the people of the faubourg. In the disturbances that rocked all the major towns of the Jura in the wake of the 1830 revolution, national guardsmen from the faubourg Faramand filled the ranks of the rioters in Arbois, angered by the reestablishment of the tax on drink. Wine producers and cabaret owners, frequent allies in protest, sparked the "tumultuous gathering" in the faubourg, from which "they descended without noise and by a circuitous route to the house of the tax collector." An officer of the national guard, when asked to take arms against the crowd, replied that the guard would do so only after the tax registers had been burned. Arbois emerged as a beacon of republicanism in the Jura.[73]

In Dole too, at the time of the tax inventory of the wine harvest, "the inhabitants of the faubourgs, armed with farm tools," threatened tax officials, before being calmed by "some respectable citizens" from inside the town.[74] In Narbonne, as in nearby Béziers,[75] the reestablishment of the *octroi* led to disturbances. With the acres of vineyards doubling over the first half of the century, the issue was of considerable importance for the agro-town. In 1831 "the peasants returning from the vineyards demonstrated noisily" initiating a confrontation in which cavalry charged the crowd—a dress rehearsal for the massive rebellion of 1907.[76]

Clermont's agricultural population of 1,200 in 1827 included vine dressers who owned land beyond the *octroi*. The hatred of these "rural" urban folk for the customs barrier reached a fever pitch after the revolution of 1830. In 1831 the vine dressers stormed the *octroi*. In 1835 a crowd attacked officials at the Montferrand gate who were trying to prevent people from bringing animals into town untaxed. The "forces of order" had to pull back "to avoid the murderous blows" of the rioters, who numbered more than a thousand. The tax office and the gates were destroyed as the taxmen fled for their lives. On September 9, 1841, nine people were killed during another series of protests against and attacks on the Clermont *octroi*. The next day the wine producers of the surrounding villages turned out in force, again destroying the barriers. Troops fired, killing 20 and wounding 25, taking losses of 3 killed and 15 wounded. Hundreds were arrested. It had been more of a pitched battle than a riot, as city and country joined forces against the *octroi*.[77]

In 1831 in Cahors, the tax collectors faced increasing resistance. First, "an insurrectionary mob," including some men in national guard uniform, stormed the town hall. After the crowd was dispersed, "the faubourgs remained in a great state of agitation; no one went to attend to his work." There were rumors that the prison, which held many peasants arrested in a previous riot in the village of Calvignac, would be stormed, with the help of villagers from outside Cahors. The rumor quickly reached Figeac that death threats were resounding in the faubourgs of Cahors. Indeed, the faubourg Saint-Georges, across the Lot, had contributed greatly to the resistance.[78] In 1841 the violent protest against the census, popularly seen as a Trojan horse for new taxes, began in the faubourgs of Toulouse, across the Garonne. The newly appointed prefect fled, and order was restored only with the arrival of a *commissaire extraordinaire* and the dissolution of the national guard.[79]

Grain riots came in waves during years of dearth—1816–17, 1826–27, 1840–41, and 1846–47.[80] The *octroi* was sometimes the site of "popular taxation" (*taxation populaire*)—protests against the departure of staples, particularly grain, bought by merchants at prices ordinary people could ill afford. The events in Lons-le-Saulnier in April 1840 are illustrative. A man selling potatoes at a high price from a wagon was recognized by the wives of some day laborers as an employee of M. de Vannois, a wealthy property owner believed to be a speculator. An angry crowd surrounded his wagons, overturning at least one. People began to carry off grain, until authorities promised that the poor would receive charitable assistance, and that hoarders would be brought to justice. Early the next morning the crowd began to form again. Swollen to three thousand, it stopped the wagons, which had been filled with more grain, presumably for the Lyon market. At the edge of the adjacent commune of Montmorot, the wagons were again attacked, and a number of soldiers sent to guard them were injured in the fracas. In nearby Courlans, the poor pillaged the château of de Vannois, the suspected hoarder.[81] In Sedan, wagons loaded with grain being shipped to Belgium were stopped at the entry to the faubourg Le Fond de Givonne and in the village of Givonne. The national guard, drawn from the *beaux quartiers*, confronted the rioters, who, some armed with rifles and pitchforks, hurriedly built a barricade. Bonbarded with a hail of rocks, the guardsmen charged the barricade, wounding twenty-five people with their bayonnets.[82]

These incidents, which could easily be multiplied, generated apprehension among urban elites of the turbulent faubourgs. During the July Monarchy the essence of what it was about faubourgs and suburbs that frightened the bourgeois began to be nuanced in an important way. Louis-Philippe's prefect, Chabrol, warned him, as noted earlier, that the factories on the edge of the city could "be the cord that will strangle us one day." The "dangerous classes" were gathered on the outskirts of the capital and of other cities as well. Saint-Marc Girardin, deputy from the Creuse, the department that sent thousands of seasonal migrants to work in the building trades in Paris each year, sounded his famous alert at the same time. He warned that "the barbarians who threaten society are in the faubourgs of our manufacturing towns, not in the Tartary in Russia."[83] They were the cabinet-makers and other workers of the lodging houses of the faubourg Saint-Antoine, whose lack of bread, Chevalier argues, "played a very large part in the political agitation in the faubourg during the last years of the Restoration and on the days of Revolution." The police claimed that denunciations of Charles X and shouts for Napoleon II had been heard, among other places, in the fearsome faubourg Saint-Marceau and the faubourg Saint-Martin.[84] In clerical Angers, deputies who had signed the provocative protest of the 221 deputies in the spring of 1830 against the government of Charles X received a hero's welcome in the faubourg Chalouère.[85]

For the urban elite of Louis-Philippe's *juste milieu,* popular republicanism after the revolution of 1830 took on the mixed image of social and physical marginality. During the protests against bread prices and taxes in Strasbourg in 1832, the prevailing rumor was that the faubourgs would rise, as young republicans circulated through the cafés, and the garrison of the frontier city was put on alert.[86] In 1835 a letter was sent to a man in Issoudun by "two of my friends living in the faubourg"; whether or not the gendarmerie exaggerated by calling it "a veritable catechism of the people," it was much sterner stuff than had appeared in the sleepy town Balzac evoked in *La Rabouilleuse.*[87] In 1838 in Blois, a petition in favor of electoral reform found no favor among the "reasonable inhabitants of this town." However, it won support "in a part of the suburbs called Les Granges, the inhabitants of which are in general not very enlightened and almost all busy with agricultural work." Since 1830, they had fallen under the influence of "men hostile to the government."[88]

When rumors had legitimist plots in the works, the locus of such conspiracies was not the faubourgs or the uncertain edge of city and town—although the popular royalism of Nîmes provides a dramatic exception—but châteaux, manors, and country houses farther out, as reflected by a denunciation sent to the mayor of Tarbes in October 1830 of a gathering of "prominent people, at which decisions were made that will be bad for all the good citizens . . . woe to us if their conspiracy succeeds."[89]

A song circulated by frustrated supporters of the Bourbons in 1832 identified the insurgents of 1830 with the faubourgs:

> And you brave men of the faubourgs
> In whom Paris during its three days
> Saw such tireless audacity,
> Believe that we render you thanks
> For not having pillaged us
> As much as you would have wanted.
>
> . . .
>
> Especially you, worthy workers
> Who live from all your trades,
> To escape from slavery
> You have lost your work
> But now you are truly
> Free to die of hunger.

Here we have a revealing combination of grudging admiration for and fear of the workers of the faubourgs, who had driven the Bourbons from the throne, but who now shared a common enemy with the legitimists—the Orleanist monarchy.[90]

As strikes became more prevalent under the Restoration, rumors of brigands, beggars, and arsonists had given way to fears of "workers" banding together to plan strikes or other mischief on the edge of town. For example, in May 1829 the story circulated in the textile town of Cholet that the workers of "the five parishes of the environs were going to meet and come demand work from the merchants."

In 1829 this seemed less threatening than the liberal political opinions of the merchants themselves. Given the dispersion of industrial work in the hinterland of Cholet, this comes as no surprise, but provides another example of the pervasive fear of the semiskilled industrial proletariat on the frontier of urban life.[91]

The strikes of the July Monarchy reflected the gradual emergence of class consciousness within the context of changes in the structure of work that placed artisans at the forefront of social protest.[92] They were often planned and sustained by meetings in the faubourgs or suburbs, beyond the prying eyes and jurisdiction of the police. There workers could discuss, debate, and organize in the relative freedom of taverns or even open spaces, sometimes posting guards to spot the arrival of gendarmes. For example, in 1840 a strike by shoemakers was planned by leaders such as "Le Nantais" in a cabaret in Flacé, a small village outside Mâcon, while in April 1845 police arrested striking bakers meeting at the tour de L'Evêque outside Nîmes.[93]

No more powerful image of fear of the peripheral could be found than that shared by the wealthy merchants of central Lyon, in the quarters of the town hall and the place Bellecour. They confronted the hatred of the silk workers of the Croix-Rousse—it was still called a "faubourg"—who came charging down to attack the *beaux quartiers* behind a banner that shouted, "Live free or die fighting!" in April 1834, as they had in November 1831. These were anything but outcasts or disorderly, disorganized workers. They were very organized, and that made them doubly threatening.

In 1841 an officer described the Croix-Rousse as if it were a foreign land with which he was at war: "the morals there are coarse and one can easily understand why. Situated near a completely corrupted large city, populated by people whose pecuniary position relegates them to the very lowest class of society and who receive little education, the Croix-Rousse is a place that can only be considered a receptacle for a sizable impoverished population. Civilization is barely to be found there."[94]

It is even easier to find fearful descriptions of the faubourgs in 1848 and during the Second Republic. Lord Palmerston, closely following events across the Channel, proclaimed that *he* was not afraid of "the scum of the faubourgs of Paris." In Paris, most of the fighting during the February revolution occurred in the central districts, following the shooting of demonstrators marching on the boulevard des Capucines. A comment by Alexis de Tocqueville reflected the passing of revolution from the center of Paris to the eastern faubourgs. On May 21 he had noted that, during the Festival of Concord on the Champs de Mars, "the bouquets of the sturdy young women from the industrial faubourgs . . . fell on the assembled deputies like hailstones, reminding the authorities that concord was somewhat less than perfect."[95] Thus the June Days, that bloody civil war that sent tremors of fear throughout much of Europe, followed the February revolution.

Much of the fighting during the June Days took place in and around the faubourg Saint-Antoine. The cabinetmakers contributed to the image of the volatile, insurgent faubourg. In 1848, fear of the faubourgs and of the edge of the city was a recurrent theme in the repression that followed the June Days in Paris and insurrections in Rouen and Limoges, in which *faubouriens* also played a prominent role. One of the two liberty trees planted in the enthusiasm of the spring of 1848 in Belfort, then a small town of not much more than five thousand, was placed between the town center and its faubourg (and the other near the church), as if to establish harmony between the two. Neither the liberty trees nor the harmony lasted long.[96] Several of the prominent "banquets of the people" of the Republic took place on the edge of the capital, as for example "at the *barrière* of Pigalle, where the newly formed association of cooks prepared their first meal for the saddlemakers," or "in the faubourgs of La Villette, where the carriage joiners welcome the Representatives of the People for lunch in their workshops. The frugal meal offered by the fraternal workers takes on the smell of Sundays in the countryside, echoing the miracle of the bread and consecrated wine"—but in this case with "citizens," not waiters, serving their equals in the Republic.[97]

Municipal authorities in normally placid Caen must have been surprised to see the laceworkers of the faubourgs Vaucelles and Maladrerie march to the town hall demanding work after the February revolution. When Louis Napoleon visited the city in September 1850, he was warmly welcomed in the elite quarter of the place Royale, but in the faubourg de Vaucelles he was greeted by hostile republican shouts.[98] The faubourgs of Limoges and Reims were likewise among those challenging the elites of their cities.

Despite the repression that followed the insurrection in Lyons in June 1849, across the Rhône La Guillotière remained, at least in the perception of the authorities, "a habitual center for a population of vagabonds and convicts." A leftist municipal council was reelected, despite the electoral law of May 31, 1850, which eliminated a good proportion of eligible voters. The image of marginal people in peripheral spaces threatening established order, as for instance by voting, was hard to shake.[99]

During the Second Republic social elites feared, and the police watched, closed or intimidated into closing, the *goguettes* of some of the communes of the distant suburbs of Paris. These "bacchanalian and singing associations" combined sociability and, it was assumed, politics. The members of the *goguettes* of Montmorency, Pontoise, and Franconville sported Montagnard apparel, such as red ties and belts, as they sang popular *démoc-soc* tunes. Officials bandied about the term *goguette* "to make people afraid." It was not only the peripheral and thus less policed location of the *goguettes* or their generally popular social composition that caught the attention of the government. Popular associations themselves, part of the "apprenticeship of the Republic," were suspect.[100] A subprefect put it this way in 1850: "these associations quickly degenerate into cells preparing for revolution, if they lack proper leadership and enlightenment." Their peripheral nature seemed, at least to authorities, to "deprive" them of both. *Goguettes* were banned during the state of siege imposed by Louis Napoleon and gradually disappeared, perhaps also victims of the popularity of the *café-concert.*[101]

After the coup d'état of December 2, 1851, the few remaining Montagnard militants of Le Mans went to the villages east of the city in the hope of convincing the weavers there to attack Le Mans on behalf of the Republic. But the "descent upon the city"—the nightmare of the bourgeois elite—never took place.[102]

We can carry this association between social and geographic marginality and the challenge to urban elites further in time. During the Second Empire Baron Haussmann unleashed "urbanism through demolition"—the phrase is that of Pierre Lavedan[103]—and chased thousands of poor workers from the crowded central and eastern districts of the capital to the faubourgs and suburbs, particularly those of the north and northeast. Some 350,000 Parisians of modest means were exiled to the periphery. There were still hundreds of thousands of workers in the capital, but a geography of class segregation clearly emerged. As T. J. Clark puts it, "Paris was all traffic, all 'circulation'; and between the great avenues were separate cities, rich and poor, where one could walk for half an hour without seeing a *blouse,* and then another hour in a different direction with never a private carriage or a rolled umbrella, or even the shiniest, most threadbare of *redingotes!"*[104]

By the late 1860s it seemed to many that "the plebeian is now camped in the environs, in Montmartre and Belleville, and from these desolate heights threaten the flat, richer spaces of the central quarters."[105] Gérard Jacquemet tells the story of the development of Belleville, already notorious for its wine merchants: "In the beginning, Belleville was a place where one amused oneself, or took a walk, or where lovers arranged to meet: 'From the entrance to the faubourg to Temple up to the plateau of Belleville, one could see a swelling tide of workers, bourgeois, clerks, *grisettes,* good children, and soldiers, all of whom laughed, sang, chattered, and flirted.' Later, toward the end of the Second Empire, things changed. Belleville no longer breathed joy, but a sinister odor of oozing crime. . . . [The quarter of America] and its quarries were all the while the asylum for vagabondage, theft, and crime." At least that was its image—a place that had long been "a den of brigands."[106]

The social and political threat, in any case, seemed real. Residents of Belleville, with its Club des Montagnards, 1,200 strong, and its 5,000 laborers in the National Workshops, took an active part in the insurrection of June 1848.[107] In the elections of 1869 Léon Gambetta and Henri Rochefort, hardly favorites of the emperor, were elected by Belleville to the Corps Législatif; a contemporary wrote, "however, we still did not know what sense of terror would be produced in the provinces by the name of Rochefort; it represented all of the distrust and hatred that Belleville inspired. The public meeting movement in Paris that followed the application of a more liberal law in June 1868 moved to the more proletarian periphery of the capital. The dance halls and warehouses in which workers debated economic, social, and political issues were "like detached forts of socialism surrounding central Paris."[108]

In a sense, the Paris Commune of 1871 that followed can be considered "the revenge of the expelled," of those described earlier by the *Journal des débats* as "outside the city," for whom the decision of the provisional government to allow landlords, despite desperately hard times, to demand immediate payment of back rent was an outrage and a disaster.[109] Particularly given Belleville's active role during the Commune, it is appropriate that among the last barricades to fall during bloody week of May 1871 were those in Belleville and near the cemetery of Père Lachaise; the Mur des Fédérés, where insurgents fell before firing squads, still stands in memory of those slaughtered—at least twenty-five thousand—and also as a reminder of the relations between center and periphery in transforming Paris.

"Radiating from the faubourgs, poverty," in the eyes of upper classes, "came to carry sickness, crime, and civil war to the heart of the fancy neighborhoods, which thereafter worried about their health and security."[110] The future *journées* of the capital would be the work of the right—February 6, 1934, above all—more than of the left, at least until 1968.

The "Belle Epoque" in Paris was, among other things, the heyday of the *apaches,* bands of thugs from the suburbs. The Band of the Four Paths of Aubervilliers, the Wolves of the Butte, and others have been described by Michelle Perrot: "young marauders of the faubourgs . . . (who) saw themselves in this Indian image, which they claimed as a symbol of their defiant mobility and their brawling spirit . . . the 'zone' was their frontier and they were actors in an urban western."[111] In the first decade of this century, the term "apache" came to mean, as defined by a newspaper in 1907, "the swindler, the ruffian, the clever, informed smuggler, the burglar, the rascal with the hidden knife, the man who lives on the edge of society, ready for any shady task so as to avoid regular work, the scoundrel who picks a lock or disembowels a passerby, sometimes for nothing, simply for pleasure."[112] The apaches, "a microsociety with its geography, hierarchy, language, and code," were marginal in two senses. First, they rejected—and were obviously excluded from—the bourgeois society of the heart of Paris. But they also stood apart from working-class culture, rejecting work itself, and were better dressed, albeit exotically, than workers, while sharing a similar resistance to industrial discipline, bourgeois moralization, and the police. The apaches went into Paris as marauders: "Coming from the heights of Belleville, Ménilmontant, or the Butte, they were fond of the center—the Maub, Montparno, the Mouffe—coming to prowl in the Latin Quarter, laying siege to Les Halles, making Sébasto their *ramblas.* The apaches were no longer content with the *barrières,* noisily taking possession of the center of town, from which their fathers had been expelled."[113] They were feared by Parisians, as by many residents of the suburbs as well, representing the uncertain edge of urbanization, the disorganization of the frontier of urban life.

The anarchist Emile Henry, about to be guillotined for tossing a bomb in the Café Terminus near the Gare Saint-Lazare in Paris in 1894, also conjured up the image of the impoverished periphery: "The bourgeoisie must finally understand that those who have suffered are at the end of their rope; they are showing teeth and striking as brutally as those who have been brutal to them. . . . It is not we who carried out the bloody week [in 1871] or Fourmies. . . . Are they not innocent victims, these children who slowly starve to death of anemia in the faubourgs because bread is rare in their house; these women who are wasting away in your workshops to earn a few cents a day, still grateful that misery has not yet pushed them into prostitution?"[114]

In that same year, 1894, the bourgeois moralist Henry Leyret moved—at least for five months—into the peripheral quarters of Paris. To understand working-class life, the people Georges Clemenceau had called the fourth estate, he took out a license to sell liquor. A bar seemed the perfect place to get to know the workers of the margins of urban life: "Far from the boulevard, in the middle of the faubourg, I planted my tent under the sign of a wine merchant." During the winter and beyond, he observed workers and their families from the other side of his counter, "big children with large hearts, eager to work, easy in love, if occasionally cheats, even occasionally bullies [*si casseurs*]!" Shocked by the grinding poverty of the separate world of the faubourgs ("in these poor, perched lodgings of such misery")—with its own argot, such that he provided translations for many terms and words—he expressed surprise at the workers' patience. But how much longer could it go on? "Too much misery inevitably will end their long submissiveness." Leyret too expected the explosion to come from the outside, from the floating worlds of the periphery.[115]

Jean-Claude Perrot's comment on the significance of town walls for bourgeois urban dwellers in the eighteenth century echoes even more for the period of the great growth of the faubourgs in the nineteenth: "The ramparts . . . retain in the landscape an eminent place . . . when they lose all military value, the *barrière* still protects the bourgeoisie from the riffraff of the faubourgs."[116]

Faubourgs and peripheral communes lacked the cultural infrastructure of urban life. If some, like the faubourg L'Houmeau in Angoulême, approximated bourgs with a bourgeois elite drawn from the ranks of commerce, most lacked voluntary associations such as reading clubs that provided some sort of continuity. A deputy mayor of Bercy reported in 1827 (in response to a request for information on outlets for liberal newspapers and brochures) that there were no reading clubs or bookstores there. There was only Pierre Raphanel, who ran a tobacco shop; "having been forced to take in payment several collections of novels" from a schoolteacher, he had begun a small reading club, renting books for a small sum.[117]

Rare were developing industrial faubourgs in the first half of the century that had churches, the kind of symbol of order that the upper classes found reassuring, whether they attended them or not. This seemed to make it even more difficult for urban elites and officials to "moralize" the people of the periphery. Thus in the wave of public penance that accompanied outright repression after the Paris and provincial communes of 1871, the Catholic elite hurriedly constructed churches in faubourgs (in the industrial quarters of Montluçon on the left bank of the Cher, in the faubourgs of Limoges, and so on), and established religious associations for workers, themselves becoming watchful honorary members. Building parishes was another thing. Instead of voluntary associations, with statutes and lists of members registered with the prefecture, the faubourgs still offered people of small means open spaces and rough cabarets, *guinguettes* and *bouchons,* beyond surveillance and police jurisdiction. What went on there many people of the central city could only guess, but they had their suspicions.

It was precisely the double life of the faubourg that made it as suspect to contemporaries as it is intriguing to us. Kaplan suggests that what made the faubourg Saint-Antoine the "revolutionary quarter par excellence" was not its role as "traditional core of popular agitation," but rather its complex situation as "bastion of independence, center of uncontrolled work, hiding place for fugitives of all sorts, nursery of discreet rooming houses, and sanctuary for illegal gatherings." Kaplan asks if its residents had "developed a sense of their difference, of relative autonomy, and a type of political conscience vis-à-vis central authority that had made them sensitive to the defense of their rights. The daily counterculture of the faubourg, sharpened by its ambiguous relationship with town and state, had engendered this spirit of independence and cleared the way for its revolutionary vocation.'' The faubourg Saint-Antoine had an image that was ''double and contradictory: on the one hand, as a Parisian avant-garde, a martyr of liberty, victorious over despotism; on the other, as a sewer pipe of disorder, nonconformity and a place of chronic instability.''[118] This ambiguity of image, but also of reality, became even more complex with the large-scale industrialization under way in many places during the first half of the nineteenth century in Paris but, even more telling, in many provincial cities and towns.

4

Center and Periphery:
Contrasts in the West—Poitiers,
Châtellerault, and La Roche-sur-Yon

A View from the Center of Poitiers

Born in 1807, Anne-Latrelle de Cisterne de Courtiras Poilloüe de Saint-Mars grew up within the narrow confines of Restoration Poitiers. The social and spatial perimeters of her world were those established by the aristocracy and clergy of one of France's ecclesiastical centers, which was also a town of landlords and officials. The memoirs of this daughter of a noble, published posthumously under the nom de plume of Countess Dash, reflect the physical and social isolation that characterized elite quarters unchallenged by working-class concentration within the city or faubourgs. Poitiers was one of those towns—like Avignon, Aix-en-Provence, and Bayeux—in which the presence of an urban nobility and the continuing preeminence of the clergy seemed to have successfully turned the clock back to the ancien régime. An "insurmountable wall" stood between the nobles and everyone else. But the survival of elite urban neighborhoods was similar to other city centers dominated by a more bourgeois elite.[1] Poitiers had two "faubourgs Saint-Germain," the quarter of the cathedral of Saint-Pierre and the rue des Hautes-Treilles,[2] with other noble town houses near the romanesque masterpiece of Notre-Dame-la-Grande.

The noble Irland de Bazoges, former *député-suppléant* in the elections to the Estates-General and an émigré who returned to become mayor of Poitiers in 1807, resided in a splendid house built at the time of Louis XIV near Notre-Dame. Guests entered from the street through the monumental gate to the garden, which, typical of noble town houses in the region, was enclosed by tall walls sheltering guests from the sight and most of the sounds of ordinary people who lived, as in the seventeenth-century Marais in Paris, not far away. Visitors reached the residence itself by a magnificent stone staircase with an elegant railing of forged iron. The countess recalled the interior of the hotel with awe: "the furniture, the conspicuous ostrich eggs, stylized mirrors, large, overstuffed armchairs, canopy beds, and the petite wife of the worthy man in a dark purple-brown dress with a small white shawl, always gay, ever sprightly''—all brought back her childhood.[3]

The countess's family lived slightly less elegantly on the rue du Moulin-à-vent. Their friends were several other distinguished families also known for their devotion to the king. De Chassenon, a former magistrate, lived in a "superb" residence near Saint-Hilaire, when he was not at his château of Curzay near Lusignan. There were very few shops on their street to break its image of a noble enclave protected by location and walls from the hustle and bustle of commerce and artisanal work. The nobles generally shunned both the Cercle Littéraire, founded in 1816, and of course its liberal rival, the Société Littéraire. They limited social activities to their private gatherings.[4]

The Revolution had devastated the nobility of the Poitou, dispersing its scions across the frontiers. Late in the Empire a sufficient number of nobles had returned to form a "charming nucleus" of the social elite. The old routines of elite sociability began again, after having been so rudely interrupted by the Revolution and its most terrifying symbol, the guillotine that had stood on the place du Pilori. Now, as before, the families of the old noblesse went off to visit their friends after Mass and dinner, to chat or play cards in "the smartest houses," hosting in turn. With the Restoration, more nobles returned to Poitiers, some from abroad and others from châteaux in rural Poitou where they had managed to avoid discovery by revolutionaries.

The patriarchs of the *haute noblesse* formed what the countess remembered as the "salon of antiquities," wearing knee breeches, silk stockings, square-styled jackets, and three-cornered hats on top of powdered wigs: "they repressed the lost years, some thirty of them, and returned to the joys of being twenty years old again." Some of the women dressed in old silk gowns, which had been hurriedly packed and survived in musty-smelling trunks in someone's attic or *cave,* or had been sufficiently treasured to be taken into exile. Gradually the nobles reconstituted their fortunes; soon there were again a good number of "rich people, with excellent houses," where the right people were "perfectly well received in the very best company." Once again, it was a time of "excellent dinners (in a region of good living) and magnificent balls accompanied by splendid suppers, where galantines, turkeys with truffles, and hams provided dancers with energy until five and six in the morning. There were a number of attractive women, as many unmarried as married, and enough men to court them all." The countess enjoyed innumerable occasions to observe all of this firsthand while growing up; her mother hosted a small gathering each Saturday, a dinner once a month, and a ball during Mardi Gras, with the common masked revelers of the streets kept out by an imposing gate and walls.[5]

Despite the return of altar and throne to power, powdered wigs and fancy breeches could not alone erase the terrible memories of the Revolution for the nobles of Poitou. Even in the reassuring confines of the convent school of the Dames de la Foi, the young countess could not avoid the shadow of the Revolution. The children told stories of nuns who had disappeared into the caves along the Clain river, near the abbey of Sainte-Radegonde. They listened to tales of the heroism of the faithful who served the Bourbons and the Church during the bad years. A friend of the family, the abbé Marin de la Bessière, was said to have miraculously survived the September Massacres in Paris after being left for dead among the corpses of other priests. The girls wept each time they heard the stirring

story of a beautiful young servant in Poitiers who refused to escape the executioner's ax by denying, even when encouraged by her accusers to do so, that she
had assisted an escaping noble; "I did my duty, why should I hide it?" she
innocently stated, before being dispatched by the tearful executioner. It seemed
only reasonable to such listeners that a republican conscript found his arm
paralyzed as he began to chop down a statue of the Virgin Mary and the Infant
Jesus on the place du Pilori.

The children recounted the misdeeds of a local regicide, cautioning their cats
not to venture onto his property, where evil lurked. Not long after the monarchy
returned, the guillotining of the disloyal General Berton on the place du Pilori
served to remind all of what God had in store for those who violated His law on
earth. Although it is most unlikely that she attended the execution, Anne-Latrelle
had been told how Berton gasped violently when he first saw the scaffold and the
infamous, terrifying instrument of execution before which "even the most fervent
royalists held their tongues," and how one of his accomplices had committed
suicide the night before the day of justice, avoiding the scaffold but not the wrath
of God. Public executions—there were 34, including 7 women, between 1811 and
1848 in Poitiers—and the public exhibition of lesser criminals on the place Notre-
Dame, reminded people that there was a God of vengeance. Anne-Latrelle and her
friends spoke about such things in hushed tones in their convent school. There they
longed for the dolls in their rooms at home that they had named after famous
noblewomen such as Mlle de Montmorency and Mme de Rohan, dolls that they
had baptized in small private ceremonies.[6]

That the clergy's influence extended to most of Poitiers reassured the nobility.
If nothing else, Poitiers was a place of religion, and had been a "town with
abundant priests and monks"[7] and a fervent belief in saints for centuries. No less
than five bishops lived there during the Restoration, among them de Bouille,
bishop of Poitiers; the bishop of Luçon, who spent no more time in Luçon than had
his distant predecessor, Richelieu; and a retired prelate who preferred Poitiers to
anywhere else. A fourth bishop, de Vareilles, was grateful to have escaped Gap,
his former episcopate, and regaled suitable company with stories of his youth in
Metz ("he had the supreme manners of the ancien régime, a true priest of the
eighteenth-century court") in his family's residence on the rue Saint-Paul, just off
the rue de la Cathédrale. Finally, Brumauld de Beauregard remained in Poitiers
while awaiting official confirmation of his appointment to Orléans. Each Sunday
morning he said Mass at eight o'clock in the cathedral "for the women of the
people and the servants . . . he saw their side of things, speaking to them
familiarly, even questioning them"—which seemed odd enough that the girl
mentioned it. While not a familiar sight on most of the streets, the bishops in the
deep colors of their episcopal garb frequented the noble salons, several themselves
hosting gatherings.[8]

In 1817 the prefect's annual report, with a certain edge to it, seemed to confirm
what the young countess deeply believed: "no part of France is more under the
direct influence of the clergy than Poitiers. I doubt even that there is a town in Italy
where this influence is so marked."[9] What even this prefect of the early
Restoration considered a return to the mysticism and asceticism characteristic of

the twelfth and thirteenth centuries provided arms to the enemies of the Church. The Restoration brought a flurry of religious ceremonies that combined a sense of expiation for the "sins" of the Revolution with the symbolic reconquest of the public space of the city—a reconquest as determined and relentless as that of the dechristianization campaign of the year II. The traditional Easter Monday procession, now organized by a new confraternity, celebrating the deliverance of besieged Poitiers by the Holy Virgin in 1200, returned to the streets "in the spirit of reparation for the crimes committed during the Revolution." The cult of the Sacred Heart found renéwed enthusiasm in the cathedral and other churches and chapels of Poitiers.[10] The high clergy of the diocese complained to the king in April 1817 that a rumored new and relatively inexpensive edition of the complete works of Voltaire would put within the reach of the people that "antisocial and anti-Christian writer" who had "prepared the scaffolds for kings, chains for pontiffs, the triumphs of impiety, and the calamities of the people." When the godfather of a newborn forgot the prayers he was to say at the baptism, the priest refused to perform the ceremony. It was also war on nude bathing in the river. And when the harvest failed, a priest of Poitiers announced that God was punishing his people for the sins of the Revolution; only devotion to the Sacred Heart could put an end to this "public gangrene" and restore prosperity.[11] It was that kind of time in that kind of town.

No phenomenon more symbolized the spirit of Restoration France than the missions. As resentment, hostility, and even open opposition to them offered something of a gauge of political mobilization against the Restoration, so did an outpouring of manifest faith reflect the persistence of traditional religious values. The mission of 1817 pushed the clergy of Poitiers to something of a frenzy. The arrival of the mission was one of the most vivid childhood memories of the pious young countess, who need not have added that she had never read the *Declaration of the Rights of Man* or the *Social Contract,* and had been taught to believe that it was a felonious crime—worse, a mortal sin—to disobey the king. Just about everyone attended the missions, where the renowned abbé de Janson inveighed against "all kinds of pleasures, preaching penance and privation." She also remembered that there had been some "a small number of opponents who attempted several demonstrations, one when the mission cross was erected near Saint-Hilaire; the authorities set them straight right away."[12]

Thus with the Restoration, Poitiers "returned to its countenance of a peaceful town, with sleepy, medieval charms." Much of the town stood on a steep and irregularly shaped hill. Its streets were winding and narrow, and offered imposing inclines ("poorly built, insufficiently accessible, even more inadequately paved, without noteworthy public squares," went the military survey, almost by formula, in 1841). Buildings seemed huddled together, as if for protection against the outside world—which was, after all, the origin of urban settlements: "ramshackle houses leaning against public buildings, as if one day they simply ran out of space within the walls." Notre-Dame-la-Grande only shed the structures propped against its chevet in 1849, twenty years after the municipal council first approved the work. Not until 1850 could one travel directly from the pont Neuf to the place d'Armes, long after the bridge had been completed. Despite a plan for street align-

FRANCE PITTORESQUE

View of Poitiers.

ment drawn up during the Empire, and a municipal edict of 1818 that new streets had to be at least eight meters wide, only the expansion of the quarter of Blossac countered the prevailing image of total immobility and stagnation.[13]

That Poitiers during the Restoration still in some ways resembled a town of the Middle Ages pleased the nobility, the clergy, assorted rentiers and functionaries, and Anne-Latrelle, but not everyone. In January 1817 the prefect of the Vienne, Louis du Hamel, had confirmed in his "Reflections on the Situation of the Town of Poitiers" the municipality's dire predictions of 1790: "lacking commerce, without industry, without even any desire to acquire these means to prosperity, the population of this town vegetates, returning to its habitual lethargy."[14] Aside from artisanal production for local consumption, the only industry of any consequence in the vicinity, cotton spinning, was located in the commune of Biard outside Poitiers. It languished until 1828, when it received a contract to make pants for the army. In 1845, 485 residents of Poitiers worked for the manufacture in Biard, 400 of whom were women who trekked there carrying work done at home.[15]

The center of town, unchanged for centuries, seemed to preserve what one fervent contemporary called "the moral character of the *cité*," closely tied to the Church. Even when the prefecture was later constructed on the bluff above the station, it was apparent that the town's population did not justify the construction of a new adjacent quarter. But gradually the ecclesiastical center of the old town withered, not only because of its lack of economic dynamism, but because the route from the porte de Paris to La Tranchée and the road to Bordeaux crossed the newer upper town, not the urban nucleus "at the foot of churches from which the somber toll of bells was heard on the hour." The Café des Trois Pilliers, which would become the center of radical republican activity during the Second Republic, and a number of stores benefited from this new traffic, however modest. The result was that "everyone saw that the life disappearing from the old quarters was moving above the *cité,* from the center toward the edge of town." As the center of Poitiers moved away from the ecclesiastical center, the result would be, a contemporary feared, an inevitable weakening of what he considered the moral traditions of old Poitou.[16]

In 1817 the prefect blamed some of the suffering on the fact that the poor seemed to have retained the ancien régime habit of depending upon the thirty-six religious communities in bad times. Although there were now less than half as many residents of convents as before the Revolution, the old habits of "laziness" had been retained. So had popular religious superstitions that du Hamel found offensive to "Our Holy Religion." The upper classes were hardly immune from this "monastic virus." The noble families had no taste for the arts, commerce, or what du Hamel called "the mechanical arts," by which he meant industry informed by science. A few wise men had created useful establishments, but these merely provided a "shocking contrast with the rest of the town."[17] In addition, Poitiers was "the refuge of rentiers," many of whom owned considerable holdings in the countryside, and itself retained a sizable agricultural population.[18]

It was the prefect's informed opinion that Poitiers's development had been arrested in the fourteenth century, unlike that of Tours, Angoulême, and even Limoges, its prosperous neighbors and gentle rivals. Poitiers stagnated. The monarchy should rescue it by establishing an arms manufacture in the departmental capital, instead of in nearby Châtellerault. Such a step could, he reasoned, change the attitudes of the people, offering the poor the chance to work for an honest wage. At the same time he cautioned the government against authorizing more religious congregations to move to Poitiers. While stifling commerce and industry, they made his administrative tasks more difficult because of their outspoken intolerance toward even the simplest of secular pleasures such as dances and the theater, both of which the nobles too avoided. The clergy were now attacking him for his spirited defense of the municipal theater, a move that motivated his frank and —for the time—surprisingly blunt attack. The isolated and self-satisfied clergy, with the nobles of the Hautes-Treilles quarter, seemed to condemn Poitiers to remain in another century.[19]

Indeed, there are few cities in France today where the ecclesiastical heritage remains so vividly imprinted on even secular stones, beginning with the remnants near the cathedral of the fourth-century baptistery of Saint-Jean, considered the oldest church in France. With its war on the Church in a town that had been a capital of the Counterreformation, the Revolution made ecclesiastical architecture part of the fabric of urban life. In 1790 Poitiers had twenty-four parishes, in 1815 but six (Saint-Pierre, Notre-Dame-la-Grande, Montierneuf, Saint-Hilaire, Saint-Porchaire, and Sainte-Radegonde). These six had been rebaptized Liberty, Fraternity, Equality, Unity, Republic, and Federation in 1792, before all of them were closed in December 1793. The church bells, which had seemed to ring day and night, were melted down. In 1790 the convents of the Visitation and of the Feuillants had been converted into prisons. The Grand Séminaire and the convents of the Carmelites and the Filles-de-Notre-Dame were employed as barracks for troops en route to fight in the Vendée, who kept their horses in the church of Montierneuf, and their supplies in the bishop's palace and the Carmelite convent. Church property represented part of 281 sales of land between 1790 and 1800. Yet despite the loss of many buildings, many signs and symbols remained evident of the Church's special position in this town with a modest, declining population of 27,000. Like Le Puy, Poitiers seemed less a town than an ecclesiastical *cité* on a hill. In addition to the six surviving parishes and a number of chapels, fifteen religious congregations remained, at least until 1848.[20]

The nobles and clergy counted other losses upon returning. Proud Poitiers had lost its status as a regional capital and intendancy, and lucrative fiscal agencies. It was left with an inadequate consolation prize of being the departmental capital of the Vienne. Even the personnel of the prefecture and the new appellate court could not compensate for the large staffs of lawyers and other auxiliaries that had been lost. In 1790 the municipality had protested to the National Assembly that Poitiers could least afford to lose its status because it was "deprived of all the resources that elsewhere generate the fruitfulness of commerce and industry." The petition predicted that Poitiers would soon fall into an irreversible "languor," if its ecclesiastical institutions were closed. It was an accurate prophecy. The structure of local power itself was altered, a fact that even the return of the Bourbons and many of the prerogatives of the Church could not change. The bourgeoisie, particularly moderate merchants and lawyers, many of whom had purchased *biens nationaux*, profited from the "downfall of the nobility and clergy" to rise slowly to predominance.[21]

Not much had changed by 1841. The town had a smaller population then— 22,376—than in 1823, and grew at a snail's pace in the decades to come.[22] The only sound one heard at night was, it might have been claimed, the wind whistling through the cassocks of the clergy as they scurried off to vespers. The town still seemed

> the cadaver of a large town. The old capital of the region no longer has enough life to survive. It has no industry, its provisionment is difficult and its markets limited. It exists not by itself but only from the importance stemming from its royal court, school of law, medical school, and administrative person- nel . . . its existence as the first town of the department is artificial. Witness Bourbon-Vendée, take the example of Montbrison in the Loire, which is nothing when compared to Saint-Etienne or even Roanne.[23]

Within its physically large dimensions—six kilometers in circumference, not including the faubourgs[24]—there remained considerable room for gardens and even small fields. No one clamored to live in Poitiers. The town itself was still surrounded by walls, however dilapidated in places. The gates slammed shut at night as the bells of Notre-Dame sounded the end of the day, and one by one the candles lit by the faithful stopped flickering in the darkness of cathedral and church. The gates had been replaced by new *octroi* barriers, but they too were closed at night.[25]

Poitiers from its hill dwarfed the small faubourgs that lay across the sharply winding Clain river. These small faubourgs were poorer than the central city, inhabited by workers and peasants and some who were both. Beyond the pont Neuf and the Clain river lived most of the three thousand parishioners of Saint-Radegonde, a stone's throw from the cathedral of Saint-Pierre, but reflecting a distinctly different social composition, "having only laborers as inhabitants." This peripheral parish along the Clain was the poorest, and had been so in the previous centuries; in June 1825 its priest, despite thirty-seven years of service, complained that he did not have enough money to live on.[26]

In 1820 the nobles spent carnival season in their town houses, as usual; it would have been inappropriate for them to appear, even in disguise, at the masked ball at the theater, a festivity reserved for "students and *grisettes.*" Those gatherings were irreverent, common, anxiety-provoking: "one really didn't let go in Poitiers, morals there were quite strict." As was traditional, some revelers marched through the town, singing. One of them paused in front of the house of the young countess, where, shutters tightly closed, there was no sign of carnival. He shouted, it was said, "Tomorrow we shall bury carnival, but there could be others at the same time." At least that was how the victims of this "nasty joke" chose to remember it, after news soon struck with a devastating blow that the Duc de Berri had been assassinated outside the Paris Opera by Louvel that very hour. In the noble salons and the conversations of the young girls, there was idle speculation about dark conspiracies involving the liberal sons of commerce and the students they so hated: "Was it indeed chance? Did they know in advance about the murder?"[27]

Countess Dash described Poitiers as "one of the most turbulent towns in France." It might have seemed that way to the nobles, because of the "chivalrous temperament" of the young students and the soldiers in the garrison. Political divisions, as well as social rivalries, led to fights, occasionally to duels, which she recalled as having occurred in 1820. Liberal and royalist students each had their own clubs and cafés; when one side became enamored of an actor or actress at the theater, the other took pains to show disdain for the same performer. The nobles considered the students, too, beneath their class, whether royalist (and few were) or not. They also believed the prefects beneath them, their posts having been a creation of the Revolution. They refused all invitations to the prefecture, while the wife of the prefect Moreau de la Rochette wept bitterly.[28]

In Restoration Poitiers the nobles thus continued to isolate themselves, as much as possible, from all but their servants. They did not try to cultivate the popular royalism characteristic of Nîmes and other cities of the Midi. Poitiers had no tradition of religious wars, at least not since the days of Charles Martel in A.D. 732. The nobles had little to do with the middle ranks of society, "the bourgeoisie, all those perched on the threshold of the palace, people with money, including many functionaries and merchants." The countess recalled that "one would rather have received the seamstress at table than the wife of a parvenu. I am not judging, only relating." If social distance had not provided sufficient reason for these parvenus to be ignored, their hostility to the Bourbons—"here already were the elements of Orleanism"—left an enormous gulf between them. The countess later would contrast the "old inflexible nobility" of Poitiers with the nobles of Moulins, whom after a short stay she believed to be unique, because "anyone who could be admitted to the inner circle by birth, industriousness, or fortune gathered together."[29]

But as in Nîmes, Toulouse, Montpellier, and other centers of passionate royalism, the nobles of Poitiers patronized merchants and artisans who, by loudly proclaiming their affection and loyalty to the Bourbons, earned the right to supply the Hautes-Treilles quarter. As the countess later recalled, that quarter "was not allowed to buy elsewhere . . . the opposite clique had their own [merchants] but the others held the first rank." In the countryside the nobles rewarded faithful and dutiful peasants who filled the churches, inviting them on certain religious holidays to come to the château, or at least near it: "they danced before the iron gate, drinking barrels of the good wine of the region."[30]

During the Restoration, liberals dominating one of the town's two *cercles*, the Société Littéraire, which counted among its members the unfortunately named regicide Cochon de l'Apparent, who had first authorized the association when he was prefect. Here they read *Le Constitutionnel, Le Courrier français*, and whatever forbidden brochures the police were not able to discover and confiscate on the road from Paris to Bordeaux. Above all, liberalism under the Restoration, like republicanism during the July Monarchy, was transient, finding support among the three hundred to four hundred university students in temporary residence, lodging with lawyers, notaries, and other respectables, but not with noble families. These students boosted the local economy but also whistled and shouted in the theater. Their heated discussions and occasional shouts from their clubs and cafés, the Pupile, the Flore, and the Duschêne, or from the street, sometimes reached the walled gardens and salons of the nobles. Yet only in March 1821 did the students cause a major disturbance, when thirty-one of them were arrested, following their protest that their vacation during carnival had been cut. Their political opposition was limited to oblique "agitation." The nobles, having obtained the closing of an *école de l'enseignement mutuel*, began to inveigh against the university itself, particularly the law school.[31]

Not surprisingly, the middle classes of Poitiers were happy to see Charles X driven from the throne. Some members of the national guard even constructed barricades, hoping to assure the defeat of the Bourbons.[32] The nobles and clergy were stunned by this unthinkable act of God. In September 1830, legitimists disrupted the ceremony in which the magistrates of the court took their oaths of loyalty to the new regime; a majority of the magistrates refused to attend the commemoration of the first anniversary of the July Days.[33] Some royalists fought back; the *Gazette de l'Ouest* (circulation 630) heaped scorn on the regime of newcomers, echoing the contemptuous opinion of the salons of the Hautes-Treilles that the interests of Poitou were being lost "in the vast chaos of centralization"—a common Bourbon lament in the nineteenth century. The nobles continued to live "apart,"[34] probably even more isolated from a town whose administrators represented the *usurpeurs*.

Legitimist banquets on the feast day of "Henry V"—108 people at the Hôtel de France in 1837, and 80 the following year—were far more annoying than dangerous to the July Monarchy. Twelve workers at the latter banquet—a halting step toward popular royalism—stood ill at ease among the de Vaucelles, de Curzays, de Fayolles, and de Cuissards, who were all decked out with white and green ribbons, preparing to toast the 800,000 Russians who might restore monarchy to France. A letter signed ''Leproy,'' who was certainly a police spy, warned of ''secret scheming of the old nobility and the legion of Carlists of this town.'' The nobility of Poitou, ''numerous and wealthy, assisted by this ignoble tribe of priests,'' retained ''an extraordinary influence on the lower classes.'' This was old news. Several legitimist law students were arrested on the feast day of ''Henry V'' for inopportune comments. The rumors of a Chouan insurrection in the Vendée, which indeed followed in 1832, contributed to renewed fears of a local aristocratic plot. Loyalty to the Bourbons remained the dominant sentiment of the Poitiers elite.[35]

But political change swirled around the nobles and the clerical fortress. The students of Poitiers remained a minor center of republicanism, which developed at least a weak following in Poitiers after the revolution of 1830. In 1832, a year of republican demonstrations in France and of Chouan movements in the Vendée, itinerant singers strolled through the streets singing couplets ''insulting for the government,'' hoping to sell the printed lyrics. In February a crowd shouted encouragement beneath the window of a magistrate living among the nobles on the rue des Hautes-Treilles; he had been insulted the night before by his legitimist neighbors. In March a crowd presented a charivari to the president of the appellate court. A republican gathering place was closed down in May. Several minor republican demonstrations occurred at the place du Marché that month. On May 16 more than twenty students and workers greeted a legitimist deputy with the rough music of the charivari. On the following night the crowd was much larger—almost five hundred, ''composed entirely of ordinary people,'' shouting against Chouans and Jesuits in front of the homes of prominent legitimists. When the mayor forbade the singing of the ''Marseillaise'' in the theater in December, forty young men left a café to demonstrate in front of his house, shouting ''Down with the mayor!'' and ''Down with the *juste milieu!*''[36] Shouts of outrage, official posters torn down, and smashed busts of Louis-Philippe demonstrated republican opposition to the repression of the Lyon insurgent in April 1834.[37]

One source of discontent was the faubourgs. The issue was the *octroi,* which had been moved farther out. The residents of the faubourgs, people of extremely modest means, protested that life had then become significantly more expensive for them. Taverns there lost their trump card in attracting thirsty clients, gaining only an increased police surveillance they did not want. Early in January 1832 a throng of residents of the faubourgs—some three hundred to four hundred strong—poured into the courtyard of the town hall and surrounding streets to protest a rise in the *octroi* tax and the way it was collected. The prefect and mayor agreed to hear out a deputation from each of the four faubourgs. Sixteen men, ''presenting themselves decently and politely,'' were chided for having participated in a ''tumultuous gathering.'' The delegates then returned to their ''constituents'' to shouts of ''Down with indirect taxes!'' The following evening the people of the faubourgs, particularly the faubourg de la Cueille, returned to the customs barrier and carried its registers off to the main tax office. Although none of the registers was damaged, the armed national guard was sent to the faubourg de la Cueille, "where people were the most exasperated by the tax collected at the *octroi*. . . . [W]e came upon a mob of angry people completely deaf to the voices of their magistrates." The residents had constructed barricades but, after hurling a few rocks, dispersed after a first warning. Authorities were at something of a loss to understand the resistance of the faubourg de la Cueille, which was known to be favorable to the "patriots," that is, the Orleanists. It was easier to understand the resistance of the other two major faubourgs, Montbernage and Saint-Saturnin, believed to be more sympathetic to the Bourbons. There barricades had appeared, from behind which the *faubouriens* hurled rocks and insults at the "forces of order" until the third and final warning.[38]

The revolution of 1848 barely shook the calm of Poitiers. Although there were short-lived republican clubs, including the Club de Poitiers,[39] republicans and Montagnards found little success in Poitiers, but more in the faubourgs, helped by old memories of hostility between town and faubourgs over the extension of the radius of the *octroi*. A gendarme's report, describing "the greatest peril that can threaten society—the men of the democratic clubs," placed them in the faubourg de la Cueille.[40] The faubourg of Montbernage attacked the *octroi* of the pont Joubert on March 27, 1848, hurling the barriers into the Clain and demanding the elimination or at least reduction of the tax on drink. In October the people of the faubourg de la Cueille joined those of Montbernage in a march on the tax offices; they made off with the registers, carrying them to the smaller offices at the *octrois*.[41]

Despite the mobilization of the faubourgs over the issue of taxes, with few workers, no base of potential support for the left existed in Poitiers. Even after the 1848 revolution, one could have arrived in town and thought that the Bourbons were still on the throne. That year the feast of the Ascension was celebrated in the streets "for the fulfillment of the vows of Louis XVIII," while it had been forbidden by the Orleanist prefect during the last regime.[42] Louis-Edouard Pie, a controversial and aggressive counterrevolutionary, was named bishop of Poitiers. Given the history of the town, it seemed appropriate. His motto was "Christ must reign also upon earth."[43] Pie was welcomed to Poitiers in December 1849 by Vicomte Emmanuel de Curson: "*Benedictus qui venit*. . . . Enter the walls which saw the birth and death of Hilary and which guard the tomb of Radegonde. . . . This ancient soil of Poitou, which once gave birth to giants who knew how to fight and die for their altars, is ready to flower again at your voice and your blessing."[44] Crosses and fleurs-de-lis adorned the noble and ecclesiastical center of old Poitiers. The influence of the clergy on the lower classes could not be shaken. Three political newspapers battled in print without engaging the local population. The "party of order" formed, joining Orleanists, moderate republicans, and a number of legitimists, who looked increasingly to the authoritarian structures of the proto-Empire as a guarantee of social order. Even counting the students, the number of republicans remained small. Seditious shouts in Poitiers were more likely to be the "Long live the King!" heard on the promenade de Blossac, not far from the rue des Hautes-Treilles.[45] When Louis Napoleon Bonaparte came to inaugurate the railway in Poitiers on July 1, 1851, he had more reason to fear the thinly veiled hostility and sarcasm of Bishop Pie than the hostility of Montagnards and other republicans. The shutters of the noble residences were tightly closed in disrespect.[46]

Led by Pie, some legitimists now actively entered the political fray. During the carnival of 1851, three royalists dressed as women had mocked Louis Napoleon and the socialists. Such behavior would not have been acceptable thirty years earlier, if Countess Dash's recollection of noble disdain for street performances during earlier carnivals is correct. Legitimists now left their town houses to establish an association, the Amis de l'Ordre, in October 1851, which they hoped would win the lower classes over to their cause, but it was dissolved at the time of the coup d'état, before it had begun to consider how to achieve this task.[47] Over the billiard table in the residence of a prominent legitimist defiantly hung a portrait of the Comte de Chambord dressed as a Vendean general. But, despite Pie's attempt during the Second Empire "to turn Poitiers into the capital of French legitimism" and to bring Chambord to the throne as Henry V,[48] the time of heroic counter-revolution, the stuff of the dreams of Anne-Latrelle and her friends, lay in the ever more distant past. Countess Dash, who had long since left Poitiers, might still have felt at home in the residence of Cardinal Pie.[49] Ironically, it was the nobles of the Hautes-Treilles who became marginal, at least politically, as the century slowly but surely passed them by.

Châtellerault's Faubourg

If Poitiers, a town of nobles, clergy, officials, and rentiers, in many ways evoked the ancien régime, the small neighboring commercial and industrial town of Châtellerault, thirty-two kilometers away, defiantly announced the nineteenth century, its bourgeoisie, and its working class. When Captain Thiébault arrived in 1841 to survey the region, he emphasized that the "bustle of its streets contrasts with the silence of those of Poitiers, on which it is dependent." Châtellerault, with a population just over nine thousand, seemed so young and with such a bright future "that it grows from day to day." It was well situated for commerce and industry, located on the main road from Paris to Bordeaux, and on the Vienne river. Long a center for the manufacture of cutlery, the town was further boosted by the government's decision early in the Restoration to establish a major arms manufacture there, although most of the skilled workers had to be brought in from outside, and the municipality had to buy the land at considerable expense. At the time of the officer's visit 2,000 people, including 1,300 workers, were lodged in the buildings of the manufacture.[50]

The Vienne divided Châtellerault into two parts: the old bourg on the right bank and the growing, industrial faubourg of Châteauneuf on the left, linked, as today, by an old stone bridge. The bourg, of rectangular shape with its center of population close to the river, was reached from the north by a boulevard that had replaced the town walls. Turning left, a visitor plunged into a "type of labyrinth in which it is difficult to find one's way, composed of a great number of groups of houses separated by alleys that are inaccessible to wagons, with the exception of two or three into which one can venture if quite sure one won't encounter a driver

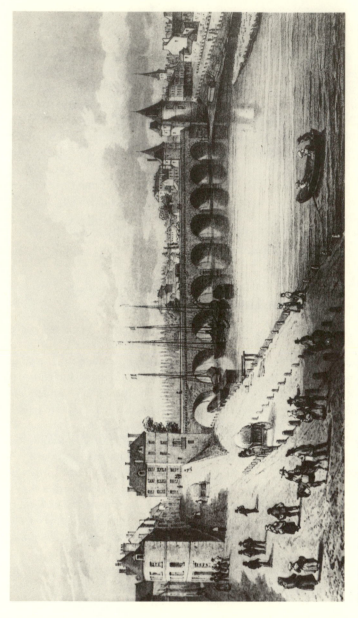

Châtellerault: the pont of Henri IV spanning the Vienne, with the faubourg Châteauneuf on the right bank. (Roger-Viollet)

coming boldly from the opposite direction.'' Across the bridge to the faubourg Châteauneuf stood buildings and houses of considerably more recent construction. Many—indeed most, on some streets—housed cutlery workers, or those from the arms manufacture who did not live in its buildings.

Even at the time of the 1851 census, when the number of cutlery workers had already declined considerably, there was little doubt about the concentration of the industrial population in the faubourg. Day laborers, male and female, and weavers and armament and cutlery workers were, in that order, by far the largest number of residents, particularly on certain streets like the rue du Ligue and the rue du Thuré. They clustered on the rue de Bultes, as well as the rue d'Antran, the rue Madame, and the rue de l'Abattoir. Within the walls of the arms manufacture, virtually all heads of household were armament workers of some kind, with or without families.[51] The faubourg finally gave way to gardens and rural property (called ''enclosures'') owned by residents of Châtellerault, to the *octroi*, each gate of a single barrier of wood, and beyond, to the ''countryside of Châteauneuf.''[52]

Scanty reporting suggests that the growing faubourg was a center of wide-open leisure: the mayor complained in September 1823 that in one cabaret ''great quantities of wine'' were consumed. There one also found ''fallen'' women, and some of the young men of Châtellerault attracted to their way of life. The noise irritated neighbors and, if it did not travel across the bridge to the center of Châtellerault, news of public scandal did.[53] In 1840 the subprefect requested that a number of houses, cabarets, and cafés at the end of the faubourg be added to the jurisdiction of the police commissioner, although they were located in the commune of Naintré. This spot, known as pont d'Etrée, was close enough to the arms manufacture to be worrisome, and lay eight kilometers from the center of Naintré: ''this continuation of a populous faubourg, these inns and cabarets exempt from the *octroi*, can sometimes attract a bad lot who, in this manner, belong to the town of Châtellerault without being subject to the daily surveillance that is so necessary.'' The authority of the police commissioner was extended to include the troublesome appendage.[54]

The bourg, or *cité*, of Châtellerault underwent a political evolution characteristic of commercial and industrial towns in the first half of the century, passing from liberalism to republicanism. A couple of families claimed to be noble, making much of being distantly related to a mayor of Poitiers ennobled in the eighteenth century. There was, however, ''a sizable bourgeoisie, permanently settled in the *cité*, of mediocre fortune, yet without aristocratic pretensions.'' It resented ''the arrogance of the nobles, the extravagance of the clergy, the burden of war, tithing, and feudal obligations.''[55] Alfred Hérault, later elected deputy, described the bourgeois world in which he grew up:

> To live a calm, peaceful life in one's little town, to maintain cordial and pleasant relations with one's family and friends, to avoid risking money in hazardous speculations (the possibilities of which, in any case, hardly ever present themselves), to aim for local responsibilities, several honorific functions, such as being on the municipal council or serving as an administrator of the hospice, to grow old in this way, honored and esteemed, then go to final rest in a vast

cemetery alongside one's grandparents. In the middle of the nineteenth century, this remained the ideal existence of a solid bourgeois of Châtellerault.[56]

In old Châtellerault, relations between bourgeois and worker in the century's first decades were cordial. "Feelings of solidarity" were encouraged by the fact that, in a town whose residents, in the opinion of one official, pursued money with great determination, there were few or no great fortunes; "bourgeois and worker thus passed their existence side by side. Ideas, reasoning, the way of looking at life were hardly different for the one or for the other." If the workers were uneducated, "the cultural baggage of the bourgeois, despite several odds and ends of Latin, was not very heavy. Their tastes were similar. Both loved the good life, outings in the countryside, great gaiety. Between the café and the cabaret, only the furniture differed." Men of means could join one of two clubs or *cabinets de lecture* to read, play cards, or enjoy conversation. The Sociéte Littéraire had existed at least since the year VIII; its members, described as "the most worthy bourgeois of town," gathered in a room rented from a *limonadier*. Its friendly rival, the Cercle Littéraire, met in a café. The two clubs had about eighty members between them in 1822, merchants, magistrates, and property owners of the bourg. In 1828 the Société d'Emulation, Science et Littérature met for the first time, stating the goal of learning more about those disciplines "and of the various phenomena that recur." One of its first topics for discussion was a *Précis sur la Révolution,* a phenomenon that many thought could be repeated.[57] The bourgeoisie was somewhat "Voltairean in general"; the lower classes seemed to have attended Mass regularly. But social and political antagonisms had not yet driven the interests of the two classes apart. They were not yet, but would become, "enemy brothers."[58]

In Châtellerault, commerce and industry served as "the foyer of liberalism," which the Restoration government viewed as an example of perfidious ingratitude, having established the national arms manufacture in the town.[59] The middle classes considered the nobility exploitative, and the clergy haughty and out of date. Anticlericals protested a priest's refusal to bury either a former clergyman who had married, or a liberal who had loudly denounced the "foolishness" of the clergy.[60] In 1819 *Le Propagateur de la Vienne* offered a clever account of the missions, written in the form of a theater review: "The mission ended in Châtellerault and the troupe, under the direction of M. Lambert, closed its run on Sunday, May 2. This troupe of four is decidedly second-rate; two new actors who had not yet appeared arrived for the staging of the planting of the cross. We are astonished that the directors, with their impressive offices in Poitiers, sent so few extras for this great day." The final procession included women allegedly "disguised as virgins."[61]

The "bad" newspapers, particularly *La Quotidienne* and *Le Globe,* arrived regularly from Paris, and were read in the "bad" cafés and at the Société Littéraire during the "muffled agitation" of 1827 by men of commerce and industry. The next year another reading club was formed in the faubourg Châteauneuf by fourteen or fifteen people, not bourgeois, but "well-off workers who rented a room in a café in which to read *Le Constitutionnel*" and to complain about the curé of Châteauneuf.[62]

Early in 1830 a petition against the payment of taxes was circulated in town by leading liberals.[63] Among others, the 150 who signed welcomed the July Revolution as their own. By 1833, public opinion was divided between the *juste milieu,* a few legitimists referred to as the "Ultras," and the men of "movement," who had become republicans. Yet each reading club included members of different political views, complementing Hérault's recollection of calm, if not consensus, in the Châtellerault of his childhood.[64]

Much of that changed with the revolution of 1848. Alfred Hérault remembered the festive mood that followed news of the February Revolution: "acclamations, songs, shouts of 'Long live the Republic!', the parade of armed men, the flash of bayonets, the roll of drums, music, and especially the roar of two canons." Yet for people of means, this mood gave way to "anxiety and fear."[65] Châtellerault was the only town in the region in which the Montagnards held the upper hand during the Second Republic. Shortly after the February Revolution, the workers of the arms manufacture joined the activities of the Club de la Fraternité, closed by the government in July. Some of the workers demonstrated before the arms manufacture against their director and tried to plant a liberty tree.[66]

At the time of the municipal elections of July 1848, the munitions workers, joined by many others from the faubourg, marched across the bridge to the Palais de Justice to vote, seven or eight hundred strong. A few stormed into the electoral hall, shouting "Down with the royalists! Into the water with them!" and—appropriate for a cutlery town—"Let's cut them in two!"[67] A year later the subprefect stated that "the town is in an exceptional position, dominated by its working class, principally drawn from the (arms) manufacture." Lists of political suspects compiled by the subprefect during the Second Republic invariably included workers living in the faubourg and working for the arms manufacture.[68]

By February 1849 the socialists had successfully recruited among the armament workers and in the faubourg Châteauneuf, "where anxiety reached its peak . . . the workers are unemployed, publicly announcing their intention to march on the town at the first occasion. Our reds are jittery, as if it were the night before a battle."[69]

The Club de la Fraternité became the Societé de Prévoyance, a mutual aid association. Suspected by the police of being affiliated with Solidarité Républicaine, its headquarters was the café Le Petit Bordeaux in the faubourg Châteauneuf. Socialists found at a bookstore "appear to be citizens of the town, go-betweens between the workers of the arms manufacture and the (other) population of the faubourgs." The "section" of Châteauneuf seemed alive with political gatherings before the election, with shouts in the various meetings heard along the quais. A thousand people attended a banquet in June 1849 in honor of the socialist Pierre Pleignard, a former representative and member of the General Council. A month later the subprefect based his request for additional troops on the situation in the faubourg.[70]

By 1850, politics had divided Châtellerault into "two hostile camps."[71] The Vienne too seemed to divide them, as socialist propaganda inundated the town and its environs. Socialists from Limoges, tried and convicted in Poitiers for their part in the April 1848 insurrection in that town, were greeted as long-lost brothers in Châtellerault. In April 1850 workers shouted republican slogans outside the church, while the faithful sang a Te Deum inside; a few months later the workers burst through the doors. Workers from the faubourg sang "Les Vignerons" and other revolutionary songs "everywhere, in public places," particularly around the fountain of Châteauneuf. A song of seventeen couplets, "somewhat burlesque in nature," it ridiculed the honor guard organized for the arrival of Bishop Pie.

With the repression of associations and public meetings, following the national pattern, a cabaret of the faubourg became the focal point of Montagnard activity. The police raided it, following complaints of "bloodthirsty songs, including that of the guillotine," as workers were planning a banquet there. The police arrived to find a tailor, Marcellin, standing on a table reading a newspaper to about a hundred people assembled beneath a portrait of the socialist Raspail. There was stupor when the police burst in, then defiant shouts for the Montagnards and against the royalists. When the moderate republican Garnier-Pagès arrived in Châtellerault at the beginning of May 1851, he was warmly greeted by Pleignard and the other bourgeois republicans who had been part of the provisional administration after the February Revolution. But, reflecting the split between bourgeois leaders and workers, "the workers of the arms manufacture and, in general, the inhabitants of Châteauneuf, greeted this traveler cooly."[72]

In response to Montagnard strength, in June 1851 the prefect asked for a permanent garrison in Châtellerault. The next month Louis Napoleon himself met a hostile reception, including some guardsmen, when he came to open the Tours-Bordeaux railway line. This was not a happy visit for the Prince President, who, to the great embarrassment of local officials, was both lectured to and then ignored by Bishop Pie in Poitiers. The national guard, which had not been permitted to drill for some time, was disbanded and disarmed in the fall.[73]

Together, Poitiers and Châtellerault would have been a classic nineteenth-century city, if the eighteen miles between them could have been bridged. The noble quarter and ecclesiastical urban structure of churches and convents in Poitiers exemplified the classic elite quarters of the ancien régime, lingering on in the nineteenth century. The *cité* or bourg of Châtellerault was an example of a relatively prosperous bourgeois quarter typical of nineteenth-century towns. Across the Vienne, the locus of large-scale industry would then have nicely represented the class and neighborhood dimensions and solidarities of artisanal cutlery workers and factory workers, skilled, semiskilled, and unskilled.

The evolution of France between 1815 and 1850 might also be seen in their different political outcomes. Poitiers, a town of nobles, clergy, and landlords closely linked to the ancien régime, perfectly symbolized the spirit of the Restoration, as described by Countess Dash. The bourgeois of the *cité* of Châtellerault, was at home in the Orleanism of the July Monarchy, were threatened by the radical republicanism of the workers of the faubourg Châteauneuf. Forms of social organization, too, can be contrasted. The informal salons of the nobles, attended by some of the high clergy, had little in common with the reading clubs of the bourgeoisie of Châtellerault or, for that matter, those of Poitiers. The mutual aid association that became a political club, and the boisterous cafés of the faubourg, in the shadow of the arms manufacture, helped shape the workers' political mobilization in the Second Republic. Neighborhood solidarities—the sense of belonging—in the faubourg Châteauneuf, about which we have only indirect evidence, certainly contributed to class solidarities and facilitated socialist influence.

The Faubourg Without a Town: La Roche-sur-Yon on the Edge of Urbanity

La Roche-sur-Yon offers a third, if somewhat bizarre, contrast. La Roche-sur-Yon might be described somewhat whimsically as a frontier faubourg without a town. In 1790 the National Convention voted to divide France into departments, thus for administrative purposes eliminating the traditional provinces—Languedoc, Picardy, Limousin, Burgundy, Poitou, and the others—associated with regional privileges and inequities. Each department—their names taken from rivers, mountains, the sea, or other geographic characteristics—had one city or town designated as the *chef-lieu* or departmental capital, to house the administrative apparatus of the more rationally organized government. Some *villes parlementaires* were inevitably chosen, despite their aristocratic traditions. It was unthinkable that Dijon or Rennes not be the capitals of Côte d'or and Ille-et-Vilaine, however much the National Convention wanted to eclipse the parlements themselves. In most departments, even those without a spectacularly important claimant, the choice seemed quite clear; Agen, Auch, and tiny Mende and Guéret eagerly became capitals. Each awaited the economic advantages that would come from the arrival of more officials, military officers, magistrates, and lawyers, enhancing the town's new status and filling the coffers of its merchants. In cases where two or more towns seemed reasonable candidates, the claimants set forth their case to Paris with as much passion as reason. Among the most notable losers were Reims and the port of Brest, the latter's residents being aghast to learn that Quimper had received the prize.[74]

For the poor, marshy, western department of the Vendée, the choice was extraordinarily difficult. There were no towns of more than a few thousand people. Luçon was a bishopric, but its days of relative glory in the time of Richelieu had long passed. Fontenay-le-Comte—the largest town, with a population of about five thousand—stood near the southern edge of the new department not far from Niort, the capital of Deux-Sèvres. Less likely contenders included Saint-Gilles, which had applied without really understanding for what it was applying; Saint-Hilaire, already protesting that "personal interests" were conspiring against it; Les Sables d'Olonne, trumpeting its modest commerce; and the bourg of La Roche-sur-Yon, fifty of whose five hundred inhabitants signed a petition in 1790 asking that their town be selected.[75]

"If this town, the oldest and once the largest in this part of the province, is not what it once was," this last petition frankly admitted, La Roche-sur-Yon stood squarely in the middle of the Vendée, as any "impartial glance at a reliable and accurate map would show." The petitioners asked the "courageous and immortal National Assembly" to take into consideration that its central location would lessen the journey of most travelers to the prefecture; it was nine leagues from Fontenay-le-Comte, six from Les Sables d'Olonne, and eight from Saint-Gilles.

In the middle of a vast meadow, La Roche-sur·Yon stood on a modest hill on the left bank of the river that gave the town its name. The Yon, however, is hardly more than a stream, despite the brave claim of the petitioners that it was navigable. Living in the marshy and humid Vendée, they nonetheless sought to demonstrate that the number of old people living in the bourg proved that the air was healthy.[76] Despite the fact that the town was "in the countryside," its residents were "honorably lodged" in and on the outskirts of the bourg. Many local property owners would be delighted to offer lodging to arriving officials; wood and stone were readily available for new constructions, "no doubt even less expensive than elsewhere." La Roche-sur-Yon was close enough to the Vendée's main roads to expand its slight commerce, which, it was confidently stated, would be enhanced by a market every Thursday and two annual fairs. There were two churches, a post office, even a small literary society. The petitioners, including a priest, were careful to note that they took the liberty of presenting their observations "assuredly not because of their own interests, but for the general good."[77]

Learning of this petition, the other claimants renewed efforts to be named the administrative capital. One of these petitions from "our rivals jealous of our local advantages" had the bad grace to refer to La Roche as a "hamlet" or "village," bringing an indignant response; the bourg's mayor reminded the deputies that their town had at least thirty "bourgeois houses, which, if not luxurious, offer at least a certain comfort that would be difficult to find elsewhere."[78] La Roche-sur-Yon was disappointed. Fontenay-le-Comte became the capital of the Vendée, despite its peripheral location.

Three years later the civil war in the West broke out, the department of the Vendée lending its name to the insurrection which extended far beyond its boundaries.[79] The republican General Turreau burned La Roche-sur-Yon to the ground on March 2, 1794, its 434 people finding safety where they could. Fontenay-le-Comte—briefly known as Fontenay-le-Peuple during the Terror— emerged unscathed, safely removed from most of the fighting.

The Directory feared another uprising behind religious banners and crucifixes in support of an invasion by an army of nobles—like the one which landed and was destroyed at Quiberon in Brittany in July 1795. The function of the departmental capital took on a critical function: that of serving as a base for the maintenance of public order. Napoleon too feared another Vendean insurrection. Early in 1804 he sent General Gouvion to assess the political situation. While reporting that the clergy and even some émigrés appeared to have accepted the regime because of the Concordat with the Church, Gouvion returned with an idea that he thought would prevent further uprisings. The Vendée required a new prefecture in its geographic center, a town with a watchful bureaucracy and a substantial garrison that would maintain order. His choice fell upon La Roche-sur-Yon, then amounting to barely six inhabitable houses and some rubble. New roads could be built, old ones widened and paved. The hedgerow country of the *bocage,* itself "an obstacle to civilization," would no longer be isolated from the rest of France. New schools would provide a beacon of light in what was considered the most backward part of the region. Commerce and industry would surely follow, helping to civilize the Vendée. The emperor readily accepted the idea. On May 25, 1804 (5 Prairial, year XII) he promulgated a decree ordering the construction of the Vendée's new capital alongside the ruins of the old bourg.[80]

Instead of city fathers, the town had the state, upon which it remained dependent. La Roche-sur-Yon became, with Pontivy in Morbihan, the first planned town in France since Richelieu and Vitry-le-François. Like those two modest monuments to early modern urban planning, the new La Roche-sur-Yon fully reflected the imperatives of power. It was to be rectangular, with the exception of that corner including what remained of the old bourg. Its street plan therefore took the shape of a trapezoid. Wide boulevards were to surround and parallel wide streets. Troops would pass in review on the place d'Armes, the largest square. Two secondary squares were planned, one in front of the prefecture, the other to provide space for the market. Fifteen thousand residents were expected to flock to the new town within a matter of years.

La Roche-sur-Yon emerged as perhaps the ultimate example of the imperialism of the straight line, a throwback to the Baroque planning of the seventeenth and eighteenth centuries. There was nothing of what Lewis Mumford calls "the organic city" to impede the imperatives of centralized power.[81] Appropriately, construction first began on the prefecture, the tribunal, and the prison; the garrison, a warehouse for military supplies, a military hospital, a lycée, and an *auberge* were not far behind. An "imperial hunting lodge with garden and park" was also planned, in anticipation of the emperor's first visit, as well as buildings to lodge officials and gendarmes. Upon the request of the prefect, Merlet, Napoleon consented on 10 Fructidor, year XII, to having the town bear his name; it became known as "Napoléon-Ville" or, more often, "Napoléon-Vendée."[82]

Prefect Merlet quickly learned, as reports reached Fontenay, that it was far easier to plan a town of straight lines and right angles than to actually create one. He asked for a delay in the transfer of the prefecture. For one thing, his subordinates were refusing to follow him to such an uncertain new assignment. The reply from Paris was curt and to the point: "The political motives that determined [the transfer of the prefecture] require that its execution not be deferred, especially at the outset." The prefect's immediate presence would furthermore encourage the rapid completion of the first constructions. Merlet's request for leave in Paris, where he could steel himself for the move, was likewise turned down.[83] He arrived, after complaining of being ill on the way, to find little more than the skeleton of the new prefecture, an empty plateau marked by ditches, with piles of building materials here and there. He was housed in part of the old château spared by the fires of 1794.

Merlet presided over the official ceremony inaugurating the new town, one that attracted an audience of curious countrymen. But the town's problems had only begun. The bishop of Luçon refused to move the seminary to the new town; it remained in Chavagnes, near Montaigu, another of La Roche's resentful rivals. Several *conseillers de préfecture* and employees of the prefecture resigned rather than take up residence in the unfinished town. Those who arrived found "no lodging, no *auberge*, no suppliers: one can find necessities only at great cost, and the difficulty of transportation makes the salaries of officials and employees quite inadequate.'' Soon the single *auberge* housed a few visitors, but there was no room at the inn for officials forced to reside in the town.[84] Construction of the town, which began a year late, moved very slowly, at least partly because it was difficult to attract building workers. The construction of the barracks, completed in 1810, had revealed that the brick and masonry selected by Cretet, the general director of the Ponts-et-Chaussées, for use by masons from Lyon, crumbled in the humidity of the Vendean marshes.[85]

Napoleon had specified that the construction of Napoléon-Ville was not to cost an exorbitant amount; but costs soared beyond the 300,000 francs allocated annually for ten years, particularly as construction dragged on hopelessly. The prefecture, which opened its doors but a little more in 1810, absorbed over 500,000 francs by 1818, three times the amount allocated. Completion of the hospital in 1814, which turned out to be a big year for military casualties, absorbed more than twice the anticipated 194,000 francs. The Grande Place or the place d'Armes turned out to be a relative bargain at twice the estimate.[86]

In 1808 Napoleon, with a little time on his hands after the Treaty of Tilsit, arrived in the pouring rain to inspect the town that bore his name and was intended to bring centralized order to the Vendée. After passing through a makeshift *arc de triomphe,* he found even the completed buildings disappointing. They reminded him more of common barracks than of stately memorials to his glory. He could not have been unaware of the grumbled complaints of those officials not yet suitably lodged in the sixteen houses that had been completed. The director of taxes, for one, had dressed for the occasion in a room in a common cabaret. Napoleon rode quickly around, inspecting the ditches that indicated where roads were planned, barely pausing to acknowledge the townspeople who had been herded together at the unfinished prefecture to honor their emperor. He rode out of town almost immediately, mumbling, it is said, that Rome was not built in a day and that even Paris was unfinished.[87]

Napoléon-Vendée was unlike any other town in France.[88] Its first inhabitants shared little except lots of space; the wide, largely unfinished boulevards, streets, and squares, expected to accommodate fifteen thousand people, seemed empty to one-seventh that number. There were officials and soldiers—fewer of the latter than expected, because of the Peninsular War and the Russian campaign—as well as building workers, and the prostitutes who followed them. Merchants who moved to the town expecting a bonanza failed; only several tanners who set up shop in 1812 did reasonably well. The completion of a new road between Nantes and Bordeaux in 1813 did not significantly reduce the costs of transporting goods to and from Napoléon, which remained high, as with any colony. Many roads were impassable at least six months of the year. Despite the government's attempt to attract residents by exempting them from property taxes for fifteen years, advancing one-quarter of construction costs, and permitting the construction of houses with straw roofs of peasant style, until the Restoration the population remained less than two thousand, which in 1841 became the minimum for a commune to qualify as ''urban.'' Not a single *notable* had been willing to follow the prefect's suggestion by buying property in or near Napoléon and moving there.[89]

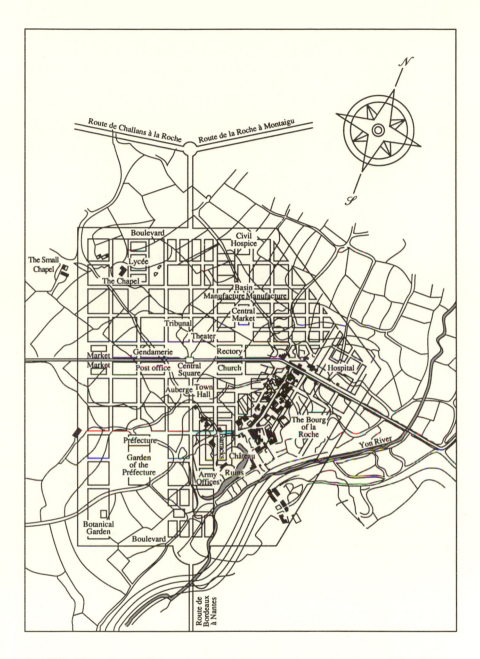

An 1804 military survey of La Roche-sur-Yon and the projected town of Napoléon-Vendée.

The emperor's characteristic optimism that the Yon could be made navigable had proven ill-founded. In any case, what could be exported from the region? Only hemp seemed likely, and perhaps some wool, but no fortunes would be made there.[90] In any case, the town lacked that most fundamental characteristic of burgeoning urban life for such ventures—capital.

In 1812 there were 1,902 residents of Napoléon-Vendée, drawn from 46 departments. Of these 434 had lived in La Roche-sur-Yon—some could remember fleeing in 1794—or had been born there. Another 337 were from the adjacent Loire-Inférieure, almost all building workers from Nantes. There were 612 from the Vendée, including 114 who had behind left the gloom of discouraged Fontenay for the desolation of Napoléon-Vendée when the prefecture moved. Early in the Restoration the population increased modestly at least partly because of the completion of the lycée. It too was no bargain; one contemporary described it: "the rain pours in from all sides, the rooms are submerged, the general humidity threatens the health of the students." Students who wished to pray for better things found no chapel, for lack of money.[91]

Housing remained inadequate; the most desirable rentals were auctioned off to desperate officials, so not everybody won. In the first year of the Restoration, an undignified free-for-all occurred involving officials and magistrates; claimants invoked official function, family size, and every other possible reason. One such conflict almost ended in a duel; several functionaries threatened to resign because of the lack of progress.[92] Soldiers were no better off than civilians; the captain undertaking a survey in 1826 described the ground floor of the barracks as "uninhabitable." In the dormitory the unfortunate soldiers melted in summer and froze in winter.[93]

La Roche-sur-Yon/Napoléon-Vendée remained a colony—an unsuccessful one at that—in the midst of marshland and *bocage*. On the map drawn for one of the military surveys, some of the squares representing blocks along the two main axes were filled in, with the prefecture standing at the edge of the settled areas; but about half of them remained blank, unoccupied. For the next twenty years the town stood unfinished, appearing to be a construction site abandoned in winter, a faubourg without a town, the periphery lacking an urban center. One early perfect described living in "a little town—a type of colony offering me nothing, having for its 'society' only individuals who, for the most part, have neither the tone nor the manners of the world in which I have spent my life." While gallantly accepting his fate and vowing that he would die for his principles, the prefect did indicate that he would "bless the hand that transferred him."[94]

The experience of the capital of the Vendée from the fall of Napoleon to the proclamation of the Second Empire in 1852 was not much happier. In 1814 Fontenay-le-Comte put forth another claim to the prefecture, complaining that it had been transferred "in contempt for the law and by the whim of a tyrant from whom France has just been so happily delivered." The "several millions madly and uselessly spent" by Napoleon could not overcome the well-known disadvantages of its unfaithful and unworthy rival, including infertile soil and inadequate roads.[95] Fearing that the town would lose its status as prefecture, the inhabitants, at the first news of the emperor's return to France in 1815, rushed into the streets

La Roche-sur-Yon/Napoléon-Vendée: Nineteenth-century view of the church of Saint-Louis, with the statue of Napoleon and the place Napoléon.

"drunkenly saluting the return of their benefactor, carrying his bust in triumph crowned with laurels."[96] Yet even after Waterloo, through the intervention of the new prefect, Frémin de Beaumont, and the royalist deputy Fougerais, La Roche/Napoléon-Vendée renamed Bourbon-Vendée, kept the prefecture.[97] The Restoration too found administrative centralization an effective means of establishing and maintaining its authority.

Yet the Bourbon Restoration eliminated the town's raison d'être: monarchy, Church, and countryside now held the upper hand. Merchants and café owners suffered because there were fewer troops to spend money in town. The revenue from the *octroi* was halved. The mayor, Tortat, implored the government to maintain a permanent garrison, not to protect the town (although that thought must have entered the minds of some townspeople amid fears of royalist vengeance), but to spend money. Sixty officers and four hundred soldiers would yield, he reasoned, an extra 12,000 francs in tax revenue. Land values would rise because of the rent paid by officers. The mayor warned that if the population, then slightly more than two thousand, did not increase, "unfavorable" comparisons might be made locally between the monarchy and the empire. This could hurt government candidates in the elections. In 1818, when rumors that the garrison was going to be eliminated completely began to worry merchants, a "mob" of townspeople had gone to the town hall to protest. In Paris Tortat convinced Decazes to leave the garrison in Bourbon-Vendée.[98]

Bourbon-Vendée staggered on, with completion of the town's half-built structures suspended. Tortat organized the first voluntary associations—that mark of urbanity—a masonic lodge, in 1818, and the departmental Société d'Agriculture. Both provided a degree of sociability in a town where there was little to do.

The mayor also bravely requested in 1817 that Bourbon-Vendée be granted the title of a royal *bonne ville,* an honor bestowed by the king. To no one's surprise, he was turned down.[99]

Little seemed to go well. Some of the roads had to be repaved because of the sandy soil, humidity, and unevenness of the terrain.[100] The town had no slaughter-house until the 1830s. the prefecture was surrounded by holes in the sandy earth and mud. The place des Exécutions was no more cheerful than its name. Unfinished public buildings looked "as if standing alone in the desert." The departmental lycée awaited the denomination of a *collège,* another small source of income. Commerce floundered. After a delay because the municipality could not pay building workers, the town hall was finally finished and a modest landscaping effort provided a botanic garden. But in 1828 a frustrated municipal council refused to vote its budget, to protest the failure of the government to come to the assistance of the "colony" of Bourbon-Vendée.[101]

Even the liberals complained that the church, begun in 1808, remained unfinished. In the meantime the faithful continued to squeeze into the dilapidated parish church of old La Roche-sur-Yon, rebuilt after the fires of 1794. When the prefect warned that local grumbling might be felt in the elections, the lumbering church of Saint-Charles and Saint-Louis (two saints so popular in the Vendée that it was too difficult to choose between them) was quickly finished in 1829 and blessed the following year. It loomed above a town one-fifth the size for which it had been planned.[102] The cumbersome structure of grimly classical style typical of the Restoration (somberly represented by the Palace of Justice in Mâcon) was described by one enthusiast of suspect taste as "beautiful and vast"—it is certainly the latter—and as one of the most impressive monuments of the young century. But it seemed a massive shell. There was virtually no internal decoration or ornaments; it had no bells. No paintings of Saints Louis or Charles, or even of Saint Hilaire, the former bishop of Poitiers, were forthcoming from Paris, despite requests from the curé and the church council.[103]

The uprooting hypothesis suggests that La Roche-sur-Yon, which grew up from practically nothing and then doubled and tripled in size, should have been, however modest its population, a very dangerous place. But despite its reputation as a colony of *marginaux,* townspeople had virtually nothing to fear from other permanent residents or transients. They had, however, reasons to fear the countryside. Nowhere else could the political conflict between city and country have been worse than between the Vendée's department capital and its hinterland of *bocage* and marsh, isolated hamlets and unproductive farms. Bourbon-Vendée, intended to represent the revolutionary victory of town over country, felt the revenge of the countryside with the Restoration. The townspeople were under-standably nervous about the return of the king, fearful of a White Terror. The Duc d'Angoulême was "very cooly" greeted upon his arrival in September 1814, but he may not have noticed owing to the presence of "a mass of peasants who, with their enthusiasm, overcame the indifference of the inhabitants."[104] Dressed in their Sunday best, in coarse white shirts, short dark coats, striped pants, and enormous sabots, with long hair flowing from under their wide-brimmed round hats, and sporting red handkerchiefs made in Cholet, the men saluted the return of royalty.[105]

The Hundred Days made the Chouans more determined to exact their revenge. The tocsin ringing in the *bocage,* proclaiming the return of the king, sounded terror for the townspeople. Some who had purchased *biens nationaux* hid in Napoléon, as their harvests were systematically destroyed.[106] Mayor Tortat and other relatively moderate officials succeeded in preventing the soldiers of the army of the Vendée from coming to town to settle scores. The king's order, in July 1815, that "irregularly constituted" forces be disbanded was generally followed in the Vendée.[107]

In September 1816 a new prefect, Ferdinand de Waters, emphasized the political division between town and country; the people of the latter were described as "trustworthy, but those of the towns and part of the bourgeoisie cause us to suspect their principles, particularly those of Bourbon-Vendée." The rural population "would take advantage of trouble to destroy this . . . colony made up of outsiders who have not given the government proof of their loyalty and who do not in general have an excellent reputation."[108] In October he warned that the inhabitants of Bourbon-Vendée "leave much to be desired so far as their political views and conduct"; like the people of all colonies, they were "people of suspect morality" requiring active surveillance.[109]

The national guard was dissolved, its members "disarmed in their houses, humiliated, insulted, treated as conspirators."[110] Armed men arrived at Bourbon-Vendée's cattle market to frighten away prospective buyers and sellers. In April 1816 an armed force was rumored to be marching on the departmental capital, where "the faction that has just been defeated a second time still retains a great number of followers."[111] The immediate reason for their anger was the pardon given General Travot, "implacable enemy of the Vendée," and the impunity of the purchasers of *biens nationaux.*[112] The harvest failure of 1817, marked by grain riots in Les Herbiers, increased tensions between the "true" royalists and those who had purchased church or noble property; several of the latter were grain merchants accused of "wanting to starve out the people" and telling the poor, "Go find your nobles so they can feed you."[113]

In self-defense, Bourbon-Vendée became a modest island of liberalism during the Restoration. The members of the masonic lodge opposed Ultra influence, leading to its temporary closing by the prefect in 1822.[114] In 1828 liberals on the municipal council led in the refusal to pass the annual budget, and merchants castigated the government for insufficient attention to the town. A reading club newly authorized that year provided a forum for liberal complaints. Bourbon-Vendée by now had a nucleus of eligible voters, who made possible the election of two liberal deputies in 1830, to the consternation of most of the department, which dismissed the town as "a heap of ruined men, adventurers of all kinds without any sense of morality, all devoted to the revolutionary party."[115]

The Vendée's strange capital had poor relations with the countryside for another reason as well. To survive economically, it needed lively markets. As it struggled to rise from ashes and mud, the town had no grain market, only a cattle market in early spring and thrice weekly markets for everyday supplies, including Sunday (which the Church was forced to tolerate, because people in the surroundings came to church in town).[116] In 1812 an imperial decree had established a grain market on the second Monday of each month, and five other fairs. To give the fairs of Napoléon-Vendée a chance to survive, the imperial government had suppressed a number of the other regional markets. But just one of the fairs, that of June 8, attracted sellers and buyers; the others existed in the departmental almanach only; "not a single pair of cows were brought to market." Mayor Tortat wrote the priests, cattle merchants, and wealthiest property owners of the region, encouraging their participation. He persuaded merchants and innkeepers to donate money for prizes for animals brought to the fair. Gradually more people came to buy and sell in Bourbon-Vendée, particularly as the roads improved.[117]

The revolution of 1830 turned the tables again. The prefect fled, and the notable residents, led by Tortat, created a provisional administration, awaited the new prefect, and hoped for the best amid inevitable rumors of nobles, priests, and peasants taking arms in the mists of the *bocage*.[118] Yet Bourbon-Vendée benefited from the threat of insurrection in the West. Troops searching for Chouan bands in 1831 and 1832 provided good business for the town.[119] Having the upper hand, the town antagonized its old enemy, the countryside. On August 26, 1838, Bourbon-Vendée provocatively inaugurated a statue honoring none other than General Travot, the "pacifier" of the Vendée during the Revolution.[120]

The population of Bourbon-Vendée finally reached 5,000 in 1839, but still "literally bent under the weight of its repairs."[121] The remains of the old château, most of its stones used in the construction of the new town, could be seen until the early 1840s. Now the "iron hand" of another government appeared to block progress. The municipal council claimed that the town had never been reimbursed for almost a sixth of the more than 12 million francs spent between 1804 and 1813. The prefect, Count Emmanuel de Hermine, agreed that the plans of "the genius" Napoleon had "already born fruit"; his town had served as the "flame destined to enlighten the savage and superstitious population that surrounds it." Now it was time for the plans of "the great man" to be completed.[122] Only the barracks, appropriately enough, stood proudly, a massive edifice of three wings and four stories surrounding a square courtyard.[123] In 1845 the government authorized the leveling of existing streets and the creation of new ones, including several near the Yon with an eye toward the construction of the long-awaited canal; the indebted municipality had to pay for the work.[124] The theater was completed in 1846, with the help of increased *octroi* revenue from the growth in population. In 1844, when the army agreed to locate one of its largest stud farms in Bourbon-Vendée, the town had to go even deeper into debt in order to contribute its share of 98,000 francs for the enterprise. An asylum for insane women outside town also brought a modicum of income.[125] But a stud farm and an asylum do not make a town.

With the revolution of 1848, Bourbon-Vendée petitioned to be known as "Napoléon-Vendée"—one official quickly crossed out "Bourbon" on his official stationary, replacing it with "Napoléon" in anticipation. Finally the town could be confident that there would be no new royalist insurrection, although legitimists still held sway in much of the countryside. The military survey of 1840 suggested that Napoleon had been correct; in the long run, new and better roads brought commerce and respect for, or at least obedience to, the law, to the previously impenetrable *bocage*. In the officer's assessment, "the old Vendean . . . each day is losing some of his originality." Peasants no longer believed the promises of the nobles that they would remain unscathed by bullets, however much religion remained "a fetish" in the region.[126] The bishop of Luçon now set the tone for the clergy, calling for "peace, unity, calm, and moderation."[127] Napoléon-Vendée briefly boasted two political clubs in 1848: the moderate republican Club Démocratique Central of "workers and young men," and the conservative Club du Commerce, "principally made up of small-time merchants and property owners." This minor outburst of organized political activity seemed unexpected: "such emulations of Paris are indeed new in the Vendée."[128] It was a sign not only of the political awakening of 1848, but of urbanity.

The Republic came and went quickly in Napoléon-Vendée. There were no workers' associations because there were so few workers. The artillery company of the national guard was disbanded in 1849 because of its chaotic organization, not for lack of loyalty to the conservative regime. The publication of *Le Démocrate vendéen* in the fall of 1850, printed in La Rochelle and edited by a certain Napoléon Gallois, received more attention in Paris than in Napoléon-Vendée.[129] One innocuous café gathering at the time of the June 1849 insurrection in Paris was the extent of dissident political activity. A Club des Amis de l'Ordre formed by functionaries, lawyers, magistrates, and *chefs d'ouvriers* represented the current of opinion, not the small banquet without speeches or toasts in March 1851 that celebrated the Republic.[130]

With the proclamation of the Second Empire, the municipality confidently petitioned Louis Napoleon shortly after the imperial plebiscite for help so that it could continue its "civilizing work." After tracing a history of broken promises made to this town "conceived of in the American way," the entreaty ended, "such is the unhappy state of the town of Napoléon." Napoleon I had wanted a "town flourishing through its endowment and its revenue"; instead, there were massive debts, and the bitter claim that the state owed the municipality almost 2 million francs. The emperor had wanted spacious boulevards bordered by elegant buildings to be "the ornaments of the town." They were barely functional, anything but elegant.[131]

Napoléon-Vendée had barely six thousand inhabitants. Some of the squares formed by the streets originally planned remained uninhabited. There was not a single fountain, and the water available from three pumps had an odd taste. The limpid waters of the almost comically narrow Yon generated no industry. A canal had been promised from distant Paris. Commercial exchange was limited to local consumption, as was the limited production of pottery, cloth, beer, and building materials. The last of the officers ordered to carry out a survey mentioned only its stud farm and asylum as of interest. In many ways, Napoléon-Vendée still resembled "a faubourg of Paris"—not a compliment—with its crouching houses of a single story or two at best. One encountered a handful of property owners, a good many functionaries, hopeful merchants from various parts of France doomed to disappointment, a small number of workers concentrated in the building trades, a few soldiers, and an agricultural population including day laborers and share-croppers. There were "almost no Vendeans, but rather a mixture of customs and behavior impossible to find elsewhere. One can say of the people of Napoléon-Vendée that they still have no historic character; it remains a new colony transplanted in the middle of an ancient people."[132]

A statue of Napoleon I was then erected in the center of the place Napoléon, paid for by local contributors, in the hope that the new emperor might reward the loyalty of the town to his uncle. (The sculptor, the Comte de Nieuwerkerke, had demonstrated his political versatility by submitting a bust of the Comte de Chambord for a salon in 1843.) The extended right hand of the emperor points to where the new town was to be built. The statue was inaugurated with the roll of drums, cannonfire, and a military review as part of a lively celebration on September 19, 1854. For the first time, the streets of Napoléon-Vendée were full of people, some from the countryside. Napoleon III, who had promised to come, never showed up.[133]

5

Quartier Blanc, Quartier Rouge: Cultural Marginality and Popular Politics in Perpignan

In Perpignan, marginality had a strong cultural and spatial component. Neighborhood life there provided traditions of familiarity and solidarity embedded in collective memory. The Catalan neighborhoods within the ramparts of the fortified town were sometimes referred to as "faubourgs" because these two quarters, Saint-Jacques and Saint-Mathieu, were the residences of ordinary laborers who, in many if not most towns, would have resided on the outskirts of town. The population of an agro-town, with many people living from work on the land outside, in some ways resembled the traditional faubourgs of the ancien régime. Rural life remained, as we have seen, an integral part of cities and towns well beyond the middle of the nineteenth century. Economic and social changes in the texture of urban life increasingly made rural people residing on the edge of cities seem archaic, even marginal. They seemed even more out of place, at least to administrators, social elites, and well-polished visitors, when they lived inside cities in neighborhoods thatt were villages. In Perpignan, as in the other agro-towns of the Mediterranean, the village nature of "rural" neighborhoods—for example, the *îlots* of Narbonne—helped sustain social, cultural, and political solidarities. This was even more the case in Perpignan, because the culture of these rural urban residents remained defiantly Catalan; they were thus marginal in a second way. Saint-Mathieu's embracing of democratic socialism during the Second Republic provoked the wrath of the government of Louis Napoleon Bonaparte and so made ordinary people in that neighborhood, and others as well, marginal in a third way. Through systematic repression, the French state tried to impose its order.

Neighborhood loyalties in Perpignan were rooted in spatial identities; *quartier* loyalties, in turn, helped determine the evolution of popular politics. Saint-Jacques was the parish of popular royalism, while Saint-Mathieu was that of the left, evolving from a generalized support for Bonapartism to republicanism and, during the Second Republic, to democratic socialism. The bitter and often violent rivalry that opposed the two neighborhoods was, like the development of popular politics, rooted in and reinforced by traditions of Catalan popular culture. Successive regimes demanded the obedience of ordinary Catalans; during the July

Monarchy and the Second Republic, political leaders espousing the national ideologies of royalist legitimism and democratic socialism sought their allegiance.

Neighborhood in an Agricultural Town

Perpignan's peripheral location and its vibrantly Catalan culture defined its uneasy relationship with the French state. Perpignan had been the capital of Northern Catalonia, or Roussillon, which became part of France with the Treaty of the Pyrenees in 1659.[1] Vauban carried through the construction or refurbishment of the series of frontier forts, including Mount-Louis, Villefranche, Prats-de-Mollo, Port-Vendres, and the citadel of Perpignan. The intendants of Louis XIV and their successors had tried to impose the French language on Roussillon, establishing a *collège* in which instruction was given only in the dominant idiom, requiring that sermons in the cathedral and the other parishes of Perpignan be given in French, making its knowledge a prerequisite for a lawyer or member of any other liberal profession, and requiring that all public acts, including records of births, marriages, and deaths, be written in French.[2]

The eighteenth-century intendant Boulainvilliers assessed the French state's unwilling province: "The People of Roussillon call themselves and value themselves as Catalans, and would regard as a degradation or an insult the name French or French Catalans. . . . Barcelona is their compass, so much so that with regard to fashion and taste they give their approval only to what comes from this town or is practiced there. . . . It is a common proverb that a Catalan must not go beyond the fountain at Salses [the superb Mozarabic fortress north of Perpignan, which marks the northern frontier of French Catalonia] without having left a will."[3]

Though Perpignan's population doubled between 1801 (10,415) and 1851 (21,783), its most salient characteristics persisted: the prevailing presence of the French state, the Catalan language and culture of its lower classes, a close relationship with the rural world, and neighborhood—indeed village—solidarities among ordinary people.

Michel Brunet describes Roussillon as "a sort of protectorate . . . a microsociety associated with France without being totally annexed to it. It largely preserved its particularisms and fierce independence by playing on its historical ambivalences, its remoteness, and its frontier location that has alternately, and sometimes simultaneously, made it a zone of transition or a deadend."[4]

The French Revolution extended control of the French state over Catalonia. When the provinces were divided into departments in 1790, most of Roussillon became the Pyrénées-Orientales.[5] The first prefect arrived in 1800, when Napoleon created the prefectorial corps, like a satrap in a foreign land that had far more in common with Spanish Catalonia than with the land of the conquerors. French civil, military, and ecclesiastical administrators voiced condescending, stereotypical views of their Catalan charges. They considered them excitable, termperamental, "Spanish." To an officer carrying out a survey in 1824, they were "naturally proud and stubborn; they have profited less than other people from the advantages of civilization. They don't like outsiders very much and welcome them only when it is in their interest to do so." The Catalans seemed to lack "the manners that distinguish the French and all other peoples.'' In the early 1830s Abel Hugo, in his *France pittoresque,* described the Catalan thus: ''impetuosity of character, bluntness in social relations, a high opinion of himself, such are the distinctive characteristics of the Roussillonnais, everywhere where education has not brought its level. What he loves above everything is independence . . . he is lively, irascible, and the friend of soft indolence.''[6]

The officer quoted above described their language as a ''corruption of Latin''; their ''lack of culture [had] left them in their primitive poverty; they can express nuances of thought only with the help of French—thus their language includes a great number of corrupted French words.''[7] An imperial prefect in the year X called Catalan ''harsh for the outsider who happens to hear it, never to become familiar enough with it to speak it.''[8] At the time of the Revolution the nobility still spoke Catalan, while merchants with commercial links to the north had found it advantageous to learn French.

After visiting the town early in the July Monarchy, Prosper Mérimée seemed surprised that 150 years of French domination could not ''completely rid this province of the character of strangeness that is conserved in its countenance, language, and the habits of its lower classes.'' His was a Parisian view. The Roussillonnais still called northerners *''gavatx''* (*gavaches*), which was not, Mérimée added, a compliment: ''he who employs this term does not have a good opinion of the nation.''[9] The term *gavacho* went back to at least the seventeenth century; it was used in early nineteenth-century Cerdagne ''as a term of abuse'' which ''could be extended, metaphorically, toward any outsider; but it commonly meant the French—the peoples from beyond the Pyrenees.''[10]

French remained the language of administration and the state, ''relegated to the courts and several salons.'' The French government ''had taken little control over daily life.'' Most people in Perpignan ''understood and spoke a little French''—one of the unanticipated results of the arrival of first royal, then revolutionary and later imperial, armies, the latter claiming French as the language of ''the nation.'' But after the Revolution as before, the language of the vernacular remained Catalan ''the only language of oral communication currently used.''[11] Because of long traditions of popular culture, the slow advent of primary education in French in Roussillon, and the disruption brought by the turbulence of the revolutionary and Napoleonic eras, this remained true to the beginning of this century.[12]

The tension between the French-speaking or bilingual elite and the Catalan people was particularly noticeable in religion. The language and culture of Catalonia defined and perpetuated popular religious traditions that were often at odds with what the French ecclesiastical hierarchy had in mind. When Perpignan again became a bishopric with the Restoration (another means of exercising control over the region), the bishop was, as much as before, an outsider, a Frenchman. In contrast, the ordinary clergy of Roussillon were drawn exclusively from the Catalan-speaking population. In 1814 Catalan was still the language of religious instruction and of the sacraments in all parishes in the Pyrénées-Orientales except the cathedral parish of Saint-Jean in Perpignan.[13]

The Catalan nobility and bourgeoisie, on the other hand, had proudly assimilated the culture of the French; certainly the bourgeoisie spoke the language well by the Restoration, which had not been the case before. The arrival of new bourgeois families in Roussillon, enriched by *biens nationaux,* and the presence of merchants from Languedoc and a certain number of retired officers further distanced the elite from ordinary Catalans. Jaubert de Passa, noble and local scholar, and Théodore Guiter, a future deputy whose brother had served in the National Assembly during the Revolution, had grown up speaking Catalan but adopted French while studying in Paris. Of the families of long-time residence, the "well-off" (*gens aisés*) had abandoned Catalan dress in order to "emulate French fashions." Now "the red cap, short vest, close-fitting pants or breeches with leather gaiters rising to the knees, red belt, and espadrilles belonged to the lower classes alone."[14] The process of Frenchification continued.[15]

Perpignan stood south of and on the right bank of the Têt river, which was often little more than a dry riverbed. There was another "river" as well, the aptly named Basse, made rancid by the grim tasks of the tanners. It too was sometimes bone-dry. Yet in 1846 Ibrahim Pacha, son of Mehemet Ali, on visiting Perpignan allegedly exuded, "I could be on the Nile!" Irrigation contributed to agricultural production on about 8 percent of the land of the environs. Perpignan's hinterland produced grain and olive oil, in addition to wine. Another visitor described Perpignan as "standing in the middle of a forest of fruit trees." Not far beyond the ramparts, truck farmers and gardeners grew fruit and vegetables—particularly beans, onions, and increasingly artichokes—on 168 hectares of gardens. Some of the finest gardens were those of Le Vernet, "the pride and opulence of the town," beyond the Têt, and those of Saint-Jacques, beneath and beyond the church of the same name, outside the walls, owned or tended primarily by the men of that parish. During the first half of the century, vineyards doubled in area and gradually came to dominate the regional economy. François Durand, whose commercial ventures, including smuggling, supplying the French armies had made him the wealthiest man in the department, owned vineyards among these vast holdings. He is usually credited with finding a market for the wines of his adopted region, somehow managing to convince even Thomas Jefferson, who fancied himself something of an expert on wine, that "the best wine is that of Perpignan and Rivesaltes from the harvest of M. Durand."[16] After 1830 the local distilleries, one of which was in the old cloister of Saint-Martin-de-la-Merci, produced the sweet, potent wines still found in and around Banyuls and Rivesaltes.[17]

After the disruptions of the wars, Perpignan maintained its role as a major administrative, commercial, and military center and prospered as a conduit for trade with Spain. It maintained its role as a major administrative and military post. It also still benefited from smuggling, which remained the largest source of revenue for the small coastal towns of Banyuls and Cerbère and the mountain communes of the frontier, through which "legal contraband" had passed under the Continental System and during the imperial wars.[18]

Like Béziers, and to a lesser extent Montpellier, northern neighbors along the relatively urbanized Mediterranean, Perpignan depended upon extremely close economic, social, and cultural ties with its hinterland. The town resembled a large rural bourg. Its population in 1819 was 12,499, just about what it had been on the

View of Perpignan. (Bibliothèque Nationale)

eve of the Revolution. There was very little industry to sustain a larger population—Perpignan produced common cloth, candles, leather goods, and chocolate—and no workshop employed more than ten people.[19] Nobles and bourgeois,
particularly merchants, bought land beyond the walls, especially in the coastal
plain, for prestige, enjoyment, and above all profit. They owned most of the land
within fifteen kilometers of the town, including much of the communes of
Toulouges, Pézilla-de-Conflent, Saint-Laurent-de-la-Salanque, and Elne. Seven
Perpignanais owned a third of Cabestany to the southeast and the holdings of four
others represented three-quarters of the commune of Alénya closer to the coast.[20]
If the wealthy merchant Pierre Méric drew his large income from commerce,
his status came from the ownership of property in Bompas, Elne, Millas, and
Pézilla-de-Conflent. In 1835 the vast majority of municipal taxpayers owed their
electoral eligibility to their rank as property holders, most paying taxes on property
in three or four nearby communes. Durand paid only 15 percent of his 8,035 francs
in taxes in Perpignan, the rest being assessed on property in ten other communes,
including Elne, Collioure, Thuir, Salses, and Saint-Laurent-de-Salanque; only
336 francs of Durand's taxes were for the business tax (*patente*). Adrien Anglade
d'Oms, *propriétaire* and, like Durand, member of the departmental general
council, paid more taxes in Perpignan itself than anyone else, but also owned
property in Bompas, Pézilla, Elne, Toulouges, Villemolaque, and Céret. The
Restoration deputy Joseph Lazerme, of noble stock, paid his 4,603 francs in six
communes, including Perpignan. For Lazerme too, the business tax accounted for
a small fraction of his taxes.[21]
Despite the massive transfer of land during the Revolution, there were few
property owners of great wealth. Rich landowners had been able to buy chunks of
land belonging to wealthy émigrés, poor peasants that of small property owners.
But the "dismantling of great property" did not occur.[22] Property in Roussillon

Table 5.1. Occupations of the Leading 400 Municipal Electors in Perpignan, 1835

Occupation	Number
property owners	121
goldsmiths	7
merchants	39
notaries	7
officials, functionaries	23
pharmacists	7
doctors	10
manufacturers	6
army officers	10
haberdashers	6
shippers	10
clergy	6
innkeepers	10
grocers	6
bakers	10
harness makers	6
masons	10
druggists	9
lawyers	8

Source: 2M5 20, *Tableau des électeurs municipaux,* 1835

remained "very divided, and fortunes limited, [with] few wealthy and few indigents." The former included property owners, wholesale merchants, and prosperous shippers to whom the Revolution and imperial wars had been kind. The Restoration and July Monarchy brought, however, a rise in the fortunes of the wholesale merchants and, in contrast, the marked increase in the number of poor property owners and artisans who had nothing to leave to their heirs.[23]

Yet investment in rural property by the urban bourgeoisie characterized most cities, not just agricultural towns. Perpignan also had a sizable agricultural population living within its ramparts—at least 16.9 percent of the population in 1820.[24] This number included 428 *brassiers,* or landless—with some exceptions[25]—laborers who worked the fields and vineyards of the hinterland "with their own arms"; 224 of the 293 for whom we can identify place of birth had been born in one of Perpignan's quarters, their village. There were also 118 cultivators, 114 gardeners, and 96 others whose fates were tied to the land, including other rural workers, sharecroppers, and shepherds.[26] By 1846 the agricultural population had increased to 18.7 percent of the total.[27] A study of the wills for the town puts the percentage even higher: 27.1 percent for "the population dependent exclusively upon the land (property owners, small producers, gardeners, day laborers)."[28] There were other signs of rural life as well. Country people flocking to Perpignan's markets and fairs contributed to its image as a slightly overgrown bourg. As the vineyards in the region increased by at least 50 percent between 1825 and 1850,[29] winegrowers brought their increasing harvests through the gates to their *caves,* while complaining about the tax levied on them by the state. Pigs and

Table 5.2. Social Structure of Perpignan, 1820

Class	Number	Percent
Upper classes		
property owners	373	8.35
commerce and industry	204	4.6
		13.0
liberal professions	181	4.0
functionaries, officials	152	3.4
		7.4
Petite bourgeoisie		
shopkeepers	337	7.5
employees, clerks, summoners	137	3.1
		10.6
Working classes		
artisans (tailors, 118; shoemakers, 100)	896	20.0
workers	350	7.8
agricultural occupations (428 laborers [*bras-siers*], 114 gardeners, 118 cultivators)	756	16.9
household servants	817	18.3
		63.0
Others		
clergy	63	1.4
military (including 69 retired)	140	3.1
miscellaneous: (Spanish refugees, beggars, etc.)	60	1.3
		5.8
	TOTAL	99.8

Source: A. M. Perpignan, Municipal census of 1820 (N = 4,466 heads of household)

chickens ran freely through the streets of Saint-Jacques and Saint-Mathieu.[30]

Even more than in most French cities, Perpignan's fortifications represented an unnatural barrier between the agricultural town and its hinterland. In some ways, it had not always been so. During the eighteenth century the conflict between town and countryside seemed endemic because of the privileged position of its urban elite. This elite had paid few or no taxes (being spared from the *dîme* and even certain taxes on land); had maintained the right to call upon the "garden overseers" (*surveillants des jardins*) to adjudicate contested rights over land and water (the *privilège des estimes*); and had profited from entry taxes on peasants from the environs coming to market their goods. They were beneficiaries of a disproportionate amount of the region's meager water resources, and lordly monopolists of such education as was available. In short, to rural people—and to the urban poor as well—Perpignan was the home of the powerful (nobles, ennobled bourgeois, high clergy) who bought up the finest land of the hinterland, enjoyed jurisdiction over the limited water of the stream Las Canals, and seemed to dip into the pockets of the poor.[31]

The Revolution, however, eroded the reputation of Perpignan as "a tentacular town, a town devouring men and wealth, parasitical and oppressive,'' by ending vexing privileges while increasing the power of the state. Ordinary rural people who had claimed to be the ''poor third estate of country people'' victimized by the city's nobles now complained about the state.[32]

Perpignan and the French State

The dominant presence of the state was immediately apparent to anyone approaching Perpignan. Vauban had imposed its military physiognomy in the seventeenth century. Brick ramparts of an oval shape flanked by six towers, with an external moat, protected the town from external assault. Etienne Arago, whose prominent family lived in nearby Estagel and who would be named director of the national postal service by the provisional government in 1848, described the approach to the town: ''A sky almost always pure and transparent, splendid sunshine, bringing alive the gleaming nuances of the old ramparts of brick or worn stone of the fortifications. The slopes and the glacis of the fortification, everywhere graced by a grassy green rug, two magnificent promenades . . . all lends the town an air of movement, life, and gaiety.''[33]

Perpignan had three gates: the porte Notre-Dame, through the tower of the Castillet, led to Narbonne and eventually to Paris, 900 kilometers to the north, a world away; the porte de Canet pointed toward the village of the same name, a short distance from the Mediterranean; the porte Saint-Martin hurried travelers on the road to Spain. A fourth gate, the port de Sel at the pont de l'Assaut, had once served as the main gate, before the ramparts were extended in the previous century. At the highest point of the town stands Vauban's citadel. Ironically this massive fortress, once the Palais des Rois de Majorque, the capital of the Catalan empire in the fourteenth century, now garrisoned French troops. Each night army drums sounded nightfall in the small square in front of the church of Saint-Jean, as the guard returned to one of the two large barracks within the walls.

The state did bring Perpignan some benefits. Merchants supplied the large garrison, normally several thousand troops but reaching as many as 25,000 during the French intervention against Spanish liberals in 1823. War was good for business. But what many Catalans saw as a military occupation by a powerful outsider posed significant problems for the town. There were frequent brawls between soldiers and civilians, particularly at the place du Puig (puig = small hill), situated outside the barracks of Saint-Jacques, in a neighborhood of cabarets and brothels. In 1820 a brawl began when a soldier declared, ''Catalans are brigands, scoundrels, canaille!'' Four years later a man was accidentally shot by an imprudent soldier during the festival of Saint Louis. Many incidents occurred during the July Monarchy, when the garrisons were again swollen. The most serious of these resulted in the shooting deaths of four peasants in May 1833.[34]

The fortifications (which survived until the end of the nineteenth century) blocked Perpignan's expansion: ''urban life is submitted to the constraints of a military regime.''[35] Army engineers forbade building within several hundred meters of the walls, so that besieging armies could not put such structures to use. This accentuated the shortage of space within the walls, particularly as Perpignan's population doubled during the first half of the century. With the exception of a few buildings tolerated along the three roads to the city and some isolated houses in the countryside, there were no faubourgs to absorb newcomers.

Two small territories Le Faubourg and Les Blanqueries, extended into the countryside, but, lying within the extended ramparts, offered little space. In Le Faubourg one found some of the occupations characteristic of faubourg life: saddlemakers, blacksmiths, wheelwrights, innkeepers, café owners, and others catering to travelers and country people. Les Blanqueries encompassed the tanneries, two public baths (which stood too near the sights and smells of the tanneries for the comfort of the more delicate French clients), botanical gardens, and several private gardens.

There were other sources of tension between the state and the municipality. In some ways, military utility dictated and defined exactly what the state was prepared to undertake in building or improving roads. The state invariably turned down municipal requests for building permits. The ministry of the interior took its time in approving even the simplest request for minor changes. In 1807 the council had voted to purchase a house so as to permit the expansion of the square then called the place Napoléon; this relatively simple transaction was not approved until 1824. The old cemetery near the fortifications provided a second example of an arbitrary response to the town's needs. The cemetery, too small to accommodate a population swollen by the Peninsular War, had no walls. The municipality's lack of funds during the Empire had prevented establishment of a new cemetery. Yet toward the end of the Empire, the army refused to allow the enclosure of the old one, claiming that its walls might provide protection for an attacking army. As a result, nothing prevented pigs from wandering in to unearth the remains of the deceased. In 1822 the state again refused to authorize the construction of a wall.[36] During both the Restoration and the July Monarchy, the army ignored a municipal request to remove a wall made obsolete by the expansion of the ramparts around Les Blanqueries, so that a few more houses could be built.[37]

The ramparts themselves, their gates closed at night, intensified endemic popular hatred of the *octroi*. That smuggling had been a way of life for hundreds if not thousands of Catalans further contributed to popular resentment of the state and its tax apparatus that went far beyond official protests of the municipality. As Brunet has demonstrated, the people of Roussillon were at best reluctant *adminis-trés*. Resistance to taxes was chronic and often violent; on July 27, 1789, five hundred people joyfully smashed a statue of the *fermier général*, a powerful tax official, at the town hall, before attacking the tax offices and lodgings of officials. Roussillon was "a classic land of resistance (*insoumission*)."[38]

Perpignan, proud of its long tradition of municipal liberties in the now remote past, had other grievances. The army expropriated buildings, and the municipal budget was insufficient to construct new ones to replace them. Military law still specified penalties—principally fines—for civilian violations of the zone of the fortifications, although the army no longer confiscated animals that wandered into the restricted area.[39]

Most people in Perpignan also resented the army's arbitrary claims on water, a scarce resource in an arid climate. The arbitrary power of the state wielded from distant Paris through the prefecture became a political issue in the late 1820s, mobilizing local liberals against the government of the Restoration. When the gates slammed shut at night, townspeople lost access to the two fountains outside the walls. By day they had to share these with the horses of the garrison, which reduced the supply available to civilians. The uncertain water of the Basse served, at best, only one-sixth of the people of Perpignan. Much of the water of the Têt—when its bed was not dry—was intercepted by those living at the slightly higher elevations to the west, or was diverted for irrigation. The army claimed the right to have the water supply declared to be in the public interest and then help itself. In 1822, after a drought of eighteen months, army engineers considered ways of bringing water up the hill to the barracks of Saint-Jacques, which angered the other quarters, not the least Saint-Mathieu, as only their enemies would receive the run-off. The municipality dug through ancient records, presenting the army with titles and records of privileges dating to the Middle Ages, which mentioned Perpignan's right to water from the streams, small canals, and rivers. But to no avail.

These issues, as it turned out, came to a head in the spring of 1830, when army engineers again asserted that the state had the right to take what water it wanted for the citadel. Citing charters from 1488 and 1510, the municipal council hoped to bring water to Saint-Mathieu through a canal from the stream. It flatly refused to recognize the authority of the state over the water. The army engineers, however, claimed half that water. They cited an order signed by Vauban in 1679, which proved only that the state had used a portion of the water from the stream, without demonstrating its right to do so. The municipality was willing to allocate part of the water to the citadel, but only in proportion to the respective populations of town and garrison (15,000 and a maximum of 2,500, respectively, or 6:1). Further-more, the state refused to pay more than half the cost of repairs to the aqueduct. Perpignan lost.[40]

In 1830 another conflict between the municipality and the state affirmed Perpignan's powerlessness. The municipal council refused to cede the Hôpital de la Miséricorde, which housed foundlings and to which the town held the title. The state intended to refurbish it as the bishop's residence, since it was adjacent to the cathedral. The prefect "authorized" a council meeting—the required formality—in order to approve its plan. A municipal commission demonstrated that Perpignan had held title to the building since the twelfth century; it rejected the proposed transfer of the foundlings to the dilapidated hospice of Saint-François, the final home of incurables. Without a suitable dwelling to house incurables or beggars, it seemed "an irreparable evil" to leave two hundred foundlings without shelter in order to provide a more elegant palace for the bishop, particularly a prelate who had tried to curb popular festivities during carnival. Confronted with municipal opposition, the prefect simply annulled the council's deliberation; from the state's point of view, it had never taken place. Perpignan lost again.[41]

Perpignan's Neighborhoods

Perpignan was divided into four parishes, each of which was considered a quarter, and each of which had medieval origins, as well as Le Faubourg and Les

Blanqueries, both of which also lay within the ramparts. Saint-Jean was the focal point of political power, with the prefecture, the cathedral, the bishop's residence, and the town hall. The wealthiest parish, it offered the principal urban amusements for the elite, including salons and the theater. The elegant place de la Loge was the center of the quarter and of Perpignan itself; its name came from the presence of the Loge de Mer, built at the end of the fourteenth century to house the *tribunal de commerce*. On Sunday afternoon and virtually every summer evening, bourgeois strolled around the place de la Loge before stopping in one of its elegant cafés.

Perpignan's elite lived in Saint-Jean, as did many shopkeepers and artisans, but few manual laborers. In keeping with the social structure of the quarter, one found a good number of household servants living in the houses and apartments of their masters on the major squares and streets of Saint-Jean (19 residing on the place d'Armes in 1820, 34 on the place Royale, 20 on the rue Notre-Dame, and others on the commerical rue des Marchands, the rue des Trois Rois, the rue Saint-Dominique, and so on). The similar but smaller and somewhat less elegant parish of La Réal lay to the south.[42]

Saint-Jacques and Saint Mathieu were Perpignan's two most plebeian quarters. These also included shopkeepers and artisans catering to local needs. Unlike Saint-Jean and La Réal, however, Saint-Jacques and Saint-Mathieu were known for concentrations of rural laborers, including *brassiers* and gardeners. The only other concentrations of rural day laborers were to be found on the rues Coste Saint-Saveur and Amandière in the La Réal quarter, with 5 and 14, respectively, in 1820. Few servants resided in Saint-Jacques and Saint-Mathieu (16 and 29, respectively), only 4.7 percent of those listed in the 1820 census for Perpignan; in any case, these may have worked in La Réal or, more likely, in Saint-Jean.

Saint-Jacques and Saint-Mathieu were, in a sense, villages, and their *places* resembled village squares; "except in winter the men, young and old, their workday over, gather on the village square, which serves as a rustic forum. Awaiting the evening meal, they talk in groups, exchanging news and excitedly discussing politics."[43] These two "faubourgs," particularly Saint-Mathieu, helped give Perpignan its rural air, as the trek to work beyond the walls and the pursuit of leisure took its peasant population back and forth between neighborhood and countryside. At the same time the term "faubourg" seemed appropriate because Catalan ethnicity and popular culture seemed marginal or peripheral to the French culture identified with the dominant class and with the state throughout the period 1815–51. The contrast between the habitués of the place de la Loge and the "peasants" of Saint-Mathieu was another dimension of the friction between the administrators of the French state and the people of Catalonia.

The heart of the quarter lay beyond the modest church of Saint-Mathieu, rebuilt after the original church was demolished in 1639, in the southwest corner of the city. Saint-Mathieu was formed by a series of parallel streets (rues de la Lanterne, du Four Saint-François, and du Puit-des-Chaines) with cross streets (such as the rues de l'Hôpital and Dagobert) that formed rectangular blocks. The porte Saint-Martin stood beyond the barracks of the same name. With the

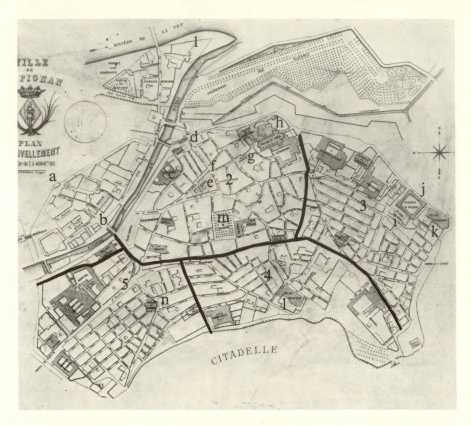

1. La Faubourg
2. Quarter of Saint–Jean
3. Quarter of Saint–Jacques
4. Quarter of La Réal
5. Quarter of Saint Mathieu

a. Les Blanqueries
b. pont d'en Vestit
c. Prefecture
d. Castillet and porte Notre–Dame
e. Town Hall
f. place de la Loge
g. place d'Armes

h. Cathedral of Saint–Jean
i. place du Puig
j. Barracks of Saint–Jacques
k. Church of Saint–Jacques
l. Church of La Réal
m. place de la Liberté
n. Church of Saint–Mathieu

Perpignan in the middle of the nineteenth century. (Bibliothèque Nationale)

124

exception of its boundary with La Réal, the parish stood by itself, bounded by the ramparts and the Basse.

In the year IX, a report to the prefect noted that "local expediency" required that the church of Saint-Mathieu be elevated to the rank of a parish: "it has around it a population of four thousand people, most of whom are agricultural workers who often need to be reminded of the moral principles on which laws are based." Saint-Mathieu was the quarter of the *brassiers;* 96 of them lived there in 1820 and 177 in 1846, probably reflecting the increased production of wine in the hinterland. Each evening the agricultural laborers without work for the following day awaited property owners offering jobs across from the convent of Merci. In 1820 there were also 6 gardeners and 5 shepherds living in the quarter. In 1846 the neighborhood also included 101 day laborers (*journaliers*), most of whom probably also worked in the countryside, and but 1 gardener. There were fewer cultivators, too, living in the quarter; of the 11 residing on the rue Four Saint-François in 1820, but 1 remained in 1846. The rue Puit-des-Chaines, which included 13 cultivators in 1820, had none in 1846. The others may well have sold their land or turned it over to the production of wine.[44]

The quarter of Saint-Jacques was considerably larger than Saint-Mathieu. Its houses too "resembled those of the countryside, low, dirty, and occupied by peasants."[45] The church of Saint-Jacques had been founded in the thirteenth century, following the expansion of the medieval town to the east. It stood at the back of the quarter, adjacent to the barracks, virtually against the fortifications. It had been known as the parish of the weavers, very few of whom were now left in Perpignan, and of the gardeners, many of whom worked in the gardens below the ramparts.

The church and barracks of Saint-Jacques bordered the place du Puig, the center of neighborhood life. The porte de Canet lay beyond the place du Puig, to the right of the church. With the fortifications forming the quarter's exterior limit, the rues Bastion Saint-Dominique, du Ruisseau, and de l'Université divided it from its neighbors. Like Saint-Mathieu, the heart of the quarter consisted of parallel streets (the rues Saint-François-de-Paule, l'Anguille, de l'Aloës, Farine, Paradis, and Porte-de-Canet, and the Grande Rue Saint-Jacques below the church and the barracks). Some of these crossed a steep hill (and streets like the aptly named rue des 15 Degrés), culminating in the place du Puig.

In 1820 at least 203 *brassiers* lived in Saint Jacques (47.4% of that occupation), 72 gardeners (63% of those in Perpignan), 21 *agriculteurs,* and 2 cultivators. By 1846 the number of *brassiers* had more than halved to 100. Despite the rapid conquest of the hinterland by vineyards, as in much of the Mediterranean, an expansion in acreage devoted to garden farming maintained the place of gardeners in Perpignan, particularly in Saint-Jacques.[46] The number of hectares cultivated by gardeners had increased from 81 in 1750 to 168 in 1826, then to 914 in 1855, with 536 on left bank of the Têt and 378 on the right bank, producing fruits and vegetables, particularly artichokes. The day laborers (*journaliers* and *manoeuvriers*) then working in Perpignan numbered 115, and gardeners 103 (another source counts 171 in 1840). For example, on the rue Jésus den Boudeille (renamed Sentier in 1830), 25 *brassiers,* 5 gardeners, and 1 *agriculteur* were

Mid-nineteenth-century view of the church and quarter of Saint-Jacques. (Roger-Viollet)

among the working population of 49 men; the rue Bénaventurats (Binabantouats, changed to Cuirassiers after 1830) included 16 *brassiers* and 3 gardeners among the 28 people with occupations listed in 1820; the rue Bente Farine had 7 *brassiers* and 8 gardeners among 35 heads of household. In 1846 at least 103 of the 137 day laborers (excluding *brassiers*, whose occupational designation refers specifically to rural work) lived in Saint-Jacques, and another 92 in the *extra-muros* sections of Perpignan, compared to but 1 in Saint-Mathieu. In all, the agricultural population of Saint-Jacques may have accounted for over 40 percent of the quarter in the early 1840s.[47]

Saint-Mathieu, the quarter of rural day laborers, and Saint-Jacques, that of the gardeners, shared a mutual hatred rooted in the past, even though the two quarters were not contiguous.[48] Speaking of the Cerdagne, on the Spanish frontier to the west in the Pyrenees, Peter Sahlins has underlined the "corporate character of the Old Regime village communities," which was "most in evidence in their elaborate sense of village patriotism . . . the defense of village parochialism was often the domain of the young men. Responsible for the ritual and symbolic initiation of 'outsiders' who settled into the community, they also defended the rights of their villages against neighboring communities, especially during festivals and fairs." In Catalan villages "the sense of local identity was grounded in a specific if disputed local territory and its boundaries," accentuated by "the idea of an enclosed territory."[49] This sense of enclosed territory and rivalries characteristic of village traditions is also applicable to the urban villages of Saint-Jacques and Saint-Mathieu, despite the fact that the neighborhoods had no corporate tradition outside of their status as parishes.

The problem of defining a neighborhood and its limits is intriguing. How do we understand and document a sense of solidarity with neighbors, and against others? In Perpignan this sense of belonging, readily apparent in these two warring villages, was enhanced by physical features which formed decisive boundaries. The ramparts formed the exterior boundary for each quarter, the corset of a fortified town. Each quarter corresponded to a single parish, at least after the Revolution, which contributed to a sense of belonging. Relatively large commercial arteries formed internal boundaries for Saint-Jacques and Saint-Mathieu, streets that were more heterogeneous in population than each of those quarters, representing a social frontier between them and the more elite quarters of Saint-Jean and La Réal.

Yet the different role of organized religion in the quarters also contributed to the rivalry. Unlike Nîmes and Montauban, among other cities of the Midi, both quarters were Catholic. But unlike Saint-Mathieu, the parish of Saint-Jacques had long been renowned for intense religiosity. This was symbolized by its Gothic retable, which also may have reflected the relative wealth of its parish council, though only when compared to Saint-Mathieu, as indicated by the fact that Saint-Jacques was able to reconstruct its church organ in 1816. Before the Revolution Saint-Jacques, like Saint-Jean, sponsored an annual lottery for the benefit of a poor girl from the parish. The candidates dressed in white on the big day; the winner received clothes and some money—a less imposing payoff than another lottery where the winner took home a large pig. Whereas all but one priest from Saint-Mathieu had taken the oath of the Civil Constitution of the Clergy during the Revolution, the clergy of Saint-Jacques, like that of most of the region, had not.[50] In October 1824, confraternity members of the chapel of Christ celebrated a solemn service for the soul of Louis XVIII in Saint-Jacques; no such ceremony occurred in Saint-Mathieu. Saint-Jacques was rewarded by promotion in 1825 to the status of a parish of the "second class," equal to La Réal.[51]

The Confraternity of the Sanch (Sancha), or of the Holy Blood ("du Très Précieux Sang de Jésus-Christ," also known as the black penitents), had been established in Saint-Jacques at the beginning of the fifteenth century, probably through the efforts of Saint Vincent Ferrier. Its chapel had been separated from the nave by a wall until the Revolution. The members of the Sancha traditionally escorted the condemned to the scaffold in Perpignan and the other towns of Roussillon, and continued to do so throughout the nineteenth century.[52]

The most fervent rituals and ceremonies of Holy Week were found in Saint-Jacques. The parish faithful washed the feet of a statue of Christ on Holy Wednesday. At 10 p.m. every Holy Thursday, the parishioners enacted the mysteries, carrying life-size statues of saints through the streets of the neighborhood. Organized by the Confraternity of the Sanch, the procession snaked through the streets, stopping at four churches and three convent chapels. The procession had changed little since that described in 1787.[53] Two trumpeters led the way, dressed in red, with two of the black penitents carrying black banners with images of the instruments of the Passion (hammers, lances, and ladders), followed by other members of the confraternity with red candles, and children with small crosses. A large cross came next, with more instruments of the Passion carried by the confraternity of gardeners. In this group marched the Regidors, the officers of the Confraternity of the Sanch, their faces uncovered (unlike the other penitents), one of whom hoisted a black standard. The rest of the black penitents followed, marching two by two, with burning white candles, some of whom carried representations of the mysteries—"des Misteris"—of the cross. These representations included the Garden of Olives (presented by the gardeners of Saint-Jacques), the Flagellation (the cabinetmakers), the Crown of Thorns (in the ancien régime, the *procureurs*), and the Ecce Homo (nobles, at least before the Revolution). Next the clergy appeared, subordinate as always in the festivities to the lay confraternities they struggled to control, each in a cassock and square hat, interspersed with the musicians. Fifty Roman soldiers followed, commanded by a centurion with a flag representing ancient Rome. In their midst walked a man dressed as Christ, carrying an enormous cross on his left shoulder, preceded by three women of Jerusalem in black; one of them, dressed as Veronica, showed the crowds an imprint of the face of Christ. Jesus was accompanied by Simon and followed by Mary, Mary Magdaleine, and Saint John the Baptist.

More black-garbed penitents followed, some in bare feet, a few carrying representations of death and crucifixes, and several carrying Christ on the cross, on a cart draped with black velvet. The Flagellants accompanied Christ, "richly robed in fine white cloth . . . faces covered with a white veil, flagellating themselves with a *discipline* of eight to ten cords with points of iron." An observer of the procession during the first half of the nineteenth century recalled that "the crowning moment for the flagellant was to have his shoulder nicely flayed and his robe bloodied." The clergy of Saint-Jacques brought up the rear. Along the route of the procession and its various stops, the assembled population sang "popular religious songs, or '*goigs,*'" as they were called—mournful tunes (despite the origins of the word in the Latin *gaudium,* "joy") in verse; these "tunes owed much more to the popular songs of the old troubadours than to the classic canticles of the church," and related the Passion and helped popularize its cult in Roussillon. In 1842 one observer considered them "only a very pale and distant imitation of those of old," however much they remained an important part of the culture of organized religion and festivity in Saint-Jacques.[54]

Did identifiable social factors account for Saint-Mathieu having been the *quartier rouge* and Saint-Jacques the *quartier blanc,* instead of the other way around? Both quarters had a concentration of rural laborers. The number of *brassiers* in Saint-Mathieu, most of whom were propertyless, increased considerably between 1820 and 1846, while there were virtually no gardeners in the neighborhood (only one in 1846). Saint-Jacques had few *brassiers* in 1846. Most of the *brassiers* of Saint-Mathieu were propertyless.

As the above suggests, in contrast to Saint-Mathieu, Saint-Jacques retained much of its reputation for religiosity, the white robes of some of the flagellants being still blood-red. Many of the gardeners of Saint-Jacques owned their own land and had maintained fidelity to the Church. More than likely, they remained indebted to wealthy legitimists in vertical solidarities of patronage. Saint-Mathieu retained the horizontal solidarities of equals; relatively few day laborers owned land.

The gardeners of Saint-Jacques, the parish of the northwestern quarter of Perpignan, worked some of the lands that lay toward the marshy Salanque in the plain, an area of fervent royalism, as the Second Republic would confirm. There the "domination by royalist landholders from Perpignan and by the clergy was, in general, unchallenged."[55] Saint-Mathieu's links were to a different countryside. Many of its *brassiers* worked in the Ribéral region west of Perpignan, along the Têt river, an area that included the radical town of Millas. There where winegrowing as a cash crop had increasingly pushed aside other kinds of agricultural production, the left easily won recruits.[56]

Catalan Popular Culture

Catalan popular culture facilitated resistance to the French state and reinforced neighborhood rivalries. It was an outdoor culture. Prefectorial reports describing its manifestations reflect distance, condescension, and sometimes sheer amazement at what was considered troublesome by virtue of being "exotic." Listen to the police describing Easter Sunday, 1826:

> An extraordinary performance took place on one of the public squares of Perpignan, by authorization of the mayor. An enclosure was formed for this purpose and the public admitted for the price of 50 centimes. The number of actors was from 70 to 80, from the class of workers and agricultural laborers, all more or less *travestis*. The performance lasted several hours without interruption, despite individual brawls and some petty thefts. This event was similar to those that have been reported to your ministry before. Written in Catalan, in a gross and licentious style, the origins of the play are lost in the night of the years, and its memory remains only because of popular tradition.[57]

During Lent, the people performed Mysteries; at sometime in the past, such performances had moved out of the churches into the open air, to improvised theaters or makeshift stages in the streets, as had the procession of the Sanch. Leaving the churches was symbolic as well as practical. These performances trumpeted the quasi-independent popular religion disapproved of by the clergy: "driven from the temple, the religious drama takes refuge in a profane space." The rupture between the official Church and the people, accentuated by the Revolution, added to the distance between the hierarchy and popular religion in Roussillon: the Civil Constitution of the Clergy, the closing of churches, the emigration of priests, a marked decline in vocations, and an aging priesthood all took their toll. So did anticlericalism, and perhaps disbelief as well.[58]

The charivari too, a form of ritualized drama, enjoyed a rich tradition in French Catalonia; ordinary people openly mocked transgressions against what seemed to be the natural order of domestic and community affairs. In Perpignan, charivaris took on a theatrical air. For example, in January 1817 young men organized a charivari in front of the residence of a servant who had married her former employer, a blacksmith. The next morning the street was littered with rocks, some quite large, that had been hurled in anger against the door. The bridegroom's daughters, who disapproved of the second marriage, were suspected of arranging for the charivari. Then in May of that year a crowd of six to seven hundred gathered to "offer" a charivari to a widow who had recently married for the second time. The police, fearing that the incident might lead to more serious disturbance, took care to light all nearby streets and passages to facilitate the identification of participants. They removed a makeshift stage that had been placed in the middle of a street for "a play in Catalan verse, very indecent, and insulting for the couple who had just married." Immediately after the first firecrackers exploded, the police broke up the crowd.[59]

Singing was an intrinsic part of the oral culture of ordinary people in Catalonia. Songs not only reaffirmed collective identity, they also were "small acts of vengeance" directed at people against whom grudges were held. In Perpignan they were part of the war of words hurled back and forth between the two quarreling neighborhoods. Songs recounted local events, quickly entering the collective memory. For example, in the spring of 1818 five peasants from Saint-Mathieu were arrested for singing songs "about a woman, songs contrary to good morals." Songs served as insults in the oral culture, setting off disputes, exacting vengeance, initiating brawls, especially during carnival, when singers enjoyed masked anonymity.[60]

Dancing was inextricably part of Catalan popular culture. Abel Hugo, visiting Perpignan in the early 1830s, reported that the Catalan "loves dancing passionately; he indulges in it to excess."[61] Catalans danced to the music of bagpipes, tambourines, flageolets, and oboes. General Castellane, no friend of ordinary Perpignanais, extolled the graceful and athletic character of the dancing: "they stroll in a circle and then toss the women into the air!" During carnival and in summer, the dances rotated again from parish to parish: from Saint-Jacques to La Réal, Les Blanqueries, Saint-Jean, Le Faubourg, ending with Saint-Mathieu. Each lasted three days. The feast days of the artisanal *corporations* offered more occasions for singing and dancing.[62]

Sometimes fights broke out, as at the dances of Saint-Jean in July 1818, between two groups of dancers who had "purchased" certain dances. The musicians had become confused about whose turn it was; the police intervened. Confronting the disappointment and anger of the poor, who had been excluded from dancing because two dancing groups in the wealthiest of parishes had purchased all the dances for themselves, one of the groups tried to solve the impasse "by paying for the dances of the common folk." The police ended the festivities early. The entrepreneur complained that the hasty conclusion to the event had deprived him of the anticipated return.[63]

Popular culture in Perpignan thus helped define and perpetuate this sense of belonging in these two *quartiers*. The dances of carnival and of the summer months intensified neighborhood rivalries by establishing the "outsiders" as rivals vying for the attention of the women of the quarter, just as festivals in the countryside pitted in courtship the young men of rival villages against each other.

Carnival, above all, was the season of festivity. On its last day people went outside the walls to eat, drink, and dance some more, yet again affirming close ties between the people of Perpignan and the hinterland. A contemporary claimed that the capital of Roussillon was perhaps the town in France where the taste for masquerade was "conserved in all its energy," calling it the "Venice of France" (albeit it a rather dry one). Far from waning, the popularity of carnival seemed to soar to new heights each year:

> To wear a mask here is a need, even more for the people—it makes them delirious. When the new year arrives a sort of frenzy grips the population. Thousands of masks are displayed, and many stores for costumes open up in each quarter. Everyone puts on Saturnalian garb, everyone disguises himself with a mask, from simple cardboard coarsely darkened to the finest velvet. The masqueraders bound through the streets shouting. From the first day of the year until Ash Wednesday hardly a day goes by without masks in the streets in small or large numbers, above all on Sunday. As everywhere, the banquets multiply and game quadruples in price. When the last week finally arrives, pleasure no longer knows any bounds. As carnival nears its end . . . everyone's head is inside out. Hundreds of drums parading through the streets emit a deafening roar. . . . Masquerade parodies are now performed [only] in public places.[64]

The bourgeois sometimes cast disapproving glances on these noisy parades of masked people through the streets, following by "all the rascals of the town." Masked balls, open to the public for an admission fee, concluded the festivities. These, in the opinion of one bourgeois observer, generally brought out disreputable people. In 1829, soldiers and prostitutes caused "disturbances" at the dances beyond the porte de Canet. In contrast, private balls remained the privilege of the elite, and there the most elegant and expensive costumes were seen.[65]

Traditions of masquerade and disguise also offended those officials, military officers, and high clergymen singled out for the deadly serious mocking afforded by grotesque costumes and biting songs and chants.[66] The Church hierarchy protested against the anticlerical tone of carnival, as well as its length. Carnival was "the madness of the people of Perpignan"; the clergy complained that it began just after New Year's Day. The procession of the Sanch on Holy Thursday, described earlier, had become a point of contention between the bishop and the faithful. In the year X, a prefectorial report had noted complaints that "festivals and processions were really only an occasion for public amusement and good times." Those marching through the streets traditionally carried "small kegs of wine ready to quench the thirst of the participants in and spectators of these religious ceremonies." In June 1818 the Restoration prefect expressed his exasperation that the processions of the penitents, back in full force, "infinitely resemble a masquerade." He had been promised that the faces of the participants would not be masked, "but despite this promise I was obliged to look the other way because . . . this tradition is very old indeed."[67]

In 1826 the minister of the interior reminded local officials that municipal edicts could "ban dances and other profane amusements from churches and other places consecrated to prayer." In 1827 the bishop, Jean-François de Saunhac-Belcastel, objected to the fact that the Jubilee, an official Church celebration of great pomp, would overlap with the carnival celebrations; he had good reason to fear that the religious "festival of Zion" would be overwhelmed by the profane "festival of Baal."[68]

Baal, as always, won in a rout. The Jubilee was celebrated inside the churches, leaving to ordinary people the run of the streets. The bishop complained bitterly about the "profane songs, sung to the tune of canticles," and reported that "a grotesque personnage had performed the part of a sick priest." This notorious public scandal seemed the result of "the dark and perfidious plots of the impious" who took such delight in carnival. The mayor, Baron Desprès, had banned masks and disguises at the end of January, having learned that "a scandalous performance tending to ridicule the practices of our holy religion" was in the works. He thus forbade "all type of distinctive mark, ribbon, or anything else which alluded to religious practices," and threatened transgressors with severe penalties. But the decree banning such popular pastimes "that have been in the possession of the people for centuries" faced such heated opposition, even from the upper classes, that the mayor relented; "hardly had the first announcement been made at the town hall, than masks suddenly appeared, marching peacefully through Perpignan's main streets." Ordinary people of Saint-Jacques and Saint-Mathieu took symbolic possession—at least temporarily—of the fancier quarters of Saint-Jean and La Réal.[69]

The solidarity, organization, and festivities of Perpignan's Catalan "faubourgs" of Saint-Mathieu and Saint-Jacques could anger French prefects, police, and bourgeois. But neither group of "outsiders" would have considered the "peasants" of Saint-Mathieu and Saint-Jacques "dangerous," but only marginal in the sense of being rural and "backward"—that is, not French—plebeian, lacking deference, troublesome. In a region to which the whims of war had so often sent Spanish exiles and French armies, the peasants of Saint-Mathieu and Saint-Jacques may have seemed a picture of stability; at least their patterns of work, leisure, and quarrels were expected. Proximity to the border, the comings and goings of ordinary people between the countries, and the persistent political crises in Spain contributed to an image of the marginality of this frontier region. During the latter periods, the French military presence in Perpignan increased rapidly, and police surveillance of potential political activists was enhanced.

What about those people who belonged to no neighborhood, who were truly marginal, outcasts, *les exclus?* What about the "dangerous classes"? Crimes in Perpignan were considered rare—not a single murder in the department in 1818.[70] Bad times brought an increase in theft, as in the winter of 1817, when "the hunt for beggars from the outside and those of the town not wearing a[n identifying] medallion" began with eighty arrested in one sweep early in October 1817.[71] Beggars came and went, as everywhere. The police threatened to arrest "three or four peasants of the town who were seen two or three days in a row at nightfall going to beg from door to door."[72]

For example, in 1819 there were complaints about the arrival of countless impoverished pilgrims going to Saint-Jacques-de-Compostelle who had been turned back at the Spanish border. Beggars customarily received a few cents once a week on Friday from certain residents: "thus on that day the town offers the hideous sight of a swarm of beggars of every age and sex tumultuously running through the streets and squares." They then left until the following Friday, marauding during the interval in the gardens, fields, and vineyards outside the walls.[73]

If any group corresponded to the "dangerous classes" in Perpignan, it was the gypsies. They sold what they could, battling each other for space at the market, begged, and were accused of thieving. Rumors of their misdeeds abounded, spreading with incredible speed, as for instance one report that a group of gypsies had roasted and eaten a small child stolen from a village in the Hérault. They were "denounced" in the vicinity of Figueras, in Spanish Catalonia, by a young woman who "had refused to take part in the meal." The details she provided led to the arrest of a certain Cigibano and his family, but no prosecution followed.[74] The police occasionally rounded up gypsies and made those without work leave town.[75]

Vice lurked on the outskirts of Perpignan, where prostitutes, some of them gypsies, "habitually hang out in the woods and near the promenades."[76] In December 1816, girls of eight to ten years of age, were arrested as they solicited passersby "to all sorts of indecencies which take place in the orchards." The previous month, a police sweep in a meadow outside the walls led to the arrest of eleven people, mostly beggars, including Grace Casanove of Rodez (almost certainly Rodès, near Ille), homeless, a victim of epilepsy, "living from charity"; Marie Angélique *dite* del Fouste, sixteen years, traveling with her two younger sisters; Marie Gleize, with one child; Eulalie Bonaventure and his wife and two children, who had been expelled from Perpignan on three previous occasions; Catherine Fabre, a known prostitute, convicted of theft and begging, with three children, each identified as a beggar and vagabond; Jean-Marie, fourteen years old, traveling with his eight-year-old brother; Magdeleine Brial from the Aude, with two younger children; Pierre Robel, a crippled beggar sixty years of age, from Perpignan, but with no place to live; Sébastien Gauchan, a former domestic from a nearby town, surviving through begging; and Narcisse Frèches, a Spanish woman on the road with her two young children, living in the fields, who claimed to have resided in Perpignan itself for seven years, and whose husband hawked needles and thread in the countryside. It was a typical group camped on the outskirts of the town. They were the truly marginal—the excluded, outcasts, beyond the gates.[77]

Quartier rouge, quartier blanc:
National Politics and Catalan Culture in Perpignan, 1815–51

The *faubouriens* of Perpignan may have lived within the ramparts, but their world of work was the fields, the gardens, and increasingly the vineyards beyond Vauban's fortifications. To the French state, the ordinary Catalans of Saint-Mathieu and Saint-Jacques were in some ways no less marginal than the transient outcasts, including gypsies. Yet in sharp contrast to the latter, ordinary Catalans, with well-established traditions and solidarities, would play a crucial role in the political awakening and struggles of common people during the first half of the nineteenth century. They would generate a strong, interventionist police response on behalf of the third and most powerful party, the French state.

The emergence of the left in Perpignan during the Second Republic at first glance might be explained by the political activity of a republican bourgeois elite rooted in the centralized tradition of Jacobinism, an elite that found support among the *menu peuple*. However, the model of "democratic patronage" brilliantly presented by Agulhon would seem only partially applicable in Perpignan and Roussillon. Despite the progress of Frenchification at least partially imposed from above by the centralized state, Paris-centered bourgeois republicanism neither effaced nor absorbed Catalan popular culture during the Second Republic.[78] Nor can Catalan nationalism explain the militance of ordinary people in Perpignan. Ethnic identity was present, despite the allegiance of the local Montagnard leadership to the Jacobin tradition that looked to Paris and its idea of the French nation, but not political Catalan nationalism. While many local Montagnard leaders, like their disciples, spoke Catalan, the Workers' Society of Perpignan in March 1848 insisted that "above all, we are French." No one could have been more Paris-oriented than the Arago family.[79] Catalan has been described as "par excellence the language of political action; when one wants to ask the masses for obedience and submission, one addresses them in French, but when wants to rouse indignation, provoke derision, or obtain the active participation of the public, it's better to address them in the only language that is emotionally effective."[80]

The conflict between *les blancs* and *les rouges* in the department may have in itself contributed to the (re)flowering of popular culture. Jalabert, a local scholar, noted in 1819 that the *barrentina,* or red cap, worn by males on feast days was disappearing as the headdress of the rural laborer. By 1850 the color red was again firmly in place as that of ordinary people in Catalonia, at least partially because of its identity with the left in the tradition of the Phrygian cap of the Revolution.[81] Among the symbols of the Montagnards were red wine and the thyme plant of "potency and hardiness": "We will plant some thyme, it will take root, the Mountain will burst into flower."[82] Here Agulhon's analysis of the relationship between "the apogee of folklore" and the way in which the Republic came to the village after the revolution of 1848 applies not only to the bourgs and villages of the Var—and Roussillon—but to Saint-Mathieu.

The rivalry between Perpignan's two urban villages, enmeshed in the routines of everyday life and in the calendar of popular festivity, also contributed to Montagnard allegiance during the Second Republic. As the police of Louis Napoleon Bonaparte quickly discovered, the neighborhood solidarities of Saint-Mathieu helped democratic socialism take hold. The Republic came to the village; the village lay within the fortifications of Perpignan. But in Saint-Jacques these solidarities helped solidify the tradition of popular royalism. Social and political conflict in Perpignan was rooted in the rivalry, often violent, between the two neighborhoods. There was nothing haphazard or random about this violence; rather, it emerged out of the solidarities of place.

The results of the French Revolution again concern us here in two ways. The Revolution furthered the reach of the French state and enhanced the predominance of a French-speaking bourgeoisie. All the successive regimes of the revolutionary era looked to Paris, none more than the Jacobins and Napoleon. The Revolution also forced ordinary Catalans to take sides: Saint-Mathieu became identified with radical republicanism, Saint-Jacques largely with popular royalism. The cultural dichotomy between elite and popular politics is apparent in the subsequent political evolution of Perpignan. The Restoration found a centralized bureaucracy based in Paris an admirable instrument with which to hound and repress its political enemies. It thus is somewhat ironic that ordinary Catalans were among its most fervent supporters. In the realm of elite politics, the liberal opposition to the Restoration was based in the bourgeoisie, drawn largely from commerce. But strong antiroyalist feeling remained entrenched in Saint-Mathieu, shaped by the rivalry with Saint-Jacques. The revolution of 1830 would be an unchallenged defeat for Catalan ethnicity: one of the very first preoccupations of the new municipal council was to change Catalan street names to French. The liberal and republican political opposition to the July Monarchy, too, rejected Catalan ethnicity. Following the revolution of 1848, popular political allegiance to the democratic and social Republic took root in Catalan culture and in the neighborhood solidarities of Saint-Mathieu. The repression undertaken by the imperial presidency of Louis Napoleon Bonaparte thus takes on the dimensions of a cultural struggle between the French state and what it considered to be the "marginal" culture of the Catalans.

Who had supported the French Revolution in Roussillon? Not the small but powerful nobility of Roussillon, whose ranks included a number of ennobled bourgeois, among them the "nobles of the ramparts," families that had provided the Crown with land for the fortifications constructed during the seventeenth century.[83] While Roussillon elected no nobles to the Estates-General, the monarchist Club de la Paix won the election of 1790.[84] Members of the two masonic lodges (L'Union and Saint-Saveur), particularly the *mercaders* and other wealthy merchants of Saint-Jean, who had spread "disbelief" in the last decades of the ancien régime, pushed the Revolution forward. By the end of 1790 the Société Patriotique—later the Société Populaire—was firmly in political control, its numbers swollen by the arrival of troops sent to the border regions.

The parish of Saint-Mathieu was in the forefront of popular support for the Revolution. The division between juring and nonjuring clergy further embittered relations between Saint-Mathieu and Saint-Jacques. Two priests had been among the leaders of the Société des Amis de la Liberté et de la Constitution, which had established its headquarters among the *brassiers* of Saint-Mathieu.[85]

The Revolution ended Roussillon's few remaining privileges and deprived it of the headquarters of a military division.[86] It also entailed an enormous transfer of land through purchase of *biens nationaux*. From no other department in France did more émigrés depart. Not all fled because they were against the Revolution; some believed they were safer from the Spanish armies in Spain than in France. Almost all left because of the war. At least six thousand people crossed the frontier—which was infinitely fluid—into Spanish Catalonia, beginning in the winter of 1790–91, but particularly when the Spanish invaded in 1793 and, in response, a hundred "suspects" were rounded up in Perpignan. Most wealthy landowners left, especially after the Spanish army withdrew following its defeat at the battle of Peyrestortes and that of Orles, which became known as the "Catalan Valmy." The exodus was thus not limited to the nobility or other wealthy property owners; ordinary people made up the majority of émigrés.[87]

About thirty thousand people profited from their absence and the nationalization of Church property to purchase a total of more than 20 million francs in property. In no other department did so much land change hands. Although the prefect exaggerated in 1816 when he claimed that virtually all property found new owners, entailing "a complete upheaval in the social order," the social and political consequences of the emigration were significant.[88] Peasants, sometimes even groups of peasants, were able to purchase the land of émigré peasants. The purchase of *biens nationaux* did not destroy the wealth of the few large landowners.[89] It did, however, enrich the bourgeoisie, with François Durand at the summit.[90] The wealthiest merchants and transport entrepreneurs, in the top rank of the *haute bourgeoisie*, had become the "kings of the day," offending the few remaining nobles by their "primitiveness" and their fortune.[91] These new "kings" thought of themselves as French, speaking the language of the state whose conquering presence had been one of the most salient outcomes of the Revolution.

Exhausted by war, Roussillon longed for peace. But ordinary people continued to resist the demands of the state, as they had by fleeing conscription during the revolutionary and imperial wars. In May 1814 a crowd including "heads of family, workers or day laborers respected for their work," and women and boys attacked the tax offices, the *octroi,* and the state tobacco stores, hauled the tax registers to the place de la Loge, and burned them. But the municipal council had barely drafted a letter proclaiming fidelity to the Bourbons and receiving a delegation of tailors expressing eagerness to make uniforms for a company of "royal volunteers," when three imperial generals arrived, gave the prefect six hours to get out of town—he took but one—and ordered away all émigrés who had come back since the return of the king. The new prefect organized irregular troops, the Miquelets, to fight the royalist volunteers and prepared Perpignan's defenses. But news of Waterloo sparked yet another wave of desertions in the imperial army in this classic region of resistance against the state.[92] One brief popular demonstration of enthusiasm for the Empire was followed shortly by the news of the Second Restoration. The very number of purchasers of *biens nationaux* helped avoid the White Terror that bloodied the streets of other cities in the Midi.[93] What prevented Saint-Jacques from taking terrible revenge on Saint-Mathieu, as their Catholic counterparts did in Nîmes? As violent as the rivalry between the two parishes sometimes was, both were Catholic, as well as Catalan. Unlike the inhabitants of Nîmes, they stopped short of massacre.

As the minister of the interior read the prefectorial reports on "public spirit" in the first years of the Restoration, he formed a picture of the crucial frontier department. Much had changed in the years of turmoil, but much had not. Catalans remained reluctant charges, at best. The rivalry between Saint-Mathieu and Saint-Jacques had been intensified by political division. A tricolor flag affixed to the house of a rural laborer of Saint-Mathieu had reflected residual popular Bonapartist sympathies. In that quarter the white flag of the Bourbons was torched on another occasion; songs eulogizing Napoleon still resounded in the safety of the night.[94]

The purchasers of *biens nationaux,* to say the least, "had not seen the émigrés' return without some sadness!" Many émigrés had lost at least some of their wealth, a few nobles having been reduced to living in relatively modest apartments. While a few found some humor in their new situation, others, including some "condemned to misery," reacted "with hatred and threats." Fear that the Ultras might force the return of the lands to their original owners gave the Restoration liberals a firm base of support among the *censitaires* of the region.[95] In 1820 rumors, however farfetched, that announced the return of the tithe, feudal obligations, and even of *lettres de cachet* did not help the Bourbon cause. Nor did the influence of Spanish liberals engaged in struggle across the border. While the Carbonari plots went virtually unnoticed and the lengthy report after of the elections of 1821 claimed that "public spirit is generally good and the mass of the population asks only to be left in peace," the reign of Charles X, as in most towns, brought more visible signs of liberal opposition.[96]

The dissidents, largely drawn from the world of commerce, elected Durand deputy in 1827. Property owners and merchants blamed the government because their olive oil, wool, and wines did not sell. Anticlerical liberals opposed the Church hierarchy on matters of education policy.[97] They insulted the faithful during the missions of April 1828.[98] At the theater, applause and whistles greeted even the vaguest political allusion.[99] Artisans were becoming interested in politics, "on the side of the opposition, even if," the prefect thought, "they do not understand anything." The young too were turning against the government,[100] staging a boisterous charivari in February 1830 for Lazerme, a deputy and member of a powerful royalist family.[101]

The revolution of 1830 brought defeat for Saint-Jacques, a bastion of support for the Restoration. Men from the neighborhood had stood near the mission cross during the incidents of 1828, ready to protect the women praying at its base from insults.[102] Now the clergy quickly and quietly moved mission crosses into the churches, hoping to avoid trouble, and the bishop of Perpignan fled for his own safety, not returning for several years. On September 9, 1830, shortly after a liberty tree had been planted, a crowd at the pont d'en Vestit, pelted tax employees with rocks, and then reassembled in front of Saint-Mathieu after being dispersed. On the evening of December 9, 1830, at the time of the trial of the last ministers of the Restoration, "a great number of unknown people drawn from among the poor" arrived at the door of the *procureur*, Lacroix, demanding that he arrest the Carlists of Saint-Jacques and release people arrested in incidents in the nearby towns of Elne and Pia. When Lacroix refused, the crowd of three to four hundred, gathered on the esplanade behind the prison, had to be dispersed by armed troops after an exchange of gunfire.[103] Abbé Carbasse of Saint-Mathieu faced the hostility of his own parishioners. In 1825 he had refused to bury a juring priest, Batlle (then a common name in the region, spelled as such), who was followed to his grave in the part of the cemetery reserved for Protestants by "a mob of peasants and children." Receiving threats from his parishioners, Carbasse now fled Perpignan, returning only a year later.[104]

Anticlericalism held the alliance of liberals together, as the new municipal council worked to reduce the influence of the clergy.[105] Yet despite the municipality's bitter dispute with the state over water rights, briefly described earlier, the revolution of 1830 was, to repeat, anything but a victory for local autonomy or an affirmation of Catalan culture. The bourgeois liberals who became Orleanists, and the few who became republicans, looked to Paris, not to Catalan traditions and culture. This tension between French Jacobinism and Catalan radicalism has persisted to this day.[106]

On November 11, 1830, the mayor, Lacombe St. Michel, the son of a member of the National Convention, proposed that the council change the names of seventy-four streets in Perpignan, a logical and popular way to commemorate the Revolution. Names associated with the Bourbons and the Church were obviously out, Orleanism and the Empire in. In the quarter of Saint-Jean, the rue Notre-Dame became the rue Lafayette; the rue des Trois-Rois, the rue des Trois-Journées; the rue de Croix-Blanche, the rue des Ecoles Vieilles; and the rue du Duc de Bordeaux, the rue Foy. In Saint-Mathieu, the rue Saint-Martin became the rue d'Orléans. Some streets with conventional names received patriotic ones. The rue del Bon Aïre became the rue Queya, named for the first man who fell in the attack on the Tuileries palace in 1791. The rue d'Ortaffa became the rue Dagobert, commemorating a revolutionary general killed in the department during the Napoleonic wars. Likewise the rue de Chavigny, named for a former prefect, became the rue Rigaud, after the Perpignan-born painter. The rue Grosset, in honor of a Restoration mayor, became the rue Camille Jordan. The street named after Villeneuve, a former prefect, became simply enough the rue Neuve; the place Royale became the place de la Liberté; part of the rue des Juristes took the previously unthinkable name of Voltaire; the Grande Rue des Jésuites also obviously had to be renamed.[107]

The new municipal council did not stop there. Many Catalan street names were arbitrarily changed to their French equivalents. Paris-centered nationalism won a resounding victory over ethnicity. The rue Fabriques d'en Nadal became the rue des Fabriques de Nadal; the rue de las Cases Crémades, the rue de l'Incendie; the place de las Cebes, the place des Près; the rue de la Creu de Fuste, the rue du Maçon; the rue del Carre Estret, the rue Etroite; the rue de la Pedre Fouradade, the rue de la Pierre Trouée; and so on. Though without doubt the vast majority of the people of Perpignan continued to call the streets by their Catalan names, the Frenchification campaign launched by the municipal council was a sign of things to come.

Now it was the turn of the prefects of the July Monarchy, like those of the Restoration, to complain about the "spirit of independence" that characterized the Catalans. Prefect Edmond Méchin claimed in 1831 that this "sort of independence . . . seems to push them ceaselessly toward a system of social equality."[108] For the first time, a major demonstration included men from both Saint-Mathieu and Saint-Jacques, although royalists still dominated the latter quarter. Saint-Mathieu remained the center of the popular left in Perpignan, a gathering place for "sedition."[109] To eliminate signs of republicanism, the administration had to wage war on Catalan popular culture. As carnival approached in 1833, the mayor banned the improvisation or reading of scripts "that bring to life family quarrels." Among the traditional uses of the charivari, "private family dissension should never be the source of public amusement." He likewise banned "any disguise that could trouble public order, including those alluding to religious establishments, even those suppressed, or which could refer to well-known people, or that offend any individuals or class of citizens, or finally which could offend decency or morality."[110]

Organized republicanism may have begun in 1831 with informal links with the Paris-based Society of the Rights of Man—the police claimed three hundred members in Perpignan—and the Association for the Freedom of the Press. The republican party found some support among the *censitaires* of the place de la Loge. The few legitimist electors posed a limited challenge to the Orleanists; the plebeian Carlists of Saint-Jacques were more of a threat to the quarter of Saint-Mathieu than to the state.[111]

In 1833 police dispersed a crowd preparing to stage a charivari for an Orleanist deputy from the Hérault, and to protest a trial of officers who had signed a republican petition in Limoux.[112] The charivari, a traditional means by which ordinary people expressed their sense of justice, had become part of political life in Perpignan.[113] There were other incidents, as well, that year. In May, some of "the most turbulent people in town" arrived at a baptism wearing red ribbons.[114] After midnight, the "Marseillaise," "Le Chant du départ," and a chorus of shouts for the Republic echoed in French at the annual summer dances at Les Blanqueries. Just as the police managed to stop the singing, "a transparency was placed in the middle of a dance floor, representing the goddess of Liberty, coiffed with a Phrygian cap, having at her feet a representation of Lyon with the inscription, "July 27, 28, and 29, 1830.""[115]

The Arago family of Estagel, northwest of Perpignan, led the political opposition to the July Monarchy. François Arago was elected deputy in 1831. Profiting from an expansion in the number of electors following increased economic development, and drawing legitimist support against the common enemy, Arago subsequently bested each challenger the government put up to oppose him, including Durand, and ran unopposed in 1837 and 1842.[116] Though he sat with Garnier-Pagès on the left in the Chamber of Deputies, Arago in 1844 called a constitutional, hereditary monarchy "the only one that can take root and bear fruit in France." At a reform banquet in 1840, Arago's moderate speech contrasted with that of the republican activist Corbière.[117] Six years later he advised the workers "never to be won over to antisocial views or communist ideas attacking the principles of family and property."[118] The Arago family and the bourgeois republicans associated with him played an ambiguous role in the left's success. Arago gradually lost some support among ordinary people. Yet in other ways his personal popularity helped mold the popular republicanism of Saint-Mathieu: "The Arago of the popular demonstrations before and after 1848 was a social reformer and a republican, even if the great man was neither." The family popularized the image of the Republic, one "unstained by the memory of the Terror." In short, Arago mirrored, or harvested, the republicanism and the then democratic socialism of Roussillon.[119] Both, like Arago, looked to Paris for inspiration, as the following Catalan song of the late July Monarchy reveals:

> I want to depict the life
> of a woman in Paris
> Who is from Estagel . . .

Marianne is her name . . .
Her godfather, who baptized her,
Gave her this name
When she left for Paris.[120]

Popular Political Culture

If, in the opinion of a newly arrived prefect writing in June 1828, ordinary people in Perpignan were "generally too little enlightened to be concerned with politics," the municipal police knew better.[121] Privileged observers, they watched and listened as national political debates reached the lower classes, reinforced by the rivalries between Saint-Mathieu and Saint-Jacques. During the years of great political contention in the city—1815–20, 1830–33, and above all 1848–51—politics and daily life seemed to converge. For example, in the last two years of the Restoration, hostility to the Bourbons seemed rampant among the lower classes. It mattered little that they did not read the opposition papers of the salons and reading clubs of the place de la Loge, to which they did not belong. They did not read French, if they read at all. But they listened in cafés to newspapers being read aloud, translated into Catalan.[122]

The political participation of everyday people was closely tied to expressions of Catalan popular culture in public places: "modern political life was born and expressed itself in this social life, inherited from the eighteenth century." Peter McPhee's comment on "such regions of substantial, clustered peasant communities" also applies to Perpignan, where "public life was centered on outdoor socialising and, in particular, the rhythm of religious and secular communal festivals, with their complex and vibrant pattern of processions, songs and dances. While . . . committed catholicism seems to have been well in the decline by the middle of the nineteenth century, religious rituals and festivals, as part of popular culture, had retained their symbolic and social importance."[123]

We return once again, with the revelers and the police, to carnival, where street masquerades ridiculed the clergy. In Roussillon, as in other regions,

> [t]he essence of Carnival lies in its parody of the constraints of the real world: by inverting and mocking reality, Carnival creates a new world. To a world of sickness, poverty and hunger is opposed one of indulgence and excess. To social hierarchy, laws imposed by outsiders, and intrusive police, Carnival opposes egalitarianism, communal autonomy and popular justice. Via masquerades and transvestism, sexual taboos are transgressed and sex roles reversed. The elaborate rituals culminate on Ash Wednesday with the judgment of the Carnival symbol, the *mannequin* or dummy, and its punishment by drowning, burning, beating or beheading.[124]

In Perpignan, the small squares and narrow streets provided the stage for popular culture and popular political culture. Masquerades, play-acting, charivaris, singing and dancing, and the wearing of red apparel reflected and accentuated the development of the political life of ordinary people. The symbolism of Catalan popular culture threatened the elite. For example, popular dancing was one of the images of fear affecting royalists, who believed that an insurrection was imminent after the Hundred Days. Rumors spread among royalists in July 1815 that Bonapartists were dancing the farandole, the snakelike celebration in the streets taken to be a dance of death against royalists. In October 1815 a vineyard guard, Poume, called Moulate, had bragged that he and four hundred like him "would make the royalists of the town dance." Royalists would "dance" from the end of a rope, while the Bonapartist rabble would prance in triumph around their dying victims.[125]

After the revolution of 1830, attacks on Church property represented a *carnaval enragé*. In February 1831 the residents of Le Faubourg and Les Blanqueries gathered to plant a liberty tree beyond the porte Notre-Dame on military land. The crowd, already edgy because the ceremony had to be delayed three days until official permission was received, marched to the seminary and, finding the doors open, entered and broke some windows. Furniture, beds, silverware, books, ornaments, and practically everything else was burned, some of it being hauled first to the place de la Loge. When the national guard was summoned, only 200 of 1,500 appeared—others were already there, part of the crowd. The army patrolled the streets and guarded the houses of two religious orders.[126]

The War of Words: Popular Political Culture and Neighborhood Rivalry

In the oral but hardly inarticulate culture of the ordinary people of Catalonia, singing was inextricably linked to politics, being a weapon of the weak against the state and the upper classes, as also against rivals of equal strength in the streets and squares of Perpignan.[127] During the Revolution, singing and dancing had been identified with radical republicanism in Saint-Mathieu, as the Revolution moved from Girondin supremacy to the revolutionary tribunal of the Terror. The corruption of the mournful chants of the people, the *goigs* of the procession of La Sanch on Holy Thursday, were part of their political repertoire. Early in the Restoration royalist songs resounded through Saint-Jacques, particularly at night, "for the pleasure of those who share their opinions, and to impose them [on their enemies], particularly when [the royalists] have heard good news."[128] But throughout the Restoration most songs and chants heard in the streets of Perpignan were hostile to the Bourbon monarchy, being sung by people from Saint-Mathieu.[129] These and other local events as well entered verse and the collective memory. An example is the musical vilification of witnesses who testified in court proceedings against those arrested from the quarter.[130]

What degree of political awareness did the songs heard in Perpignan reflect? The songs were more than vague affirmations of political preference, such as the standard shouts "Long live Napoleon!" or "Down with the *aristos!*" Some were simple allegories, such as the couplets entitled "L'Oiseau désiré," about a bird now forced to perch on distant Saint Helena. Yet at the same time, a sophisticated account of the Congress of Vienna of 1815 resonated in the streets of Saint-Mathieu. It was difficult to catch the singers *en flagrant délit,* and thus to record the exact words of a song considered seditious and incendiary. Very few "texts" were ever found. In August 1819 the ministry of interior received copies of a number of such songs that had been sung by opponents of the Restoration, songs which "have no other goal than to revive painful memories, and revive those divisions that have tended to weaken each day." Among them were "Ullysse et Télémaque" or the "Nouvelle Chanson," referring to "the *campagnons* of his bravery, their noble countenance covered with glory."

The police forced one man arrested in 1818 to sing the song so that it could be written down and translated into French: "There I was, quite ensnared, the 9th of March, they forbade me to sing. I don't know how to prepare myself. One day I will sing again." And: "I heard Rossignol [a republican general known as the 'scourge of the Vendée'] singing in the *bocage,* I want to join in the good Rossignol." In July the police were still searching—in vain—for a copy of another song in Catalan heard virtually every night in Saint-Mathieu; they hoped to catch someone whom they could force to sing before a scribe.[131]

The confined streets were anything but calm in the first years of the Restoration. For example, in 1818 *brassiers* from Saint-Mathieu sang in the streets on April 30, encouraging a later performance by residents of the enemy quarter. On the feast day of Saint-Jacques, the peasants of Saint-Mathieu taunted their rivals with song in their own quarter. About sixty men from Saint-Mathieu marched to the dances of the rival parish, singing "offensive" songs. At the dances of the porte Notre-Dame in September 1818, a *brassier* of Saint-Mathieu, Pierre Gatounès, sang in a cabaret, "One lives forever in history when one dies for the emperor," before being silenced by the national guard.[132]

After the revolution of 1830, a victory for Saint-Mathieu, the songs of popular republicanism now echoed in the streets during the first years of the July Monarchy, particularly in 1832 and 1833. There was so much singing and other disturbances at night that the commander of the departmental gendarmerie ordered nightly patrols to arrest anyone on the streets after 10 P.M. without a lighted lantern, singing, making other noise, or carrying arms.[133]

Ordinary people appropriated republican or Bonapartist songs but usually sang them in Catalan. In April 1831 the *commissaire* encountered on the place de la Loge "a band of young peasants from the parish of Saint-Mathieu who were singing a Catalan song; one of the couplets praised Napoleon II." He arrested one of the singers at the porte de Sel and ordered him to appear in his office the next day to sing the entire song, so that the words could be written down. Then he let him go, "so that his comrades, frightened by his arrest, would sound the alarm in the quarter."[134] The disturbances, which lasted several nights, included a round of songs celebrating the short-lived victory of the Poles in their rebellion against Russia, a cause dear to French republicans. Once again, national political issues quickly reached ordinary people. On April 14 "a crowd of about sixty men, all workers and residents of the faubourgs Saint-Mathieu and Saint-Jacques," carrying sticks, marched through the streets from 11 P.M. to 2 A.M., singing a song that ended with republican shouts. The processions and singing went on with virtual impunity; despite a prefectorial decree and the commander of the gendarmerie's order that the police break up any such demonstration, the night guards, "fearing the inhabitants of these faubourgs, did not arrest anyone." A man playing the violin led the next night's festivities.[135] Men described as of "an obscure class, without influence" agitated among "the working class," circulating "compositions in the Catalan dialect [sic], sung to the tunes of [17]93."[136]

Ritualized Violence and Popular Neighborhood Politics

The feuding quarters not only hurled songs and shouts as insults, they used fists as well. Once again the first years of the Restoration provide numerous examples. In February 1817 a confrontation at the place des Trois Rois pitted a group of *brassiers* from Saint-Mathieu against royalist artisans in the national guard. Four days later the laborers took revenge, attacking a royalist with "the most terrifying threats," while a laborer proclaimed with bravado that there would be another revolution, "and we will begin with you!"[137]

The war of words, songs, and fists continued in 1818, particularly during carnival and the summer dances. In March a former soldier from Saint-Mathieu battled a day laborer on his own turf. Early in January 1819, a band of twelve to fifteen workers entered a cabaret in Saint-Jacques and began singing "La Guinée," an antiroyalist song, attracting twenty or thirty local men armed with sticks. A fight and a chase followed, with threats of revenge hurled in the night. The next night an inhabitant of Saint-Mathieu, "right-thinking and of integrity," was attacked by a man named Clara from Saint-Jacques. "Peasants" and a baker of Saint-Mathieu intervened, hauling Clara and his sword to the police. Fists were one thing, a deadly weapon another. Inevitable threats of revenge were exchanged, including a boast that all royalists would be led to the scaffold. Singers taunted Saint-Jacques with "La Guinée." More fighting broke out on the rue de l'Anguille later that night when two men of Saint-Mathieu found themselves surrounded by peasants, "against whom they defended themselves with their fists." About the same time, on the rue des Quatre Coins, a group of young men tossed a white cockade that had been "defiled by garbage" through the window of the house of a royalist tailor, an émigré, singing "songs so abominable that decency does not permit me to quote them."[138]

It went on. During carnival, twelve to fifteen laborers from Saint-Jacques marched to the rival neighborhood in two lines with a drum. They stopped in front of the cabaret Lo Galeode Fouste, demanding wine. When their rivals responded with "La Guinée," a royalist from Saint-Jacques shouted his fantasy of washing his hands in the blood of the men of Saint-Mathieu (there were naturally two different versions of this), which was characteristic of the violent, theatrical rhetoric of popular culture. The two sides were separated without bloodshed, but several days later were at it again, after a royalist *brassier* called Cami or Canni had written his own lyrics to "La Guinée": the royalist "Contre-Guinée" of Perpignan was born.[139]

The ritualized violence of neighborhood politics often took place beyond the walls in the countryside. For example, in February day laborers from Perpignan were greeted with "La Guinée" when they appeared in the commune of Saint-Estève with a white handkerchief provocatively tied to a hoe or shovel. Yet a month later, "La Guinée" seemed to have disappeared from the musical repertoire of Saint-Mathieu, replaced by "other couplets in the same spirit," these composed by a day laborer from Saint-Mathieu. Late in April, "insignificant songs, but which tend to revive political feeling," echoed in the streets of Saint-Mathieu, sung by fifty to sixty peasants gathered before a cabaret. In November these "peasants" were singing "offensive songs" again. The children of the two quarters followed the example of their families, engaging in rock fights, a "small war" waged on the terrain of the fortifications beyond the porte de Canet.[140]

Despite the clear identification of Saint-Jacques with support for the Bourbons and of Saint-Mathieu with hostility to the Restoration, the political boundaries between the quarters were not, of course, absolute. In one incident the singers of Saint-Mathieu had been joined by some young men who had broken with the royalist traditions of "honest legitimist families" in Saint-Jacques.[141] For example on Sunday night, February 2, 1817, a fight broke out between peasants within Saint-Mathieu. It was carnival, a time when "the animosity between the two parties was increasing each day." Words were exchanged in a cabaret behind the barracks; several national guardsmen took offense when insulted. Gendarmes, sent to assist the police, were in turn attacked. Three days later the participants went at it again at the porte de Sel, as the laborers returned to Perpignan at the end of the day. François Millet "suddenly leaped from his donkey to attack" André Salès. The latter held his own, until felled by a large stick wielded by Millet's brother-in-law.[142] Another such brawl between peasants, in March 1817, occurred at a spot called Le Puits de las Cadanes, one of those places where laborers usually awaited daybreak and work in two groups, "not wanting to mix with each other." In this case, fifteen young royalists from Saint-Mathieu took advantage of higher ground to defend themselves against twice their number whose songs had insulted them. The lack of work in a time of drought seems to have compounded the heat of the passions of carnival; perhaps the royalists were being hired by royalist property owners, while Bonapartists—described as remaining in their houses while their enemies awaited the start of the workday outside—were not.[143]

Furthermore there were also many people within both quarters who were neither part of the "rural" world nor belonged to either party. Not all minor dramas—*les choses de la vie*—in the life of a quarter had a political content. Day laborers brawled for other reasons at the pont d'en Vestit, one of the *points chauds* of Perpignan. In February 1817 a man had been seriously injured when struck by a stick during a fight among several agricultural laborers, the kind of event viewed by the prefect with disgust: "the peasants, accustomed to drink, very irascible, of a tempestuous nature, rarely take their leave in this region without several quarrels which are almost always accompanied by blows." A fight between a peasant of Saint-Mathieu and another from Saint-Jacques at the bastion of Saint-Dominique might have had political overtones, but did not; the man had attacked his sister's lover.[144]

Other incidents reflected resentment against that third and most powerful party, the state. During carnival in 1817, three soldiers began to "amuse themselves at the expense of a peasant by blocking his entry to the house of a bookseller of Saint-Jacques." Each time he attempted to escape his tormentors, they cornered him. He was rescued by the arrival of three peasants of his quarter. A brawl began;

the soldiers soon found themselves badly outnumbered and surrounded by "a large mob of spectators, composed for the most part of peasants who proclaimed themselves on the side of the three others." A detachment whisked the brawling soldiers away as more peasants from Saint-Jacques arrived to join the fray.[145]

The Revolution of 1848, Popular Culture, and Neighborhood

Dynastic opposition and bourgeois and popular republicanism came together during the 1846 elections to the Chamber of Deputies.[146] In the hope of electing de Contades, the grandson of an émigré and the son-in-law of General Castellane, the government held out the possibility of extending the railroad beyond Narbonne to Perpignan—the so-called "Contades amendment"—to woo local voters. Castellane put the military division under arms in an attempt to intimidate those who might waver. François Arago, candidate of the dynastic opposition, was elected by 343 votes to 192. Six thousand people packed the place de la Loge to celebrate the government candidate's defeat, before being dispersed after three warnings from the troops.[147]

The February Revolution of 1848 in Paris brought the same coalition into the streets of Perpignan again, beginning "the great political mobilization" of the Second Republic. This, even more than the events of the previous regimes, was rooted in Catalan popular culture and in the rivalry between Saint-Mathieu and Saint-Jacques. The state became the final arbitrator.

Peter McPhee has demonstrated how Perpignan's exceptionally close relations with its hinterland worked to the advantage of the Montagnards.[148] The expanding market economy during the July Monarchy provided channels for the subsequent political mobilization that spread from Perpignan and other towns and bourgs; ordinary people were drawn not only into markets but also into politics. "Aux paysans" and other radical brochures read by the "habitués of the [place de la] Loge" in Perpignan turned up in the villages of the department.[149] The landowning peasants and landless rural proletarians of Roussillon supported the radical bourgeois and artisans of the towns, particularly in the lowlands. The democratic socialists "worked" the surrounding areas, with the greatest success in small towns.[150] Some of the intermediaries were poor workers familiar with city and country.[151] Rural residents attending the fairs and markets of Perpignan offered an opportunity for proselytizing among those described by a policeman as "these wretches of the countryside who are always looking for bad news." The Montagnards "strolled all day on the fairground, offering countless handshakes, stopping a moment with some and then moving on to others. The most influential returned to the Café de France."[152]

The economic program of the Montagnards appealed to ordinary people: they promised war on usury, the abolition of the tax on drink and the reduction of other indirect taxes, increased credit facilities, a progressive tax on the rich, and anticlerical measures.[153] The state's considerable economic power in the region—extracting taxes, garrisoning troops, assessing tariffs on foreign goods—made it a natural frame of reference for the political concerns of people whose modest livelihoods lay open to sudden economic reverses.

A general awakening of a sense of solidarity among ordinary people, urban and rural, developed, but not class consciousness per se in a region with virtually no industries of size or concentration. But, to repeat, solidarity and demands for social reform cannot alone explain the strength and persistence of democratic socialism in Perpignan. Nor can the traditions of republicanism, now well established in Roussillon. Nor did Catalan nationalism emerge as a movement against the French state, although ethnic identity became inextricably linked to Montagnard expression and originality, and helps explain its resilience in the face of repression directed by French authorities. We must look to popular culture and to neighborhood solidarities for an explanation.

Within and beyond the gates of Perpignan, Catalan popular culture—dances, songs, and charivaris—was particularly conducive to the flowering of political contention. Catalan popular culture was anything but ''a disappearing relic in a changing society but, for a time at least, was the collective, ritualistic framework for the expression of new ideas about politics and society.''[154]

The brawls between quarters, provocative incursions into enemy neighborhoods, political songs in Catalan (which popularized Ledru-Rollin, Raspail, Barbès, and other national figures among the Montagnards), songs that simply served as insults, and the contempt bred by years of distant familiarity—all revived. Now, however, the radicals of Saint-Mathieu found some allies in Saint-Jacques. Neighborhood solidarities contributed to—and may even have been decisive in—the triumph of popular democratic socialism, while Catalan ethnicity provided the means of its expression. The old rivalry between the two ''marginal'' neighborhoods, *quartier rouge* and *quartier blanc,* would become a source of strength for the left.

In February 1848 the angry crowds that confronted Castellane's troops two years earlier suddenly found themselves masters of the street, and the moderate and republican bourgeois followers of François Arago took political power in Perpignan. Théodore Guiter, former opposition deputy, called the municipal council together, proclaimed the Republic, and served as its *commissaire.* Crowds threatened all the symbols of the power of outsiders: the prefecture (quickly vacated by the prefect), the *octroi,* the bishop's palace, the seminary, and convents. Two clubs, the moderate Club des Amis du Peuple and the Club Démocratique, selected candidates for the legislature.

Arago won in the expected landslide, but, in keeping with his Paris-centered political vision, chose to represent the Seine, where he was also elected.[155] With the Republic itself under assault following the June Days and the election of Louis Napoleon Bonaparte to its presidency, the radical Comité Central Démocratique worked to counter the efforts of committees of legitimists, Bonapartists, and the moderate ''men of order,'' some of whom supported Arago.[156] The ''party of order'' in Perpignan was greatly outnumbered; the conflict remained one between royalists and their socialist enemies.

Celebratory toasts in the wake of the fall of a common enemy could not efface the rivalry between Saint-Mathieu and Saint-Jacques, exacerbated by the expansion of the revolution in the first months of the Republic. On Sunday, June 4, the day of the by-election to the National Assembly, the national guard company from

Saint-Mathieu, "known and identified," in the words of the state prosecutor, "as contributing to disorder," went into the countryside for a banquet. Their return, marked by guns fired in celebration in the air, began the incident briefly mentioned in chapter 1. When a policeman, Vidal, reprimanded the revelers, Cyprien Dominique, a blacksmith of twenty-two known as Limagne, threatened him. The policeman, unpopular in Saint-Mathieu, arrested Limagne with the help of the colonel of the national guard. But on the way to the police office at the porte Notre-Dame, his friends from the parish, a few in guard uniform, jumped the police, knocked down the colonel, and freed their friend. "A mob of ordinary people" from Saint-Mathieu then marched on the town hall, demanding the replacement of Vidal, the policeman. The roll of drums summoned the entire national guard to the town hall to keep order. When confronted by guardsmen from other quarters, the men of Saint-Mathieu returned home to get arms themselves. The guardsmen of Saint-Mathieu tried to force their way into the courtyard. One of them who fired a shot was disarmed and arrested. Fearing bloody trouble between enemies with long memories, the provisional commissioner of the Republic released Limagne and sent the national guardsmen home. Suspicion of Saint-Mathieu was such that the prosecuting attorney claimed that the Montagnards of Saint-Mathieu had hidden arms and munitions in their quarter.[157]

The next evening, residents of Saint-Mathieu forcibly disarmed guardsmen, wounding one posted at the town hall. Despite a warning from someone ("In the name of God, don't go into Saint-Mathieu or you'll get your throat slit!"), a patrol of two hundred troops and guardsmen set out and was attacked by workers from Saint-Mathieu armed with swords and pistols, wearing red caps and shouting in Catalan at the entry to the quarter on the rue Saint-Martin near the rue des Jemappes, another of those streets renamed after the July Revolution. A subsequent patrol was assailed with rocks "in one of the streets of the faubourg Saint-Mathieu, and after negotiating with men armed with rifles trying to block its passage."

Among those now sought by the police, a certain Monier was easily recognized because of his long beard and white felt hat; he quickly sent his hat—too valuable to discard—back to the village of Peyrestortes, to the northwest, with his sister, and shaved off his beard. Yet the police were able to identify and track him down. Others of those who attacked the patrol were also from Peyrestortes, including one wearing a red hat who had threatened to go to Peyrestortes to get the people there to "do justice" to the authorities in Perpignan. Here again, the close ties between town and country were demonstrated. "The entrance of certain inhabitants of town" through the porte Notre-Dame and the porte de l'Assaut subsequently was closely watched.[158]

Artisans and workers supported the Montagnards, joining radical bourgeois in the heady days of the spring of 1848. Even more, the Montagnards drew their strength from "the poorest class, all agricultural laborers who live in Saint-Mathieu."[159] Saint-Mathieu seemed as distant from the social and political life of the place de la Loge as Catalan popular culture was from the dominant culture of the French. The sense of neighborhood was much stronger than that of class, beyond the sense of ordinary people united against a state dominated by the interests of the wealthy. The collective memory of the past and the traditions of popular culture informed the rivalry between quarters, its political content, and resistance to the state. When the national guard was dissolved on June 23, 1849, following a tumultuous gathering at the prefecture and town hall at the time of the insurrection that month in Paris, it was largely because the government feared Saint-Mathieu.[160] The guardsmen of the latter seemed little disposed to return their rifles, and several arrests followed. The police suspected the existence of a secret society: its "composition would be most dangerous, almost all of them from Saint-Mathieu."[161] The world of the day laborers of Saint-Mathieu centered on proletarian squares where workers awaited daybreak or celebrated the end of the day, on the quarter's cabarets, and on the countryside beyond the fortifications, those arbitrary and misleading barriers between city and country. The quarter seemed fertile ground for socialist propaganda, largely oral, such as that provided by a certain Montagnard named Planès, who went, if a policeman is to be believed, "every day into the cabarets of Saint-Mathieu, spreading the most awful propaganda."[162]

The most militant workers frequented the Café Allègre on the rue de la Lanterne.[163] The Montagnard leaders, like the Restoration liberals, held court in the relatively fancy cafés of the Loge. The Café Desarnaud became the "salon of the democratic socialist aristocracy." The masonic lodge of Saint-Jean stood accused of serving as a center of Montagnard activity, or at least a place for socialists to meet, drawing some members from "the lower class and particularly the workers."[164] When the results of the 1850 Paris elections were known, workers from the popular quarters went to the Grand Café, "where all the Montagnards gathered; all day and until midnight this café served as a tribune for predictions, each one improvised, with some promising the inevitable fall of the government . . . the people, as usual, gathered on the Loge."[165]

The democratic socialist mutual aid society La Fraternité, founded on May 31, 1850, provided a basis for popular organization, at least until its dissolution. Of more than one hundred members of La Fraternité, a policeman noted that, "except for six or seven bigwigs, all the rest belonged to the class of men I encounter every night in the street or in the cabarets."[166] The committee that drew up its statutes, as required by law, "was composed chiefly of the more militant *rouges* of Saint-Mathieu." A magistrate claimed in December of that year that its actual membership far exceeded the 600 names registered at the town hall and may have approached more than 2,000, although such frightened and sometimes inflated official estimates have to be taken with a grain of salt. Almost all the thirty-four popular associations in Perpignan in 1850, including mutual aid societies begun during the July Monarchy, were on the left.[167]

The notable exception was the Société Saint-Michel, founded by legitimists in April 1850, ostensibly a mutual aid society to counter Montagnard strength among the Catalans. It soon had seven hundred members, many drawn from Saint-Jacques. Typical of associations of patronage, it included honorary presidents and members, among them clergymen, and was organized for—not by—workers who could demonstrate "a proper life, good morals," and who evidenced a proper political orientation. Like other such organizations in the Midi, its real goal was to "stand up to anarchists, if they attempt to disrupt public order." But the gap between the activities of such leading royalists as Paul de Lourdoueix, editor of *L'Etoile du Roussillon,* and the parishioners of Saint-Jacques remained wide. While Montagnard peasants and workers fought it out with legitimists near the citadel, conflict within the royalist camp between intransigents and moderates, as elsewhere, damaged the Bourbon cause.[168]

Politics even reached the brothel. A fight started when a prostitute wearing some sort of pin decorated with the color red was confronted by a royalist, who asked her, "I'd really like to know who gave you *that.*" The reply came all too quickly from another, wealthier, client within earshot: the *rouge* threw the *blanc* against the wall, breaking his shoulder.[169] Baptisms too reflected the mass politicization of Perpignan: legitimist green hats abounded in some ceremonies, red caps and red-coated sugar almond candies in others.[170] So many fights occurred almost nightly that it seemed a "civil war" was about to begin.[171] In 1849 workers wearing red caps danced around a liberty tree singing "Long live the red Republic!" A large crowd first demanded news upon learning of events in the capital in June 1849, and then the replacement of the military posts in Perpignan by the national guard. When day laborers in bands of from fifty to a hundred went to Pia and other communes, they asked for work or money and, being refused, began "to bring in the harvest without the assent of the property owners." The prosecuting attorney blamed this action of the poor on "the instigation of the baneful theories on the right to work."[172]

Carnival facilitated a systematic, symbolic expression of allegiance to the democratic socialist Republic in Saint-Mathieu. Once more we listen to the police, this time during the heyday of Catalan popular political culture—1850, under the Second Republic:

> On the return of the population from the tree nursery, a dozen children aged nine to thirteen crossed the place de la Loge in the following order: three of them, the one in the middle taller than the others, marched arm in arm in front and, opening the procession, carried on their shoulders another child standing up; [she] was dressed as a goddess, wearing a Phrygian cap, her right hand holding in the air a bough of laurel. Those following sang the "Marseillaise," and the many people who came to watch opened their ranks to let the goddess pass.

The marriage between popular culture and politics was complete. When a policeman grabbed the young goddess and removed the red cap, "the people, at first so content, changed character"; there was trouble the next day.[173]

In the dances that rotated from parish to parish, political songs and slogans added to the cacaphony of music. Political division intensified old rivalries that ordinarily would have brought the men of one neighborhood into another as challengers for the attention of the local women. At the dances held on the place de la Liberté at the beginning of September, again in that troubled year 1850, one hundred socialists complained that the police refused to throw out royalists who were causing a commotion; instead the police dispersed the Montagnards with the now frequent three official warnings.[174]

Two weeks later, "political symbols were perfectly evident during the dances yesterday in Le Faubourg. The socialists wore hats and red ties . . . the legitimists wore green hats, without ties." Fights followed.[175] In September 1850, police with tricolor sashes confronted a sea of red at the dances at Saint-Mathieu, the last of the year, "one of these frenetic dances so characteristic of this region." When the police waded into the crowd to arrest those wearing "social decora-tions . . . the dancers did not hesitate to adopt a provocative pose vis-à-vis the police agents, gendarmes, and particularly the two police agents who were watching them. After outrageous and seditious shouts in Catalan, a young woman walked in front of one of the police commissioners, hissing, 'To the guillotine!'"

The police arrested the woman, Thérèse Lafon, but the crowd rescued her. Her rearrest brought half the parish of Saint-Mathieu to the place de la Loge to protest. Troops succeeded in dispersing the crowd after the third and last official warning. A policeman then managed to stop the band from playing "L'Air des Girondins." As he left the dance, the remaining revelers shouted after him—"To the Mari-anne [guillotine], Chicoulate!"—"Chicoulate" being the name of a Carlist bandit guillotined in 1846 for murder. The name stuck; "Chicoulate, Chicoulate!" echoed after the beleaguered commissioner as he made his way through the streets.[176]

Revolution and singing went hand in hand in the Second Republic. Songs sparked many of the fights between the *rouges* and *blancs* of the two warring neighborhoods. In 1850 few days went by without brawls and other incidents. Thus on May 20, after a group of military replacements had marched down the rue de l'Argentière singing and shouting for the Republic, confrontations occurred in Saint-Jacques. The next day a police patrol prevented a fight from starting on the place du Puig as the antagonists were taking off their coats, and some four hundred people were settling down to watch. There, in the heart of Saint-Jacques, the royalists held the upper hand. Elsewhere a man injured in a brawl two days earlier came upon one of his attackers and took revenge "with interest." Several days later a hundred royalists gathered to sing on the place du Puig, as people from the commune of Millas arrived with a tricolor for a trial of one of their own. On May 29, among those "massed" on the place du Puig were "the most infamous inhabitants of Saint-Mathieu," the usual suspects. On the Grand Rue Saint-Jacques in July, fifty Montagnards attacked several of their badly outnumbered enemies.[177]

Most incidents of violence between the two quarters began with a provocative incursion by a band of singers into the enemy quarter, or their arrival on contested neutral space. When a group of royalists arrived on the place de la Liberté to serenade a leading legitimist on his feast day, their enemies were not far behind to drown them out.[178] After the statutes of the mutual aid society La Fraternité were approved at a mass meeting in a meadow outside the city walls, the members returned to town singing "the same songs heard every day." Entering by the porte Saint-Martin, some three hundred of them marched up the rue des Augustins singing "death to the royalists," the kind of song sure to bring a response. In one case, the prosecutor reported, "the Montagnards, more numerous and audacious, went into the quarter of Saint-Jacques to provoke and attack the royalists, singing songs that ended with the refrain 'war to the death.' The royalists defended themselves. The police intervened on several occasions and the police commissioner, as well as his agents, were abused in a violent manner. There were many arrests."[179]

Confrontations between socialists and royalists of the two quarters were also occasioned by routines of work and pleasure. Day laborers brawled as they awaited daybreak at the place du Puig and the porte de Canet in Saint-Jean, and at the porte Saint-Martin in Saint-Mathieu. The ritual, boisterous return from the countryside or from the coast at Canet also sometimes led to disturbances, as when a group of people from Saint-Mathieu returned singing with a tricolor and a red flag; later that same night other Montagnards returned from the Joubert fountain outside the walls to the liberty tree on the place de la Liberté for some more singing.[180]

In the evening, disturbances were most likely to occur at the place du Puig, the location of the royalist Société Saint-Michel during the Second Republic. The square became a focus for counterdemonstrations. Hostile and sarcastic "serenades" would be followed by insults and fisticuffs.[181] Or when fifty radicals returning from the dances at Le Vernet, across the Têt, went out of their way through Saint-Jacques, so as to insult their enemies, sparking yet another fight.[182]

The larger streets, neutral turf outside Saint-Mathieu and Saint-Jacques, became scenes of daily political provocations. So also, in the evening and on Sundays and holidays, did the Platanes, the Esplanade, the place de la Liberté, and the place de la Loge. Wearing a red flower or, in defiant contrast, a white or green one, could spark a fight on such neutral space. The presence of reds and royalists in the same café was an almost inevitable cause of trouble, as when about two hundred people took their quarrel from the confines of a cabaret to the ditches beyond the porte de Canet.[183] The battles between *quartier rouge* and *quartier blanc* were not at all unlike those that were so frequent between villages in the countryside.[184]

In December 1850 there was death. For several days, children from the "red party" marched into Saint-Jacques armed with sticks and singing "provocative refrains." A man yelled at the small intruders to go home, at which point one of the band, a boy of sixteen, raised his stick, which the irritated *blanc* took from him. It happened that a man from Saint-Mathieu—known as Mata-Pouillets, Killer of Chickens—was visiting his mistress near the place du Puig in Saint-Jacques, demonstrating that love—or at least sex—can conquer all. Seeing what had happened, he ran out of his friend's room and dispatched the man with his knife as easily as he dispatched chickens, slicing two other men before fleeing. Rumors spread that Saint-Mathieu would rise as one man to slaughter the royalists of Saint-Jacques. The next day Julien Dapère, twenty-eight, was arrested hiding in his sister's house in Saint-Mathieu. He claimed to have defended himself against two men who had been alerted that someone from the enemy neighborhood had violated the quarter ("Someone from Saint-Mathieu is here—let's kill him!"). Several days later, Honoré Illa died of three knife wounds.[185] The relative calm that had lasted for about a month ended abruptly. The legitimist party turned out in force for his funeral. Dapère himself was forced by the authorities to walk through the quarter of Saint-Jacques in daylight, near the body, a move which the *procureur général* believed had a good effect in Perpignan.[186]

The Repression of Catalan Popular Politics
in the Second Republic

Faced in 1850 with a veritable crescendo of "sedition," the authorities claimed that Perpignan was on the verge of insurrection. Evidence for this assertion, however, was no more than the usual reporting of opposition political activities. One rumor had a Montagnard inventing a "very ingenious means of guillotining twelve people at once." The return of several Perpignan socialists from their trial in Rodez on June 14 led to a triumphant tour of the town after the agricultural laborers of Saint-Mathieu had gone to greet the coach in Le Vernet. The following week political discussions outdoors seemed more blatant; accounts of the trial, including a couplet in the patois of Aveyron in honor of the accused, circulated in cafés.[187]

To the police, each gathering seemed a dress rehearsal for insurrection.[188] "Bands of workers" allegedly accosted and insulted their social superiors in the streets. Workers carrying the red flag through the streets were chased and arrested.[189] In September mounted troops quelled more disorders in Saint-Mathieu; subsequent decrees banned any costumes, emblems, or other objects of a political nature in the streets.[190]

Gradually, as elsewhere in France, the bourgeois leadership withdrew from militance, no longer surveying the scene below from the balcony of the Café Desarnaud. Arago's moderation alienated the democratic socialists, particularly when he accepted a decoration from Louis Napoleon. Perhaps his obvious ambivalence toward his Catalan past had begun to irritate ordinary Catalans. If Arago's popularity and his somewhat liberal centrism was such that "the name of Arago could be utilized by various groups of any political tendency or social orientation" by the end of 1849, his popular appeal had diminished in the region.[191]

A banquet held in March 1850 reflected the waning of "democratic patronage," as well as the essential role of the hinterland in the political mobilization of ordinary people in an agro-town. The gathering took place in "an obscure cabaret outside Perpignan. Only men belonging to the most perverted and ignorant class were in attendance. The leaders of the socialist party kept away."[192] Two months later, as socialist workers provocatively strolled through the place du Puig, singing, one of them announced, "If the occasion presents itself, the workers alone will run the affairs of the country," and added that the workers now disavowed "the tophats and suits."[193] The withdrawal of "respectable" leadership contributed further to the image held by elites of the marginal nature of the democratic socialist movement.

Raising the costs of political participation, the repression gradually took its toll on the Montagnard movement in Perpignan. This made neighborhood an even more vital base for political opposition. The prefect had blamed Lloubes, Perpignan's mayor, for being insufficiently firm with the socialists. The centralization of policing through the appointment of a special commissioner in August 1850 reduced municipal authority over the police. The prefect ordered the replacement of the night guards by *sergents de ville,* since Prat, the special commissioner, claimed that the former were either too old or ineffective, or that they treated the socialists like "little saints, the famous troublemaker Gauze is considered a paschal lamb, and [a cabaret in Saint-Jacques], which has a good reputation, a den of thieves." Five additional rural guards were added to patrol the hinterland.[194] In November 1850 Perpignan's last liberty tree was cut down, because it "blocked traffic" on the rue de la République and was the site of "crowds threatening public order."[195]

Indicative of the repression was the police report of July 17: "We don't see any more of these large and dangerous crowds; they whisper and suspect their neighbors. They see police spies everywhere."[196] Bourgeois socialists stayed away from the cafés of the place de la Loge,[197] as secret agents gathered information on a variety of suspects, adding to details believed compromising provided by the regular police.[198] Thus on February 3, 1851, police reported on the activities of the Montagnard leader Corbière, who "went home at 9:30. Mouchous, leaving the Grand Café at 10 o'clock, returned home and a quarter of an hour later left again for Le Faubourg. He opened the door at number 27 with a key from his pocket. This lodging is the house of his mistress," the interior of which was happily beyond the view of the police.[199]

The prefect banned red cockades and hats, and other symbols of Montagnard politics and Catalan popular culture.[200] Although police prevented musicians from playing republican songs during the summer dances of 1851, red caps bobbed defiantly.[201] The police squinted to catch traces of red clothing in the distance and cupped their ears to hear the sedition of the Catalans.[202] At the dances of La Réal, three brothers wearing red cockades sang "insulting" songs, including one that alluded to the "murderous rack they have in store for us if they are ever given the chance."[203]

Less well policed, the countryside remained the privileged, indeed logical, place of political discussion for people whose work lay outside town. Three hundred men and their families celebrated the Republic's second anniversary at the fountains of Las Hortes two kilometers beyond the porte de Canet.[204] During carnival in 1850, rumors abounding in Saint-Mathieu that Roussillon would be placed under state of siege led to talk in much of the town that a socialist insurrection was being planned in several taverns a few kilometers beyond the ramparts, where Montagnards routinely gathered.[205] On February 26 the police went two kilometers beyond the porte de Canet and the gardens of Saint-Jacques in hopes of surprising a socialist conspiracy. Alerted by a posted guard, about four hundred people scattered through the gardens, vineyards, and ravines. The next day police broke up another "meeting" at the *auberge* La Chaumière, though it was nothing more than the routine kind of gathering that took place before or after the nightly promenade, or *paseo,* through Perpignan.[206]

The meadow of a socialist, Massot, providing for dances on Sundays and holidays was one such meeting place. In April 1851 the police claimed that those gathered on the route de Rivesaltes had discussed the political disposition of each commune in the arrondissement.[207] Later in the summer, the meetings were in the meadows and gardens surrounding the city.

The rituals of life and death became virtually the only possibilities for mass demonstrations. The baptism of a child born to a socialist baker and his wife occasioned a sizable gathering where guests downed red almond candies.[208] So did another in which the godmother was the mistress of Mata-Pouillets, the killer of Honoré Illa.[209] The funeral of a socialist militant in February 1851 attracted over two thousand people; that of a man whom the Church refused to bury, a thousand more.[210] The long walk to work took on defiantly political dimensions, as when fifty agricultural laborers went out to tend the vineyards owned by Mata-Pouillets[211]; or when Perpignan socialists crossed the commune of Pia on the occasion of a pilgrimage to a votive chapel and sixteen were arrested for "seditious shouts."[212]

The prefect ordered the dissolution of La Fraternité, the Allègre circle (whose fifteen members simply moved to the Café de France); three regular gatherings of workers were dissolved the same day.[213] Other clubs, however, survived, contributing to the government's conspiracy theory about Montagnard organization.[214]

When the last of Perpignan's liberty trees, at the pont d'en Vestit on the edge of Saint-Mathieu, was cut down, no demonstration followed. Even the feast of that parish was calm.[215] This very fact frightened the authorities, who now claimed, as during the previous summer, that an insurrection was being planned by members of the Allègre group, which had been meeting on the rue de la Lanterne in Saint-Mathieu. Vandalism against the property of wealthy property owners was blamed on the poor of Perpignan. Several civilians were rumored to have purchased cartridges from soldiers.[216] The songs heard in the streets seemed to take on a more determined and martial tone, such as "Let's put at the end of our rifles Changarnier, Radetsky, Louis Napoleon, the Pope, too!" In mid-November, even some Montagnards believed that an insurrection was planned for the end of the month "in a great part of France."[217]

There were no plans for an insurrection in Perpignan, nor elsewhere in Roussillon, despite widespread allegiance to the Montagnard cause. The plotting was in Paris—for a coup d'état by Louis Napoleon Bonaparte. When it occurred, several hundred people gathered at the prefecture in protest, before being dispersed by the army. The settling of scores that followed was not between the reds of Saint-Mathieu and the whites of Saint-Jacques, but between the third party in Perpignan, the state, with the assent of the "party of order," and the Montagnards, while the legitimists stayed discreetly in the background.[218]

After the revolution of 1848, the Republic had come to the village, but to the village or faubourg within the walls of the agricultural town. The "faubourgs" of Perpignan had appropriated national political issues and participated in the great awakening of 1848–51. Yet it should be clear by now that ordinary people in Perpignan had been quite politically awake before. The tense rivalry of the quarrelsome quarters had been inserted into national political life, reaching the desks of the ministries of interior, justice, and war in Paris. The coup d'état was directed at the Montagnards of Saint-Mathieu, and at Catalan culture as well.

It may have seemed ironic that the *blancs* and the *rouges* both lost out to the Bonapartists and the "party of order," who had relatively few followers in the region. A bitter invective penned in the North in 1848, after the events in

Roussillon, reflected the official identification of Catalan culture with revolutionary disturbances. It now seemed much more than stubborn independence and resistance to France and things French: "Catalan fury, the spirit of cruel vengeance, the frenetic mania for devastation, the ardent thirst for pillage, the ungovernable instincts of a population which, may God be thanked a thousand times, has no parallel in France!"[219]

The Jacobinism of the democratic socialists was ultimately as inconsistent with the regional consciousness of the Catalans as Bonapartism. The process of Frenchification went on, ironically assisted by the Paris-centered political vision of the Catalans themselves, closely tied as it was to the hope of joining other peoples of the left in seizing control of the French state. Yet it was among the seemingly marginal Catalan people, particularly the agricultural laborers of the quarter, "faubourg," or village of Saint-Mathieu, that democratic socialism had put down its deepest roots. In fact, there was nothing marginal about the "faubourgs" of Perpignan, old neighborhoods that fought each other and also resisted the centralized state commanded by Louis Napoleon Bonaparte.

The Second Empire came and, eighteen years later, went. Toward the end of its last decade, in 1870, as waves of political mobilization and strikes swept France in the months before the Franco-Prussian War, officials in Perpignan once again complained to Paris about a familiar subject. Said the police commissioner: "the quarter of Saint-Mathieu is completely perverted. Subversive ideas have made frightening progress there during the past four or five years. Men, women, and children claim to be socialists; the other quarter, Saint-Jacques, is more sensible." Faithful to its past, Saint-Mathieu stirred again.[220]

6

The Precocious, Violent
Faubourgs of Nîmes

Vauban's citadel, above the boulevard du Grand et Petit Cours, recalls the town's crucial strategic position on the road from Montpellier to Marseilles and Avignon, and near the Languedoc Canal and the Rhône. Standing above Nîmes, it at first appeared to have been built to defend the physically vulnerable city against enemy attack. In fact, it had been constructed "to repress and contain the turbulent inhabitants of Nîmes." Appropriately, it had been transformed into a prison that held 1,200 convicts during the July Monarchy, with another building added for the overflow.[1]

Nîmes, founded in 633 B.C., became a major Roman city with a population of at least seventy thousand. Vestiges of the glorious Roman past remained: the Temple of Diana, on side of the hill; the Maison Carrée, within the northern limits of the old town; the ruins of a Roman aqueduct, which paled in comparison to the Pont du Gard not far to the northeast; and the tour Magne, which had become a relay post for the primitive telegraph that linked Nîmes to Paris. In its great Arena, measuring 72 by 42 meters inside, twenty thousand people could watch the battles of the gladiators.

Bloodshed in Nîmes during the first half of the nineteenth century no longer took place in the Arena, now occasionally used for festivals and to shelter some of the poor, but on its boulevards, which separated its center from working-class fauborgs. Nîmes earned a reputation for being one of the most—if not *the* most—violent city in France. This violence had nothing to do with disorganization, but rather with conflicting sectarian claims in, and the collective memory of, Nîmes's precocious and turbulent faubourgs, which had grown up with the silk industry in the eighteenth century. The new gladiators were Catholic and Protestant proletarians. In Nîmes the faubourgs were not pitted against the central city; rather, religious rivalry helped link ordinary people of both faiths to elites of their confession living in the *cité*.

Like the Catalans of Perpignan, the Provençaux of Nîmes struggled against the powerful outsiders from the North, not the least of whom had been Louis XIV. The popular royalism of the Counterrevolution was at least partially sustained by resistance against the Jacobin ideal of the French nation, one, indivisible, and French-speaking. With Protestants constituting more the one-third of the population population (37% in 1851), the streets of Nîmes had been bloodied by fighting

156

and murder during the Revolution.[2] In 1790 the Protestants, almost a century after the Revocation of the Edict of Nantes, had taken revenge on Catholics, culminating in the *bagarre de Nîmes*.[3] Thermidor brought a bloodbath in which dozens of Protestants perished at the hands of plebeian Catholic bands. After Napoleon's final defeat the White Terror, organized from above by secret elite royalist groups and carried out by poor Catholics, came to Nîmes, Uzès, and other places in the Gard. Brutal murders and attacks on Protestant property in July and August 1815 were overseen by François Froment, whose father had lost his position as municipal registrar in 1784 because of complaints of improprieties made by Protestant manufacturers, among others. Froment had been a fanatical counter-revolutionary in the battles of the Revolution's first years and an agent of the royalist émigré court. Fifteen Protestants were massacred in the faubourgs on August 1, and more were dispatched during the bloodbath of the nights of August 16, 19, and 20, being dragged from their houses to be hacked to death with swords and knives. Victims included a wealthy Protestant banker, left to die on the road near his devastated estate, but many poor people as well. The sight of husbands, brothers, and sons being hacked to death outside their houses or on the outskirts of town lingered in the collective memory for decades.[4]

Royalist bands became part of the terrifying lore of the Gard. In particular, the royalist bandit Jacques Dupont, an agricultural laborer, was known to everyone as Trestaillons, because he allegedly cut his victims into three parts; the even more notorious Graffaud earned the name of Quatre-Taillons (one more slice) of Uzès. Acquitted of murder by the royal court of Riom in 1816, Quatre-Taillons lived in security in the Catholic villages near Bagnols-sur-Cèze. Shortly after the revolution of 1830, he was tracked down and beaten to death by gendarmes in the Catholic village of Courbessac, northeast of Nîmes. Trestaillons had died in 1827, his coffin escorted to its grave by one of the confraternities.[5]

On May 14, 1820, "the widows, mothers, children, and heirs of several victims of the reaction of 1815, all living in the town of Nîmes," petitioned the Chamber of Deputies for justice. The assassins of their relatives had gone unpunished. François Sauffine, a former army captain, had been cut down on the chemin d'Uzès on August 1, 1815; his widow had been driven from her home by Trestaillons, among others, and died eight months later. Pierre Courbet, stocking maker, had been murdered in the most notorious faubourg, the Catholic Enclos Rey. The nine-year-old son of Paul Hérant, silk worker, had watched his father being hacked to death, also in the Enclos Rey. Antoine Rigaud, cultivator, had been dragged from his house and killed by a royalist mob, leaving a widow and three young children. Antoine Clot, an agricultural worker, had been shot at point-blank range by Trestaillons in the Enclos Rey on July 18. David Chivas had lost his life on the chemin d'Uzès on July 21; Catholics prevented his widow from claiming the body for several hours. André Chivas had died at the Mas-de-Rouvière in his vineyard outside Nîmes.[6]

Several incidents in that same year of 1820 demonstrated that little had changed in "this place of hate and vengeance."[7] Even the clergy dreaded the arrival of the missions of the controversial abbé Rauzan "in a region where the smallest incident can have serious consequences."[8] On April 3 the quarrel of two children of different religions on the boulevard soon brought their elders into the fray. On April 30, adult Protestants and Catholics fought it out. More trouble followed in June when two young Protestants taunted Catholics, not long after the assassination of the Duc de Berri in Paris, with a song ending, "Oh, what joy, worthy Nîmois, no more king or Comte d'Artois!" Two old women also came to blows. That same month, a cultivator complained to the police that he had been insulted by a certain Louis Ribit, a shoemaker, who had called him a "brigand" and, accusing him of killing Ribit's mother in 1815, vowed revenge. The processions of the Fête-Dieu brought provocations and insults from both sides.

It went on. On August 4, 1820, Louis Segnin, a public writer who had converted to Catholicism, returned home to find four men waiting; they beat him with sticks before he reached the safety of the *octroi* office. He claimed that the darkness kept him from identifying his assailants, which may have been—or more likely was not—the case. On December 6 a brawl took place "between market women, one of whom had lost her husband during the troubles of 1815," sparked other fights. When a dozen men sang a Bonapartist song, royalist couplets sounded from other parts of the room, and a brawl was narrowly avoided.[9] It was an old story.

Events in 1826 demonstrated the persistence of religious rivalries—if anyone needed reminding—and the close association between physical space and sectarian violence, even during a time of relative political calm. On February 6 children showered a Protestant funeral procession with rocks and insults along the boulevards and out the faubourg to the cemetery, sparing neither the deceased nor the bereaved. The missions were a time of unbearable tension in Nîmes. Near the boulevard des Carmes a tailor was arrested for loudly asserting that all Protestants should be massacred. A priest in the nearby village of Dions caused commotion in the opposite camp by forcing a Protestant who had not tipped his hat to him to kneel, threatening him with the sacrilege law. The missionaries refused the sacraments to Catholics who had married Protestants. They forbade a printer to print Protestant books, ordering him to burn all the works of the philosophes in his possession. He finally was permitted to send his "objectionable" literature to Paris in exchange for books of piety, so as not to lose his investment in the inquisitorial flames. At the conclusion of the missions, "exclamations and sobs . . . echoed loudly" in response to the preaching of the priests; in their frenzy some of the faithful frantically tried to rip pieces from the priests' cassocks. The missionaries had become the "absolute masters of that part of the population susceptible to being carried completely away by the sensations of the moment."[10] Four plebeian Catholics guarded the pedestal upon which a mission cross was to be placed.[11]

Catholics hooted a mixed marriage; the bride had attended the missions with apparent fidelity and then shocked the faithful by marrying a Protestant. When the cousin of the bride, who had also married a Protestant, died after giving birth several months later, the parish priest refused a Catholic burial.[12] During the missions "a scoundrel" who had previously been convicted of theft was suspected of hanging a tricolor flag from the tour Magne, and claimed he had been paid twenty francs to do it. Because every such act generated rumor and fear, "a sort of anxiety among Catholic and Protestant alike could be felt. On May 5 a number of young Protestants from town went to one of the Catholic bourgades, where the missionaries were staying, and sang "the most scandalous songs." Reciprocal provocations and fights followed. Rumors spread in the Catholic community: that a Protestant had killed a Catholic, that the procession of the Fête-Dieu of Saint-Charles would be disrupted, that a "poster dripping with blood" had been found on the door of the cathedral (in reality, only part of a liberal Paris newspaper, the "blood" being a red string). The posting on the door of a sign "Bishopric for sale, bishop to hang!" did not help calm Catholic fears. But the procession took place with only one fight, and a brief moment of panic when women fainted at the front of the church during the final benediction, and people rushed forward, thinking Protestants were attacking them. At 11 P.M. another placard was found, this time at the town hall: "Notice to French Protestants: brigands want more murders and thefts. . . . Let us not be victims of a government which tolerates this, and which cannot last."

Pastor Emilien Frossard found it difficult even to describe the people of Nîmes—"and we undertake it with trembling." More than thirty years after the White Terror, Nîmes was divided "into two camps which economic and civic life often bring face to face." The "mob of artisans"—by which he meant the Catholics—who surged to the boulevard des Casernes hardly ever mixed with the more elegant people who strolled about the boulevard de la Comédie on Sunday evening. Even at the door of the hospital, or at the prison, "they interrogate the unfortunate person and carefully note his religion."[14]

The collective memory of religious fanaticism had far more to do with the continued antagonism than religiosity per se: "without at bottom being very religious, they are easily impassioned by sectarian rivalry." In general, ordinary people seemed, at least to an outsider, surprisingly unreligious.[15] Few Catholic men, unlike women and children, went to Mass. "In Nîmes everyone claims to be ready to die for his religion, yet there are too few people of faith disposed to live for it," observed Frossard.[16]

Yet Catholics were attached to the public traditions of their faith. "Seeing a woman of the lower classes," M. de Jouy, a member of the Académie Française, noted in 1818, "one sees immediately the religion that she professes: the Catholics wear a cross, the Protestants a golden image of the Holy Spirit, from their neck."[17] After the revolution of 1830, the municipality was free to make decisions about external religious practices that would have been unthinkable during the Restoration. It banned any kind of procession in the streets and public places. In February it announced that the clergy would no longer accompany corpses out the chemin d'Avignon, southeast of the Enclos Rey, to the Catholic cemetery. Furthermore, the defunct, who had been carried by friends to the Catholic cemetery, would be transported in a horse-drawn wagon owned by an entrepreneur who held the monopoly for this lugubrious service. A priest would meet the procession at the cemetery for the final ceremony.

Police dispersed a crowd that gathered to protest the first such burial, and others that followed. It seemed that violence more than prayers might accompany the final journey of the wife of the theater director, because of the presence of "the

women of the people . . . that is to say, the most fanatical and possessed part of
the people.'' The clergy and the municipality quickly worked out a compromise:
the priest from the cemetery would meet the body and the curé halfway along the
chemin d'Avignon. Thus not a single step would be taken without the reassuring
presence of a priest. Several thousand people who turned out for the funeral out of
faith, loyalty, or simply curiosity shouted for joy when they saw the curé appear
alongside the wagon.[18]

"What can one say about the people of Nîmes?'' a visiting member of the
Académie Française asked two people ''equally wellplaced to answer the question.'' The first described them as ''hard-working, patient, lively, industrious;
look at them in their workshops, always gay, alert, obliging, and spiritual.'' The
opinion of the second was very different: ''They are a horde of brigands eager to
murder, pillage, or set fire to something, dancing around the guillotine, and
mercilessly insulting the victim being sacrificed.'' The visitor concluded that
''they are two peoples, good or malevolent, humane or cruel, peaceful or
tumultuous, according to the circumstances in which they find themselves, the
interests that motivate them, and the impulsion they have received from those who
stir them up.'' What differentiated the people of Nîmes and the Midi from the rest
of France, he thought, was ''a fanaticism of spirit and greater effervesence of their
passions'' which surfaced inevitably when there was nothing to hold it back.[19]

Yet the poor of both religions were noted for their relative sobriety, despite the
fact that wine cost next to nothing, as well as for love of hard work (few were ever
described as ''lazy''), and morality. Religious rivalry seemed to generate charity.
Even in 1827, a bad year, few beggars were to be seen in Nîmes. As a department,
the Gard had a reputation for few crimes. The workers were renowned for their
love of festivities, including bullfights, but also purchased the cheapest seats in the
municipal theater, particularly for operas. On Sunday, if times were good, they put
aside their usual fare of the week (anchovies, salted herring, cod, dry vegetables,
salted pork) and ate pig livers, fish cooked in wine, frogs, escargots, and jam.
When on holidays ordinary Nîmois went to enjoy the good weather along the tiny
Vistre river, formed from the waters of the Fountain, the poor were to be found
along its banks in their green pants and vests, while the wealthy retreated to their
mas and larger country houses.

Some workers may have been among those owning *masets* (from *petit mas,* or
maisonnette), small square houses in the immediate vicinity, barely more imposing than the *cabanes* of the Marseillais. The *masets* were described as being little
more than ''a cube of masonry, pierced by a door in the front and a window on the
other sides, each with shutters of bright green. Around this lies a small plot of
rocky soil with a few olive trees, several grapevines, and a walkway with irises on
either side.'' By the end of the July Monarchy there were nineteen workers'
chambrées, or informal clubs, reflecting neighborhood solidarities, where workers gathered on Saturday evening, Sunday, and sometimes on ''Holy Monday.''
For the most part, ordinary people still spoke Provençal, whereas the elite of the
city had embraced French during the revolution.[20]

People from Nîmes were and still are frequently described—invariably by outsiders—as fiercely loyal in love and hate, a temperament that visitors sometimes blamed on the hot and relatively—at least for France—humid climate: "the Nîmois is lively, buoyant, a little impulsive, and even more so in his vices than in his virtues. . . . He loves with enthusiasm, and hates until death. He is entirely dominated by momentary concerns, having only his own caprice and often misdirected feelings to guide him."[21] "Warlike games," including some that were dangerous, remained popular, as well as jumping, running, wrestling, and even rapid-paced dancing, which made the army think that the Nîmois made good soldiers. Physical skill and stamina were frequently put to use in fighting on the boulevards.[22] Of public amusements, the people preferred the spectacles, races, and fights staged in the Arena as in Roman times, despite the official disapproval and the distaste of the upper classes for rowdy games. The much-beloved running of the bulls, sometimes confused by Parisian papers with Spanish bullfighting, and other violent contests featuring bulls, together with hunting and other blood sports, helped firm the sterotype of the "dangerous classes."[23]

The old town housed the institutions of national and local political power: the prefecture, the palace of justice of "elegant simplicity," the town hall, the theater, and the cathedral of Saint-Castor.[24] Although in the last years of the July Monarchy some bourgeois began to settle south of the Esplanade, where the railroad station was built, the *cité* remained "the domain of the bourgeoisie," particularly the seventh and eleventh sections. The most handsome houses stood on the boulevard between the Arena and the Maison Carrée. Here lived the silk manufacturers and wholesale merchants whose families had risen to prominence during the previous century, among other wealthy men of property and also many retail merchants.[25]

The bourgeois quarters of the original town were themselves densely packed.[26] In 1818 they were described as "a labyrinth of narrow, winding streets, a heap of old, somber, shabby, poorly spaced houses, many standing at improbable angles."[27] During the First Empire, an estimated 6.5 percent of the population lived in "spacious, well-built, accessible, clean, and properly maintained" houses of three or fewer stories.[28]

Nearly twenty years later, little had changed; the streets of the old city were described in a military survey of 1837 as "dirty, narrow, and winding," an almost routine formula in those surveys. They were paved with flat limestone and were often blocked by the two-wheel carts and mules of Provence. Nîmes smelled, particularly during the summer. Streets were difficult to clean, owing to a chronic lack of water and the existence of but one public fountain. In 1822 the mayor complained that previous measures of public health were being routinely ignored, with appalling results. Garbage was left on the streets, chamberpots were dumped here and there.[29] The moats that had once surrounded the walls were only slowly covered up; the canal leading toward town from the Fountain was stagnant in the summer, "a putrid cesspool." The silk industry, dyeing, and tanning contributed to the putrefication.[30] The wind blew a "fine dust that enters every pore . . . a veritable scourge for this town."[31]

With the exception of a handful of nobles whose public role was waning,[32]

View of Nîmes in 1840 in a lithograph by Bayot and Champin. (Bibliothèque Nationale)

bankers, wholesale merchants, manufacturers, and wealthy property owners with holdings in the hinterland stood at the top of the social hierarchy. And unlike ordinary people, who flocked from the faubourgs to the Cours Neuf and the boulevard de la Comédie, men of means more often headed for the Esplanade when the weather was good, or undertook a more lengthy *tour de la ville*.[33] On Sundays they strolled with their families in town in the Jardin de la Fontaine or along the canal below the tour Magne and mont Cavalier, examples of classic eighteenth-century restoration and town planning.[34] The men, though generally "withdrawn into family life," occasionally left home to attend the theater or go to their club to read newspapers or play games, a privilege for which they paid about forty francs a year.

Protestant and Catholic elites rarely mixed, barely greeting each other in the streets.[35] The existence of separate schools, as well as a school for Jews, reinforced antagonism within the middle class. Separate Protestant and Catholic charitable institutions also helped maintain a virtual wall between the people, wealthy and poor alike, of the two religions.[36]

In a town characterized by the rich associational life of Provence, there were six clubs in 1820. Four were royalist, including the Société Bolze, which met in a back room of the café of the same name, the rendezvous for "the elegant people of both sexes," and another, the Ultra, which had recently begun to accept more moderate royalists. Two clubs were liberal in membership: the Jardin de Gailhe, assembling Protestants from *haut commerce* and even a few Catholics (the prefect considered its members to be impassioned radicals), and that organized by a

1. faubourg de la Bouquerie
2. Les Bourgades
3. Enclos Rey
4. faubourg de Richelieu
5. faubourg de la Couronne
6. faubourg Saint-Antoine
7. faubourg de la Magdeleine

a. Gardens of the Fountain
b. Canal and Quai of the Fountain
c. place de la Bouquerie
d. Citadel
e. boulevard du Grand et Petit Cours
f. Saint-Charles
g. Barracks
h. chemin d'Uzès
i. boulevard des Calquières
j. Cathedral of Saint-Castor
k. Maison Carrée
l. boulevard Saint-Antoine
m. La Placette
n. Arena
o. Esplanade

Nîmes in the first half of the nineteenth century. (Bibliothèque Nationale) certain Jalabert, with older members. There were also two reading societies whose members included the most militant of liberals, and a masonic lodge.[37] The plebeian faubourgs had no such voluntary associations.

The bourgeois lived simply, "avoiding superfluous luxuries," showing little interest in the arts. Their houses were spacious, orderly, clean. Many of their sons became lawyers and magistrates; one, François Guizot, became a professor of history. Their wives looked after the household, assisted by servants, permitting themselves only the luxuries of coffee and chocolate. "Second-rank wholesale merchants" lived a sedentary, frugal, and precise existence, "the state of happy mediocrity," relaxing on Sundays in their small country dwellings. Unlike the rich, who had begun to eat at the fashionable hour of 5 P.M., which permitted them to do something after dinner, they ate later and more modestly. They tended to be melancholy, and less concerned with the rules of politesse. Below them on the bourgeois ladder were the clerks, "lively, fastidious," their wives "somewhat imperious."[38]

To someone writing in 1835, Nîmes had benefited from "the natural effect of civilization and above all the special civilization that distinguishes France . . . developed in an immense metropolis, and diffused from the center to the periphery by a single administration." Provincial differences were being effaced. Now Nîmes, thanks to the revolution of 1830, benefited from "the peaceful bourgeois who now govern so easily from Paris, with the help of a small telegraph placed at the top of the tour Magne." Perhaps the arrival of migrants seeking work would further dissipate "these savage hatreds," even among the lower classes.[39] Yet little doubt remained that "religious hatreds subsist and are further complicated by political antipathies."[40] The bitter antipathy between Catholics and Protestants was reinforced—if not determined—by neighborhood rivalries between ordinary people.[41]

Most workers lived in the faubourgs, in houses of fairly recent construction with one or two floors, thus smaller than the houses of the center, with tiny gardens symbolizing close ties to rural life. Nîmes, like Perpignan and other towns in the Midi, might have been called an agro-town by virtue of a sizable agricultural population, particularly in the faubourgs—6,325 in 1827, including the laborers employed by wealthy property owners on their nearby estates.[42]

Nîmes's growth and general prosperity, however uneven, had for more than a century been tied to the manufacture of silk, produced in small workshops and by homeworkers. Although a distant second after Lyon, the silk capital of France during the Restoration, the town still liked to think of itself as making Europe "tributary to its light, brilliant cloth, in which the soft cottons of the Indies mix so nicely with indigenous silk . . . worked by adroit hands." Solid, useful, common cloth of a variety of "ingenious" designs was also produced. In 1827, 15,043 of the total population of 39,464 worked or otherwise depended upon the textile industry for a living (as did many villagers producing silk in the Gard and southern Ardèche); they lived at the mercy of accelerated, brutal rhythm of peaks and valleys in the industry.[43]

Whereas there were as many as 20,000 employed in 1821, two years later the count was only 6,270, but in 1824 the industry's condition had improved dramatically, with 26,630 employed. The period 1825–35 brought less abrupt peaks and valleys, although a severe recession followed the revolution of 1830. In 1834, the year of the Lyon insurrection, the percentage of silk workers among all Nîmois workers reached its peak of 41.7.[44]

Most silk workers worked at home (with the exception of those who produced laces and rugs, as well as some hosiers). They were often vulnerable to illness—the producers of taffetas, particularly, to chest and leg problems, the latter from working eighteen and nineteen hours at a time in an awkward position. The stocking makers, who were somewhat better off, worked a few hours less when there was work, but suffered from a degeneration of their lower limbs and from eye problems. The carders had perhaps the most unhealthy jobs, suffering from chest, throat, and eye diseases. They died young. The ribbonmakers, carders, finishers, combers, and other workers as well, all suffered diseases and debilitations specific to their work.[45] In addition to the crises generated by a fall in demand, certain kinds of workers faced regular layoffs, such as spinners employed only during August, September, and October.

In the fall of 1834 the industry entered a period of crisis from which it never fully recovered. The manufacturers had reduced rates, putting more work out in the countryside—a time-tested, profitable strategy. Several thousand silk workers were out of work, and the municipal council had to provide 30,000 francs for municipal workshops. As the rural silk workers brought their work to town on Monday, which was also the day that the workers took off, two hundred Nîmois silk workers gathered on the Esplanade and the Cours Neuf to await their rivals. The police dispersed them before they could seize and tear up the work being sold to the manufacturers.[46]

The market for cloth and taffetas dwindled, and the production of shawls and rugs was mechanized. The arrival of the railway helped diversify the local economy, supporting its continued, if modest, growth and providing jobs for building workers as well as railway employees.[47] Yet in 1840 only five workshops employed more than twenty workers.[48]

The faubourgs had developed precociously during the eighteenth century, when the silk industry helped the town's population more than double from about 18,000 in 1722 to at least 49,000 by 1780. Attracting many migrants, the old town became saturated, so that some two thousand people lived in the Arena. The lands to the north and northwest—gardens, meadows, vineyards, and olive groves—were sold off as lots for houses, being purchased by masters and silk workers. Small producers set up their looms; workers lived more cheaply nearby than they could have lived inside the city. A contemporary writing in 1753 noted the rapid growth of the faubourgs, including the Enclos Rey: "Twenty years ago, twenty thousand people was about the number of inhabitants [of Nîmes]; today it has more than doubled. Two large faubourgs which together form an entire town have grown up in this short period of time."[49] In 1771 the town consuls described the residents of the faubourgs as morally as well as physically and socially marginal:

> The faubourgs [are] inhabited by a population of workers and farm laborers, attracted by the resources offered by commerce and agriculture. They form a particular kind of society which has only very limited relations with the long-time

residents and, as they live apart, determines their own sense of morality. . . . The lack of principles evident in most of these inhabitants could bring about disorders . . . their debauchery leads to laziness, and these two vices manifest themselves in thefts and other crimes.[50]

Yet the faubourgs, which lay within the perimeter of defense established by Vauban's fortifications, were precociously integrated into the life of the city. They had become neighborhoods in their own right, with churches built in the eighteenth century: Saint-Charles on the edge of the faubourg des Prêcheurs, and Saint-Paul in the faubourg de la Madeleine. The southwestern faubourgs of the Protestants had names associated with local history; the Catholic faubourgs names of apostles and saints.[51] Without imposing buildings Nîmes and its sizable faubourgs seemed to blend together into the rocks and hill during the day, and at night offered a few large shadows. As a result, it was difficult "in a glance to grasp and to understand the extent of its faubourgs."[52] De Jouy, writing in 1819, declared after a visit of eight days that "Nîmes today lies in its faubourgs."[53]

Silk manufacturers invested in the faubourgs, most of them residing in town houses but continuing to buy up land around Nîmes. A contrast existed between the "quasi-immobile center within the old walls and the very lively faubourgs," as some of the rural characteristics of the latter waned. The destruction of the ramparts in 1785–88, which the municipal council had voted in 1774, symbolized a "new conception of the town which slowly emerged during the century of light." It served as "sort of an exorcism of this almost visceral fear of the 'outside.'"[54]

The economic and administrative integration of the faubourgs into Nîmes, combined with the mutual hatred of Catholics and Protestants, reduced or even eliminated some of the tensions between *cité* or bourg and faubourg that characterized other towns with essentially proletarian suburbs, including those of Lyon, Reims, Châtellerault, and Limoges. In Nîmes the residents of the Catholic faubourgs respected, indeed revered, the Catholic elite of the central city, and hated the Protestant faubourgs; the Protestants returned the favor. Yet to some extent the faubourgs also remained a world apart, poorer, more violent, with the boulevards that divided them from the central city serving as a significant and highly contested buffer because of religious division. Although the decline of the silk industry slowed population growth, the faubourgs continued to grow through migration.[55]

The expansion of the faubourgs beyond the boulevards was limited only by hills to the north.[56] The arid *garrigue* was covered by brush and olive trees, and increasingly by vineyards, although some of these were being abandoned because a liter of wine at times brought only the minuscule return of two centimes. The *garrigue* itself offered uncertainty: for example, in 1823, two rural guards chased two thieves on the chemin d'Alais (Alès) beyond the faubourgs, after hearing the desperate shout of "Thief!" They found a knife, a pistol, and a wagoner's shirt left by a band of some thirty robbers from the Cevennes. The hill above the Fountain could also be dangerous, as a man discovered in November 1820, when he was robbed after having been invited to play cards near the tour Magne. Members of the feared Black Band lured two unsuspecting strangers to a *mas* outside of Nîmes, robbing them. A gruesome murder in February 1822 in a nearby meadow was among the isolated attacks there.[57]

The distinguished visitor De Jouy, began his tour of the town in 1818 with the Catholic quarter of the Bourgades. His walk through the "unfortunate enclosure," which he described as "a true cesspool, the aspect of which is hardly as repulsive as the men who live in it," reminded him of what he had heard about the White Terror. Here still resided "a man twenty times designated by public horror as the leader of a horde of murderers." Walking farther, he was shown on the faubourg du Chemin d'Uzès "the house of a slaughterer of Protestants." His visit then led to the palace of justice and the Arena, and then the Cours Neuf, scenes of the massacres of 1815, the details of which the author wished to spare his readers.[58]

Frossard, a Protestant pastor, described the faubourgs as the "village" standing over the town.[59] Their houses presented "so miserable a sight that you would believe yourself transported to a large village." The faubourgs were poorer than even the poorest parts of the old town; half their streets were still unpaved in 1837, and when gas lighting came to the town in 1835, only one lamppost was placed in the faubourgs.[60] These faubourgs were even more crowded than those of Paris, Reims, and Limoges.[61] Their streets were wider than those of the central city and stretched out in relatively straight lines, cut at right angles by cross streets.[62]

The greatest concentration of silk workers—one-third—lived in the faubourgs beyond the Grand Cours in the quarter known as the Bourgades, between the prison, the barracks, and mont Duplan. Workers lived closely packed together, "leaning on the first hills of the *garrigue*," in the Enclos Rey, the rue de la Vierge, and the rue de la Garrigue. The church of Saint-Charles, on the faubourg side of the Grand Cours, was their parish.[63] The Bourgades, corresponding roughly to the Ancien fauborg des Prêcheurs, had doubled in size before the economic crisis of 1835–37. The subsequent loss of population, however modest, may help account for the ebbing of popular royalism. Whereas 24 percent of the population lived in the Bourgades in 1806, in 1851 it was 21 percent.[64] These eastern and northeastern faubourgs drew Catholic migrants from the regions of Avignon, Arles, and Lyon.

Out of a population of 37,000, in 1818 there were about 12,000 Protestants, constituting the majority of the bourgeoisie, especially merchants, wholesale and retail, many of whom lived within the limits of the old town. The Protestant faubourgs were those of the western—particularly La Placette—and northwestern sections. These neighborhoods reached toward the Protestant parts of the Gard, particularly the region of Alès, and the Cevennes beyond. The Protestant sections were confessionally less homogeneous than those of the Catholics. During the 1840s about 41 percent of the working-class population were Protestant. The fact that there were so many Protestant workers undercuts the thesis that class antagonism took on strictly confessional lines, with Catholic workers resisting Protestant employers,[65] although the economic power of the latter certainly helped intensify the religious division that already existed.

Religious solidarities were therefore reinforced by those of place of origin. Yet well into the first half of the century, most silk workers had been born in Nîmes. Migrants were most likely to come from the surrounding villages, the Cevennes, or the Mediterranean littoral.[66] Protestants finished their lives separately, as well: they had their own cemetery—"sad and solemn" in the opinion of its pastor, "the view dominated everywhere by arid hilltops and bare rocks, broken by fenced-in olive trees of a pale and powdery hue."[67]

The poorest Catholic workers lived in the Enclos Rey, northeast of the boulevard du Grand et Petit Cours. After 1837 the eastern faubourgs, and La Placette to the west, developed most rapidly; with the construction of the railway bridge and station in the mid-1840s, the districts to the south followed. To the west of the boulevard de la Comédie the Protestant faubourg of La Placette grew. This neighborhood, in which about a fifth of the textile workers lived, had the reputation for being the dirtiest quarter during the Empire and Restoration. Some of the houses were below street level and accumulated the debris of chrysalids, silkworm cocoons, and stagnant water. To the east, beyond the Petit Cours, another fifth of the textile workers made their homes on both sides of the chemin d'Uzès and on the north side of the chemin d'Avignon. Many workers also lived within the Grand Cours, in the old city.

Industrial work, however, remained largely associated with the faubourgs; "a semicircular ring" from west to east, but particularly reaching toward the hills to the north.[68] Here again we return to a familiar image: workers not only on the edge or periphery of a city but above it, "a threatening microcosm . . . from which the workers come down to the center to join in the famous brawls.' "[69]

Neighborhood Violence in Nîmes

Collective memory and neighborhood solidarities shaped violence into familiar spatial patterns in the faubourgs. Space in Nîmes became, in the words of André Cosson, "an important vector of political events: it is the bearer of revolutions."[70] Patterns of residence and political allegiance were closely tied to confessional allegiance.

Boulevards circling the town traced the path of the walls demolished in the 1780s. In the evenings, particularly on Sunday and Monday, the Nîmois made the *tour de la ville* before going to bed. It was on the boulevards here that some of the ugliest incidents between Catholics and Protestants began. The boulevards played a special role in the social, political, and cultural life of the town. Roughly forming a dividing line between those of some means and the impoverished (with the exception of the quai de la Fontaine), they nevertheless provided space for sociability. On Sundays, Mondays, and other evenings as well, "the exterior boulevards of town reverberate with shouts. The masses rush forward and stampede; such are their games and pleasures."[71]

The boulevards sometimes also served as a no-man's-land for brawls between members of rival *compagnonnages*. For example, on November 1, 1820, All Saints' Day, thirty members "gathered on the boulevard and were at the point of coming to blows." The first rocks had already been thrown when the police arrived to break up the fight, arresting two men. Later in the month another fight broke out in an *auberge;* the only person hurt was a rural guard who tried to intervene. In December 1822 the *compagnons* were at it again; after their gathering on the boulevards had been dispersed by the police, they "arranged a rendezvous in the countryside with the intention of fighting," but the police prevented them from doing so. Back on the boulevards, a *compagnon* was seriously wounded by a joiner wielding a tool of his trade.[72]

In February 1830 "a tumultuous gathering of *compagnons* of the Devoir this evening greatly alarmed the quarter of the boulevard du Petit Cours, with many serious injuries occurring." Police reports describe two similar bloody brawls in 1839. The police closed two *auberges,* each serving as the local mother house of a *compagnonnage,* as well as another café at the place de la Bouquerie. After the police had gained control of "these important points," they chased the workers away and prevented them from gathering on the boulevards or the adjacent cafés.[73]

Where the boulevards divided Protestant and Catholic quarters, they were hotly contested neutral space, including the northwestern part of the boulevard du Grand et Petit Cours and above all the pont or place de la Bouquerie, at the canal de la Fontaine, between the Grand Cours and the Comédie, which separated the Protestant faubourgs from the old town. There in 1815 and 1816 Catholic dandies armed with canes protruding knives or razors strolled provocatively, their ladies in tow, daring any Protestants to come near. Band of Catholic workers waited for Protestants emerging inopportunely from La Placette, or returning from the countryside or the Protestant villages in the Cevennes.[74]

On Sunday, September 14, 1823, groups formed on the square "according to differences of political opinions." It all began innocently enough on the edge of town: young men disrupting an excursion into the countryside by throwing grapes. The grapes became rocks, snatched from the Roman ruins; for the next few days, whistles summoned both forces to battle at the place de la Bouquerie and the adjoining boulevards.[75] During the Fête-Dieu in June 1828, when the procession of the parish of St.-Charles stopped at the place de la Bouquerie, several men entered a Protestant café on the quai de la Fontaine. It stood near the remnants of another café still referred to as the Café of the Island of Elba, once the headquarters of Protestant paramilitary groups, but destroyed by Catholics during the White Terror. During the subsequent fight, Catholics fled under the blows of billiard cues.[76]

The dramatic turns of political fate in 1815 and 1830 "marginalized" first Protestants, and then Catholics. During the Restoration the Ultras held the upper hand, with the Comte de Vogüe and other like-minded friends being returned to the Chamber of Deputies by the department's eligible voters, with the enthusiastic support of the unenfranchised Catholic workers.[77] Most eligible Protestant voters, on the other hand, were liberals, wanting freedom to practice their religion, civil equality, and protection from the Catholics.[78]

The revolution of 1830 reversed the situation.[79] While tricolor symbols and placards had appeared in some quarters, the poor suffered through the winter of 1829–30 in silence. Liberal *cercles* and cafés provided forums for opposition newspapers, brochures, and ideas. Protestants claimed the revolution of 1830 as their victory; ten year later it would bring their most eminent spokesman, François Guizot, to power.[80]

Now Protestant workers strolled confidently and provocatively on the place de la Bouquerie, tricolor emblems firmly in place. They strutted proudly on the boulevards, shoulders square, cockade pinned to their coats, daring Catholic royalists from the Bourgades or the Enclos Rey to appear with the white or green symbol of the Bourbons. Catholics had again become outsiders in some respects, even if they remained a solid majority.

Trouble lasted from the first days of the new regime into the following spring. On August 4 and 5, when Protestants—including women provocatively dancing the Farandole—surged to the Bouquerie, and Catholics into the Bourgades, the elites and clergy of both faiths worked hard to maintain order, so that shouts of "Long live peace! Lond live unity!" were heard. A Protestant pastor described, not without bias, how the defiant shout "Long live the king!"—meaning the recently departed Charles X—was considered a cry "among our people of pillage and murder." In the Bourgades—"this hideous faubourg of wretchedness and filth, the scene of royalist excesses"—supporters of the deposed monarch fell upon stray Protestants as the news of the king's flight arrived. Fear of another 1815 effected a temporary reconciliation of Protestants and Catholics, but only those of "the opulent class; one now sees people joined together who have not spoken a word to each other in fifteen years." More than 150 "heads of important families . . . and with the most opposite political views" gathered spontaneously. They spread through "all the quarters of town and particularly the faubourgs, which are the most worrisome."[81]

But the reconciliation did not last long. In mid-August Etienne Honoré, a Protestant, was killed on the Petit Cours as he ran toward the Bourgades to find his brother, having heard of a stabbing there. Both Catholic and Protestant services were interrupted by disruptive intruders. On August 30 Protestants gathered at the Bouquerie, armed with rifles, swords, pitchforks, and iron bars. The Catholics of the Bourgades readied their guns, and early in the afternoon began to assemble at a windmill north of the city, with the white Bourbon flag unfurled. They attacked Protestants in a rural tavern, while Protestants chased Catholics through the vineyards in the part of the periphery under their control. Troops could not prevent the bloody fighting that followed; six Protestants were killed and twenty-eight wounded, and two Catholics killed and six wounded (probably more, as the latter hauled their own back to the Bourgades). That night, Protestants pillaged several gun shops and at dawn the next day began gathering at the Bouquerie, reinforced by perhaps as many as 1,500 men from rural villages in the Vaunage. This force spontaneously formed "national guard" camped at the Arena, anticipating an attack by Catholic forces from the villages to the west.

Yet the expected civil war did not materialize, despite incidents of varying seriousness, including devastation of the gardens of Protestants on the edge of the town by Catholics, the removal of the tricolor emblem at the *octroi,* and rumors of "women in rags . . . going through the streets dancing the farandole" in the Bourgades on September 4. Troops restored some degree of order, and the new prefect ordered away the impromptu "national guard" units from the villages of the Vaunage, after allowing them to make a triumphant *tour de la ville* in military formation.[82]

The worst was over. But in the months that followed, the "seditious shouts," provocations, and acts of violence reflected the same spatial patterns. Several families of the Bourgades and the Enclos Rey spent the night in their vineyards, fearing attack. Early in October a Corsican known as Bastian was stabbed to death. Here too, "politics played the largest part in this affair." The boulevard des Calquières was the scene of near clashes. Later in the month a rumor reached the Protestant quarters that a crowd had forced gendarmes to flee the Bourgades and the Enclos Rey. Protestant demonstrations and more fights followed, including a full-fledged duel.[83]

During the July Monarchy legitimists retained control of local political life, particularly when they allied with the small group of republicans, holding about half the seats on the municipal council and publishing a provocative Carlist newspaper.[84] The continued strength of popular royalism led to masquerades being banned during the 1831 carnival. Busts of the new royal family were smashed by those loyal to the old one.[85] On March 10, 1831, when the Catholics "from the poorest class" of the Bourgades learned that the mission cross was to be taken down, they gathered for several nights on the Grand Cours and the Esplanade, shouting "Long live the Cross! The Cross of Death! Long live Charles X!" Two days later a noisy crowd, largely women and children, gathered, some carrying wooden crosses. The women sang "canticles followed by dreadful vociferations." To one gendarme, "everything seemed to indicate preparation for a war of religion. There were no expressions of pain, rather of ferocity." Troops stood in formation near Saint-Charles and guarded the principal intersections of the boulevards. Three other crosses were also moved into the churches. As the first cross was taken down, someone set fire to the store of a man who had been burned out in 1815. The silence of the church bells the next day, Sunday, protested the removal of the crosses. Subsequent incidents included the burning of a Protestant's country house, a stabbing, and a rock fight on the Cours-Neuf. As a large crowd of both faiths watched, François Bigot, a former member of Trestaillon's band, took advantage of the melee to fire a shot at a Protestant.[86]

In August 1832 several days of violence occurred in the quarter of Cours-Neuf, where Protestants and Catholics both lived. Twenty people were subsequently placed on trial—ten of each faith—with the legitimists accused of forming an association of "evildoers" that devastated the property of Protestants in the neighborhood. In revenge, Protestants attacked a mill where their enemies sometimes met; its owner barely escaped with his life. A gang of Protestants beat a Catholic, shouting "Assassin of 1815!"—which was before their victim, age sixteen, had been born. Police whisked the boy to safety only by pretending to arrest him. Similar incidents continued for a week.[87]

In June 1833, green and white became the colors of the day, as the parishioners of Saint-Charles celebrated their new church bells. Protestants ventured into the Bourgades to insult their enemies, but the day passed without serious trouble. The next month, legitimists marked the festival of "Henry V" by shattering the windows of a Protestant café on the chemin de Montpellier. While the Bourgades celebrated, their antagonists seethed. Then on July 20 two legitimists were wounded, one critically, after straying into the Protestant quarter of the chemin de Montpellier. Rock and fist fights continued, some of them started by Protestants who were unhappy that the municipality had limited celebrations of the July Revolution, while the prefect had seemed to tolerate boisterous Catholic proclamations of loyalty to the pretender.[88]

In 1847 what turned out to be the last official anniversary of the revolution of 1830 demonstrated that the old hatreds were still alive. Protestants provocatively celebrated the fall of the Bourbons in festivities virtually ignored in most French cities after the mid-1830s. Young Protestants who arrived in the Bourgades singing the "Marseillaise" were greeted with a shower of stones. On July 30 and 31, Catholics and Protestants marched from their respective faubourgs to confront each other at the Bouquerie. On August 1 three warnings were required before the two hostile crowds dispersed; the Catholics refused to back down until the departure of their adversaries, who taunted them with republican songs.[89]

The revolution of 1848 and the Second Republic in Nîmes and the Gard—the subject of several studies—continued these familiar patterns of confessional, political, and spatial rivalry. In his thesis on the origins of republicanism in the Gard, Raymond Huard discusses the rivalry between royalism and democratic socialism. Republicans were drawn in small numbers from the petite bourgeoisie "recently risen from the people" and the ranks of the *artisanat.*"[90] The political clubs created in 1848 became "the privileged place of quasi-direct democracy," essential in the evolution of nineteenth-century republicanism. Yet despite well-organized and well-attended political banquets and the success of the Club des Travailleurs in familiarizing some workers with concrete aspects of the socialist vision, "the mental universe of the legitimist workers remained impenetrable to republican propaganda."[91] The ideas of the utopian socialists had only been weakly implanted in Nîmes.[92]

Yet there were certain signs of radicalization, beginning with the acceptance of the "right to work" in the context of specific demands of workers. In October 1848 the Société des Travailleurs attempted to form a producers' cooperative of three hundred workers in the building trades, a number that grew to nine hundred, offering what Huard calls "a relatively coherent image of socialism."[93] Protestant workers followed the radical republicanism and democratic socialism of some of the Protestant elite. Protestant mutual aid societies paralleled Catholic religious associations. Old hatreds and neighborhood solidarities probably remained more important than ideology.

After the Protestant and Catholic faubourgs celebrated the fall of the July Monarchy, they turned on each other again.[94] On March 20 a young legitimist stabbed a Protestant; a magistrate subsequently faced threats for having imprisoned the man.[95] A reenactment of the bloodbath of 1815 yet again seemed possible at the time of the legislative elections; on April 27 a crowd of working-class legitimists from the Bourgades and the Enclos Rey taunted the habitués of the Café Gibelin. There was an exchange of shots; "within an hour . . . both communities were armed and facing each other across barricades thrown up hastily at either corner of the Place de la Bouquerie." Three Catholics were dead by nightfall.[96]

In June, after a Catholic was attacked while crossing the place de la Bouquerie, Catholics and Protestants "as if by common consent, retired and set up sniper positions on the rising ground on either side of the main road to Alès,'' which led to the square.[97] More disturbances occurred in August, when the boulevards were ''literally encumbered by groups of people talking together . . . the cafés and the boulevards were overflowing with people.'' At the place de la Bouquerie, near the liberty tree planted in honor of the Republic, shouts for Napoleon and against the legitimists and a Catholic deputy mayor echoed. Yet in all, there was far less violence than that which had followed the revolution of 1830, and nothing like that of 1815–16.[98]

Protestant neighborhoods remained the bastion of the left. The republican clubs were in the western part of town, near the Fountain or in La Placette, in the predominantly Protestant quarters. The most radical club, the one founded by Germain Encontre, met in his bookstore on the rue Gretry near La Placette. Formerly the Club de la Fraternité, it bested the more moderate Club Gibelin, which had met in the café on the place de la Bouquerie. The Club Martin *cadet,* near the Fountain, renamed the Cercle des Travailleurs in 1849, became the center of socialist organization in the Gard.[99] Montagnard electoral ballots were distributed from a café in La Placette, among other places.[100] In Nîmes, politics and sociability mixed with the ease of absinthe and water.

In September 1848 cockades—red or white (or sometimes green)—seemed more than ever ''the subject of every conversation.'' Socialists and royalists planned provocations, as women and girls prepared corsages and other sartorial accouterments in anticipation of aggressive promenades on the Esplanade, La Plateforme, the quai de la Fontaine, and the boulevards. Royalists wore the fleur-de-lis, sometimes embroidered with the figure of Christ. The women of La Placette planned to go to the Esplanade coiffed in hats with red ribbons, while their men stood ready to fight anyone who made unflattering remarks. When the police intervened to force someone to remove such provocative symbols, a large crowd quickly gathered, either to note the response of the police (traditionally accused of favoring one party or the other), to cheer, or to jeer.[101]

The boulevards, the place de la Bouquerie, and the Esplanade thus remained neutral spaces open to symbolic conquest by one faction or the other. Against a backdrop of red flags, red caps, and other symbols of '93, a socialist banquet on October 30, 1848, was held behind the Protestant cemetery, after the prefect had refused to allow it to be held at La Plateforme. Leaving the banquet, several hundred participants formed a column, hoping to make the ritual, triumphal walk around the boulevards. Led by several trumpeters from the national guard, with banners and flags, and shouting praise for Barbès, Raspail, and Robespierre, they were stopped at the *octroi* by troops. The officers told them that banners and flags were illegal, ''not meeting the regulations,'' and that such a procession could bring civil war. Soldiers fixed bayonets, but the column, its numbers now swollen ''by all the party of Protestants,'' had briskly moved past the outnumbered soldiers, stopping at the Bouquerie to insult prefect, police, and gendarmes before dispersing. In the Bourgades more than six hundred Catholic workers were massed to prevent any attempted incursion into their neighborhood.[102]

The neighborhood character of popular royalism also remained strong, centered in the Catholic Bourgades and Enclos Rey.[103] Legitimists utilized their associations created in the July Monarchy to perpetuate vertical solidarities of patronage that characterized popular royalism.[104] The Club Central des Ouvriers, founded after the Revolution, built upon the hostility of Catholic workers toward the Protestant bourgeoisie, particularly the manufacturers. The Sentinelle, established in June 1848, proclaimed itself a society "of Catholic fraternity." Other associations, notably the Cercle du Droit National, subsequently carried the cause of "royalist democracy" in Nîmes and the Gard, as legitimists attempted to maintain the allegiance of workers by promising them that a restored monarchy would bring them better economic conditions. The royalists retained control of the national guard.[105]

Legitimist festivals reinforced religious, political, and neighborhood solidarities. On Ascension day in May 1849 the Bourgades came alive with the usual talk of vengeance and provocative revelry, including the farandole and the erection of a royalist arch of triumph. The Protestant workers in turn were ready, announcing that if the Catholics came to challenge them, "they would be caned like dogs." The police closed off the boulevard Saint-Antoine and the chemin de Montpellier to keep the two sides apart.[106]

The workers of the Bourgades joined the elite in the celebrations of the feast day of Saint Henri—and therefore that of the pretender Henry V—each July. The Enclos Rey celebrated their holiday with ostentatious verve in 1850. Catholic workers longed to settle old scores with Protestants, "to fall upon the rich who dismissed Catholic workers." Wealthy legitimists attended Mass and then banqueted at the Croix de Fer near the *octroi*. The legitimist leader Comte H. de Lourdoueix was welcomed by "a young girl of eight to ten years, entirely dressed in white, wearing a straw hat, decorated by three large white cockades." Then Lourdoueix and his colleagues returned to the faubourg stronghold of legitimism, which became almost impassable because of the crowd shouting against the Republic.[107]

Catholics favored their own places of leisure outside town, including the tour de l'Evêque, where they sang royalist songs. The Protestants went beyond the barriers of their own quarters, or beyond the Esplanade.[108] A police report of September 1848 suggests division by religion as well. The police told two prostitutes move their business from the old city to the peripheral neighborhoods, one to the faubourg Cours-Neuf, the other to the faubourg d'Uzès.[109]

The government, that powerful third force between *rouges* and *blancs,* sought to dismantle the organizational networks of both, beginning with the left. By the elections of May 1849, all the clubs had been closed; the Club Martin *cadet* became little more than a regular gathering of political militants in the café of that name.[110] The Société des Amis Réunis, founded in October 1850, lasted only a few weeks, its statutes being confiscated and its meetings banned.[111]

The leftist Cercle des Travailleurs, with more than a hundred members, lasted until November 1850, when the so-called "Plot of Lyon," allegedly organized by Alphonse Gent, launched another wave of police action. Its members were later accused of participating in the secret Nouvelle Montagne.[112] The Montagnards retreated into allegedly nonpolitical associations.[113] On November 16, 1850, the *commissaire central* closed and sealed the doors of the Club Martin *cadet* at La

Plateforme, and the Cercle des Amis Réunis at 23 rue Saint-Paul.[114] The former transformed itself into a mutual aid society, in the hope of avoiding prosecution. Some of its members joined a club on the chemin de Sauve, again on the Protestant side of Nîmes, or the one on the rue Gretry. Montagnards kept meeting in cafés, like the one that had housed the Cercle des Travailleurs, or that of the Montagnard Broussel on the Cours-Neuf.[115] For the police compiling a file on socialists, information received from the cafés of the boulevards was essential, including that of the Café Clavel on the boulevard Saint-Antoine.[116]

Royalist organizations fared only slightly better. Alizier (led by Lourdoueix) and Le Droit National were closed down. Three more royalist organizations followed in July 1851, including Cercle de la Concorde, above the Café Guibal on the boulevard du Petit Cours, its meeting place adorned with paintings or drawings of Queen Marie-Thérèse, the Comtesse de Chambord, and La Rochejacquelein and Lourdoueix.[117]

In the meantime the Montagnards had expanded their influence in the department from Nîmes and other towns. They won over much of the peasantry in the Protestant west of the Gard with a political program focusing on specific economic issues, attacking a recent rise to two francs in the cost of hunting permits, protesting the government's prohibition of bullfights, and supporting the cause of the indebted rural poor. Celebrations in 1851 of the anniversary of the February Revolution brought police intervention at La Placette and on the Cours-Neuf, while a "ball of democrats" went on all night in a tavern on the rue de l'Embarcadère.[118] In March a rumor had it that the Montagnards of Saint-Césaire, just to the southwest, were going to dance the farandole on the day of the military lottery. They promenaded about the Cours-Neuf and La Placette wearing red belts and ties.[119] In La Placette and on the Cours-Neuf, too, the anniversary of the proclamation of the Republic was celebrated with verve in May.[120]

Late in 1851, officials helped orchestrate a mood of social fear, alleging popular preoccupation with "the coming distribution of public wealth, of the plundering of the rich for the benefit of the poor," and rumors of hushed gatherings of the secret societies, particularly in the wake of the insurrection in Largentière in southern Ardèche.[121] The coup d'état of December 2 led to an attempted defense of the Republic in the Gard. Confronted by a ready military force and the unlikely support of the legitimist-dominated national guard, a second, countermanding order went out, as a small group of Montagnard insurgents was dispersed on the road from Alais (Alès) fifteen kilometers from Nîmes.[122]

As elsewhere, a fairly clear separation had occurred between the radical bourgeoisie and "those revolutionaries who emerged from the people." The unwillingness of the Protestants, whose legalism characterized radicalism in Nîmes during the Second Republic, to commit themselves to insurrection, combined with intimidating military measures, prevented serious resistance to the coup d'état.[123]

Huard suggests that the brawls between the faubourgs ebbed during the Second Empire, because the state represented a neutral third party, in constrast to the Restoration and the July Monarchy. The Orleanist bourgeoisie rallied quickly to Louis Napoleon. Yet the confessional and neighborhood division within political life in Nîmes survived. Leslie Moch characterizes "most Catholic neighborhoods as the most conservative and the Protestant neighborhoods as the most liberal at the turn of the century." In the legislative election of May 1906 the socialist candidate, François Fournier, won 70 percent of the vote in La Fontaine and La Placette quarters, on the southwest and west side of the old city. The Enclos Rey supported the nationalist candidates; there Fournier won but 16 percent of the vote. The results of the election brought throngs into the streets for the traditional triumphant march around the boulevards, while the supporters of the defeated nationalist candidate Ménard consoled themselves in the southeastern neighborhoods. *Le Petit Midi* described the electoral victory of Fournier as "the victory of La Placette." True to tradition, fights broke out between the two sides.[124]

In Nîmes too, the urban periphery emerged as the locus of social and political conflict. The people of the faubourgs added new chapters to the collective memory of neighborhood rivalry, struggle, and violence. Precocious faubourgs and neighborhood solidarities contributed to the political awakening of ordinary people. Unlike Reims, the faubourgs of which challenged the center for political power, the Catholic and Protestant faubourgs of Nîmes, long since integrated into the city economically, each with ties of religion and also probably of economic patronage to wealthy people of their own confession in the center, fought each other. The waxing and waning of their respective political fortunes in the decades of revolution alternately marginalized them, at least in a political sense. As in Perpignan, both reds and whites ultimately lost out to that most powerful third party, the Bonapartist state.

7

Reims and the Challenge of Its Industrial Faubourgs

Reims had a long tradition as a major ecclesiastical and commercial center, and had gained a certain renown for the bubbling white wine named after the region of Champagne. But more recently it had become known for the manufacture of textiles, particularly woolens. Reims experienced one of the greatest rates of population growth of French cities during the first half of the nineteenth century. The urban experience of that century was most vividly seen in the new spaces of the industrial periphery, the locus of industry and working-class organization, pitting, in sharp contrast to Nîmes, faubourg against central city.

Preparations were well under way for the coronation of Charles X in Reims on May 30, 1825. Great care had been taken to duplicate, as much as possible, the ceremony in which the Capetian kings had been anointed in the cathedral of Notre-Dame, which towers over Champagne's largest city. Six triumphal arches had been erected for the occasion. It had been almost fifty years since a monarch had been crowned in France; the subsequent period had not been a happy one for the Bourbons. Louvel's murder in 1820 of the heir to the throne, the Duc de Berri, was on the minds of those responsible for the elaborate security precautions for several days of festivities. Plots against the monarchy by Carbonari and military conspirators who longed for the time of Napoleon—the "Usurper," as the Bourbons called him—had been discovered several years earlier in the Loire country and the capital. Troops, gendarmes, and police *commissaires* and their agents from all over the North of France poured into Reims.

The office of the *haute police* in Paris, under the direction of the prefect of police, coordinated the security operations. But the prefect of the Marne knew that security for the coronation and the prevention of "all crimes or disorders that could trouble the august ceremony" were his personal responsibility. The minister of the interior warned him to go through the lists of former convicts and known Bonapartists in the North of France. But in particular, the prefect was to watch "the working class, in general ill-disposed." Reims was becoming a working-class town. It was not the common criminals of the lower classes who were worrisome: indeed, less than a week before the ceremony, Charles had pardoned forty-seven of them. The "bad spirit" of ordinary workers required special attention.[1]

The elaborate coronation went smoothly, combining, in the opinion of the event's official historian, medieval pageantry and nineteenth-century luxury. The new king was anointed with holy oil from the same container provided by a dove for the baptism of Clovis by Saint Remi in 496. It had been kept, according to legend, in the good saint's basilica, that magnificent structure that so gracefully witnesses the evolution from Romanesque to Gothic architecture. Saint-Remi stands on the southeastern edge of Reims, a considerable distance from the cathedral and the place Royale in the central city. Charles may or may not have noticed in the shadow of Saint-Remi the small, crowded houses, most of whose occupants were textile workers, that had come to form the quarter of Fléchambault.

Twenty-two years later, a crowd at the town hall acclaimed the provisional municipal government after the February Revolution of 1848. Without a garrison and with the gendarmerie busy elsewhere in the department, not even the addition of several socialists to the short-lived provisional municipal administration could stop the outbreak of popular exasperation that quickly followed. On February 25, during a demonstration calling for the replacement of the municipal government, a crowd of workers confronted the fixed bayonets of the national guard, which had arrived "to drive it back toward the high quarters of Saint-Remi and Fléchambault." Retreating to the latter, angry workers carefully chose their target, the factory of Félix Croutelle, where power looms had first been set up in 1838, and set fire to it.[2] Back in town, workers broke streetlights, threatened a convent, disarmed several guardsmen, and pillaged a grain merchant's store. Finally, "the agitators were pushed back, bayonets in their ribs, to the ramparts, which they tumbled over to scatter rapidly into the countryside." A semblance of order restored, the bourgeois republicans planted a liberty tree not far from the center of town on the allée near the porte de Mars, where a mission cross had stood between 1821 and the revolution of 1830. In the upper town not long afterward, four thousand workers celebrated the dramatic events with a banquet on the rue Saint-Nicaise in the heart of the proletarian third arrondissement. But in Reims too, the unity of citizens after the February Revolution was precarious, at best. Differences between two conceptions of the Republic were reflected there and would be accentuated by the contrasts between center and periphery.

Between the coronation of Charles X and the coup d'état of Louis Napoleon Bonaparte, Reims emerged as an industrial city, its workers largely concentrated in its upper town. Textile workers went out on strike in the 1830s, and challenged the Reims elite for power after the revolution of 1848. To the bourgeoisie, the "dangerous and laboring classes" about whom one heard so much from Paris were massed in the upper town.

The working-class challenge did not come from the densely packed city center, chronically inundated by waves of beggars—outcasts—nor from artisans from the traditionally militant trades. The woolens workers of the rue and faubourg Fléchambault, the faubourg de Cérès, and others on the city's edge threatened the wealthy of the place Royale and the elegant quarters near the cathedral.

The coronation ceremony of 1825 emphatically proclaimed the restored

View of Reims in 1844. (Bibliothèque Nationale)

Bourbon monarchy's attempt to reestablish the baroque piety that was assumed in retrospect to have characterized the ancien régime. Charles prostrated himself before the archbishop of Reims, a gesture bound to offend even many uncritical royalists. The anointed king promised, "all that I will do for religion, I will be doing for the good of my people." Before going to pray in Saint-Remi, Charles stopped at the chapel of Saint-Marcoul, where he took holy water provided by the *grand aumônier* and entered the hall of Saint-Agnes. With a royal gesture unseen in France for centuries, he reached out to offer the sick and crippled the "healing touch" of the kings of France. The poet Béranger, eloquent enemy of the restored Bourbons, would mock this attempt to turn the clock far back with blistering satire in "The Coronation of Charles the Simple."[3]

More than tradition might have dictated the choice of Reims for such a coronation. The city had long been one of France's most prominent ecclesiastical centers. More than fifty crosses stood at intersections and on public squares. At the time of the Revolution, almost a thousand clerics were supported by the city's many churches and convents.[4] The Church remained the city's largest property owner. The clergy, particularly the archbishop, benefited from tax revenues on grain and provided six members of the town council. Resentment against the Church was such that nobles, woolens manufacturers (*fabricants*), and wealthy merchants, instead of battling each other, coalesced against the Reims's most powerful order in the first years of the Revolution. This, in turn, may have defused potential popular hostility against the wealthy.[5]

Reims, like Poitiers, never recovered the status it enjoyed during the ancien régime. In 1790 it lost the struggle with Châlons-sur-Marne for the departmental seat of the Marne. It was small consolation that it became—and still is—France's largest subprefecture and that it received the departmental civil and criminal tribunal. Châlons, which had been the *généralité* of Champagne, won the prize by virtue of its location in the center of the department on the main road to the east from Paris—which is why Louis XVI and the royal family stopped there briefly in June 1791, while the horses of their coach were changed in such great haste.[6]

The Church lost badly during the revolutionary period. In 1789 there had been fourteen parishes in Reims; after the Revolution there were but four: the cathedral of Notre-Dame; Saint-Remi, not more than three hundred meters away; Saint-Maurice, closer to the center; and Saint-Jacques, west of the cathedral. Twenty-nine churches and chapels had been auctioned off as *biens nationaux*. Many were torn down, including the basilicas of Saint-Timothée and Saint-Hilaire, and several churches dating back to the time of Clovis. Convents and abbeys enjoyed a better fate; their size and the cost of building identical new structures made them attractive to the state and to merchants. The abbey of Saint-Remi became the hôtel-Dieu, while the hospital became the convent of the Jacobins, the meeting place for the Société Populaire in 1791–93. Textile manufacturers transformed the convents of the Capucins, Clarisses, and Carmelites into warehouses and workshops. La Veuve Cliquot champagne was stored in the old church of the Temple inside the northern rampart. The congregations of Notre-Dame and the Visitation returned at the beginning of the Restoration to find that their convents had been sold.[7]

In the same year as the coronation of Charles X, Mayor Ruinart wrote to protest that Reims had been dropped from the list of *bonnes villes* by the king, a list that included such lesser lights as Besançon, Bourges, Grenoble, even Clermont. "No Frenchmen," the mayor wrote, "can be unaware that Reims is one of the oldest towns in France . . . known for its unrelenting attachment to the august family of the Bourbons." This seemed an easy case to make. After the Hundred Days, the prefect and mayor appointed by Louis XVIII had eagerly eliminated remaining symbols of the Revolution. The municipality had repaired cherished statues of the kings, smashed by "the storms of the Revolution," so they could be "exhibited once again for public admiration." A statue of Louis XV was reinstalled in 1818. Reims had done faithful penance for the sins of revolution.[8]

Early in 1821 the mission had come to Reims: a team of fifteen priests preaching dramatic interpretations of the glories of heaven and the anguish of hell. Communicants renewed their baptismal vows, and were urged to offer "honorable amends to expiate the outrages suffered by the Church" during the revolutionary era. After six weeks, the missions culminated on February 23. A giant cross, a veritable calvary with a base weighing more than seven thousand pounds, was built from materials from the church of Saint-Nicaise and from a statue of Louis XV, both of which had fallen to the Revolution. A large team of strong horses hauled the cross to one of the tree-lined walkways beyond the porte Mars. So many faithful marched in the procession that those at the head of the cortege arrived before those at the end had left the cathedral.[9]

Like the coronation four years later, the procession and ceremony would have been perfect, had it not been for the disruption caused by some workers who joined a merchant's son shouting against the mission. One of the workers was convicted of a sacrilege committed inside the church of Saint-Remi. He and the other workers were believed to reside in the poor quarter of Fléchambault, just inside the *octroi* barrier.[10] Arrests that month included a certain Bognet who, in the company of another man, had insulted a missionary in the church of Saint-Jacques. Sebastien Rollin, living in the other large workers' quarter, the faubourg de Cérès, on the northeastern edge of Reims, likewise faced prosecution "for having publicly made insulting and seditious remarks at the foot of the calvary."[11]

The contrast between Reims's ancient center, home of the most prosperous manufacturers, and its expanding, plebeian periphery was already apparent in the last decades of the ancien régime. Roman and medieval Reims comprised the central neighborhoods, including the place Royale, the town hall, the cathedral, and the grain market. These were the wealthiest districts, served by most of the city's domestics. The planning for the coronation had provided impetus and money for repairing damage to the cathedral and Saint-Remi, for embellishing the place Royale and rebuilding the ancient town hall, where the municipality greeted the new king. In anticipation of his coronation, Charles contributed sixty thousand francs to laying out a new street that would directly link the place Royale to the town hall.[12]

Relatively few textile workers resided in the privileged central quarters. They had settled on the periphery, particularly in the faubourgs of Cérès and Fléchambault, where life was cheaper. At the beginning of the Revolution, it was from the upper town that the textile workers of Reims "fell on the city hall, where they invaded the meeting of 'bourgeois' citizens. . . . in this way the unemployed and propertyless made their political voices heard." The section of Fléchambault became a Montagnard section, also called "Sans-Culotterie." During the Empire, Jean-Nicholas Ponsardin, who became mayor in 1809, earned the reputation of a "worthy person of wealth" because he distributed food "to the poor of the faubourgs." Napoleon's sudden return to France provoked great anxiety in Reims. But the women of the quarter of Saint-Remi expressed their joy, angered by the harsh treatment meted out to the faubourgs by the Russian cossacks defending the restored Bourbon monarch.[13]

Reims Under the *Monarchie Censitaire*

Reims had long been renowned for the wines of Champagne. Vineyards surrounded the city on all sides. In 1828 a hundred wholesale wine merchants were storing wine in the vast chalky caves on the edge of town.[14] Yet even more so, Reims's reputation during the Restoration rested on its woolens. The industry stretched into the hinterland. Hand-spinning not only persisted but prospered. The industrial revolution in many parts of France was, after all, largely the intensification of forms of industry that had long existed. Merchant capitalists found a ready work force in the hinterland, particularly between the Vesle and Suippe rivers north and northeast of the city. The production of merino woolens had begun in

1. faubourg de Laon
2. faubourg de Cérès
3. faubourg de Fléchambault
4. faubourg de Vesle
5. The Upper Town (*la haute ville*)

a. Canal de l'Aisne
b. Town Hall
c. Place Royale
d. Cathedral of Notre-Dame
e. rue du Barbatre

f. place Saint-Nicaise
g. Saint-Remi
h. Hôtel Dieu
i. Porte Dieu-Lumière
j. Vesle River

Reims in 1844. (Bibliothèque Nationale)

Reims, but gradually moved into the countryside during the Restoration, reaching into the Ardennes.

An officer conducting a military survey in 1828 of the area from Reims to the hamlet of Les Petites Loges, almost halfway to Châlons-sur-Marne to the southeast, noted that even in the richest farmland supplying grain and cattle for the Reims market, "there are few rural communes that do not include several weavers and combers working for the manufacturers of Reims." Paunay, just above the Vesle, produced grain, but its population also included weavers and combers. The 20 weavers of Wez turned out 21,000 meters each year. In the villages of Verzenay and Verzy on the edge of the montagne de Reims, one found 15 and 20 weavers and combers, respectively. Approaching Reims, there were 12 looms in Courmelois, a hamlet of 124 people, and 28 weavers and combers in Cormontreuil, just beyond the Reims *octroi*. Twelve weavers (and one manufacturer) lived in Sillery, but the 50 looms found in that commune of 440, and their annual production of 54,000 meters, suggests that another 30 or so wove part-time. It was the same in Puisieulx, Taissy, Beaumont, Sept-Saulx, and Villers-Marmery. Remuneration for cottage industry was sufficiently attractive (1.50 to 2.50 francs a day) that property owners found it difficult to find workers for the fields. Despite competition from British and Parisian producers, the closing of the Dutch and Belgian markets, and the decline in demand for cashmere and other products, woolens manufacturing remained the principal source of wealth, offering a livelihood, however modest, for workers in the faubourgs of Reims and in the countryside, where most spinning continued to be done.[15]

Mechanical spinning had been introduced in 1807, first on the small rivers on the edge of town, and then gradually in the city. In the year X, 384 woolens manufacturers or, more properly speaking, merchant capitalists, lived in Reims. A few of them had already begun to bring their workers into large workshops, well before mechanization necessitated such a change as a means of more efficiently organizing and overseeing production.[16] The first mechanical spinning factory started up in 1812. During the Restoration, one enterprising manufacturer began to produce cloth called "novelties" (*nouveautés*), a combination of cheaper cotton warp yarns and weft wool (*circassiennes*). Soon another entrepreneur had developed *napolitaines*, carded-wool cloth made from yarn spun by machine, which became "the merino cloth of the middle classes." These new products and the traditional production of merinos and flannels embellished Reims's reputation and enriched its manufacturers.[17]

Yet the production of textiles declined dramatically from 18 million francs in 1808 and about 11 million early in the Restoration to 6 million in 1820. English goods and high Spanish and Lombard customs duties hurt the woolens industry; so did the competition of inexpensive cotton clothes, what the subprefect denounced as "a type of organized brigandage," taking advantage of government policies that seemed to favor cotton over wool.[18]

Mechanization came to the rescue, along with the greatly increased production of *nouveautés*. By 1828 there were 181 spinning workshops in Reims, most powered by steam engines; two-thirds of the 1,250,000 kilograms of wool was spun by machine. By 1835 only a handful of the 45 spinning mills in Reims were not mechanized. One of Reims's most innovative manufacturers, Croutelle, president of the Société Industrielle of Reims, developed the spinning of shorter wool fibers that he produced for less in his mechanized factory on the Vesle river at the end of the faubourg Fléchambault.[19] He set up mechanical looms in 1838, and two years later first produced cloth completely fabricated in one location. By 1844 Croutelle's factory housed 100 looms.[20]

Industrial concentration continued: 156 out of 238 woolens manufacturers employed more than 100 workers, some in workshops, some at home. During the 1840s the textile industry became increasingly mechanized; most of Reims's 3,000 spinners, men and women, worked in factories, while some 7,500 wove in smaller shops.[21] During the 1840s the woolens industry moved increasingly beyond its traditional manufacture of flannels, cashmeres, and merinos to the production of *nouveautés* of wool and a mixture of wool and cotton.

In 1846 Reims's mayor estimated the total number of woolens workers at 15,000, compared with about 4,500 people working in other crafts and industries.[22] With the implosion of work to the edge of the city, the population of Reims doubled between 1820 and 1850. The fields within the southern and southeastern ramparts disappeared. Workers filled the quarters of Barbatre and Saint-Maurice on the south side, and swelled the population of the faubourgs: "a subproletariat of carders and hand-spinners, brought together in shops, overseen by foremen who negotiate with the merchant manufacturers." Of 125 workshops, two-thirds were within the shadow of Saint-Remi.[23]

The majority of textile workers thus resided in the upper town, the third arrondissement, which comprised about forty percent of the territory of Reims. It included the quarters of Saint-Maurice, Saint-Nicaise, and of the rue and faubourg

Entrance to Reims by the pont de Vesle in 1850. (Roger-Viollet)

of Fléchambault, the latter lying beyond the old walls. Although remnants of the fifteenth-century ramparts remained until 1880, the demolition in 1840 of the walls separating the town from the Vesle river, to facilitate the construction of a canal linking the Aisne to the Marne, contributed to the expansion of Reims into the surrounding countryside.[24] The proletarian neighborhoods and streets seemed a world away from the place Royale and quarters near the cathedral, symbols not only of the previous country, but of the wealth of the woolens manufacturers. Other faubourgs also were the locus of woolens work, particularly the faubourg de Cérès, north of the Esplanade de Cérès, the smaller faubourgs of Rethel and Laon, and the quarter of Jard, where blankets were produced.

Saint-Remi loomed over the delapidated buildings of the upper town and the adjacent Hôtel-Dieu, the latter a monument to the misery of the inhabitants of these quarters.[25] These neighborhoods were noteworthy for a homogeneity of social composition probably unmatched in all of France. There were hardly any people of means living anywhere in this district in 1841, not a single banker, wholesale merchant, or lawyer, and extraordinarily few rentiers or other property owners. There were no streets in the third arrondissement in which woolens workers were not the majority of residents. Only a handful of domestics lived in the upper town, and most of these, more than likely, worked during the day for families of means in the central town.[26]

For example, on the rue Dieu-Lumière, which led to the gate of the same name, of 122 heads of household, there were 41 male or female weavers and another 17 doing other jobs in the industry. Heads of household living on the rue du Moulin included 35 weavers, 28 spinners, 20 day laborers, almost certainly employed in the industry, 7 winders, 5 combers, 6 other woolens workers, and 21 other textile workers (shearers, winders, warpers, thread-twisters), for a total of 119; only 60 heads of household were not textile workers, 20 of them being gardeners. The single rentier may have felt increasingly out of place in the world of industrial work.

The long rue du Barbatre, a continuation of the rue Neuve, formed the main artery from the lower town. More than 90 percent of the heads of household living on the street and its adjacent courtyards were workers (particularly its upper reaches, farthest from the center of town, with 71 weavers, 46 day laborers, 15 winders, 16 wefters, 21 spinners, 14 combers, and a variety of pinmakers, scourers, and other woolens workers). On this long proletarian artery there were but 7 rentiers, 1 property owner, and 1 domestic, and these relatively close to the center of Reims. It was the same for the rue Fléchambault: 71 weavers, 23 spinners, 17 wefters, 15 day laborers, 5 combers. To take the example of a single building, at 33 rue Fléchambault lived André Gauvry, shearer, with his wife, a thread-winder, and three sons, one a comber, another a weaver, and the third, no age given, who was not working. In the same building lived 8 other heads of household whose occupations were working-class, and a ninth giving no profession. On the rue de Normandie 15 weavers, 9 combers, and 9 day laborers lived among 61 heads of household, not a single one of whom—with the possible, though unlikely, exception of a "musician"—was not working-class.

The social composition of other streets reveals the same patterns, including the impasse Chénia, the rue and cour des Quatre-Chats-Grignants, the rue Perdue, the rue and impasse Saint-Julien, the rue des Salines, the rue Bailla, the rue du Grand Cerf, the rue de l'Esquerre, the rue Neuve, the rue Ruisselet, the rue Tournebonneaux, the rue Saint-Jean Césaré, and the place Saint-Nicaise. The proportion of textile workers would certainly be even higher if other family members were counted, since households of artisans usually included at least one textile worker. What is surprising about this is not so much the large concentration of workers on the edge of Reims, but the remarkable homogeneity of the upper town.[27]

The Dangerous Classes: The Outcasts

During High Mass in the cathedral, the choir was sometimes overwhelmed by the "vociferations and continual shouts of the prisoners" in the jail, which practically leaned against Notre-Dame's ancient walls.[28] With its rate of population growth, Reims might well have represented a classic case of the uprooting hypothesis. The poor inundated the city, particularly during times of crisis, but indeed most of the time. A harvest failure could still push working-class families below the margin of survival. During the first nine months of 1820, several woolens manufacturers were forced out of business, while others cut back. The number of impoverished people coming from outside the city to beg increased noticeably. In 1820 these included Italian peddlers selling ink, cheap lithographs, or prints—anything they could—some trailing their families and animals behind them, many "covered with rags." When they had nothing to sell, or no one was buying, they begged. Sometimes the police led them out of town, but more often let them stay until they had accumulated enough money to move on to their next uncertain stop. This was the city's first reflex, with the support of the state: to expel beggar and vagabond— in short, anyone without a fixed residence.

In 1817 the prefect had forbidden the poor to beg outside their canton of residence. Gendarmes led away people like the Pole Joseph Larvenonski. In 1822 Larvenonski was arrested and imprisoned after having begged for several days. With a passport issued in Strasbourg, he had gone to Paris looking for work as a draper and, finding none, received a passport at the Russian embassy to return to Poland. He then fell sick, delaying his departure. Claiming to be unable to ask if he was on the road to Châlons, Larvenonski ended up in Reims, where someone probably told him he might find work.

In Reims he begged at the doors of the "finest commercial houses" with a note beginning, "Take this and read it," which related his sad story and asked for money and work. He did not do badly, since he stayed in a cabaret that took in poor lodgers. Indeed, he had the suspiciously large sum of forty francs when arrested, including several pieces of bullion. But Larvenonski also had frightened some people, perhaps because he could not speak French, and they complained to the police. Gendarmes escorted him back to the frontier at Strasbourg.[29] Despite being Polish—this was before the wave of refugees from the uprising against Russia reached France in the early 1830s—he was perfectly typical of the "professional stranger" who was part of the urban landscape in Reims and other places, begging in the doorways of the cathedral and of the homes of the wealthy of the central districts.

Even in good times there were more than 2,000 indigent families in Reims, about 6,000 people "of every age and sex," some temporarily unemployed, others unable to work. The city's reputation for charity was widely known and therefore attracted the poor of the region and beyond. About 8,000 people received some sort of assistance there each year. Saint-Remi remained the poorest parish. But even in Reims, as in Strasbourg, which probably was the grand champion of organized charity among French cities, the needs of the indigent, including "an infinity of beggars, organ grinders, and outsiders after something," far exceeded the resources of local charity.[30]

The city's charitable institutions did their best. The Bureau de Bienfaisance provided bread, flour, wood, and clothes in winter and distributed bouillon to the sick. It organized dances and theatrical performances for the benefit of the poor. The Bureau assisted from 4,500 to 5,500 indigents between 1834 and 1840; during the period 1830–34, the number ranged between 7,300 and 9,591. The appropriately named "Festival" association organized charitable pleasures during Mardi Gras.[31] The Société Maternelle, founded in 1810 by the Dames de Charité, helped 118 mothers during 1820, providing each with a layette and a little money for the first six months. But the funds allocated in the municipal budget, 10,000 to 12,000 francs, seemed to run out earlier with each passing year.[32]

There were other possibilities as well for the poor, however inadequate. The ancient Hôtel-Dieu could accommodate about 250 people at any one time; in 1820, more than 3,000 people received some sort of care there (291 died). The adjacent institution of Saint-Louis each year took in about 400 children less than twelve years of age. A small hospice for the mentally impaired had been moved to the peripheral Hôtel-Dieu in the old abbey of Saint-Remi. The Hôpital Général housed more than 300 indigents, mostly the elderly who had resided in Reims for some time, and children. In the hospice Saint-Marcour, the sisters of the Order of Béguines looked after those diagnosed as having scrofula, the disease that the newly crowned kings of France had tried to cure with their "healing touch." In 1820 sixty of them awaited some sort of miracle. In the same year the municipal council voted to reestablish the municipal pawnshop that had disappeared with the Revolution. Charity workshops, however, could employ only about 150 men, planting trees and looking after roads and paths in the spring and summer and clearing snow and ice in the winter.[33]

The parishes provided another source of charity. The Dames de l'Oeuvre de la Miséricorde, founded in 1837 by the bishop, tried to coordinate aid given within each parish, compiling information, including attendance at Sunday Mass, on each family applying for assistance. Reims's five parishes—Saint-André had recently been created in the faubourg de Cérès—assisted 2,320 families and single indigents over a three-year period during the July Monarchy.

There were three other religious establishments of charity. The Dames de la Compassion on the rue de la Vignette had arrived in 1834 to help the indigent sick. But the mayor considered their operation more of a business enterprise than a charity; since they took in paying apprentices and sold the lingerie they produced.

The Maison de Bethléem cared for foundlings sent by the Hôtel-Dieu and other children placed there by their parents or charitable adults who could pay 150 francs per year. With 46 young borders, including 3 child "criminals" in 1840, making shoes and weaving, it anticipated the construction of a new home in the faubourg de Cérès, where their services were particularly needed.[34] The masonic lodges sometimes took care of needy members and contributed to the Bureau de Bienfaisance. Thirteen workers' mutual aid associations, including as members 1,000 to 1,200 woolens workers, during hard times may have kept some workers from falling into the ranks of the begging poor.[35]

It is easy to see how people of means might have believed that their city was being inundated by the poor, and that the situation was getting worse. By 1840 the population of Reims had swollen to 38,359, of whom about 21,000 were workers, another 8,000 indigents, and 200 beggars. In a year of economic, social, and political crisis, the ministry of the interior requested an assessment of the situation in the provinces. The acting mayor of Reims, de Marceaux, blamed the plight of the poor on, in order of importance, laziness, the rising cost of living, the lack of "order and prudence," too many children, and immorality. Some families had come to consider begging a profession, even forcing their children to beg; it was then but a short step to delinquency or even criminality. The center of Reims felt victimized by "professional beggars and the shameless poor" who hung around the streets and at the doors of charitable institutions; when they were given, or obtained by other means, anything of value, such as winter clothing, they quickly pawned it and drank away the proceeds. The acting mayor had little sympathy: "The conduct of the poor man is perfectly calculated, he holds on to nothing—he says to himself, I want to remain lazy. If I am hungry, they will feed me."[36]

Many poor women survived through prostitution. Police tolerated the ancient trade, provided a prostitute was registered, worked in brothels, stayed off the streets after nightfall, and did not attract potential clients in lewd, provocative ways.[37] The Maison du Bon Pasteur took in repentant prostitutes and those whose background, or the company they kept, seemed to destine them to a life of sin. Most of the 69 women lodging there had to come up with 200 francs a year, although some were taken in for less. Yet in the fall of 1826, the beginning of another round of hard times, the subprefect claimed that "few weeks go by when the promenades and other public gathering places are not the scene of scandalous or even violent scenes, of which [the prostitutes] are the cause or occasion." Some prostitutes stole and fought for turf. Most drank, and many seemed to "carry in their wake a bevy of dishonorable men, without regular work, inclined to excesses of a more or less serious nature."[38]

Several months later the police arrested Victoire Eugénie St. André for vagabondage. Half paralyzed by the age of thirty, she was now rejected by her former clients and everyone else, even her own family; her sister was a prostitute, and her father and uncle survived by traveling through the countryside enticing people to play roulette. The police, having saved the poor woman from freezing to death in the street, asked the departmental workhouse (*dépôt*) in Châlons to take her in, which, for one thing, would remove her from Reims. But such arrests and various decrees and waves of police activity against prostitution served, at best, only to keep prostitutes out of public places during the daylight hours. So did the occasional roundups of those with venereal disease, and their incarceration in a special ward at the Hôtel-Dieu.[39]

Twice since 1830, the municipality had posted the relevant sections of the law and regulations forbidding begging and begun to round up violators in the hope of eliminating the waves of "peddlers, wandering musicians, and vagrants who harass our people and extract money from the inhabitants of the countryside."[40] The result temporarily reduced the number of chronic beggars from 400 or 500 to about 180. But repression was not enough; how—and this was the purpose of the ministry's official survey—could begging be eliminated? In 1833 the municipal council allocated ten thousand francs toward this goal, but never came up with specific plans. In 1837 a commission planned to organize a municipal workhouse, but nothing was done.

Several years later, even after the worst of the economic crisis had passed, "hordes of vagabonds" were still to be seen. In 1846 a temporary *dépôt* opened its doors in Reims, but the municipality resisted a plan that would have enlarged the building and turned it over to the state, fearing "an invasion" of those almost eagerly anticipating the shelter and meals, however unappetizing, that would come with incarceration. The departmental institution in Châlons, toward which Reims contributed ten thousand francs each year, closed down. Finally, the departmental general council decided to contribute to that of the Aisne in Montreuil-sous-Aisne at an annual cost of 30,000 francs, which would reserve 100 of the 323 places for beggars from the Marne.[41]

These were "the dangerous classes," the very poor who broke the law and even the limits of public toleration by causing public scandal or committing small thefts. They flocked to the center of Reims, where the money was, before beating a hasty retreat during periods of repression. But these dangerous classes were not very dangerous, however annoying their presence. Despite the city's population, the mayor reported with more than a little pride that only one felony had occurred in 1820, a mysterious, unsolved assault on a young man of twenty in a wealthy neighborhood. The court heard only one case of murder that entire year, and that from another district. There had been, of course, a good many misdemeanors, such as begging and violations of municipal regulations.

Despite the growth of Reims during the 1820s, no surge of crimes or infractions followed.[42] Complete police reports have survived for the three-month period beginning with July 1825. Besides felonies, police concerned themselves with four general kinds of misdemeanors: thefts, fights and simple assaults, nighttime noise, and public health violations. In these three months there was but one large theft—large indeed, at 13,000 francs—plus one assault, a prostitute arrested for corrupting a minor, seven arrests for vagabondage, as well as one suicide and one attempted suicide. There were thirty thefts investigated or thieves arrested, not many for three months in a city of over 30,000 people. There were twenty citations for reasons of public health—emptying chamber pots indiscriminately, failing to sweep in front of shops, blocking streets, or randomly dumping garbage; fifteen cases of fighting, usually involving relatives or people who worked with or otherwise knew each other; and fourteen cases of nocturnal noise. There was also a smattering of other transgressions, including working on Sunday, keeping cafés open after hours, breach of trust, cheating on weights and measures. It was all pretty routine. During hard times, such as the winter of 1827–28, thefts and attempted thefts increased; then the national guard reestablished night posts, and such crimes fell again. But even then there was no evidence of any kind of "crime wave" sweeping the city.[43]

Incidents of collective violence too were rare, although in 1817 there had been a grain riot, when a crowd forced grain merchants to sell their products at less than half the going rate and then resisted the national guard when it was called in to restore order.[44] In February and May 1818 two more grain riots marked another period of shortage and hardship. In one case the poor of Fléchambault, as early in the Revolution, charged into the center of the city, sacked several shops, freed a woman arrested by the police, and knocked a cross to the ground. This latter gesture—the ultimate insult to the religion of Saint Remi and Clovis—particularly galled the clergy, who were at the time demanding the prosecution of those who failed to kneel in the presence of the Blessed Sacrament.[45]

But in general the national guard, 140 strong, had virtually nothing to do. In 1820, vacancies in the prestigious officer corps went unfilled.[46] In any case, the center increasingly looked with apprehension toward the upper town. It had little or nothing to do with criminality, but with collective action by the city's working class.

Changing Politics

Political life in Reims reflected its economic, social, and spatial transformation. The wealthy, innovative woolens manufacturers of the central city stood at the top of the social ladder, thus increasing their influence on "the middle classes of the town and countryside." By 1827 their "manner of thinking and reasoning" had become the "general view" in the region.[47] Even if only a minority of these powerful men actively opposed the government, they were active and well represented on the municipal council and led the political opposition to the ministries of Charles X.

In 1822 the subprefect noted that almost all of what he still defiantly—as if nothing had changed—considered the "first" class, "educated men and wealthy property owners," supported strict censorship to neutralize the political opposition. Their enemies were drawn from the middle classes, particularly the manufacturers. When a retired liberal wholesale merchant drew up a protest in 1826 against a rumored proposed law on primogeniture, most who affixed their names were drawn from the middle class.[48] During the 1820s, wealthy property owners who had requested the privilege of leading the procession of the mission cross in 1821, were supplanted in local political life by merchant manufacturers who had been "shocked" by the fire-and-brimstone mission that seemed to date from another age.[49]

As the elections of 1827 approached, liberals increased their own electoral ranks by encouraging registration. Reims's relatively low status as a subprefecture worked against the government; there were not many officials and state employees available to counter the opposition of businessmen. The court magistrates, in any case, had little influence on the political life of the city. The liberal manufacturer Jobert-Lucas was returned as deputy in the pivotal elections of 1827, supported by woolens manufacturers concerned about the economic downturn and the government's decision, in favor of conservative rural interests, to increase the import tax on wool. As the political situation worsened for the government, "social harmony" suffered because workers faced rising prices just when there was little work. Yet aside from an occasional "seditious" placard and an increase in petty theft, there were no signs of any sort of imminent upheaval, merely grumbled complaints.[50]

The revolution of 1830, news of which sparked an attack against royalist symbols, a grain riot, and the reorganization of the national guard, marked the victory of the commercial and industrial elite over rural interests and the Church.[51] Popular resentment immediately surfaced against the clergy. Opponents of the Bourbons had believed that "no quarter is exempt from this reminder of the power of the Church," including those of the upper town. Now, in 1830, the bishop agreed to cooperate with the provisional administration, while urging that the clergy be given passports so they could leave town following a rumor of a cache of guns in the seminary. A placard left on the rue de Tambour on August 4 did not help, though it might have been the work of a provocateur: "A cross on our hearts, let's arm ourselves with knives for the defense of our King and our Holy Religion!"[52]

The mission cross beyond the porte Mars was the most obvious symbol of the Restoration. Several days earlier, someone had begun to dig around the base of the cross, as if to place powder to blow it up. Scrawled threats appeared, "the means employed each time to make known the schemes of the people." But before the provisional authorities could move the cross inside one of the churches, a crowd destroyed it. This event, on August 16, took on aspects of a popular festival. The "ceremony" stood the pomp and solemnity of nine years earlier on its head, "taking on the ambiance of a fair, with peddlers of songs and snacks setting up on the grounds, selling their merchandise during the demolition work." For the people of the faubourgs it was a ceremony of popular justice whereby they took symbolic control of their town by destroying a symbol of the ancien régime. The cross was knocked down, the figure of Christ torn away, its pieces paraded through town to the gates of the archbishop's palace. The cross was then carried to the rectory of Saint-Jacques, where the crowd collected a "tribute" of twenty-five francs from the curé. The next day, crowds threatened the convent of the Carmelites. This time the national guard answered the call and arresting alleged "convicts" who resisted them.[53]

The woolens manufacturers dominated political life during the July Monarchy.[54] Dependent upon the state for assuring their protection against their workers, they became Orleanists. They were opposed by the resentful advocates of the Bourbon monarchy and a small party of "movement" that included several woolens manufacturers of more modest means. A street-lighting entrepreneur, Nicolas Houzeau-Muiron, won election to the Chamber of Deputies in 1842, representing Reims *extra muros*, "campaigning as a friend of innovation and progress and the opponent of a backward-looking conservative establishment."[55]

At the same time, the lethargy of municipalities during the first years of the July Monarchy only reinforced the unchallenged authority of the centralized state. One reason municipalities saw their autonomy further eroding during the first half of the nineteenth century was the difficulty in finding someone to serve as mayor. Rare were those willing to tackle the fiscal problems of their towns, particularly as municipal posts were unpaid. For several years Reims suffered "veritable anarchy . . . the mayor, deputy mayors, and even the municipal counselors remained in their positions no more than several months, refusing to meet, deliberate, or administer."[56] Thereafter government conservatives, legitimists, and the dynastic opposition fought it out in Reims, the latter two forming an alliance in the 1846 legislative election in which the future Bonapartist enforcer Léon Faucher was elected deputy.[57] Workers remained excluded from the political process. In 1834 an Italian republican refugee, Hippolyte Tampucci, arrived to publish *Le Grapilleur,* which called for "love and devotion for woman and for the proletarian who suffers," and appealed to other equally "generous hearts" to answer the cries of the masses.[58] He directed his appeal to the workers of the upper town, particularly those called the "black hussars," workers who had migrated to Reims. But Tampucci found very few followers and virtually no subscribers.[59]

During the July Monarchy, as the faubourgs increasingly became the locus of the woolens industry, workers gradually developed class solidarities. For workers, the time of Louis-Philippe was anything but a time of prosperity. The economic crises of 1840–41 and 1846–47, begun by harvest failure and compounded by mechanization, outside competition, overproduction, and the ability of the manufactures to draw upon a vast, unemployed proletariat in the hinterland, reduced wages between 20 and 33 percent in the ten years following 1837. The cost of living continued to rise.[60]

The discouraging material conditions of life for the woolens workers have often been described.[61] Combers worked in small, badly ventilated rooms, breathing carbonic acid from the heated wool; the spinners inhaled machine oil and, by the mid-1840s, gas from the lights, while absorbing the disagreeable odor of the wool. Bleachers labored in an atmosphere of gas and sulfuric acid.[62] The municipal pawnshop endured as an important resource of the laboring poor.[63] Prostitution remained a recourse of desperation for marginal female workers as for the outcasts, *les exclus.* Louis Villermé, an indignant, problematic, but not necessarily inaccurate polemicist, wrote of female workers: "one says that she is going to put in the fifth quarter of her day. This expression makes me smile, but you can't help having a terrible feeling when you see very young girls, some whose small size shows them to be no more than twelve or thirteen years of age, offer themselves in the evening to passersby."[64]

Workers' housing remained grossly unhealthy and inadequate in every respect well through midcentury. Not surprisingly, the cholera epidemic of 1832 struck hardest in the cramped and sordid quarters of the laboring poor, killing 2,885 in the arrondissement of Reims by the end of October.[65] If the 1850 law forbidding the renting out of unhealthy housing had been applied, many if not most workers would have been left without any shelter at all. The city's increased physical size and population made the situation acute in the faubourg de Cérès and other peripheral neighborhoods.[66]

Large-scale industrialization thus created a second, proletarian city, one in which, "despite the efforts of the liberal bourgeoisie at the time, class struggle really existed." If strikes and other signs of discontent and consciousness were absent after the economic crisis of 1837, "the proletarians of the old quarter of Saint-Remi remained ready to revolt."[67] The mobilization that followed the revolution of 1848 must be seen not only in the context of the mechanization of the woolens industry, but also in the locus of work and shared work experience and patterns of residence. The insurrection of the Lyon silk workers in 1834 may have given the workers of Reims, some of whom donned red caps, a sense of a common national struggle against the manufacturers. Two strikes by woolens workers took place that year, followed by smaller movements in 1837 and 1841.

The strikes of 1834 reflected occupational or craft consciousness, and perhaps even some degree of generalized class consciousness, too, as spinners resisted wage cuts and mechanization.[68] Although the background to the movement is obscure, toward the end of May 1834 manufacturers, blaming competition from ready-made clothes, reduced their spinners' wages, or piece rates. Perhaps inspired by the recent events in Lyon, the employees of two manufacturers walked out, receiving some financial assistance from other spinners. On May 29, more workers announced they would not work until they too received the former rates. The next day, during which fourteen arrests were made, workers gathered inside town and then marched through the city gates, their numbers swelling with shouts against the mechanical spinning mills. Closely followed by gendarmes, who suspected they were headed for one particularly large factory, the workers changed direction and headed for Pontfaverger, eleven miles northeast, their number swollen to about six hundred. The subprefect, prosecutor, national guardsmen, and gendarmes caught up with them several miles from their destination and prevented them from destroying the mechanical looms. That night, following another arrest, workers hurled rocks at guardsmen. The mill owners may have agreed to the demands of the spinners.[69]

A second walkout in August 1834 was larger, again following the employers' posting of lower wage rates, despite the agreement apparently made in May. After attempting to get the prosecuting attorney to intervene on their behalf,[70] about a hundred workers of one manufacturer met in woods outside of town and then returned to the upper town. After the next workday they gathered again beyond the ramparts and left undecided as to whether they should refuse to work or smash the machinery blamed for their plight. The next day some workers convinced others to stay out. The strike lasted seven days. Accusing the wealthiest manufacturers of flaunting "a scandalous luxury," the spinners paraded through the streets, singing a song to the tune of the "Marseillaise":

> Onward, spinners, take courage!
> The hour of vengeance has arrived
> Break the chains of slavery
> From which we want to free ourselves.

Stand up, working class
With honor we'll follow the path
We must smash the big looms
Leaving nothing but dust.

Refrain:

On guard, spinners!
Let's take action
Rather death, indeed rather death
Than the reduction
For ten full years.
Your situation is well known.
Alas! How we have suffered!
Now, what can we eat?
We will have to eat stones
We would be happier to die
Than to live in such misery.[71]

The next morning the police and guardsmen broke up the workers' meeting and arrested some strikers. Workers went from house to house collecting money for those out, benefiting from what the subprefect called "an inappropriate sense of humanity." Other spinners went into the surrounding countryside looking for food and work. One hundred workers who tended the mechanized looms also joined the strike; authorities viewed them as particularly dangerous, since many were from Lyon and Paris. Troops were billeted in surrounding villages. Following some concessions, by September 6 only the metal workers remained out, returning to work by the 11th.[72]

Several things are noteworthy about the strike. First, the meetings of the workers, frequent and well attended, took place almost every day on the edge of town in the woods beyond the faubourg Fléchambault and the porte Dieu-Lumière. Thus the challenge of the organized outsiders—in some ways, not unlike the symbolic incursion of the prostitutes of Verdun with whom we began—was launched from the periphery. Second, the strike demonstrated the solidarity of the hand-spinners with the mechanized spinners. The semiskilled machine tenders also went out, though not necessarily just out of support for the spinners. Third, the workers' song reflected at least some degree of class consciousness among the woolens workers. This song symbolizes the sense of belonging, and a sense of "us" versus "them" now embedded in the popular culture and collective memory of at least the spinners. In this way the workers of Reims helped define the perimeters of their community and defend themselves, building a working-class identity while defying the manufacturers.[73]

Several other incidents that occurred during the July Monarchy at least suggest not only the adoption of republican symbols, but also a sense of belonging and cohesion among workers in the upper town. In 1838 rumors that a priest from the Bordeaux region, a missionary preparing to plant a giant cross, had in a sermon insulted the memory of Napoleon brought "several thousand workers pouring down from the faubourgs" to attack the church of Saint-Jacques. The national guard, drawn from the elite quarters below, could not prevent the crowd from storming the sacristy and smashing the furniture; there were injuries on both sides, arrests, and several subsequent incidents over the next two days.[74]

In August 1840, a year of economic and political crisis, bands of workers met beyond the city near a cemetery to the north, after their employers lowered wages. They returned to town carrying a black flag, threatening damage to the factories of the rue du Barbatre and those of the industrial suburb of Tingueux. One workshop was struck briefly. One of those arrested had attempted to affix the black flag to the statue of Louis XV in the center of the place Royale. Another walkout, this one of five days, occurred at two mills the following February.[75] In January 1844 a demonstration of workers at the place Saint-Nicaise demanded employment; workers sang the "Marseillaise" in the streets. Threats of arson and insurrection underlined not only the social crisis of unemployment and deprivation but also the resentment they felt toward the *beaux quartiers*. On January 23 of that year another poster, practically illegible, was left in front of a café relatively close to town on the rue de Vesle, warning the woolens manufacturers to lock the gates of their city, because their enemies, the workers, were at hand. Present here, as in the French Revolution, was the sense of attacking the city from the exterior.[76]

During the harsh winter of 1846–47, in which the municipality organized charity workshops to assist with canal digging and distributed bread, the workers of the faubourgs protested again in the streets. On one occasion, about eighty met at the porte de Fléchambault, marching around the exterior boulevards to the faubourg de Cérès singing the "Marseillaise." After arresting two of the "mutineers," the police were assailed with rocks—readily available in the wake of the demolition of the ramparts. The police prevented a second gathering at the place Saint-Pierre, between the central city and the beginning of the rue du Barbatre. Once again, all beggars were expelled from Reims and patrols were increased in the surrounding communes, frequently the refuge of beggars or idle workers. During the next few days a crowd of about one hundred gathered at the Esplanade de Cérès—the intersection between the old town and the faubourg de Cérès. Groups of workers roamed through the central districts, singing republican songs to the tune of church hymns.[77] At about the same time, workers met at the old rampart of Fléchambault and sang the "Marseillaise," maintaining their distance from a reform banquet where Léon Faucher was in attendance.[78] Here too we see evidence of the adaptation of popular culture to an ongoing political transformation of ordinary people, as in the second strike of 1834.

The increasing concentration of work, the ravages of mechanization on workers, the organizational basis represented by mutual aid societies,[79] the impact of utopian socialism during the last years of the July Monarchy (however much the events of 1848 bypassed Cabet and his followers[80]), and the efforts of republican shopkeepers and artisans immediately after the 1848 revolution all contributed to the mobilization of Reims's woolens workers. This was manifested by support for Montagnard candidates for the Assembly and by continued defiance and organization. But the spatial concomitants of large-scale industrialization and urban growth also contributed to the social and political conflict that followed the revolution of 1848. Class antagonism assumed a geographic dimension. The story of Reims in the Second Republic is, above all, one of the mobilization of the second, proletarian city, beginning with the pillage of Croutelle's factory briefly described in chapter 1. How much of a role did neighborhood solidarities, and the sense of common exclusion from the fancy quarters by virtue of their class and occupation, play in the precocious mobilization of the upper town, the proletarian third arrondissement?

During the Second Republic the workers of Reims's faubourgs were the most militant and organized in the North and East, and perhaps in all of France.[81] Formal organizations—mutual aid societies and an ambitious new cooperative, the Association Rémoise—coexisted with traditional, informal ways of getting together; the cafés of the upper town served as the highly informal "parliaments of the people."[82] Workers such as Armand Moret, wool-comber, and Genin, lithographer, whose father had been the bellringer in the cathedral, now challenged the center from the periphery. Soon after the February Revolution, the club of the faubourg de Cérès vigorously protested the outcome of a meeting of clubs in Châlons to select candidates for the legislative elections.[83] When the economic crisis accentuated with the revolution, the upper town became the site of the largest of the national workshops in Reims.[84] On April 10 it was workers from the charity workshops of Fléchambault who began a protest against wages and conditions of work. About two thousand workers barricaded themselves in the work area before being ousted by national guardsmen, with injuries on both sides.

The democratic socialist ideology that won a following in the faubourgs, reflected in the legislative elections of May 1849, drew upon class antagonisms. The spinners claimed that, because of the attempted insurrection in June 1849, employers did not want to reach an agreement with them over wage rates; they accused them of having "no sense of justice, much less fraternity." The police *commissaire* for the proletarian south district wrote that the workers' anger should not be dismissed out of hand, and that they "viewed themselves as slaves to the wealth of their bosses."[85] The bravado of extravagant threats by workers, part of the oral culture of the poor, frightened and angered the elite. A day laborer employed on the rue de Cérès said that, if he could not find work, he would have to be a thief; he then promised that within forty-eight hours there would be another revolution: "And this time, things won't be like last February—you will all dance [from a rope]." Many of the workers of the upper town had enrolled in the charity workshops, and this too frightened the wealthy of the central districts. The size of the faubourgs and the considerable circumference of the city made it, even in ordinary times, more difficult to police.[86]

The Association Rémoise provided the focus for working-class organization in the city. Its goal was to establish consumer and producer cooperatives that would unify the workers and eliminate the middleman, thus providing food and other goods at lower prices than those of the Reims merchants. Cooperativist ideology followed from the probable diffusion of utopian socialist ideals in a city where Cabet's *Le Populaire* enjoyed a popular following.[87] It also reflected a continuing model of radical bourgeois patronage of the workers' movement, in contrast to that proposed by middle-class moralists seeking to "moralize" the workers.

Agathon Bressy, an eye doctor, had moved to Reims in October 1848 at the age of forty-two, after the case against him for participation in the June Days collapsed.[88] Espousing an ideology of corporatism, he saw voluntary associations "as an infallible means of amelioration and well-being." Accepting the inviolability of private property, Bressy believed that the proletariat, like the bourgeoisie before it, would attain its own emancipation through voluntary associations. Bressy was described as "a very adroit and most influential man," and as "a large man with a great red beard and blond hair falling to his shoulders." In the words of a hostile police observer, "his articles, read and discussed in town, profoundly moved the proletarian masses of the faubourgs."[89] As he helped mobilize the faubourgs, Bressy followed the links of the textile industry into the countryside, turning up on market day in the villages and sending friends to other communes and factories. Although the police sometimes exaggerated the spread of socialist propoganda and the danger of strikes, they insisted, with reason, on the "perfect" organization of workers in Pontfaverger, Boult-sur-Suippe, Selles, Epais, Bazancourt, and Saint-Masmes—indeed, in "dozens" of nearby villages.[90]

Influenced by Proudhon's proposal for a credit bank for the poor, Bressy created an umbrella structure that brought the existing workers' organizations into the Association Rémoise and encouraged the creation of others. The latter were essentially mutual aid societies, the number of which fluctuated between thirteen and twenty-one, each administered by a committee of five. During the winter of 1848–49, the association's Société Rémoise d'Assistance Fraternelle provided help to unemployed workers and their families. In January 1849 Bressy and his collaborators Louis Lecamp, a worker, and Eugène Courmeaux, deputy conservator of the municipal library, published *L'Association rémoise*, which reached 1,400 subscribers, in sharp contrast with the 49 copies of Cabet's *Le Populaire* received in Reims during the 1840s.[91] Later in 1849, a small producers' cooperative began to manufacture woolen clothing. Six hundred families joined the cooperative bakery, which rented a house with two kilns on the rue de Fléchambault, drawing complaints from the competition. A cooperative grocery, established on the rue Dieu-Lumière attracted workers from all over the city.

The association, organized by men whom even the officials had to admit were "men of merit," threatened to take hold in all the working-class neighborhoods in and around Reims. Bressy's goal was to establish branches of the association in the industrial towns of the North and Northeast, beginning with Rethel, Vouziers, and Sedan. Not only would it challenge local commerce, but it seemed to bring together, in the eyes of the authorities, "all the elements necessary to achieve the triumph of the most harmful doctrines."[92] Bressy, Courmeaux, and Lecamp organized a Comité Electoral Permanente to sponsor Montagnard candidates in the legislative elections of May 1849. The Montagnard slate won in Reims but was defeated in the department as a whole.[93]

State and center struck back. In June 1849 Bressy, Courmeaux, and several others were accused of preparing an insurrection in coordination with the ill-fated attempt in Paris. The prosecution claimed that fifteen to eighteen thousand workers had prepared to "descend into the streets" in revolt. Bressy and other delegates of the Comité Démocratique Institué pour la Défense de la Constitution had allegedly presented a petition to the municipal council denouncing the dispatch of French troops to defend the Pope, had vilified the subprefect, and had called for workers to take arms. Arrested and charged with conspiracy, Bressy and the others were finally acquitted in December by the court in Melun.[94] At the time of the inauguration in 1849 of the statue of the Orleanist deputy Drouet d'Erlon, "the workers of the faubourgs of Reims flocked en masse" to the prison where one of the Montagnards arrested in June was being held.[95]

By 1850 the association claimed five thousand active members, despite hard times. A new cooperative bakery had opened in the faubourg de Laon. The weavers of the association, with eight looms, sold their products to a branch in Rethel. Bressy worked tirelessly to organize the workers into a single association, drawing up a general set of regulations for unemployment insurance for all the workers' associations. When a large strike appeared inevitable in the fall of 1850, following wage reductions and the introduction of new machinery into the woolens industry, the Chambre du Travail of the association began to organize a strike fund. Bressy next planned to help the clerks and employees of Reims join the association.[96]

Cafés on the edge of the city served as meeting places for Montagnards. Bressy and his friends cultivated workers by going to the "lower class" cabarets, such as one on the rue de Vesle, where poor weavers gathered; the faubourgs of Paris, Fléchambault, Cérès, and Barbatre also had their cabarets, like the one on the rue Neuve, where Bressy "shakes hands and cultivates popularity." At another such spot run by Cellier, a search in October 1849 turned up a large number of newspapers, brochures, and engravings. Cellier had briefly owned the Guinguette de Reims in the peripheral commune of Cormontreuil, to which he hoped to attract members of the association, but he lost out to a baker across the street who sold better wine at a lower price. Cellier's modest undertaking also suffered from constant police surveillance and harassment.[97] Bressy and his friends also opened about fifteen cabarets, including one in Cormontreuil, employing weavers unable to find work in their trade. The cabaret was large enough to accommodate meetings of five hundred to six hundred people, and served bread provided by the cooperative bakery. The prefect ordered the place closed.[98]

The elite's hopes of "moralizing" workers fell by the wayside. The municipality had established so-called "little theaters" that apparently offered the workers entertainment stressing the virtues of order and obedience; they had not only failed, but lent themselves to "sedition." It had been hoped that the people could be attracted to the music ("singing improves morality") sponsored by the Société Philharmonique, particularly on Sunday and Monday, the days of rest.[99] But workers resisted such patronage; they rejected a government plan for the creation of "official" savings associations; the mutual aid societies, particularly, did not want to yield to the prefect the right to elect their own president.[100]

Bolstered by the overwhelming support of "the middle classes"[101] and by the efficient centralization of the municipal police through the creation of the post of central police commissioner, the repression took its toll. Police watched the workers' organizations, expelled propagandists from the city, and searched houses and cabarets for political pamphlets and brochures. The jurisdiction of the police was extended into the entire arrondissement, a move that—like the political influence of the Montagnards of Reims—followed the close economic, social, and political ties between the capital and its region.[102]

The *procureur* prosecuted Bressy, first for "illegally" practicing his profession. The Association Rémoise was forced out of business in June 1850 by repeated court condemnations and large fines (2,000 and 3,000 francs). Remaining copies of the newspapers were seized in July 1850. No printer would dare take on such a client in the mood of repression. Bressy countered with an *Almanach démocratique* which was widely distributed in and around Reims. On August 19, 1850, all the workers' associations founded in Reims since 1848 were banned, as well as that of Pontfaverger.[103]

Bressy's organization, now reconstituted as the Chambre du Travail, was banned on December 26, 1850, by virtue of the law against political clubs. The masonic lodge L'Union Parfaite to which Bressy and several other militants belonged, was locked and sealed by the police. Yet another cabaret, Le Progrès, was closed down in August 1851, like most of the meeting places of the association. Bressy tried again, opening the café-restaurant Le Nouveau Monde in October 1851, while bitterly complaining of "the incessant surveillance to which men sharing my views are subject."[104] The economic crisis, compounded by further mechanization of wool combing, also worked against the Association Rémoise; most workers could ill afford either to pay their dues or to buy the products of the cooperatives.[105] Begging increased, but not crimes against property. The police remained far more concerned with the "marginal" people from the "floating world" of the periphery than the outcasts.[106]

Louis Napoleon Bonaparte's coup d'état had been long anticipated in Reims.[107] Unlike the departments where armed resistance to the coup occurred, no secret societies existed in the Marne, despite the obligatory official claims to the contrary, which focused on the links between the association and its branches in other towns.[108] On December 4, 1851, military units surrounded public buildings in the center of town against to forestall any insurrection.[109] Bressy met with his political friends in his café, which the police had closed the previous night, sent emissaries to several industrial communes in the vicinity, and organized a demonstration on the place Saint-Nicaise in the early afternoon.[110]

As rumors circulated that loyal democratic socialists would be arriving from the villages of the countryside, Bressy, who had first tried to rally the roofers working on the cathedral in town, arrived on the square amid cries of "We'll march for our rights!" and "Napoleon is a traitor!" He was joined by Lecamp in his national guard uniform. Bressy tried to get the crowd to follow him to the rue Saint-Sixte, and presumably down the rue du Grand Cerf and the rue Neuve toward central Reims and the residence of the subprefect. But the crowd scattered "like a flock of sheep" when the gendarmerie arrived.[111] The mobilization of the upper town in defense of the Republic ended with Bressy's arrest, followed by his exile to Algeria and premature death shortly thereafter.[112]

The descent, by then almost traditional, into the fancy quarters of Reims from the upper town never took place. The coup d'état overwhelmed the faubourgs. The Orleanist manufacturers accepted the Empire because it seemed to guarantee "social peace," or at least sufficient repression, and to protect them from the workers of the faubourgs. Their solidarities of neighborhood and sense of exclusion played a major, perhaps even determining, part in their social and political mobilization, with Bressy's Association Rémoise providing both ideological and organizational coherence.[113]

On January 1, 1852, the archbishop of Reims celebrated a Te Deum in celebration of the coup d'état, and the "Domine Salvum Ludovicus Napoleonem" was sung. To the great surprise of those attending the service in the half-filled cathedral, the workers did not come pouring down the rue Barbatre from the upper town, Reims's second, unequal city, to fill the place du Parvis in front of the cathedral in protest.[114]

8

The Conquest of the Urban Frontier

On January 1, 1860, Paris completed the conquest of its near suburbs. Montmartre, Grenelle, Vaugirard, La Villette, and Belleville, not long before mere villages, became part of the City of Light. Although an increase in tax revenue and the inability of those communes to provide desired services are the reasons usually cited as motivating the decision, another dimension of the predator instinct of state and city played its part. It is impossible to understand or explain Haussmann's rebuilding of Paris without reference to his desire to combine what he considered the aesthetics of long, wide boulevards with the imperial desire for social control. Haussmann plowed through working-class quarters and forged arteries wide enough that armies could be easily mobilized to counter insurrection. Across such boulevards it would be difficult to build barricades.

Similarly the annexation of the near communes facilitated the extension of police authority into the uncertain edge of urban life and throughout the central city as well. Both kinds of police action were related to the fear of the "professional strangers" of the "floating worlds" of the periphery, and, even more, of organized workers beyond the effective reach of police control. This process had begun decades earlier. From the first years of the Restoration, when *commissaires de police* were largely political appointees sent with ambiguous authority to positions of uncertain administrative responsibility, through the decades of marked police professionalization, to the period of the centralization of police authority and intense political repression that followed the revolution of 1848, urban elites and administrators were increasingly preoccupied with the policing of faubourg and suburb. Fear of the unpoliced periphery had taken on a political dimension.

Demands for improved and more efficient policing of the fringe of urban life came from people of means living on the outskirts, such as prosperous farmers and owners of country houses, as well as affluent residents of the city itself, fearful of escaped criminals fleeing the capital. Estates, country houses, and modest garden plots gradually had been overcome by the lengthening shadow of the urban periphery.[1] Images of fear held by city people changed: the hit-and-run highwayman was replaced by the seemingly permanent presence in unanticipated numbers of proletarians dependent upon a fluctuating market for industrial labor. The urban future in some ways appeared less than reassuring.

In the eighteenth century, in the words of Arlette Farge, "the street worries the rich, its disorder and daily uncertainty represent a constant threat."[2] During the first half of the nineteenth century, some of the focus of elite fear—but obviously not all—turned to the outside, particularly because, in Paris but elsewhere as well, geographic segregation had begun relentlessly to separate wealthy neighborhoods from poor ones. In old Paris the open street had been the refuge for the poor, who had very little or no private space. For the police, the goal was to "separate" the spaces, diluting challenges to the private space of the elite, while preventing or intervening in situations in the public space of the poor that might push things out of control. At the same time they recognized the right of ordinary people to utilize the only true space they had: public streets and squares. "Urban space is the place of private life for those who hardly have any at all, the obligatory space for those who possess absolutely nothing at all."[3] The faubourg and the edge of the city took on something of that same role, as we have seen, providing space for those without access to it.

In principle, a commune was eligible to have a *commissaire de police,* whose salary and expenses it had to pay, when its population reached five thousand. Demands that the state provide—and, in some cases help pay for—a policeman for communes with a smaller population was one dimension of the call for extended policing. The request that the jurisdiction of the police be extended beyond the limits of the commune, into the threatening margins of urban life, was another.

In 1817 the subprefect of Corbeil, eighteen miles from the gates of Paris, asserted the need for additional surveillance there. Corbeil had several mills, but also "a great number of factories employing many workers." The large cotton manufacture of Chantemerle, "so precious for the working class of Corbeil and the vicinity, has the disadvantage of attracting many vagrants"—"as all good things have their other side," he added philosophically. The factory brought together under one roof "a prodigious number of people, sometimes as many as 1,500," yet "there is never any disorder, no riotous event."[4] Corbeil received a policeman whose salary came out of its municipal budget.

Two years later the same official complained that the single, aged policeman of Corbeil was "worthless" and that "immorality, theft, and brigandage are the children of begging: this is what causes a frightening number of crimes." After another two years, Corbeil's situation looked even more desperate: the "nonentity" of seventy-four was inadequate to his assigned tasks. Because of Corbeil's proximity to the capital, its vagrants included many people up to no good, as well as some people placed under official police surveillance. This situation prevailed "in a town with large and expensive warehouses and, like the entire suburban region of Paris, almost entirely lacking in religious principles." No longer a rural bourg, Corbeil was part of the suburbs of Paris, and a threatening one at that; its manufactures were "too often a school of impiety and an open den of debauchery."[5]

Even if Corbeil was adequately policed, what about Essonnes, not far away, on a major route to and from Paris, likewise "surrounded by manufactures and factories employing a large number of workers"? Essonnes's policing was the responsibility of the mayor, who was, logically enough, far more interested in looking after his own enterprise. By the time a new policeman was appointed to Corbeil in the mid-1820s, Essonne's population had climbed above four thousand.

The subprefect's view of industrial work was even more pessimistic: "The growing number of factories bring a swarm of disreputable people who often then disappear after running up debts." The problems were exacerbated by a large number of ex-convicts forbidden to reside in Paris but "free to take up residence on its periphery." Since many, if not most of them, could not find work, "they return to a life of crime," or at least violated the residency requirements that had been legally imposed upon them. Essonnes in 1823 resisted the authority of the police of Corbeil, claiming to be "essentially agricultural." In 1835, although its population still fell below the five-thousand minimum for a *commissariat,* the municipal council of Essonnes was willing to pay a policeman's salary because of the commune's proximity to Corbeil, the number of its workers, and its location on a major route to and from the capital.[6]

Mennecy, a few kilometers to the south of Corbeil, also attracted "turbulent" individuals. In addition to its market, the manufactures of Echarcon, Ormoy, and other nearby villages brought to the region "a large number of outsiders." There were many travelers along the road to Milly who authorities thought should have their papers checked. Its "fixed" population too was growing. But the municipal council was divided as to whether it could afford a policeman.[7]

On the northeastern edge of the capital, Belleville had finally received its own policeman in 1822; there one found, a local notable insisted, "the very worst people of the capital and the most turbulent of the workers from the faubourgs." By 1832 Belleville's population had soared to almost 10,000; even more troubling, its transient or "mobile" population had reached 1,971. It was the same in industrializing Puteaux, on the Seine just west of Paris, where an officer contended that its future seemed "rosy, and in twenty or thirty years we might be able to speak of Puteaux as another Saint-Etienne." Its population appeared to increase each day, but could also fall, since its floating population of workers followed the demand for labor. Puteaux, like other suburbs, thus embodied the unexpected—even the explosive. Authorities now had to assure "peace and order, which might one day be disrupted by strikes." They recommended the establishment of a permanent garrison.[8]

In 1822 the mayors of the communes bordering Paris to the south railed against the *guinguettes* of the environs, some of which stayed open all night. The "worst" time of all was Mardi Gras, which began even earlier for the habitués of the taverns. "In the present circumstances," one could not help be alarmed by "a concentration of more than 80,000 people thrown together in a hundred public places fairly close to each other beyond the walls of Paris, offering no guarantee against immoderation besides the presence of a few gendarmes scattered here and there." The masked balls were particularly disconcerting; disguises, often offensive and insulting to the upper classes, officials, and clergy, made repression even more difficult.[9]

In Vaugirard, the assassination of the Duc de Berri in 1820 had led the mayor himself to undertake frequent "nighttime searches of all the rooming houses" and to arrest all beggars without papers and/or without "means of existence."[10] In 1825 the newly appointed police commissioner of Vaugirard explained that his job was difficult, among other reasons, because he had to watch over three hundred drinking places, including more than a dozen *guinguettes* that offered dancing, many of which never closed, at least during the revelry of Mardi Gras.[11]

The official population figure of almost 6,500 for Bercy, a major Seine port and market, was recognized as inaccurate. There was really no way of counting accurately the "transient population composed of workers staying in rooming houses." In 1832, a year of rebellion in Paris, the mayor lamented the "moral situation" of Bercy. One could count on the "wealthy wholesale merchants, who could only lose if there is trouble," as well as the garden farmers kept busy and prosperous feeding Paris. But in Bercy one also found at least fifteen hundred to two thousand workers. For the moment they were "more crude than evil," but they could jeopardize public order if there was insufficient work at the port to keep them busy. Each of five gates—Rapée, Piquepus (Picpus), Bercy, Charenton, and Reuilly—required surveillance, for there were "vagabonds without fixed residence and generally culpable," but of what, he did not say. When they had a little money, such people could afford to rent from "the least respectable in the commune, and they move when they think that they are being observed by the authorities." They would not organize plots against the government, but might serve as a dangerous army for conspirators. Bercy stood between (what were until 1860) the eighth and twelfth arrondissements: "The cheap price of wine outside the *barrière* brings us drinkers on Sundays and especially Mondays," people who could be tempted by outsiders with money to participate in virtually any disorder— or so at least it looked from the town hall of Bercy.[12] The community required better policing, which the mayor and his deputy, being unpaid administrators, merchants devoted above all to their businesses, were unlikely to provide. The rural guard had little authority and even less respect; suburban growth had already exceeded the town's means.

Bercy did not obtain a policeman until 1837. Even that did not seem to be enough. In June 1841 a new mayor noted that "the ever greater importance of work on the port and in the warehouses of Bercy attracts a great number of workers totally unknown to us." The result was, he insisted, brawls and strikes at a time of economic, social, and political crisis in the capital. He issued a decree reminding all workers that they must carry a *livret* and a medallion issued by the police, which, as in the case of Jews under Vichy, was to be worn at all times so that it could be easily seen by all.[13]

In Enghien, not yet even an independent commune, we see the role of terrified local elites in the quest to obtain a *commissariat*. In 1839 a group of residents of the sparsely populated village north of Paris petitioned *against* having a policeman. Since the establishment of thermal baths in 1820, the hamlet had become a small resort: "The mere title of a police commissioner is enough to cost us industry; as a result, visitors will say that there is danger here . . . we would really have to have some plot uncovered in Enghien to justify such an appointment . . . a police commissioner is an extraordinary authority, one that is badly viewed here as a tyrannical authority. . . . In order to have one here, we would have to anticipate events capable of compromising public order, and nothing like that is to be feared here." A private guard was sufficient to watch over the boats for rent on the lake.[14]

By 1843 the situation had changed. Shrewd management of the baths had brought an unexpected influx of visitors; some had built houses there. The railroad was being built, bringing many workers to Enghien, including ditchdiggers who frightened the new property owners with threats of arson—not something to be taken lightly. The property owners asked the mayor of Deuil for protection. Eighty national guardsmen were available, but more regular policing was required. When a local woman fled her husband and father, a full search of all the inns and rooming houses had been virtually impossible, at least partially because the effort required the coordination of the mayors of three communes.

The new prosperity, however welcome, now had an unpleasant side to it as well. Quarrels and fights abounded in the cabarets of Enghien, open long into the night. All sorts of unlikely people were free to rent skiffs on the lake. Men jumped into the water in the nude. Worse, "people observed two men and two women from the same skiff alternately swimming and walking about completely nude," to the great scandal of others walking along the dike and the owners of the houses on the lake. "Finally, if one can believe one of the witnesses, a very worthy man, they committed the most base indecencies in the water." The only solution was to create a new *commissariat,* as was finally done in 1843. In 1850 Enghien became a separate commune.[15]

In 1838 Meudon, not far from Paris, asked the minister of the interior to establish a *commissariat,* although its population of four thousand fell short of the normal minimum: "misdeeds and acts of brigandage have been multiplying at a dismaying rate." The five gendarmes not only had too much to do in the vicinity, but were frequently called to Sèvres when Louis-Philippe—upon whose life an attempt had already been made (and there would be more)—passed through. One factory now employed more than three hundred workers. Railroad work brought in a "nomad" population, including, it was always assumed, "numerous evil-doers." Two "riots" had taken place the year before, with the railway itself and a convent school apparent targets. Now someone had shattered the shutters of a house in an attempt to burglarize it. Perhaps because Meudon's population included people of "a thousand different occupations," it was witnessing crimes against property, "brawling and scenes of immorality," and more suicides than ever before. Understandably, there were complaints about the lack of effective policing.[16]

West of Paris down the Seine, Mantes-la-Jolie in 1826 was concerned about the wide-open cabarets of the quarter of porte Rosny and of the faubourg Saint-Lazare in Mantes-la-Ville. These were beyond the jurisdiction of the police of Mantes; the deputy mayor of Mantes-la-Ville, entrusted with policing the commune, insisted that he had better things to do than spend his time checking up on the cabarets. The subprefect received an extension of police authority into Mantes-la-Ville.[17]

The capital and other cities of a growing concentration of industry did not have a monopoly on complaints about the urban frontier. The nascent suburbs of Tours, too, gave the impression of being out of control. The gendarmerie had too much to do on the open roads of the Indre-et-Loire to pay sufficient attention to the edge of town. Tours, a center for the *compagnonnage,* attracted a steady stream of workers perfecting their skills on the *tour de France*. Its faubourg, Saint-Symphorien across the Loire, "includes a certain number of disreputable people."[18] Among those thieves who did fall into the hands of the law was Pierre Pianno, an apprentice or journeyman barrelmaker who lived in the faubourg Saint-Eloi. He was arrested "on public outcry" at the *octroi* in 1831 with 145 francs that he had stolen in town.[19] The mayor of each village was left to his own devices to maintain order, with the sometimes uncertain assistance of the underpaid, overworked, and often incompetent rural guard. Often he assigned responsibility for policing to his deputy mayor.

Monitoring the inns remained an essential part of policing the suburbs of Tours. Each inn was required to keep records of its lodgers, but in the case of La Riche in 1822, where the mayor was eighty years old, illiterate, and almost blind, such lists were turned in to him only twice a month. In a week's time, anyone wanted by the police could be far away. The search for criminals stopped at the gates of Tours.[20]

In the early 1830s pressure began to mount to extend the authority of the police into the suburban communes.[21] During the cholera epidemic of 1832, it appeared wise to facilitate the surveillance of outsiders. No legislation gave the Tours police the authority to carry their investigations, even hot pursuit, beyond the gates, although special authorization had occasionally been given in Lyon, Bordeaux, and Paris, in view of "the cabarets and public places open beyond the gates of these great cities." One of the *commissaires* of Tours, the intelligent and thorough Cazeaux *père,* had requested permission to go into the suburbs to assist tax officials in "visiting" certain merchants "who move outside the *barrières,*" as well as a number of "sellers of drink and other items suspected of engaging in fraud." He also wanted to, but could not, watch the *auberges* that lay beyond the gates, "the haunt where suspects we have reason to monitor find refuge."[22]

The mayor of Saint-Symphorien expressed indignation when authorities in Tours complained that policing in his commune was inadequate, claiming that he personally checked the inns and cabarets every day. He had found no vagabonds lodged there, and had expelled those that he found on the road, and other "disreputable people," from Saint-Symphorien. The local starchworks too were subject to regular surveillance to make sure they were washed out in the interest of health, and he had fined a resident who had not followed health regulations. He watched, when there was time, the traffic passing through his commune on the way to the market of Tours, and oversaw the unloading of boats on the Loire. The mayor insisted on the competence and dedication of his rural guard, a former officer in the gendarmerie.

It would be useless, the mayor stated, to give the arrogant police of Tours "rights in our countryside"; during the previous hunting season they, with friends and dogs, had tramped through the property of two wealthy residents of Saint-Symphorien, mocking the guard who tried to stop them from trespassing. Furthermore, granting such authority to the police of Tours would amount to a censure of his administration. The mayor of Saint-Cyr echoed similar irritations: such an extension of jurisdiction would suggest "an attack against the freedom of his administration." He had himself recently expelled vagabonds and other unwanted people from his village. He insisted that there had been only a couple of thefts of cattle in his commune, and two vagabonds had been arrested and taken into Tours. Saint-Cyr even had a national guard unit ready to defend order.[23]

But despite calls for increased surveillance and the indignation of the mayor of Saint-Symphorien, only forty-three police complaints had been issued in the surrounding communes in a period of twenty-two months; forty had been the work of gendarmes, but only three of mayors, and all by the mayor of La Riche. The rural guards had not turned in a single formal complaint. The authority of the police of Tours was first extended to La Riche and Saint-Pierre, and then, in 1844, to Saint-Symphorien and Saint-Cyr.[24]

Were the prefect of the Indre-et-Loire and others correct in thinking that "evildoers" were poised on the edge of Tours, ready to do bad things? Were Saint-Symphorien and Saint-Cyr well policed, as their indignant mayors claimed? Undeniably, there were many cheap cafés and cabarets on the outskirts, to which soldiers, workers, and prostitutes flocked. If the suburbs of Tours were the equivalent of the "American Far West," it was only in that revelry was unrestrained. The image of the dangerous edge of urban life once again seems far greater than the reality. Yet the very absence of systematic policing contributed to that image.

The case of the unusual relationship between Mâcon, a center of commerce on the Saône with a population of about eleven thousand, and its unwanted faubourg of Saint-Laurent, lying across the river in the department of the Ain, is also revealing.[25] In the 1830s Saint-Laurent, with fifteen hundred residents, was spared an *octroi*. This gave its merchants a great advantage over their rivals in Mâcon, whose prices they could undercut. The bakers of Saint-Laurent were not obliged by law to keep a certain amount of bread in store and paid a smaller business tax, therefore bread was cheaper across the bridge than in Mâcon. So were certain kinds of suspect meat that the butchers of Saint-Laurent were not above selling. The people of Saint-Laurent enjoyed another advantage, as well, not having to lodge troops.[26]

By contrast, Mâcon claimed to be "trampled by the passage of troops and burdened by all kinds of taxes and other obligations." The merchants of Mâcon bitterly resented their rival's favorable situation, claiming that the shopkeepers of Saint-Laurent took unfair advantage by going out of their way to bring to their stores every item taxed at the Mâcon *octroi*. They also accused the merchants across the river of engaging in fraud, of hiding caches of goods, of secretly and illegally sending their produce to Mâcon to be sold. A number of merchants and other residents had even moved to Saint-Laurent, because of its lower prices. The mayor of Mâcon complained that "every day we see our population decimated by emigration to the opposite side" of the Saône.

There were other bones of contention as well. It cost less to drink in Saint-Laurent than in Mâcon, and the cabarets of the former were open long into the night, "bringing to our town the noisy results of intemperance." Some residents of Saint-Laurent, in turn, complained to their prefect about drunken Mâconnais blighting their peaceful bourg. With only fifteen hundred inhabitants, Saint-Laurent had no police. The Mâcon police had no authority in Saint-Laurent, the source, they insisted, of most problems of public order. Sometimes suspects sought by the police in Mâcon slipped across the bridge to safety. Even swimming posed difficulties between the two. The more proper Mâconnais were shocked that the "ruffians" of Saint-Laurent swam nude in the Saône. As the prefect of the Saône-et-Loire put it in 1838, "the inhabitants of Mâcon and Saint-Laurent represent to some extent two different peoples."[27]

The rivalry was an old one. In 1790, when France was being divided into *départements*, the deputies from the Mâconnais petitioned that Saint-Laurent, which they referred to as nothing more than their faubourg, be "reunited" to—that is, absorbed by—Mâcon. They pointed out that Saint-Laurent had little (legal) commerce and absolutely no industry. It did have a grain market; another petition based part of its case on the need, in the interest of order, to prevent the hoarders of Saint-Laurent from "exciting the alarm" of the honest Mâconnais. In any case, the enormous changes sweeping France meant that old rivalries would disappear: those considering themselves to be living in Bresse would henceforth, like the Mâconnais, be Frenchmen, with hearts beating to the same interests. There was thus no reason not to attach Saint-Laurent to Mâcon. Another petition argued that if the "faubourg" remained separated from Mâcon administratively as well as by the Saône river, it would continue to be a center of smuggling. It was not fair that Saint-Laurent should remain in such an advantageous position—"enriched at the expense of her neighbor"—without making the same sacrifices imposed on Mâcon by the state. Nonetheless, Saint-Laurent became part of the department of the Ain, while Mâcon emerged as the capital of the Saône-et-Loire.[28]

Saint-Laurent's rivalry with Mâcon remained intense, even bloody. Brawls were frequent, and had been for as long as anyone could remember. The barrelmakers of Mâcon's Compagnie du Broc particularly hated the young men from across the Saône. They sometimes fought their "less civilized" opponents from Saint-Laurent, who waited until they recognized some of their enemies coming across the bridge to the cafés. In July 1834 men from Saint-Laurent and Mâcon fought at a Sunday dance held in Clément-les-Mâcon; a young barrelmaker was attacked with a knife. In retaliation, the Mâconnais wrecked preparations for Saint-Laurent's ball, which was to take place in Mâcon—a recipe for disaster—because the only available band refused to play across the river. There was no serious disturbance, but tensions remained high.

The next day the lottery was held for men from one of the cantons of Mâcon eligible to be drafted. As was customary, the vulnerable paraded with a flag through town and the faubourgs, led by a fife and drums, singing. The lottery ended, winners and losers headed across the bridge, logically enough, to the cheaper *guinguettes*. There they were attacked by "a great number of men joined by women and children." Several of them were hurt, though none badly. As troops arrived to assist the gendarmes, the young men of Mâcon plotted their revenge. Gendarmes had to protect the butchers and bakers of Saint-Laurent as they set up shop at the Mâcon market the next day.

Soon afterward a certain Guillemin *fils* of Saint-Laurent, who appeared to be drunk, insulted a national guardsman of Mâcon. Members of the Compagnie du Broc jumped the man, who, after being hit once with an ax, was saved by the intervention of several lawyers. More brawls followed. Carrying their flag, some of the barrelmakers managed to get across the bridge in search of their enemies despite the efforts of the national guard. Three warnings were required to end that particular confrontation. The prefect then banned processions in which flags or insignias were carried—in other words, processions by the Compagnie du Broc— and several cabarets were closed.

Something had to be done to restore order. There were several impediments to extending the authority of the Mâcon police to Saint-Laurent. Ideally, Saint-Laurent might be joined to the Saône-et-Loire. This made some sense, as the cantonal seat for Saint-Laurent, Bâgé-le-Châtel, was eight kilometers distant, and Mâcon just a stroll across the bridge—if no one blocked your way. The municipal council of Mâcon contended that "the natural order of things" dictated that either Saint-Laurent belong to Mâcon, or that Mâcon be absorbed by Saint-Laurent. Naturally, it now voted unanimously for the former, seconding a vote taken in 1815, adding that the poor of Saint-Laurent might benefit from the schools, hospice, and asylum for the aged. But the wishes of municipal councils, arron-dissement councils, or even departmental general councils meant nothing; such a change would have to be approved by the *conseil d'état* and promulgated by the king.

Imposing difficulties prevented the incorporation of Saint-Laurent into the Saône-et-Loire. The Saône formed a formidable barrier, and so did collective memory. Despite their being no more than a bridge apart, Saint-Laurent consid-ered itself to be in Bresse, and Mâcon in Beaujolais. A less drastic solution might be to put Mâcon and Saint-Laurent under the surveillance of the Mâcon tax collector, although it was in the Ain, but the law of December 12, 1830, had suspended, at least temporarily, the tax on drink in communes of fewer than four thousand people, so Saint-Laurent would remain untaxed unless joined to its antagonist. The other possibility was to assign Saint-Laurent a policeman to impose order on the wide-open town. Even with far fewer than the five thousand minimum population, an exception could be, and finally was, made. Tensions between Mâcon and its "faubourg" did not end, but public order was restored.[29]

In Châteauroux the situation was less complicated, but it was taken just as seriously. The commune of Déols, across the Indre river, was Châteauroux's unwanted faubourg, through which ran the road to Paris. Déols, like Saint-Laurent, had no industrial workers, but problems abounded in the kind of extramural settlement that typified the ancien régime. Its population of 2,045 raised it to the statistical level of "urban." In Déols, everyone knew, "prosperity is far from being general"; one-fourth of the population—the "infamous part"— survived by begging, or worse. Vagabonds gathered there, confident that they could dodge the gendarmes. The justice of the peace was convinced that property stolen from Châteauroux turned up in Déols, where it was sold. In 1843 the police finally obtained permission to pursue criminals, or anyone else, to Déols.[30]

The urban reflex of fear of the faubourgs and suburbs, followed by the extension of police authority into surrounding communes, could be seen in many other cities and towns of varying size. In the early 1820s the authority of the police of Niort was extended into three neighboring communes.[31] It was the same in

Epinal, which in 1847 asked for and received permission to extend police authority into its industrial suburb of Forges, as well as to Golbey, both of which "serve as a refuge for *malfaiteurs*."[32] In 1845 Bourbon-Vendée moved to incorporate part of the adjacent commune of Bourg-sous-Bourbon. The village had become the peripheral site of prostitutes serving Bourbon-Vendée and its garrison, including several brothels and a troublesome cabaret near the pont Boileau where dances were held, an easy walk from the frontier town.[33]

The Heights of Ingouville

The relationship between Le Havre and one of its burgeoning suburbs, Ingouville, provides an example of the way in which the authority of the urban police entered the peripheral realm of "professional strangers." Here the political dimensions of the extension of police authority that followed the revolution of 1848 and the concomitant centralization of municipal policing can be clearly seen. Municipality and state reached out to conquer a smaller, troublesome peripheral neighbor, particularly as the concentration of a peripheral proletariat on the edge of Le Havre became a political threat.

The fortified port had gradually recovered from the effects of the British blockade during the Napoleonic wars. Under the Restoration its population grew rapidly, as prosperity returned. The eighteenth-century Lemande plan for the construction of elegant new commercial quarters had only temporarily alleviated the overcrowding within the walls. The ramparts had been pushed northward by about four hundred meters to encompass the new streets surrounding what is now the place de l'Hôtel de Ville. These new quarters impressed a visitor in 1825 with their "regular shape. Several houses of extremely good taste can be seen here and there. The streets are wide, and their entrances placed so that winds can carry away the smells that frequently settle in such populous places." One enthusiastic contemporary in 1825 went so far as to describe the new quarter as "our chaussée d'Antin. There palaces rise up that are fit for the princes of commerce and their treasures . . . each day part of the empty space disappears in this new quarter . . . the value of the land it comprises has risen to a prodigious level: a square meter of surface is as expensive as the most desirable quarters of Paris."[34]

The land within the ramparts filled up; open space, still visible in a map of 1825, disappeared. The port itself almost doubled in size between 1815 and 1845. As property values and rents rose, the faubourgs of Le Havre developed on the other side of the moats and the military zone, between the ramparts and the northern *falaise*. With the arrival of young migrants, particularly from the Caux and other regions of Normandy, the number of inhabitants per hectare increased from 318 in 1802 to 548 at the time of the census of 1846. The city spread beyond the ramparts, particularly toward the east and north. Pushed on by land speculation, the axis of growth in the latter directions included the rue Thiers (now the avenue Président Coty) and the rue d'Etretat, reaching toward Ingouville. These quarters also quickly became too expensive for people of moderate or no means. This population now resided on the slopes above Le Havre in Ingouville and Graville, or in Leure to the east, an urbanization "of disorder and misery."[35]

Ingouville and Graville grew far more rapidly than Le Havre. They became its prolongation, despite the fortifications. The village of Ingouville lay not far beyond the gate of the same name, built in 1628. The village, which included a hospital dating from the seventeenth century and the convent of the Penitents, lay at the base and on the first slopes of the steep, imposing talus, reaching, at the top of the *falaise,* the côte d'Ingouville, marking the beginning of the plateau of Caux, from which Louis XV viewed the port far below in 1749.[36]

With the expansion of densely populated Le Havre, the porte d'Ingouville had been demolished in the 1780s, along with the old ramparts. The new gate, at the far end of the rue de Paris, while lacking the monumental style of its predecessor, formed part of the expanded ramparts after 1804. As the principal entry to Le Havre, the road, barely fifteen feet across at the gate, soon became inadequate to the task of funneling people in and out of the bustling port city. The rue de Paris, the central thoroughfare, lined with elegant shops and residences during the Restoration, received sidewalks in 1838. On one day in 1839 an official counted 1,800 wagons of all sorts, 2,800 horses, and 10,000 pedestrians passing through the gate; there were perhaps twice that number on market day. Two new gates partially alleviated the traffic problem: the porte Louis-Philippe was opened through the ramparts toward Sainte-Adresse in 1845, and the porte Marie-Thérèse to the northeast, toward Graville, in the following year.[37]

Ingouville's population quadrupled between 1815 and 1850. As it edged toward the fortifications, "the rustic village became an urban faubourg." The widening of a single street represented the first modest attempt to improve Ingouville, the population of which reached 2,000 in 1837.[38] At the same time,

The porte d'Ingouville in 1850.

several industries developed in Ingouville: shipbuilding and milling in Le Perrey, several sugar refineries, and some of the thirty-seven tile and brick works that lay outside the ramparts in 1825, including those lining the rue d'Etretat.[39]

The pattern of growth of its neighbor Graville, along the plain north and northeast of Le Havre, was similar. Workshops were interspersed with modest residences. Not long before, Graville had been little more than an overgrown village of twelve hundred huddled around an old priory; now it was a suburban town of nine thousand. Sanvic too attracted residents, permanent and temporary, to the alluvial plain between the walls and the cliff. Leure and Graville—the sites of whale-oil processing and cotton spinning respectively—ultimately emerged as the most important industrial suburbs after 1850. From Bas Sanvic, a factory producing animal charcoal exuded a thick stench trapped by the steep incline of the *falaise*. With Ingouville and Graville contributing a disproportionate share, the agglomeration of Le Havre reached over 56,000 at midcentury.[40]

Most of the inhabitants of Ingouville lived either in the bourg or were included in the section of Le Perrey, "the town of wood" with its windmills, built on the marshes at the edge of the sea.[41] In the bourg, which offered the advantage of drier soil, one found "a large number of respectable families," including property owners of imposing means. Some of the wealthier merchants of Le Havre had built, on the plateau above the city, "a number of palaces where they enjoy themselves in summer after the toils of the day." Balzac referred to these villas with their terraced gardens as "the Auteil of Le Havre." Some English families of leisure had also begun to settle there, so that, in the words of the German traveler Jacob Venedeys, "almost the whole upper part of Ingouville consists of such summer residences; and it would be difficult to find a more delightful situation." There, "every window commands views over vale and hill, river and sea, town and village." In 1824 the municipality of Ingouville counted 208 English residents with country houses. The public baths that opened at Le Perrey in 1825 confirmed the move of some people of wealth closer to the sea, particularly during the summer season. Sainte-Adresse, above all, attracted people of wealth, including the English.[42]

Ingouville, already referred to as a "faubourg" of Le Havre in 1779, long had a reputation for offering shelter to those "professional strangers" blamed for crime by the Havrais during the Revolution and the Empire.[43] The relative isolation of Le Havre from its hinterland because of imposing ramparts and *falaise* compounded the bad relations between the port city and its troublesome neighborhood.[44] During the Revolution, for example, the port workers of Le Havre sometimes battled the "floating population" of Ingouville. The presence of convicts and prostitutes added to Ingouville's unsavory reputation. The Empire did little to improve its image. In 1803 the "ravages" of prostitution in Le Havre may have reached an all-time high, particularly in the port quarter of Notre-Dame and its notorious rue de la Prison. When the police moved against the prostitutes in response to levels of venereal disease unmatched even in Paris, the prostitutes simply moved to Ingouville, where they were free to ply their trade. In 1808 gendarmes raiding several clandestine brothels discovered that "many girls of twelve to fifteen years receive lessons in the most dissolute debauchery."[45]

The last remaining windmill of Le Perrey, Ingouville, beyond the northwest ramparts of Le Havre, 1862.

As the decades passed, Ingouville's image remained one of physical and moral disorder. The contrast with the new, elegant neighborhoods of Le Havre was striking. Only one of Ingouville's streets was paved; the remainder were covered with stones, pebbles, and above all mud. One street—today the rue Thiers—was described in 1852: "Mud, night soil, refuse of all kinds that can be found heaped up on this road form a foul cesspool. We were told that across from the refinery, below the rue Joseph Clerc, the mud was heaped up almost to the height of the second floor. The pestilential odor brought by this accumulation of rubbish caused the death of a woman and two of her girls. The clergy had all the trouble in the world to open up a path in order to get to this death chamber. The attending priest had to wear fishermen's boots with his pant legs tucked in."[46]

Venedeys, the German visitor, came to know the environs of Le Havre well. He described Le Perrey: "The small, crazy huts, mostly inhabited by fishermen, ship carpenters, brickmakers, as well as the many liquor and cider shops, lead one to infer that their inmates do not belong precisely to the elite of the human race; but also that, in the hours which their labor allows them for rest, they strive, in defiance of Fate, to forget their unfortunate situation." The faubourgs of Le Havre reminded him of the outskirts of Paris. "How is it that in Paris none but the laboring people of the very lowest class are to be seen every Sunday at the *barrières,* giving themselves up like brutes to the indulgences of the animal appetites, while such as work at trades by which they can earn rather more than their daily bread are scarcely ever to be found there?" In Le Perrey "the very air which the bird breathes in its purity becomes pestilential for the poor. In large cities this is the order of the day. Here, in a village, the same circumstances struck me more strongly than in towns, for there we are accustomed to it.'' The brick kilns of Le Perrey ''continually impregnate the air with sulfureous effluvia, which attack the lungs, and excite cough.'' Ingouville offered a remarkable contrast to the fishing village of Sainte-Adresse, with its ''small, quiet valley'' with ''little cottages half covered by fruit trees. . . . The profoundest repose seems to pervade village and valley.'' Small wonder that the Impressionists later preferred Sainte-Adresse to Ingouville. By 1840 Sainte-Adresse and the Cap de la Hève had become extremely popular among the wealthy of Le Havre, who dined at the restaurant A la Descente des Phares. Sainte-Adresse offered not only shelter from the north and east winds that pounded the sea upon the rocks, but from the terrifying image of unchecked industry and unpoliced proletariat in Ingouville.[47]

Indeed, there was little reassuring about the composition of Ingouville's population. In 1841, 329 heads of household in Ingouville were male or female day laborers (of 3,790 households in a population of 9,880); even more were not heads of household. Another 115 were listed as without occupation, including impoverished widows, but also people whose status was so unpromising that they were not even listed as day laborers. There were also 53 gardeners among the heads of household, as well as many second-hand clothes dealers, laundrywomen, woodcutters, saw-pit workers, agricultural laborers, seamstresses, haulers, and water carriers, all scrambling to find work anywhere they could. Domestics and servants were employed in Le Havre, or by families of means on the Côte d'Ingouville.[48]

The ''marginal'' nature of the peripheral population thus increasingly preoc-cupied departmental and municipal officials. In 1822 the prefect complained that Ingouville ''includes a quantity of day laborers completely out of proportion to the wealthy.'' The former lived there, permanently or temporarily, because rents were significantly higher in Le Havre. Ingouville offered not only cheaper lodgings but numerous *guinguettes*. There and in Graville one could hardly avoid ''small cabarets and shady places of all kinds, where prostitutes hang out to escape our surveillance.'' Many of them lived in an ''infinity of rough huts . . . on the slope along the moat beyond the fortifications.'' Most of them worked in Le Havre, many managing to avoid not only police controls but the regular medical inspections, thus spreading venereal disease among sailors, soldiers, and civilians alike. The registered brothels had branches in Ingouville where they employed women chased beyond the walls. Others found shelter and a place to work in the residences of a variety of suspicious characters, some on the run, such as the cheats and hucksters who turned up at the annual Foire de Saint-Michel. Ingouville provided refuge for thieves who found ''safety for themselves and shelter for the fruit of their plundering.'' It was renowned far and wide as ''the repository for the impure, suspect, turbulent, and debauched'' of Le Havre; ''the most dangerous and scandalous scenes recur several times a day and at night.''[49]

What could be done? In lower Ingouville, the old chapel of the Penitents had been converted into a parish church in 1823. But Restoration officials had discovered that churches and missions were inadequate for ''moralizing'' the peripheral population. The seeming inability of anyone to control this ''excess of licentiousness'' frustrated people of means in Le Havre. When the gates of Le Havre slammed shut at night, its troublesome faubourg was left with only ''the simple and almost worthless surveillance of the mayor and his deputies'' and their beleaguered underling, the rural guard. But the latter, a mere police agent, had no judicial authority and could therefore not make arrests; he could only report a crime or person to the mayor, his deputy, or a gendarme, if one happened by, and hope for the best. One man without the power of arrest could hardly be expected to intimidate ''foreigners and other outsiders, soldiers, sailors, prostitutes, vagabonds, and even criminals.'' The owners of the cabarets, inns, and rooming houses of Ingouville could rest at ease knowing that their registers would not be checked and that their guests, suspicious or not, would not be roused from sleep by the police. The claims of independence maintained by the municipality of Ingouville, and the lack of a clear physical demarcation between the suburban communes themselves, contributed to the inability of the authorities in Le Havre to arrest suspects believed to be moving with ease from one suburban haven to the next.[50]

Much of the commune's extensive territory was unsettled and difficult to police. Within Ingouville a dichotomy existed between the bourg, where a number of ''respectable'' families lived, and the peripheral, least settled parts of the commune. The forces of order, such as they were, confronted the irregular terrain. The mayor, his deputy, and the rural guard all lived in the bourg. Most of the commune's dispersed population lived a considerable walk away, the trek northward being made extremely unattractive by the imposing *falaise* of the Côte d'Ingouville. The officials of Ingouville were thus cut off from those parts of the commune largely populated by people ''who rarely have any other property than their own persons and rarely stay six months in the same place before leaving without paying their rent. Lacking sufficient morality, they prefer to establish themselves in this quarter because not even the lowest of authorities ever appears here.'' There were endless places for *malfaiteurs* to hide, and the sea facilitated their arrival—and rapid departure—at night without being seen by ''those interested in their moral or political conduct.''[51] One day all these marginal people might come pouring down the hill and through the gates of Le Havre.

Occasionally on Sundays and holidays, when as many as several thousand people went up to Ingouville, army patrols were sent to keep order among the soldiers and sailors, ''always ready to quarrel or fight.'' However, these patrols, with no local authorities there to give them orders, usually ended up mere ''immobile spectators to disorder.'' Those described as ''honest'' people, bourgeois and workers with a trade, were assumed to avoid those cabarets and *guinguettes* that were the haunts of prostitutes and their most regular clients, soldiers and sailors. But they were joined in Ingouville by the more ''turbulent'' part of the port population looking for cheap fun beyond the ramparts. Revelers included the toughs of the port and impoverished would-be emigrants whose money had run out and now could not afford the cost of passage to the New World. Some fights occurred because the local prostitutes preferred sailors to soldiers, since sailors had money to burn after returning from lengthy voyages. Army patrols added to the tension by—unlike the prostitutes—taking the side of the soldiers in confrontations and fights. No one seemed to protect the civilians.[52]

Did Ingouville's unsavory reputation correspond to reality? Because, for all practical purposes, there was no *commissariat* in Ingouville, only scattered records exist. How typical was François Aimable Lefebvre? The twenty-three-year-old blacksmith was arrested in September 1834 for a theft in Ingouville from an enclosed garden east of the Bassin de la Barre owned by a maritime official. Lefebvre lived in Le Havre but had a female friend residing in Sanvic. There a search ordered by the public prosecutor of Le Harvre turned up a large quantity of furniture, clothes, and other items systematically pillaged from country houses and gardens owned by wealthy Havrais. His arrest, in the words of the subprefect, "finally will put the owners of the gardens of Ingouville at ease; they were with reason very frightened by his audacity."[53] The elite of Le Havre blamed Ingouville for much of what went wrong in Le Havre—it was an easy target; the police could always blame Ingouville themselves.

Yet some reality—for François Aimable Lefebvre was hardly alone—lay behind these powerful images and helped shape police attitudes. In 1823 the subprefect urgently requested that the authority of the Le Havre police be extended beyond its ramparts to Ingouville. It was after an increase of thefts in Le Havre and its vicinity that the question of expanding the reach of the police into Ingouville first surfaced. Joining Ingouville to Le Havre looked improbable, despite the wishes of some of the well-to-do of Ingouville. The latter municipality defended its independence, because its privileged tax status outside the *octroi* would disappear. If the *octroi* were moved to the edge of Ingouville, some residents would simply move beyond its limits.[54] The arrondissement council asked that a company of gendarmes be garrisoned in Ingouville, but the peripheral commune had no place to lodge gendarmes who, in any case, could not really be spared from rural policing. Further expanding the circumference of the walls to include new territory was also unlikely and would have been opposed by the military authorities.[55]

In 1836, after years of struggling along with a number of agents, Ingouville finally received its own police, but only when its population reached the magic number of five thousand. The revolution of 1848 increased the pressure for even more effective and centralized policing.[56] Now the elite of Le Havre had another, more pressing reason to fear Ingouville: its difficult suburb offered wide-open space for political meetings and discussions. As early as April 1848 the new provisional commissioner of the Republic argued that a central police commissioner (*commissaire central*) would make policing more efficient in Ingouville, Graville, and Leure, all of them "the refuge of convicts" believed to be taking refuge in the *guinguettes*, "where the sailors' orgies take place." He proposed dividing Le Havre and its environs into five arrondissements—three for Le Havre itself and one each for Ingouville and Graville.[57]

Not only were the regulations of the municipal police systematically ignored in the suburbs, but "suspicious houses and dangerous men" were "left to their own devices by the powerlessness of the authorities." This indicated that the mere extension of the authority of the Le Havre police into its seemingly turbulent faubourg would be inadequate. The policemen of Le Havre, Engramelle and

Baillard, were reliable and hardworking, but the problems of policing a large port with a "floating population" of five or six thousand, many of whom did not have passports or appear on lists of those staying in inns or rooming houses, were imposing. Just policing passengers arriving or leaving on the steamboat to and from Rouen was time-consuming, and the requests from the prefect of police or the minister of interior for special surveillance were frequent. Le Havre's population had reached almost 26,000, plus a good number of foreigners and convicts who avoided being counted.

In the spring of 1850 a signboard showing Marianne coiffed with a red Phrygian cap and marked "To the goddess of liberty" was removed from a restaurant in Leure, and the police came upon Montagnard graffiti in Graville.[58] This appeared to be another perhaps even more serious kind of "moral" disorder. In June, Engramelle was named *commissaire central* of Le Havre and its suburbs. The reorganization of the police and Engramelle's appointment soon bore fruit. The police prevented a threatened strike by weavers, forcing twelve of "the most mutinous, the most rebellious" to leave town. There is no evidence that the police, or the Bonapartist mayor of Ingouville, Boisgérard, succeeded in "moralizing" the "marginal" population of the urban exterior, only that there were no more official complaints about the political inclinations of those living in Ingouville during the Second Republic, nor complaints of criminality.[59]

In December 1850 the conservative *Revue du Havre et de l'arrondissement/ Courrier de Graville* applauded the centralization of police authority, lumping together the "dangerous classes" with the political challenge of the left: "Part of the commune of Graville had become the rallying point for a great number of people whose activities could cause some worry in a time of overheated political passions." Thanks to the energetic and coordinated repression undertaken by the police on the edge of Le Havre, "this source of democratic socialism no longer exists, but order does." Never had the region of Le Havre been so calm, despite the lingering economic crisis. The end of government-funded public works projects in the vicinity seemed a good thing to people of means, because it had "dispersed far from us these types of workers aroused by the agents of disorder who find in them adherents for their subversive ideas and projects."[60] Le Havre's periphery, where social and geographic marginality persisted on the edge of urban life, remained suspect, but it was better policed.

In 1851 the ramparts of Le Havre were demolished. Ingouville, Leure, the western part of Graville, and lower Sanvic were annexed to Le Havre, which became the thirteenth largest city in France. The conquest of the urban frontier was complete. Workers continued to move into the plain of Graville, and to the quarters, including Saint-Vincent, at the base of the cliff. Above, wealthy Protestants and more English were among those building elegant new residences on the Côte d'Ingouville. The Impressionists, men of modest means in the beginning, soon followed, at least to Sainte-Adresse.

Tensions between center and periphery were easily seen in other places as well. The suspect character of Sainte-Croix, Saint-Pavin, and Ponlieue (where prostitutes "encumbered" the road) brought in the police of Le Mans, beginning in

1832.[61] In the Jura, artisanal Saint-Claude and the vineyard town of Arbois, a renowned center of precocious republicanism where popular political militancy came to be defined as dangerous marginality, offer similar examples. In the same department the villages surrounding Lons-le-Saulnier, though an easy walk from town, were not "properly" watched by rural guards who lacked the authority to serve as political police and, in any case, were very poorly paid and often unable to read and write. In Montmorot (the scene of a riot in 1833), Macornay, Montaigu, Courbouzon, and Perrigny the price of staples—and ordinary people there considered drink a staple, if not more—was relatively low, attracting plebeian folk. During the Second Republic, the outskirts of Lons-le-Saulnier were alive with Montagnard activity. Socialists meeting near a château in Montmorot fled through the vineyards when gendarmes arrived. They frequented the cabaret of a M. Paris, located near a place where gunpowder was stored in Montaigu. "Suspicious" gatherings were also noted outside the cabaret of one Milliet in Macornay. A combination of unpoliced "liberty" and an abundance of cut-rate drink attracted—in addition to workers with strong political opinions—prostitutes (many with disease), vagabonds, convicts, and irresponsible youth. Both kinds of "disorder"—social and political—were routinely equated and had to be controlled. The police of Lons-le-Saulnier thus reached into the surrounding communes in a sort of military conquest.[62]

Such peripheral "disorder" could be found even in seemingly idyllic Argenteuil. In 1851, before the Impressionists arrived to paint some of the encounters and contrasts between city and country, Argenteuil was a town of five thousand, "almost entirely composed of cultivators, property owners, merchants, artisans, friends of order." These "friends of order" were deeply troubled by the existence of two houses, both converted into cabarets, barely a hundred yards from town. It was one of the territorial oddities generated by the winding valley of the Seine that they should lie not only in another commune, Gennevilliers, although less than two miles from the center of Argenteuil, but just across the river in the department of the Seine.

The accusations against the owners of the cabarets were familiar—they welcomed outsiders, notably the most turbulent people of Argenteuil, who turned up to avoid the watchful eye of the police and gendarmerie and committed crimes with impunity. Not only were these cabarets the meeting place of "night drinkers avoiding the police," they had also recently become gathering points for "political agitators" who had stumbled on a congenial spot to meet in relative freedom. The subprefect's suggestion appears to have been followed: that police jurisdiction be extended across the river. In any case, the Eighteenth Brumaire of Louis Napoleon Bonaparte was not far away; many cabarets disappeared, and their clients were imprisoned or exiled.[63]

Like Argenteuil, Corbeil was no longer a sleepy town beyond the southern suburbs of Paris. If, during the Restoration and early July Monarchy, concern had been voiced about the social composition of the town and the inadequacy of policing because of alleged drunkenness and debauchery, now administrative fears took on another dimension. Increasingly proletarian and each year closer to the capital by virtue of its own growth as well as that of Paris, Corbeil—indeed, the entire arrondissement—stood accused of attracting "numerous groups of infamous people affiliated and corresponding with the Parisian secret societies." The capital's emerging suburb felt itself inundated with people moving in every direction through the department who had had one or several brushes with the law; "the presence of these men depraved by crime and very familiar with prisons corrupts the population," undermining their better instincts. Even the farmers of the vicinity seemed unprincipled; frequent trips to the markets of central Paris could be blamed. The young were accused of being lazy, morally corrupt, not even above backing out of a marriage the banns of which had already been announced. Many vagabonds tramped through town. Gendarmes were obliged to spend half their time watching suspicious characters. "Public opinion" incessantly demanded the implementation of social imperialism, the expulsion of these people not only from Corbeil but even from the European continent: "In the art of healing, one does not hesitate to cut off a limb that is poisoning the individual; the farmer and the forester do the same. Why is this example not followed in the realm of politics?" Social Imperialism was born.[64]

After the insurrection of June 1849 in the capital, the police closely watched the Montagnards of Corbeil, who indeed were "so well monitored that they have had to fall back to the small neighboring village of Saintry." In the face of police repression, such an extension of radical organization into the environs of city, town, and bourg increasingly characterized the Montagnard movement in a good part of France, notably in the Midi and parts of the Center.[65] Nearby Essonnes and several even smaller places were suspect, including Saint-Germain-les-Corbeil, Saintry, Etiolles, Poissy-sous-Etiolles, and Ris. The mayor of Corbeil seemed weak, even compromised. The gendarmerie could not be everywhere at once.[66]

The canton of Longjumeau, too, had its "bad elements." Socialist leaders now headed the list of undesirables, having replaced vagabonds. The former were now blamed for "diffusing all the bad books sent by their friends in Paris." Some Parisian militants themselves had taken refuge in the vicinity, "where they believe themselves beyond the eye of the police." Whereas in the 1830s ditchdiggers had been suspected of planning arson against the property of the wealthy of Enghien, now fires being set near Arpajon were blamed on the Montagnards. As usual, there was no proof, but the story was readily believed by the wealthy. The environs of Corbeil, too, had to be brought under police control, as Paris and other cities and towns were reaching out to conquer their own peripheries.[67]

In January 1850 the authority of Commissioner Rogé was extended to the entire canton. The left protested in vain. The police commissioner was no longer an aged nonentity as in the first days of the *commissariat,* but an experienced professional eager to serve the minister of interior in political repression. A report submitted to the ministry a year later asserted that the measure of police centralization and extension had been a complete success, stymieing the Montagnards.[68]

In Enghien too there now was more to worry about than the nude bathing and 'indecent acts' of indiscreet pleasure seekers renting boats on the lake; Enghien had become the hiding place for radical workers come from Paris to work in the wine harvest. Whether they were Montagnards or not, the changing social composition of permanent residents, and the presence of so many "professional strangers," were of concern.[69] In June 1851 Beaumont-sur-Oise, "where many workers are to be found," was described as the most dangerous place in the vicinity. Although relatively far from the capital, it lay on a major route, close enough to join the outer edge of Paris's developing northern suburbs. The subprefect asked that special military preparations be taken so that troops could be sent to Beaumont from Saint-Denis and Melun, if trouble occurred there or in the vicinity.[70]

Singing, drinking, and other forms of sociability had likewise become suspect, particularly, as we have seen, in the "gatherings called *goguettes,* where, under the pretext [*sic*] of relaxing and drinking," politics was discussed.[71] That the drinking and festivity were on the edge of the capital made these pursuits seem even more threatening to those who supported Louis Napoleon Bonaparte. The images of "the drunken commoner" and "the cord that will strangle us one day" merged. The problem was simple: in the environs of Paris "the working class . . . is very numerous, even too numerous," came a report to the minister of justice at the end of October 1851, little more than a month before Louis Napoleon's coup d'état.[72] On November 25, 1851, the authorities of the communes through which the railway to the north passed, including Maisons-sur-Seine, were put on a special alert, presumably in anticipation of the coup d'état. National guard units took up posts in the stations of Enghien, Franconville, and Ermont. The orders cited the possibility that rebels might be ready to attack key bridges like the pont Bezon, and stations and tracks.[73] Several days later these crucial strategic points were occupied, not by the proletariat of the suburbs, but by troops carrying out Louis Napoleon's coup d'état.

During the Second Republic the concern with extending police control into suburbs was particularly marked in industrial regions, where proletarians made a bid for political power. If the communes surrounding small towns like Lons-le-Saulnier, and Ingouville itself, resembled faubourgs of the ancien régime, Sotteville, beyond the faubourg Saint-Séver across the Seine from Rouen, housed a concentration of proletarians characteristic of large-scale industrialization. In August 1829 and again after the revolution of 1830, disturbances in Sotteville followed the arrest of people for gathering wood "illegally" in the forest of Elbeuf. A large crowd gathered in Sotteville, walked the short distance to the faubourg of Saint-Sever, and tried to free their friends. The forest code of 1827, curtailing the access of ordinary people in royal and privately owned forests, caused "great exasperation" among the workers of Rouen's industrial faubourgs, some of whom depended on gleaning to provide fuel during the gray, damp, chilly Norman winters. In the forests of the Pyrenees and Alsace, peasants were the principle victims of the new forest legislation; it was they who challenged guards, military patrols, and charcoal-burners. Sotteville was still, at the time of the revolution of 1830, a place where the urban and rural worlds, and their concomitant poverty, met.[74]

Sotteville's rapid industrialization continued unabated. In February 1840 the municipal council petitioned for a policeman. Its claim could not be based on its population, only 3,926 in 1839, but rather on its "many factories and manufactures, of which the quantity and importance increases every day.'' This concentration of industry had attracted ''a nomadic population'' (the mayor had crossed out ''of workers'' in the first draft). Here again was the identification of the working class with a nomadic and (in the eyes of ''honest people'') dangerously marginal population ''requiring constant and active surveillance.'' It was getting to be a familiar tale. On Sundays and holidays the workers of Sotteville were joined by ''all the workers and poor'' of Rouen as well as workers who were strangers. At least the municipality's financial situation, ''without being in a brilliant position,'' was such that a thousand francs could be spared annually for a police commissioner—an appointment that was soon made.[75] Two months after France's next revolution, that of February 1848, the workers of Sotteville were prominent among the insurgents of Rouen.[76] Sotteville was subsequently brought into the network of centralized police authority extending from Rouen into its industrial region.

Burgeoning, industrial Saint-Etienne likewise reached out to control its industrial suburbs. Under the Restoration, the municipality in 1822 received permission to extend its territory at the expense of its still independent peripheral neighbors. The suburbs resisted. Their relations with Saint-Etienne had never been particularly good. Residents of Saint-Etienne plodded through the rapidly diminishing countryside in search of fresh air and leisure. The merchants of the surrounding towns did not want to pay the higher taxes that absorption into Saint-Etienne would entail, turning a deaf ear to explanations that they would benefit from more surveillance of unhealthy factories, and that a reduction in crime would follow because of more regular policing.[77]

The rationale for incorporating Beaubrun, Valbenoite, Montaud, and Outre-Furan into Saint-Etienne changed during the turbulent early years of the July Monarchy. After 1831, the principal goal was to impose social control on the edge of the city. The municipal council of Saint-Etienne requested such a change. By midcentury perhaps as much as two-thirds of the factory workers of Saint-Etienne lived in Montaud, Beaubrun, Outre-Furan, and Valbenoite. Early in the Second Empire the mayor of France's most rapidly growing city complained that the suburbs were virtually unpoliced.[78] In 1855 the suburban communes were at last incorporated into Saint-Etienne, which became, that same year, the departmental capital, supplanting sleepy and relatively isolated Montbrison. The city had much to gain from receiving the prefecture, including demand for housing, increased *octroi* receipts, and so on, not the least of which, it argued, was the possibility of increased social order in the region.[79]

Lyon's three ''faubourgs,'' the Croix-Rousse, Vaise, and La Guillotière, were ''conquered'' in the same way. During the Restoration and the July Monarchy there were myriad complaints that the authority of the Lyons police did not extend into the faubourgs, and that even the presence of a *commissariat* in each of them offered far less than adequate police protection. Villeurbanne, which included the notorious cabarets of Charpennes, had originally been placed in the Isère, further complicating, as we have seen, the problems of policing.[80]

As early as 1813 the municipality of Lyon had complained of inadequate policing in its faubourgs, described as ''the ordinary refuge of the homeless and of disreputable people fearing the reach of the law in town.''[81] There was no co-ordination beyond occasional exchanges of letters between the mayor of Lyon or his deputies and the police commissioner of each of the three faubourgs. It seemed ''perhaps an evil that the faubourgs of Lyon and the town are not united under the same municipal administration.''[82] The mayor of Lyon insisted that the suburban policemen attend the daily briefings in his office, an idea that had been vigorously opposed by the mayors of each of the faubourgs, who argued, reasonably enough, that the police could not spare the time. The *commissaire* of La Guillotière not only had fifteen square kilometers to police, but was responsible for checking the innumerable wagons and travelers passing through, as well as watching inns, cafés, cabarets, and dance halls, and much more.[83]

With the return of Napoleon during the Hundred Days, the municipality complained again that experience dictated that the authority of the police of Lyon be extended to the faubourgs of Vaise, the Croix-Rousse, and La Guillotière. The object was to control

> people who are the object of constant worry and who only want to find a way of avoiding surveillance. They are helped by the fact that our authority does not extend beyond the gates of the city. Once the guilty party has crossed that threshold, he is virtually home free. Besides, not all the crimes they are involved in take place within the walls of the city, but in the surrounding territory also. Quarrels and the trouble that follow them, affecting a sizable population, begin within the inns and cabarets that dot the faubourgs.

The periphery now seemed alive with working-class insubordination, and even organizations:

> It is there that the labor exchanges [*maisons de placement*] created by the workers are located. They meet there to plan to prevent anyone from working who, if they are in the same trade, are not members of their association. They want to join together to force pay raises and, if necessary, bring about the general desertion of their workshops, or any other measure harmful to the manufacturers. Nevertheless, the police of Lyon do not have the right to extend their measures of repression beyond their limits. The rural communes do not have the means of carrying them out. The result is that the edges of our city are places of immorality, inviolable asylums open to all disreputable people.[84]

The police of Bordeaux in 1808, the mayor of Lyon noted, had received permission to extend their authority more than three thousand meters beyond the city limits, and the police of Troyes could operate in two small communes on its outskirts, ''because of its manufacturers, whose workers are dispersed in the neighboring villages.'' The growing population and industrialization of Lyon and its outskirts provided, he thought, two compelling reasons to expand police authority, to which he added a third: ''the throng of outsiders who spend their days in town and then retreat at night to the hotels of the faubourgs to escape police surveillance.''[85] Time after time, Lyon was informed that the authority of one municipality could not extend into another.[86]

Complaints became more numerous about policing the faubourgs. In 1820, in La Guillotière, the shout of ''Help! Guards! They're killing me!'' had echoed in the night, attributable to ''people who return from excursions very late, or from the faubourgs where public places stay open after the required legal closing." Whereas the police commissioner of the Croix-Rousse had reported the owners of cabarets for staying open late, there had been no such penalties in Vaise or La Guillotière.[87] The next month there were renewed calls for better policing in Villeurbanne and Vénisseux, "where the residents of La Guillotière gather," discovering a new, more distant, and still unpoliced periphery.[88]

Not until more than thirty years later—in 1852—was the problem resolved, after not only the continued industrialization of Lyon's suburbs but the insurrections of the *canuts* in 1831 and 1834, and the working-class mobilization of the Second Republic and another state of siege. At last the government sought, given Lyon's often turbulent past, "a system offering more solid guarantees." The prefect was given authority over most police functions, especially regarding the maintenance of "public order." The mayor was left with only municipal policing, that is, streets, markets, and similar urban problems. Police authority was extended to La Guillotière, the Croix-Rousse, Vaise, Caluire, Oullins, and Sainte-Foy, Lyon's suburbs in the Rhône, but also to Villeurbanne, Vaulx-en-Velin, Brun, and Vénisseux in the Isère, and to Rillieux and Miribel in the Ain. Three months after the coup d'état, on March 24, 1852, Lyon's major suburbs, Villeurbanne, Vaise, and the Croix-Rousse, were finally incorporated into Lyon itself, and the strange pattern of competing jurisdictions resolved once and for all with a restructuring of departmental boundaries.[89] The decree, revealingly enough, added Villeurbanne, Vaulx-en-Velin, Bron, and Vénissieux "to assure 'the salvation of society' and 'to prevent odious plots.'"[90]

This conquest was an intrinsic part of the campaign for "public order"—that is, social control—in the wake of the revolution of 1848. France's *notables* rallied to Louis Napoleon Bonaparte, cheering on the repression that swept the country during the Second Republic. That repression failed in some areas, notably those in which secret societies spearheaded resistance in December 1851, and in some areas contributed to the insurrection itself.[91] As urban elites and officials demanded the closing of clubs and voluntary associations, and applauded the disappearance of leftist newspapers and the disbanding of "suspect" national guard units, they likewise vigorously approved the extension of police authority into the troubling urban periphery.

Conclusion

The grand plans of Baron Georges Haussmann and Louis Napoleon for Paris were inextricable from their desire to impose spatial order on the city of revolution. The question of whether or not the boulevards and avenues of the new Paris were made wide and straight because they facilitated the maintenance of "public order"—the imperialism of the straight line—so that it would be difficult to build barricades across them, and troops could be more rapidly sent to put down uprisings, has long been debated.[1] But it is undeniable that considerations of public order played a major—perhaps even determining—part. In his *Mémoires,* Haussmann reflected on the consequences of the construction of the boulevard Sébastopol: "It meant disemboweling the old Paris, the *quartier* of uprisings and barricades, by a wide central street piercing clear through this almost impossible maze, with communicating side streets whose continuation would be bound to complete the work thus begun. The subsequent completion of the rue de Turbigo made the rue Transnonain disappear from the map of Paris!"[2]

Large-scale industrialization and the increased reach of the centralized state were not the only dynamics of change, but were arguably the two that most profoundly affected the lives of ordinary French men and women. Many people were swept up in the resistance to capitalism and the growing power of a state that did not reflect or ignored their interests. During each successive regime—Restoration, July Monarchy, Second Republic—conservatives, liberals, and radicals fought for control. This dialectic of popular mobilization and police repression was part of the experience of France during the first half of the nineteenth century: Revolution, Reaction, Repression: 1830, 1848–51, 1870–71—a scenario centered in Paris but readily visible, at least to some degree, in much of France.

The periphery, which at first was suspect as the campsite of "professional strangers"—*les exclus* perhaps corresponding most closely to the image of the "dangerous and laboring classes"—became identified with the collective threat of the "new barbarians," as the political elite of the July Monarchy preferred to think of industrial workers. Having helped create an uncertain fringe—in some ways a nightmarish image of the urban future—state and municipality were forced to take account of what was happening. The reflex of rejection was also one of conquest in the name of social order. The creation of the "floating worlds" of the urban periphery brought a police response: that too had much to do with better organization. The extension of the authority of the urban police into the faubourgs and suburbs in the 1820s, 1830s, and 1840s represented the conquest of the threatening periphery.

David Harvey, T. J. Clark, and others have insisted on the relationship between Haussmann's urban arteries and capitalist economic development.[3] The rebuilding of Paris expelled from the center many ordinary people—the urban reflex of tossing out what was unwanted to the periphery. State and city then moved to conquer the marginal people on the edge of urban life. They attempted to impose social order on the near suburbs by absorbing them, although obviously concerns for public order were not the only reason for the expansion of Paris on January 1, 1860: the attraction of additional tax revenue also counted for something.

Plebeian Paris of course continued to expand, particularly to the north and east. The public meeting movement following the law of June 1868, which reduced restrictions on the freedom of assembly, was prominent in the *hangars* of the periphery.[4] The Commune followed, arguably the culmination of "a fierce resistance on the part of the working class to any displacement from its old ground."[5] The 1870s brought a campaign to "moralize" the faubourgs and industrial suburbs with new churches and approved voluntary associations with honorary elite members. Other conquests, large and small, followed. The ragpicker-philosopher, admired and painted by Raffaëlli, lost first his independence and then his occupation in the wake of an 1883 law covering the dumping of garbage sponsored by the prefect Poubelle, after whom the Parisian trash can is named. In 1887 the painter inscribed an etching of a *Ragpicker's Head* (1884), "I see him now as vanquished more than as in revolt."[6]

We have kept our eyes focused, for the most part, on the edge of the city, the urban frontier, and, because the two intersect at certain points, on some dimensions of cultural marginality. I have tried to suggest another way of looking at and thinking about the city, and particularly the complex, ambiguous images of faubourgs and suburbs, representing what I have called that awkward embrace of city and country, as well as of disorganization and organization.

To know the margins of urban life is also to know the center; the periphery serves as a mirror with which the upper classes viewed the most frightening images of their changing urban world, one in which the laboring classes would serve but be lodged far away and, at the same time, be controllable. Faubourgs and suburbs, the home of unwanted activities and unwanted people, seemed to represent the future of urbanization. This seemed a most unsettling process for many, particularly if the cities in question were becoming uncomfortably large in size because of rapid migration, but was the case even in smaller places, too. Michel Foucault's contention that social elites seek to purify and consolidate the social order through the creation or at least recognition of the "other"—for example, the "mad"— complements the spatial concomitants of center and periphery.[7] Confronted by the "floating worlds" of the margins of urban life, elites and authorities consolidated their domination.

The process of urbanization was arguably most fundamentally that of organization. In the end, the organization of workers on the urban frontier emerged as a dominant concern of elite uncertainties and fear. The edge of the city demonstrated its dynamism as an increasing locus for large-scale industrialization well before the Second Empire. Some working-class faubourgs and suburbs coalesced precociously, as the example of Nîmes—whose faubourgs were already well developed in the eighteenth century—suggests. The social experience of the periphery, then, was one of both marginalization and organization. Neighborhood solidarities contributed to the development of a sense of belonging that depended upon a sense of collective exclusion from—of *not* belonging to—the urban center. Here again, Nîmes was an exception, because of confessional antagonism.

Urbanization continues to create new peripheries. The *octroi* disappeared in 1939, but the problems of the suburb did not. The vast majority of the people of the Paris region today live in the suburbs, about eight out of eleven million. The suburbs closest to the capital have become less plebeian, reflected in the decline of the French Communist Party in towns that had always supported it. More and more, the middle classes have found the suburbs, linked to Paris by an extraordinary transportation network, a congenial place to live. The suburban belt has continued to grow. The relations between center and periphery remain complex in Paris and its vast region. The continued gentrification of the capital has pushed people of modest means farther out. The eighteenth, nineteenth, and twentieth arrondissements of the northeast, like Saint-Denis and some of the old red belt, remain plebeian strongholds, peripheral centers of life, for example, for many migrants from northern and black Africa.

Here the contrast with many American cities is illustrative: Grosse Pointe, Shaker Heights, Darien, and Scarsdale, elite suburbs, have had very few French counterparts, with the notable exception of Versailles and some western suburbs of Paris. In the suburbs of Detroit and other American cities in the late 1960s, the fear was that "they" would come from the inner city to "get" their affluent residents and their property. In French cities during the nineteenth century, some of the fear was just the opposite: that "they" might pour down the hill from the Croix-Rousse, or from Montmartre or Ingouville, or across the bridge from Châteauneuf in Châtellerault.

In the United States, cities were not only of more recent origin; the early growth of some was almost coterminous with industrialization, which found its locus, as often as not, in or near the center. There were no tax barriers ringing cities to encourage placing industries beyond their reach. There was considerable space, and less disparity between property values at the center and those at the periphery than in most European cities. Waves of poor newcomers—above all Irish, Italians, and blacks—settled in urban centers in neighborhoods that increasingly took on an ethnic character. In parts of New York, Boston, Philadelphia, and other cities, some people of means stayed on in fairly well-defined elite quarters, but even more moved to the periphery. The newer cities of the American West grew most rapidly in the age of the automobile. The American suburb emerged as largely an elite phenomenon, in sharp contrast to much of the European experience.

In nineteenth-century French cities, did political contention itself help these more modern threshold people enter the political arena? Did political conflict with the center represent a *rite de passage* into a wider sense of belonging, as members of a class and of a nation? The line between image and reality is difficult to establish. Marginal people created their own order in the "floating space" of the periphery, where city and country met. A sense of neighborhood, informed by the collective memory of past struggles, informed the strife between Saint-Mathieu and Saint-Jacques in Perpignan; religion made neighborhood ties even stronger in Nîmes. In Reims and Châtellerault, the sense of being outsiders who were assigned to a specific space—the faubourgs—accentuated the emergence of class consciousness, organization, and political action.

The oldest faubourg, although not really a faubourg in the proper sense, was Saint-Mathieu; from the point of view of the police, it appeared to be the most cohesive. Its long-standing rivalry with Saint-Jacques contributed to the perpetuation of that sense of belonging so consistently manifested during the first half of the century. Yet after the revolution of 1848, the police considered the *haute ville* of Reims to be the most dangerous, because of the imposing organization of industrial workers. The emerging of belonging was at least partially defined by that sense of exclusion from the political and social life of the center. Unlike Nîmes, the faubourgs of Reims seemed united in their challenge. In these three "faubourgs"—the quarter of Saint-Mathieu, the upper town and the faubourg Cérès of Reims, and the faubourg Châteauneuf in Châtellerault—the presumed threat posed by workers increased police attention and political repression during the Second Republic. In Poitiers, on the other hand, there were few workers, and the faubourgs were small; one had to go to the nearby industrial commune of Biard to find militants, as after the coup d'état of December 2, 1851, or eighteen miles to Châtellerault's faubourg Châteauneuf. In La Roche-sur-Yon/Napoléon-Vendée/Bourbon-Vendée/Napoléon-Vendée, where one might have expected to find "the dangerous and laboring classes" in a wide-open colony, *le far-west français*, the only news was no news.

The faubourg and suburb deserve attention in the historian's quest for social reality, an exploration that reflects the tension between image and reality, between text and reality. To come full circle to the prostitutes of Verdun, their little story embodied something of all three of our original possibilities. First, the prostitutes may have been "marginal," even disorderly—*"les exclus"*—by the rules of bourgeois comportment. Second, to the elite they represented a disorder and danger, one that was all out of proportion to reality. Third, they and people like them served as an excuse for the state to extend its reach, through the police, farther into the periphery. Bourgeois fears, shared only partially by the police—who were, after all, privileged observers—were to some extent imaginary and to some extent real. In any case, the central component of fear changed during the July Monarchy. "Professional strangers" such as common laborers, prostitutes, beggars, and vagabonds no longer seemed as threatening, whereas organized industrial workers were now thought to be "the cord that will strangle us one day."

Yet neither urban growth itself, nor the power of the state and its police, destroyed the faubourg, the suburb, the periphery. "Outsiders," subject to the power of capital and the expanding reach of the French state, developed self-identification and solidarities that were both social and spatial. A sense of belonging appeared on the edge of the city, among those whom urban growth and the concentration of capital had condemned to social and physical marginality.

The challenge of Belleville in 1868–71, of the faubourgs of Limoges in the decades of the fin-de-siècle period, and of Saint-Denis, Bobigny, and the other working-class towns of Paris's red belt between the two world wars provide examples of the self-conscious political challenge of the marginal people of peripheral space to the urban center and thus to the state.

In 1894 a large building with an area of about eleven hundred square meters went up for sale at 13 rue de Belleville.[8] It stood at the base of the long climb up the heights of that proletarian part of the near suburbs of Paris annexed to the capital in 1860. The brief history of that building serves as a fitting conclusion, representing crucial aspects of the experience of the urban periphery in the nineteenth century. As an entrepreneur named Favié purchased an old *guinguette* in 1830 and turned it into "an immense hall" that, refurbished once and then further expanded during the 1850s, could hold as many as three thousand people. The Salle Favié was frequented by several generations of Bellevillois and was known to many people who found occasion to spend time there—as well as suspected by a good number who had simply *heard* about it. The shrewd Favié opened a café that attracted an enormous clientele for dances, offering stiff competition to the renowned Bal or Folie-Dénoyez across the street at number 8, which became the Théâtre de Folies-Belleville during the Second Empire. By the early 1840s, the Salle Favié had developed a reputation for being something of a tough place; if anyone came "too well dressed, the regulars pointed their fingers at them, ready to do them harm." The dances of Ash Wednesday were particularly noteworthy for their revelry.[9] It was from the Salle Favié that the rollicking procession of costumed revelers began for the annual tour of Belleville "amid gibes and banter, and the shouts of a wildly enthusiastic crowd." The reputation of the Salle Favié was already such that, in 1835, a representation of its façade became the centerpiece for a play called, appropriately enough, *Les Faubouriens*. The Salle Favié represented something of a free space, although one where its clients paid for drinks and, depending on the event, for access as well.

In the Second Empire the Salle's reputation reached its peak: "workers went there eagerly with their families to put their jobs behind them." There were prostitutes and their pimps too, of course, but not in numbers or with behavior that set the tone. The dances were proper, without brawls or "dangerous tumult." When anyone got carried away, there was *père* Favié, "who knew and spoke familiarly to everyone," to grab the offender by the shoulders, usually with the help of *mère* Favié, a "worthy, large woman" who joined any fray with fists flying.

Favié made a lot of money, so much that, after the more liberal law of 1868 permitting public meetings he refused to rent his hall to the "orators of the opposition," saying, "I don't give a damn about politics. The Empire made me rich. Go take your nonsense somewhere else." Léon Gambetta, Jules Vallès, and the other spokesmen for the left, republican and socialist, denounced the Empire in the other halls of the periphery, including the one across from the Salle Favié. But during the Commune, Favié had no choice. Jules Vallès, lodged in a nearby house, spoke there, as did Jules Allix and others. On March 18, 1871, a barricade constructed by the people of Belleville stretched across the rue de Belleville, below the rue Dénoyez, defended by two large cannons, right in front of the Salle Favié. The carnival dances and masquerades of Belleville had become revolution.

Favié died, succeeded by his son-in-law, his *chef d'orchestre*. But the old days were gone. Now the Salle Favié became the site of more stridently socialist "public meetings and dissolute dances," at least in the opinion of people of means. Louise Michel was among those drawing crowds there in the late 1880s and early 1890s. "Which of the socialist and anarchist orators were not heard there? Public meetings followed public meetings, alternating with billiard matches and concerts . . . the entire aggregate of revolutionaries paraded by." In February 1888 "revolutionaries" organized a huge ball there to protest the fancy balls being held at the town hall in central Paris. In August of the same year the former Communard general Eudes thundered, "Shame on the rich! Shame on the traitors! Shame on the bourgeois—" then dropped dead, "his arm stretched out, his head fallen on the water pitcher." A gathering held to discuss the possibility of a general strike in august 1893 was the last political meeting held at the Salle Favié. Such meetings and the speeches hurled from the podiums had frightened "the peaceable man, the peaceful petty bourgeois." The Salle Favié was sold and presumably put to the commercial or industrial use made possible by its size.[10] In little more than sixty years, the hall had evolved from a rural *guinguette* into a larger dance hall and café attracting throngs of ordinary people, then into one of the vast halls offering space to public political meetings that facilitated the politicization of ordinary people. The fears of the elites and authorities of the center, too, closely followed that evolution.

No physical traces of the Salle Favié remain. The rue de Belleville is lined on that side by ghastly apartment buildings put up in the 1950s. The neighborhood is now peopled by Chinese, Vietnamese, and Turks, among others—more recent outsiders searching for a sense of belonging on the social, physical, and cultural margins of urban life.

NOTES

The following abbreviations have been used throughout the notes:

A.D. Departmental Archives (*Archives Départementales*)
A.G. Archives of the War Ministry (*Archives du Ministère de la Guerre*) Vincennes
cc central police commissioner (*Commissaire central de police*)
cp commissioner of police (*commissaire de police*)
cs special police commissioner (*commissaire spécial de police*)
int. minister of the interior
jp justice of the peace
mj minister of justice
p prefect (*préfet*)
pg prosecuting attorney (*procureur général*)
p.-v. procès-verbal
sp subprefect (*sous-préfet*)

Preface

1. The chapters that follow are based upon holdings in the French national, departmental, and assorted municipal archives. Police records and administrative, judicial, and military reporting make possible not only certain in-depth case studies but also something of a mosaic of life in and on the edge of French cities and towns. The departmental archives were particularly valuable. The military surveys carried out during the first half of the century by junior officers offer a rare view of the faubourgs of many cities. The officers who undertook the military surveys (*reconnaissances militaires,* series MR in the Archives of the Ministry of War in Vincennes) were to plan the defense of a particular town or city in case of enemy attack. The military surveys are valuable sources of information, since many of the officers were extremely conscientious, compiling statistics on population, manufacturing, local customs, habits, history, and language. Some went to the municipal libraries to read what local scholars had written, or read departmental almanachs (one complained bitterly that the municipal library was only open from 11 A.M. until 2 P.M.). Some talked to mayors and other officials, even to passersby. Since most were concerned with the roads leading in and out of major towns, maps and even occasional sketches of inns and bridges turn up along with the surveys. Many of the officers expressed class, Parisian—or at least big-city— prejudices and biases. They viewed just about everyone as rubes, or *ploucs,* just as those carrying out surveys of the countryside mistakenly came to the conclusion that everyone out there was a savage, backward, patois-speaking peasant tied to his or her own *lopin de terre.*

231

Chapter 1

1. A. D. Meuse, 71M 10, gendarmerie report, June 23, 1825; prefect, June 30, 1826. All translations, unless otherwise noted, are my own.

2. Cf. Edward Shils, *Center and Periphery: Essays in Microsociology* (Chicago, 1975), p. 3: "Society has a center. . . . The center, or the central zone, is a phenomenon of the realm of values and beliefs."

3. The *banlieue* refers to surrounding communes with independent administrative status. *Banlieue,* defined by the *Dictionnaire de l'Académie françoise* of 1694 as "the stretch of a league or thereabouts around a town," originated in the territorial reach of a jurisdiction of a *ban,* or proclamation; by the nineteenth century it referred to an administratively discrete commune (*Complément du Dictionnaire de l'Académie française,* 1862). The *Dictionnaire de l'Académie françoise* of 1740 gave the example, "this village is in the suburbs of Paris."

4. André Vant, "Géographie sociale et marginalité," André Vant, ed., *Marginalité sociale, marginalité spatiale* (Paris, 1986), p. 15. One is marginal . . . because one is incapable of reintegration in the normal circuits of production and of insertion into society" (Rénée Rochefort, "La Marginalité de l'extérieur et de l'intérieur," in Vant, ed., op. cit., p. 28).

5. Bernard Vincent, ed., *Les Marginaux et les exclus dans l'histoire* (Paris, 1979), pp. 8, 13.

6. Bronislaw Geremek, *Les Marginaux parisiens aux XIVe et XVe siècles* (Paris, 1976), p. 34.

7. Bronislaw Geremek, "Criminalité, vagabondage, paupérisme: la marginalité à l'aube des temps modernes," *Revue d'histoire moderne et contemporaine* 21 (July–September 1974), 348.

8. Raoul Perrin, "Le Commis Voyageur," *Les Français peints par eux-mêmes: encyclopédie morale du dix-neuvième siècle,* vol. 6 (Paris, 1840–42).

9. See John M. Merriman, *The Agony of the Republic: The Repression of the Left in Revolutionary France, 1848–51* (New Haven, Conn., 1978); Edward Berenson, *Populist Religion and Left-Wing Politics in France, 1830–1852* (Princeton, 1984).

10. Johan Åhr, "Passages of Influence: The Politics of Print in Revolutionary France, 1848–1851," unpublished paper, Yale University, 1989. See Laurence Fontaine, *Le Voyage et la mémoire: colporteurs d'Oisans au XIXe siècle* (Lyons, 1984), and Guy de Maupassant, *Le Colporteur* (Paris, 1900).

11. Adolphe Thiers, *Discours Parlementaires de M. Thiers* [1850–64], vol. 9 (Paris, 1880), p. 28.

12. Geremek, "Criminalité, vagabondage, paupérisme," p. 348.

13. Roger Chartier, "Les Elites et les gueux: quelques représentations (XVIe–XVIIe siècles)," *Revue d'histoire moderne et contemporaine* 21 (July–September 1974), 387. Cf. Jacques Depaux, "Pauvres, pauvres mendiants, mendiants valides ou vagabonds? Les Hésitations de la Législation Royale," *Revue d'histoire moderne et contemporaine* 21 (July–September 1974), 416: "The able-bodied beggar ceases to be a poor beggar, attached to the world of the poor, a world made up of the good and the bad poor . . . he becomes 'beggar and vagabond,' and finds himself thus linked to, without being totally assimilated by, the 'vagabonds and vagrants,' considered for a long time to be existing on the fringes of the world of criminality. He loses all ambiguity."

14. Geremek, *Les Marginaux parisiens,* pp. 34, 342. See also Jacques Le Goff, "Les Marginaux dans l'occident médiéval," in Vincent, ed., op. cit., pp. 19–28.

15. Cf. Armand Frémont, "Marginalité et espace vécu," in *Identités collectives et*

travail social (Toulouse, 1979), p. 99: "The margin can be presented as 'a blank space of a written or printed text,' but also as the 'interval of space or time, a latitude having certain limits,'" (Frémont cites the *Grand Robert de la langue française,* 1985).

16. Geremek, "Criminalité, vagabondage, paupérisme," p. 348.

17. Antoine S. Bailly, "L'Emergence du concept de marginalité: sa pertinence géographique," in Vant, ed., op. cit., p. 50.

18. Cf. André Vant, "Géographie sociale et marginalité," in Vant, ed., op. cit., p. 14: "by its etymology, marginality is inscribed first in the pairing of center and periphery. [It represents] . . . the limit or frontier, that is to say the line or confines, edge, and formerly the *marche* (with its double function of protection, and of advance base for a future extension)."

19. See Shils, op. cit. Renée Rochefort, "La Marginalité de l'extérieur et de l'intérieur," in Vant, ed., op. cit., p. 33, prefers the term "peripheral spaces . . . a spatial reality without ambiguity" to that of "the marginality of places."

20. Georges Duhamel, *Vue de la terre promise* (Paris, 1934), p. 92.

21. See Geremek, *Les Marginaux parisiens,* especially pp. 6, 34, 342–44.

22. A. D. Marne, 194M 9, int. September 5, and sp September 2 and November 16, 1834.

23. BB18 1375, *procureur,* December 13 and 15, 1838; Georges Boussinesq and Gustave Laurent, *Histoire de Reims depuis les origines jusqu'à nos jours,* vol. 2 (Reims, 1933), pp. 549–50.

24. Boussinesq and Laurent, op. cit., vol. 2, p. 516; 194M 9 (sp August 16, 17, 21, int. September 11, 1840).

25. 194M 9, sp January 24, 1844.

26. See chapter 7.

27. A. D. Pyrénées-Orientales, 3M1 74, telegrams of the *commissaire* (Hippolyte Picas), June 5 and 6, 1848; *commissaire,* June 9, 1848; BB30 362, pg Montpellier, June 7, July 17, and September 9, 1848; *procureur,* June 10, 1848; *avocat général,* June 10, 1848; U191, trial.

28. Roger Chartier, "La 'Monarchie d'Argot' entre le mythe et l'histoire," in Vincent, ed., p. 275.

29. Jean-Paul Brunet, *Saint-Denis, la ville rouge, 1890–1939* (Paris, 1980), p. 15: "Vos préfets de police laissent bloquer la capitale par une ceinture d'usines. Sire, ce sera la corde qui l'étranglera un jour." André Latrielle, *Histoire de Lyon et du Lyonnais* (Toulouse, 1975), p. 325.

30. See Micheline Baulant, "Groupes mobiles dans une société sédentaire: la société rurale autour de Meaux au XVIIᵉ et XVIIIᵉ siècle," in Vincent, ed., op. cit., pp. 78–120.

31. Victor Turner, *The Ritual Process* (Ithaca, 1969), pp. 95–96, 110–12: "The attributes of liminality or of liminal *personae* ('threshold people') are necessarily ambiguous, since this condition and these persons elude or slip through the network of classifications that normally locate states and positions in cultural space. Liminal entities are neither here nor there; they are betwixt and between the positions assigned and arrayed by law, custom, convention, and ceremonial" (p. 95).

32. Ibid., p. vii.

33. Ibid., p. 134.

34. Vant, ed., op. cit., pp. 15–18. The term "marginal"—first used in this sense by the Chicago School sociologist R. E. Park in 1928—is a "vague notion . . . made up of floating significances composed of handicap, debility, maladjustment, loss of social position, disgrace, exclusion, contestation, dissidence . . . deviance, mixed up with

evaluations and deevaluations, a homogenizing notion regrouping in an abstract category diverse social figures, present or past'' (pp. 7, 13).

35. Victor Turner, *Dramas, Fields, and Metaphors: Symbolic Action in Human Society* (Ithaca, 1974), pp. 45, 231–34, 274; ''he who is in communitas is an exile or a stranger, someone who, by his very existence, calls into question the whole normative order'' (p. 268). ''Communitas is, in principle, universal and boundless, as against structure which is specific and bounded'' (pp. 263–64).

36. Charles Baudelaire, *The Flowers of Evil,* trans. Arthur F. Kraetzer (New York, 1950), p. 132.

37. Jean Bastié, *La Croissance de la banlieue parisienne* (Paris, 1964), p. 22.

38. Robert Herbert, *Impressionism: Art, Leisure and Parisian Society* (London, 1988), and ''Industry in the Changing Landscape from Daubigny to Monet,'' in John M. Merriman, ed., *French Cities in the Nineteenth Century* (London, 1981); Paul Hayes Tucker, *Monet at Argenteuil* (New Haven, 1982); and T. J. Clark, *The Painting of Modern Life: Paris in the Art of Manet and His Followers* (New York, 1985).

39. Clark, op. cit., p. 155: ''Somewhere at the edge of that party—wanting a place in it, not sure of how to insist on one—was the odd new animal, the petit bourgeois.''

40. Ibid., particularly chapters 1 and 3 (see below). Clark notes: ''Industry [but not work] could surely be made part of the idyll if the painter tried hard enough; it could be precisely and firmly stated, but nonetheless balanced with landscape's other elements'' (pp. 188, 191). See also Dominique Rouillard, *Le Site balnéaire* (Liège, 1984), who, writing of the development of the Norman Channel resorts, describes artistic exploration as a sort of '' 'conquest of the west' like that undertaken in the same years in America by pioneers who left in search of gold''; such exploration was the goal for promoters and people of sufficient leisure to ''set up their tent'' by the sea.

41. See Michael Burns, ''Emancipation and Reaction: The Rural Exodus of Alsatian Jews, 1791–1848,'' in Jehuda Reinharz, ed., *Living with Antisemitism* (Hanover, N.H., 1987).

42. The final stanza of C. P. Cavafy's poem ''Waiting for the Barbarians'' (*Selected Poems,* trans. Edmund Keeley and Philip Sherrard [Princeton, 1972]) offers an interesting and relevant twist: ''Why this sudden bewilderment, this confusion?/(How serious everyone looks.)/Why are the streets and squares rapidly emptying, /everyone going home so lost in thought?/Because it's night and the barbarians haven't come/And some people just in from the border say/there are no barbarians any longer./Now what's going to happen to us without them?/The barbarians were kind of a solution.''

43. Marilyn R. Brown, *Gypsies and Other Bohemians: The Myth of the Artist in Nineteenth-Century France* (Ann Arbor, Mich., 1985).

44. Ibid., pp. 6–7, 23–24, 31–41. Brown notes, for example, that the liberal critic Théopile Thoré praised Adolphe Leleux's *Spanish Smugglers* of the Salon of 1846 ''as a scene of primitive rebels defending their freedom and commerce in the wild outdoors'' (p. 48), while Daumier's series *Bohemians of Paris* ''argued that social pariahs of all kinds were the product of bourgeois society itself'' (p. 51). See Walter Benjamin, *Charles Baudelaire: A Lyric Poet in the Era of High Capitalism* (London, 1973), on *flâneurs*: ''the *flâneur* still stood at the margin of the great city as of the bourgeois class. Neither of them had yet overwhelmed him. In neither of them was he at home.'' Yet the *flâneur* remained a defiantly urban type, as Benjamin suggests when he asserts that ''the department store was the *flâneur*'s final coup'' (p. 70).

45. Brown, op. cit., pp. 2–3, 4, 60; T. J. Clark, *Image of the People: Gustave Courbet and the Second French Republic, 1848–1851* (London, 1973), pp. 157–60, discussing the Wandering Jew in *The Meeting* (1854). See Brown's discussion of Edouard Manet's *Old*

Musician, pp. 85–86, and his quoting of van Gogh in 1888: "I always feel I am a traveler, going somewhere and to some destination. If I tell myself that the somewhere and the destination do not exist, that seems to me very reasonable and likely enough" (p. 97).

46. See Jerrold Seigel, *Bohemian Paris: Culture, Politics and the Boundaries of Bourgeois Life, 1830–1930* (New York, 1986), "Art and Life in Montmartre."

47. Clark, *The Painting of Modern Life,* p. 27.

48. Brown, op. cit., p. 96.

49. Ibid., pp. 31–32, 45, 95–96.

50. Beaudelaire, trans. Kraetzer, op. cit., p. 158; quoted by Benjamin, op. cit., pp. 18–19. Benjamin writes that "a ragpicker cannot, of course, be part of the *bohème*" (p. 20), although the image may have been otherwise.

51. Richard D. Sonn, *Anarchism and Cultural Politics in Fin de Siècle France* (Lincoln, Nebr., 1989), pp. 27, 52–53, 60–94.

52. Ibid., pp. 49–94, 95–114; quote from p. 52. Sonn contrasts this anarchism with the "anarchism of the elite" based in the faubourg Saint-Germain and the right-bank boulevards (p. 59).

53. Geremek, *Les Marginaux parisiens.*

54. Daniel Ligou, ed., *Histoire de Montauban* (Toulouse, 1984), pp. 220–21. Montauban's population stood at 21, 929 in 1801 and at 25,102 in 1846, an increase of 14.4%, compared to those of Toulouse (87.6%) and Albi (47.2%) (pp. 221–22). Pierre George, *Précis de géographie urbaine* (Paris, 1969), p. 55, observes: "originality and juridically, the suburban quarter escaped the taxes and obligations of the town, but also was without its privileges and protection (and thus it is with an often pejorative sense that one has spoken of the faubourg)." Georges Chabot, *Les Villes* (Paris, 1978), p. 186, states that the faubourg "is still the town, but beyond it."

55. John M. Merriman, *The Red City: Limoges and the French Nineteenth Century* (New York, 1985).

56. Vant, ed., op. cit., p. 18, quoting *Le Trimard* ("organe de revendication des sans-travail") in 1897, referring to a *sous-prolétariat* of *nouveaux pauvres*. Such a state perhaps roughly corresponds to what Turner means by "structural inferiority" (*Dramas, Fields, and Metaphors,* pp. 231ff).

57. See Antoine Bailly, "L'Emergence du concept de marginalité: sa pertinence géographique," in Vant, ed., op. cit., pp. 50–51. Bailly argues that "the present spatial disparities are not transitory, nor in a minority, but durable and sometimes even in a majority." See Manuel Castells, "Structures sociales et processus d'urbanisation," *Annales E.S.C.* 25 (1970), 1155–99, and his other work.

58. See Michelle Perrot, "The Three Ages of Industrial Discipline," in John M. Merriman, ed., *Consciousness and Class Experience in Nineteenth-Century Europe* (New York, 1979).

59. Frémont, op. cit., p. 110: "Space is this interpreted as an essential element in the strategies and techniques of domination, on the part of capitalism, and, at a world level, of imperialism. Inversely, by the poorest and most numerous masses, space is lived in the state of alienation or as the site of social struggles."

60. *Gazette des tribunaux,* April 9–10, 1838. Thanks to Cat Nilan for providing this reference.

61. Maurice Bordes, *Histoire d'Auch et du pays d'Auch* (Roanne, n.d.), p. 176.

62. Gérard Canini, "Verdun sous la monarchie constitutionnelle: aspects économiques et sociaux," in *Verdun: la société verdunoise du XIIIᵉ au XIXᵉ siècle* (Nancy, 1975), pp. 102–3.

63. Quoted from Andrew Lees, *Cities Perceived: Urban Society in European and American Thought, 1820–1940* (Manchester, 1985), p. 71. See Benjamin, op. cit., p. 18.

64. M. A. Legoyt, *Du progrès des agglomérations urbaines et de l'émigration rurale en Europe et particulièrement en France* (Marseille, 1867), p. 195.

65. Quoted by Lion Murard and Patrick Zylberman, *L'Haleine des faubourgs* (Fontenay-sous-Bois, 1978), pp. 19 and 67.

66. Paul Meuriot, *Des agglomérations urbaines dans l'Europe contemporaine* (Paris, 1897), pp. 406–7.

67. Ibid., p. 407. See Peter Gay, *The Bourgeois Experience*, 2 vols. (New York, 1984, 1986). Frégier's contentions had their counterparts in England, some of which have been brought together by Lees, *Cities Perceived*, pp. 32–34. For example, Archibald Alison, the sheriff of Lanarkshire, defined cities as places where "vice has spread her temptations, and pleasure her seductions, and folly her allurements: . . . guilt is encouraged by the hope of impunity, and idleness fostered by the frequency of example." The "passion for democracy" was among those vices spreading among urban dwellers, "among whom numbers, closely aggregated together, have awakened a feeling of strength." Robert Mudie thus described the "perfect disorder . . . desolation, where every street is a crowd; the world around, and yet comfort from no lip, and pity from no eye," and sees in it the state of nature.

68. *Tableau de l'état physique et moral des ouvriers employés dans les manufactures de coton, de laine et de soie*, 2 vols. (Paris, 1840). See William M. Reddy, *The Rise of Market Culture: The Textile Trade and French Society, 1750–1900* (New York, 1984), pp. 180–82, 229–33, for a scathing critique of Villermé.

69. Eugène Buret, *De la misère des classes laborieuses en Angleterre et en France*, vol. 1 (Paris, 1840), pp. 237–38.

70. Louis Chevalier, *Laboring Classes and Dangerous Classes in Paris during the First Half of the Nineteenth Century* (London, 1973); 1st ed., 1958.

71. From 1831 to 1836, one of the peak periods of migration to the Paris region, the excess of births over deaths accounted for only 10% of the population increase of 172,000 in the department of the Seine (Jean Bastié, op. cit., p. 18). See Louis Chevalier, *La Formation de la population parisienne au XIXᵉ siècle* (Paris, 1950).

72. Quoted from Lees, op. cit., p. 76.

73. Most recently, by Barrie Ratcliffe, *"Classes laborieuses et classes dangereuses à Paris pendant la première moitié du XIXᵉ siècle?* The Chevalier Thesis Re-examined.'' Paper presented to The Western Society For The Study of French History, New Orleans, 1989.

74. George Rudé, *The Crowd in the French Revolution* (New York, 1959); David H. Pinkney, "The Crowd in the French Revolution of 1830," *American Historical Review* 70:1 (October 1964), 1–17; and many others.

75. Charles Tilly, "The Chaos of the Living City," in Tilly, ed., *An Urban World* (Boston, 1974). Cf. the works of George Rudé and David Pinkney, cited in n.74.

76. See Richard Cobb, *The Police and the People* (London, 1970).

77. Chevalier, op. cit., p. 65.

78. Ibid., pp. 83–90. "But the whole southern *banlieue* was in a similar plight: reduced to rendering to the city as a whole the most necessary but least decent, least remunerative and, frankly, the most degrading services" (p. 86).

79. Ibid., pp. 114–15.

80. Ibid.

81. Murard and Zylberman, op. cit., p. 87.

82. Benjamin, op. cit., p. 18; the last quote is Benjamin's commentary on Frégier.

83. André Vant, *Imagerie et urbanisation: recherches sur l'exemple stéphanois* (Saint-Etienne, 1981), pp. 93–94. He explains: "Full of concern for manufacturers' central space and attentive to urban symbolism, the municipality of Saint-Etienne simultaneously threw its 'waste products' and its polluting accouterments onto the periphery."

84. Alain Faure, "Classe malpropre, classe dangereuse? Quelques remarques à propos des chiffonniers parisiens au XIXe siècle et de leurs cités," in Murard and Zylberman, op. cit., pp. 91–92.

85. Jeanne Gaillard, "Assistance et urbanisme dans le Paris du Second Empire," in Murard and Zylberman, op. cit., p. 409.

86. Daniel Arasse, *La Guillotine et l'imaginaire de la Terreur* (Paris, 1987), p. 131. The decree noted the facility of access and humanitarian reasons, in order to spare the condemned an excruciatingly lengthy trip exposed to full view and taunts in a wagon, part of the theatrical drama of revolutionary punishment.

87. BB18 1098, petition, n.d., and m.j., n.d., pg Bordeaux, July 16 and August 27, 1823.

88. BB18 1103, minister of justice, November 18, and *procureur* of Caen, November 8, 1823; A. D. Puy-de-Dôme, 7M 43, petition of February 23, 1843, and 7M 45, int. March 28, 1843 (thanks to John Sweets for this latter case).

89. *Larousse de la langue française* (Paris, 1979). The definition of *fauxbourg* provided by the *Dictionnaire de l'Académie françoise* of 1694 indicated a sense of being just beyond, even contiguous with city walls: *"On appelle fauxbourg, un assemblage de maisons qui joint par dehors à l'enceinte d'une ville."* The Academy's 1740 dictionary defined *fauxbourg* thus: *"La partie d'une ville qui est au-delà de ses portes et de son enceinte."*

90. Emile Littré, *Dictionnaire de la langue française* (Paris, 1863).

91. Ibid.; "faubourg" is noted as being influenced by *faux* by the *Grand Larousse de la langue française* (1973) and the *Grand Dictionnaire encyclopédique Larousse* (Paris, 1983).

92. Voltaire's *Candide* "entered [Paris] by the faubourg Saint-Marceau and believed himself to be in the most miserable village in Westphalia" (Littré).

93. *Nouveau Larousse illustré.*

94. *Grand Robert de la langue française* (1985), from Balzac, p. 21.

95. Ibid.; *Grand Larousse de la langue française* (1973).

96. *Grand Robert de la langue française*, op. cit., from Raymond Abello, *Ma dernière mémoire,* vol. 1, p. 47.

97. Littré, 1863.

98. *Grand Larousse de la langue française* (1979).

99. *Les Hommes de bonne volonté,* vol. 3, p. 15.

100. *Grand Larousse* (1973). The *Grand Robert* (1985) notes that *faubourg* also means, in argot, *postérieur d'une femme.*

101. 1985, quoting J. Doutourd, *Les Horreurs de l'amour,* p. 406.

102. See Michel Vovelle, *Ville et campagne as 18e siècle (Chartres et la Beauce)* (Paris, 1980), and Philip T. Hoffman, *Church and Community in the Diocese of Lyon, 1500–1789* (New Haven, 1984).

103. David Harvey, *Consciousness and the Urban Experience: Studies in the History and Theory of Capitalist Urbanization* (Baltimore, 1985), p. xii. "We consequently lack . . . the conceptual apparatus 'which would make space, and the control of space, integral to social theory'" (p. xiii).

104. Pierre Ayçoberry, "Au-delà des ramparts: 'vrais colonais' et banlieusards au milieu du XIXe siècle," *Mouvement social* 118 (January–March 1982), p. 24.

105. Quoted by Bastié, op. cit., p. 3.

106. Mary Douglas, *Purity and Danger: An Analysis of Concepts of Pollution and Taboo* (London and Henley, 1966), p. 94. She adds: "the idea of society is a powerful image. It is potent in its own right to control or to stir men to action. This image has form; it has external boundaries, margins, internal structure. Its outlines contain power to reward conformity and repulse attack. There is energy in its margins and unstructured areas" (p. 114).

107. Turner, *The Ritual Process*, p. 132. The coalescence of *les marginaux* might correspond to what Turner describes as *"normative communitas,* where, under the influence of time, the need to mobilize and organize resources, and the necessity for social control among the members of the group in pursuance of these goals, the existential communitas is organized into an enduring social system," which itself becomes a kind of *"ideological communitas."* Writing of the nineteenth century, Harvey calls them "alternative communities" based upon resistance to "the dominations of money poor, capital, and a repressive state" (*Consciousness and the Urban Experience*, pp. 256–57).

108. Turner, *The Ritual Process*, chapters 3 and 4: "Communitas breaks in through the interstices of structure, in liminality; at the edges of structure, in marginality; and from beneath structure, in inferiority" (p. 128). "Liminality," Turner writes, "is a term borrowed from Arnold van Gennep's formulation of *rites de passage,* "transition rites"— which accompany each change of state or social position, or certain points in age. These are marked by three phases: separation, margin (or *limen*—the Latin for threshold) and reaggregation" (*Dramas, Fields, and Metaphors*, pp. 231–32, 245). He thus notes "the bond that exists between communitas, liminality, and lowermost status" (p. 242).

109. Douglas, op. cit., p. 139.

110. Turner, *Dramas, Fields, and Metaphors*, p. 234; also *The Ritual Process*, pp. 108–12, 134ff., discussing " 'the power of the weak' as against the jural-political power of the strong . . . [and its] political system with its internal segmentation and hierarchies of authority."

> All these mythical types are structurally inferior or "marginal," yet represent what Henri Bergson would have called "open" as against "closed morality," the latter being essentially the normative system of bounded, structured, particularistic groups. Bergson speaks of how an in-group preserves its identity against members of out-groups, protects itself against threats to its way of life, and renews the will to maintain the norms on which the routine behavior necessary for its social life depends." (pp. 110–11)

Such a process might well correspond to van Gennep's three phases of passage, cited by Turner (p. 166), of separation, margin, and reaggregation. See Carlos G. Vélez-Ibañez *Rituals of Marginality: Politics, Process, and Cultural Change in Urban Central Mexico, 1969–1974* (Berkeley, 1983), for an illuminating comparison.

111. André Vant differentiates between "total marginality and partial marginality" (*marginalité sociale, marginalité spatiale*), p. 16. *Les exclus* correspond to one of Victor Turner's cultural triad (with liminality and structural inferiority) as "exceptionally well endowed with ritual symbols and beliefs of a non-social-structural type," namely the "state of outsiderhood, referring to the condition of being either permanently and by ascription set outside the structural arrangements of a given social system, or being situationally or temporarily set apart, or voluntarily setting oneself apart from the behavior of status-occupying, role-playing members of that system" (*Dramas, Fields, and Metaphors*, p. 233).

112. Marx and Engels's categorization of the subproletariat as "canaille in rags" duplicates this distinction between *les marginaux* and *les exclus*. See Xavier Godinot, "Le

sous-prolétariat, pierre de touche de la démocratie en Europe,'' in Vant, ed., *Marginalité sociale, marginalité spatiale*, p. 39.

113. Frémont, op. cit., p. 100.

114. Steven Kaplan, "Les Corporations, les 'faux ouvriers' et la faubourg Saint-Antoine au XVIII⁰ siècle," *Annales E.S.C.* 43:3 (March–April 1988), 353–78. See also Geremek, "Criminalité, vagabondage, paupérisme," p. 348.

115. Kaplan, op. cit., 353–78.

116. David Garrioch, *Neighborhood and Community in Paris, 1740–1790* (Cambridge, Eng., 1986), pp. 241, 243–53, 257. He adds: "Not only was [the faubourg] protected from the authorities [although, as he notes, the faubourg Saint-Antoine was the only faubourg of Paris with its own police *commissaire*], but the location of the faubourg somewhat shielded it from invasion by a transient, highly mobile population. Residential mobility remained very high, but there are some indications that it may not have equalled that in other parts of the city, or have been of the same character" (p. 243).

117. A point made by Vant, ed., *Marginalité sociale, marginalité spatiale*, p. 21.

118. André Demangeon, *Paris, la ville, et sa banlieue* (Paris, 1938); Jacques Levainville, *Rouen: étude d'une agglomération urbaine* (Paris, 1913); Paul Arbois, *Etude de géographie urbaine—Clermont Ferrand* (Clermont-Ferrand, 1930).

119. Eugen Weber, *Peasant into Frenchmen* (Stanford, 1978).

120. P. M. Jones, *Politics and Rural Society: The Southern Massif Central c. 1750–1880* (Cambridge, Eng., 1985), has studied the Lozère, Ardèche, Aveyron, and Haute-Loire, finding, not surprisingly, that Weber's thesis makes sense in those four departments. Jones's emphasis on the role of geography, religion, and family is particularly convincing.

121. Ted W. Margadant, *French Peasants in Revolt: The Insurrection of 1851* (Princeton, 1979), and Merriman, *The Agony of The Republic*, op. cit. Beyond this, Weber's implication that there was or is such a thing as a single urban culture itself is, to say the least, doubtful. Weber fails to take into consideration the persistence of rural life within and on the edge of French cities and towns; positing a one-way relationship between city and country, he ignores important dimensions of urban and rural interdependence.

122. Bastié, op. cit., p. 15.

123. See Shils, op. cit., p. 73: "Societies are characterized by the exercise of authority over the population residing within a bounded territory."

124. Vant, ed., *Marginalité sociale, marginalité spatiale*, p. 20. See also Shils, op. cit., chapter 4, on the center and resistance through secession. Also Bernard Vincent, ed., *Les Marginaux et les exclus dans l'histoire* (Paris, 1979), p. 13: "To live in the state of marginality is even more precarious, in that the marginal person cannot cut all of his links with the dominant society. He is permanently subject to its surveillance, which sooner or later leads to his exclusion or his reinsertion."

125. Demangeon, op. cit., p. 61, offers another interpretation, arguing that the peripheral villages could not provide municipal services adequate to their growing population.

126. Vant, "Géographie sociale et marginalité," in Vant, ed., *Marginalité sociale, marginalité spatiale*, p. 20. See Arlette Farge, "Le Mendiant, un marginal? (Les Résistances aux archers de l'hôpital dans le Paris du XVIII⁰ siècle)," in Vincent, ed., op. cit., pp. 312–29. The process by which the central city absorbed the faubourgs became part of the definition of "faubourg" offered by *La Grande Encyclopédie* of 1895: "The manner by which towns grow through the formation of faubourgs on the principal routes of access, the successive annexation of the faubourgs to the central city, the respective situation of the urban nucleus and its dependencies, in fortified cities, those with *octrois*, etc."

127. Jeanne Gaillard, *Paris, la ville, 1852–1870* (Paris, 1977), p. 203.

128. Colette Pétonnet, introductory section in special edition of *Ethnologie française* 12 (1982), 115: "the places of a city have a certain tenacity . . . those arriving reconstitute stable communities, an endogamy of the village, especially when a certain trade becomes incrusted in a territory. The faubourg Saint-Antoine until this day has no reason to envy the *bocage* lands of Maine. Urban communities reconstitute their rites even more powerfully as they rekindle their threatened identity. Between country and city, contiguities continue—by virtue of nature, inhabitants, exchanges—and similarities that legitimate an anthropological approach."

129. Frémont, op. cit., pp. 111–12.

130. Harvey, op. cit., pp. 14, 73–74, 92, 103, 141, 150, 183, and 204. Harvey quotes Henri Lefebvre: "Capitalism has survived . . . 'only by occupying space, by producing space'" (op. cit., p. 26). "Space can be overcome only through the production of space, of systems of communication and physical infrastructures embedded in the land" (p. 27). It is crucial to Harvey's Marxist argument that the "capitalist dynamic is forced to tear down much of what it has built in order to survive" (p. 273). See also Gaillard, *Paris, la ville*.

131. See Benjamin, op. cit., "Fourier or the Arcades," pp. 157–60.

132. Harvey, op. cit., pp. 141, 150.

133. Georges Haussmann, *Mémoires du Baron Haussmann* (Paris, 1890–93), vol. 3, p. 54.

134. Harvey, op. cit., p. 74.

135. Ibid., pp. 215–37.

136. Bernard Rouleau, *Villages et faubourgs de l'ancien Paris* (Paris, 1985), p. 215. Also p. 228: "The people of the suburbs were reputed to be ferociously hostile to any incorporation."

137. Harvey, op. cit., p. 186.

138. Gérard Jacquemet, "Belleville aux XIXᵉ et XXᵉ siècles: une méthode d'analyse de la croissance urbaine à Paris," *Annales, E.S.C.* 30 (1975), 819–43.

139. Ibid., pp. 74, 220–49. "Command over space, as every general and geopolitician knows, is of the utmost strategic significance in any power struggle" (p. 22). As Harvey notes, the amnesty for the exiled Communards before the amnesty law of 1879 was particularly strong in the *quartiers* of the northeast (op. cit., pp. 243–44).

140. Annie Fourcaut, *Bobigny, banlieue rouge* (Paris, 1986), p. 13. Cf. Tylar Stovall, *The Rise of the Paris Belt* (Berkeley, 1990). See also Brunet, op. cit., and Brunet's review of Fourcaut's *Bobigny* in *Annales E.S.C.* 43:2 (March–April 1988), 438–40; and Noëlle Gérôme and Danielle Tartakowsky, *La Banlieue en fête: de la marginalité urbaine à l'identité urbaine* (Paris, 1988).

141. Michelle Perrot, "On the Formation of the French Working Class," in Ira Katznelson and Aristide R. Zolberg, *Working-Class Formation: Nineteenth-Century Patterns in Western Europe and the United States* (Princeton, 1986), p. 102.

142. Ibid.

143. See Carl S. Schorske, *Fin-de-siècle* Vienna (New York, 1980). During the Fatti de Maggio, the insurrection of the workers of Milan in 1898, workers from the faubourgs— the *Zona Suburbana* and locus of most factories—first demonstrated outside the ramparts. The next day they attempted to march—and, when rebuffed, to fight—their way to the central city; they were blocked by soldiers whose orders were to keep them from reaching the Piazza del Duomo, the focus of public ceremonies, elite leisure, and the city's transportation network. Louise A. Tilly, "*I Fatti di Maggio:* The Working Class of Milan and the Rebellion of 1898," in Robert J. Bezucha, ed., *Modern European Social History* (Lexington, Mass., 1971).

144. Douglas, op. cit., p. 140, notes of primitive religions: "when the community is

attacked from outside at least the external danger fosters solidarity within.'' Perhaps one could even argue that the stripping of the peripheral communes of their administrative and police independence corresponds to what Turner calls ''a situation which is temporarily liminal and spatially marginal [in which] the neophytes or 'passengers' in a protracted *rite de passage* are stripped of status and authority—in other words removed from a social structure which is ultimately maintained and sanctioned by power and force—and further leveled to a homogeneous social state through discipline and ordeal'' (*Dramas, Fields, and Metaphors*, pp. 258–59).

145. Vincent, ed., op. cit., p. 12.

146. Ibid., p. 277.

147. Michel Foucault, *Madness and Civilization* (New York, 1965). See Brown, op. cit., p. 37.

148. Vant, ed., *Marginalité sociale, marginalité spatiale*, pp. 21–22.

149. Charles Tilly, review of Peter N. Stearns, *European Society in Upheaval: Social History since 1800* (New York, 1967), in *The Journal of Modern History* 41:4 (December 1969), 576. Geremek, *Les Marginaux parisiens*, p. 34, gives the example of a vagrant executed in the Middle Ages with the verdict ''useless to the world.''

Chapter Two

1. Quoted in T. J. Clark, *The Painting of Modern Life: Paris in the Art of Manet and His Followers* (New York, 1985), p. 26.

2. Eugen Weber greatly exaggerates when he writes that city walls were ''a stifling nuisance into the last third of the century'': *France, fin-de-siècle* (Cambridge, Mass., 1986), p. 179.

3. MR 1201, ''Mémoire sur la reconnaissance de la route de St.-Claude à La Meure'' (1827).

4. Alfred Lescadieu and Auguste Laurant, *Histoire de Nantes* (Nantes, 1836); André Chedeville, *Histoire de Chartres et du pays chartrain* (Toulouse, 1983), pp. 254, 262; MR 1261 (1858); MR 1245 (1835); MR 1234 his (1839). The people of Vire may have been embarrassed by something else as well, given the surveying army officer's claim that they were known for their ''depraved'' morals: ''knock anywhere in Vire, and a usurer, a prostitute, or a sodomist will pop out.'' In 1839 twelve people were arrested for sodomy.

5. Niort, a town of 16,000 in 1838, no longer had ramparts, though traces of them survived; but it had *octroi* gates, one of iron, the others of wood: MR 1302 (1838).

6. Maurice Bordes, ed., *Histoire d'Auch et du pays d'Auch* (Roanne, n.d.), p. 175.

7. Vital Chomel, ed. *Histoire de Grenoble* (Toulouse, 1976), pp. 250–52.

8. Alain Girardot, ed., *Histoire de Verdun* (Toulouse, 1982), p. 223; Gérard Canini, ''Verdun sous la monarchie constitutionnelle: aspects économiques et sociaux,'' in *Verdun: la société verdunoise du xiiie au xixe siècle* (Nancy, 1975), p. 102; Pierre Longat, Jean Lecaillon, and Jacques Rousseau, *Sedan et le pays sedanais* (Paris, 1969), p. 492.

9. Lescadieu and Laurant, op. cit.

10. MR 1243 bis, ''Mémoire sur les environs de Caen et Lisieux,'' and ''Mémoire sur les environs de Caen'' (1836); Gabriel Desert, ed., *Histoire de Caen* (Toulouse, 1981), pp. 197–200. In November 1815, the butchers of Caen had revolted against the *octroi*, drawing a large and—as always—sympathetic crowd (A. D. Calvados, M 2849, cp November 25, 1815).

11. MR 1243 bis, ''Mémoire sur les environs de Caen et Lisieux'' (1836); MR 1169, ''Mémoire descriptif et militaire sur la ville de Quesnoy et ses environs'' (1846). The

case of Caen was complicated. The municipality claimed that Vauban had established the tradition of protected military zones near fortifications, and that until the time of Louis XIV people were free to build near them, but that the château had been included only by virtue of a ruling in 1821. The director of the fortifications proposed a compromise that was apparently accepted.

12. Maurice Agulhon, ed., *Histoire de Toulon* (Toulouse, 1980), pp. 223–24, 237).

13. Jean Trenard, ed., *Histoire de Cambrai* (Lille, n.d.), p. 230.

14. Jacques Michaud and André Cabanis, *Histoire de Narbonne* (Toulouse, 1981), p. 276; MR 1220, "Mémoire sur la reconnaissance sur le levé topographique de la place de Narbonne" (1825); A. M. Narbonne, census of 1820; Eliette Berlindis, Maryse Boudet, and M.-Rose Coromina, "Contribution à l'étude démographique, économique et sociale: la ville de Narbonne de 1851 à 1871," unpublished paper, 1975. See A. D. Aude 5M 24. In the 1850s the *brassiers* were still the largest group within the agricultural sector, but were gradually replaced by *cultivateurs*. In the 1851 census agriculture represented 36.90%; *artisanat*, 34.39%; commerce, 10.51% transportation, 6.09%; functionaries, 4.17% liberal professions, 3.06%; domestics, 2.80%; and other, 0.93%.

15. Emile Jolibois, *Histoire de Chaumont* (Chaumont, 1856), p. 364.

16. MR 1233 (1836, 1842, 1843, and 1850, particularly the latter, "Mémoire relatif à la reconnaissance militaire de la Jarne à La Rochelle").

17. Jean Guilaine et Daniel Fabre, eds., *Histoire de Carcassonne* (Toulouse, 1984), pp. 146–48.

18. MR 1233 "Mémoire descriptif, statistique et maritime sur La Rochelle" (1842).

19. A. D. Indre M 2550, complaint of January 7 and 12, 1833.

20. Constant-Taillard, *Guide résumé du voyageur aux environs de Paris* (Paris, 1826); Jean Bastié, *La Croissance de la banlieue parisienne* (Paris, 1964), pp. 83–84.

21. MR 1269, "Mémoire sur les environs d'Orléans" (1837), "Mémoire sur les environs de Neuville-sur-Bois et d'Orléans" (1838), and "Mémoire sur la défense du passage de la Loire entre Orléans et Jargeau" (1843). Orléans had a population of 40,161 in 1837.

22. MR 1238, "Reconnaissance faite sur la route de Lorient, depuis une lieue en avant du village de Mordelles jusqu'à Rennes" (1822); MR 1239 (1839), "Levé expédié de la ville de Rennes" (1844), "Mémoire d'ensemble sur les levés de la 2e subdivision" (1847), and "Mémoire sur les environs de Rennes" (1858).

23. Jean Meyer, ed., *Histoire de Rennes* (Toulouse, 1972), p. 334.

24. C 954.

25. See Raymond Dugrand, *Villes et campagnes en Bas-Languedoc* (Paris, 1963).

26. A. M. Narbonne, census of 1820.

27. The territory of many cities and towns included territory *extra muros* that was largely farmland, meadows, gardens producing for the urban market, vineyards, briar patches, forests, and so on, as well as dispersed settlements that included an agricultural population. The *reconnaissances militaires* invariably gave the breakdown of land use for each commune, including city and town, surveyed. Four-fifths of the 2,169 hectares of Caen was farmland, gardens, woods, or meadows (Gabriel Desert, ed., *Histoire de Caen* [Toulouse, 1981] p. 197), and included an agricultural population counted in any census of the municipality; about 86% of the communal territory was urbanized. But I am saying more than this, and am here considering the persistence of rural life inside French cities and towns and in their faubourgs.

28. MR 1260 (1831); Chedeville, op. cit., pp. 254, 262: "by its social destination—the property-owning bourgeoisie—the new quarter of Saint-Michel remains typical of the somnolent town of the first decades of the nineteenth century" (p. 262).

29. See Michel Vovelle, *Ville et campagne au 18e siècle: Chartres et la Beauce* (Paris, 1980), p. 42.

30. Chedeville, op. cit., pp. 254–60; MR 1260 (1831).

31. Girardot, ed., op. cit., pp. 222–23; and Canini, op. cit., pp. 97–99, who argues that work on the fortifications and the construction of new barracks and other military buildings had, by 1841, increased the separation between the urban and rural worlds (p. 97).

32. René Taveneuax, ed., *Histoire de Nancy* (Toulouse, 1978), p. 357.

33. Pierre Longat, Jean Lecaillon, and Jacques Rousseau, *Sedan et le pays Sedanais* (Paris, 1969), pp. 482–83; MR 1269, "Mémoire sur la partie nord-est de la feuille d'Orléans" (1838). In Montargis, perhaps as many as two thousand residents owned or worked gardens that began on the outskirts of town and extended several kilometers in each direction along the valley.

34. Bordes, ed., op. cit., p. 172.

35. François Lebrun, ed., *Histoire d'Angers* (Toulouse, 1975), pp. 199–201.

36. Pierre Gras, ed., *Histoire de Dijon* (Toulouse, 1981), pp. 255–56. In the Second Empire, the *octroi* was moved beyond the limits of the old faubourgs.

37. Ibid., p. 256.

38. François Dornic, ed., *Histoire du Mans* (Toulouse, 1975), p. 197.

39. MR 1235 (1827).

40. Georges Dupeux, *Aspects de l'histoire sociale et politique de Loir-et-Cher, 1848–1914* (Paris, 1962) p. 133.

41. MR 1177, "Mémoire sur la reconnaissance de la position militaire de Laon" (1826).

42. Eugen Weber, *Peasants into Frenchmen: The Modernization of Rural France, 1870–1914* (Stanford, 1976).

43. See also Maurice Daumas, Jacques Payen et al., *Evolution de la géographie industrielle de Paris et sa proche banlieue aux XIXe siècle*, 2 vols. (Paris, 1976).

44. Constant-Taillard, *Guide résumé du voyageur aux environs de Paris* (Paris, 1826). Among the oddities, in Bagneux "a man 102 years of age, who has traveled the entire earth, speaking thirty-seven languages and idioms."

45. A point made in Réjean Bernard's unpublished study, "Croissance d'une commune suburbaine de Paris: le cas de La Villette, première moitié du XIXe siècle," paper presented to the Western Society for the Study of French History, Las Cruces, N.M. November 1987.

46. MR 1289, "Mémoire sur la reconnaissance de la route de Paris à Brie-sur-Marne" (1825), MR 1291 (1833).

47. Bastié, op. cit., p. 143.

48. MR 1287 (1822), "Rapport de M. Filleul, ou mémoire sur le levé à vue de la route de Paris à Aunay," and "Route de St.-Denis à Neuilly."

49. MR 1292, "Mémoire militaire sur la position militaire de Fontenoi" (1836).

50. MR 1288 (1825).

51. MR 1287 (1822).

52. MR 1287 (1820).

53. MR 1287 (1822).

54. Constant-Taillard, *op. cit.*

55. MR 1288, "Mémoire sur la reconnaissance de la route de Clichy à Maisons" (1824); MR 1291, "Mémoire sur la reconnaissance de la Seine depuis le mont de l'école militaire jusqu'à celui d'Argenteuil" (1833); MR 1294 (1858).

56. MR 1288 (1822).

57. Constant-Taillard, *op. cit.*

58. Ibid.

59. MR 1289 (1825).

60. MR 1288 (1824).

61. MR 1287 (1822). The nucleated settlement of Antony had 165 houses and 530 people, but the commune had 1,200 habitants, Palaiseau had 2,500, Massy had 1,000, Longjumeau 2,000, Grand and Petit Gentilly, 2,379, and Montrouge 2,000. Vineyards, farmland, and quarries mixed in Antony, but here too, an increasing percentage of the poor, men and women, survived by washing clothes in the Bièvre, as they did in Bourg-la-Reine.

62. Daumas, Payen et al., pp. 593–94.

63. Bastié, op. cit., p. 101.

64. Ibid., pp. 102–4, 137–60, 180.

65. Bernard, op. cit., p. 3, noting that the population of the suburbs annexed in 1860 grew by twenty-six times between 1800 and 1856, while that of the entire suburban region increased by seven times.

66. MR 1292 (1843). An exception was Villejuif, which had become the "largest village in the Paris region" because of its role supplying the markets of the capital," though quarries too were important in its economy.

67. MR 1292 (1834).

68. Jeanne Gaillard, *Paris, la ville, 1852–70* (Paris, 1979), p. 101.

69. MR 1289, "Mémoire sur la reconnaissance de la route de Meaux depuis la barrière de Paris jusqu'à la limite du département de la Seine" (1825).

70. Bernard, op. cit., pp. 3–14. The author fixes the "take-off" of La Villette's urbanization in 1824, and its intensification after 1836 (p. 11). He notes that, in 1856, 84% of adult males were workers (p. 14).

71. MR 1292 (1842).

72. MR 1293 (1844).

73. Bastié, op. cit., pp. 92–98, 161–66. Bastié notes that on that side of Paris not only did the large estates remain intact, but their *propriétaires* succeeded in adding on to them.

74. Bastié, op. cit., pp. 92–95.

75. MR 1291, "Mémoire sur la reconnaissance de la route de Neuilly à partir de l'arc de Triomphe jusqu'au pont de Neuilly" (1842).

76. MR 1293 (1846).

77. MR 1292, "Reconnaissance militaire faite par ordre" (1841). Interestingly enough, the officer carrying out a survey in 1843 referred to "the excessive sobriety that they have demonstrated, in contrast to the people of Paris. They drink very little wine" (MR 1292, "Mémoire à l'appui d'une question militaire").

78. MR 1293, "Mémoire descriptif et militaire sur le village de Romainville" (1846).

79. MR 1293, "De l'importance du pont de Créteil en cas d'invasion" (1846).

80. MR 1292 (1836).

81. Bernard Rouleau, *Villages et faubourgs de l'ancien Paris* (Paris, 1985), p. 192.

82. MR 1293 (1846); MR 1294, "Mémoire descriptif militaire" (1847).

83. Rouleau, op. cit., p. 126.

84. See Susanna Barrows, *Distorting Mirrors* (New Haven, 1979).

85. Yves Lequin, *Les Ouvriers de la région lyonnaise,* 2 vols. (Lyon, n.d. [1977]).

86. MR 1209, "Mémoire sur la reconnaissance de la route de Lyon à Baignais" (1838): "The cultivators of the environs of Lyon are almost uniquely occupied with satisfying the needs of this great city. Every day they bring to the markets the vegetables, fruits, milk, flowers, and generally that which serves the needs or desires of people of opulence. . . . Many women, children, and some men leave each morning from their

homes with beasts of burden and a certain number of small wagons to go to Lyon, where they arrive at the opening of the gates.''

87. A. D. Rhône, 4M 2, mayor of La Guillotière, September 3, 1825.

88. André Latreille, ed., *Histoire de Lyon et du lyonnais* (Toulouse, 1975), pp. 315–16, including Caluire, Ecully, Tassin, Sainte-Foy-les-Lyon, and Oullins, in addition to La Guillotière, the Croix-Rousse, and Vaise.

89. George J. Sheridan, Jr., ''Solidarities and Neighborhoods: The Case of the Silkworkers of Lyon, 1830–1880,'' unpublished paper. The Croix-Rousse was an independent commune, while the slopes of the same name were mostly within the limits of Lyon.

90. Lequin, op. cit., vol. 1, pp. 173, 180–81.

91. MR 1209 (1841); Latreille, ed. op. cit., pp. 317–26.

92. Lequin, op. cit., vol. 1, pp. 170–73.

93. MR 1208, ''Mémoire sur la reconnaissance de la route de Lyon à Saint-Laurent de Mure'' (1828), noting that of the population of 13,085 (4,200 households), 6,000 depended upon agriculture and 3,000 upon the silk industry; ''Mémoire topographique, statistique et militaire . . . aux environs de Lyon'' (1845); Lequin, op. cit., vol. 1, pp. 170–80; Sheridan, op. cit., who offers an illuminating contrast between the Croix-Rousse and La Guillotière and Brotteaux.

94. Lequin, op. cit., vol. 1, p. 182.

95. MR 1208, ''Mémoire joint au levé à vue de la route d'Iseron à Lyon'' (1825); Latreille, ed., op. cit., pp. 315–16: ''Each faubourg thus constituted its own personality, created by the conditions of work and by the nature of the immigration that it received''; MR 1209, ''Mémoire militaire sur le terrain compris entre Vaise et Limonest'' (1850). The port of Vaise was completed in 1829.

96. MR 1209, ''Mémoire militaire sur la vallée de l'Yreron et la défense de Lyon vers l'ouest'' (1851), giving the population of Lyon as 221,609, counting La Guillotière, the Croix Rousse, and Vaise, *''autrefois ses faubourgs,''* and the number of looms as 30,000 in Lyon and another 10,000 in the environs.

97. Jacques Levainville, *Rouen: étude d'une agglomération urbaine* (Paris, 1913), p. 342.

98. MR 1245, ''Mémoire sur la reconnaissance de Rouen à Bonsecours'' (1824, 1834, 1835); Henri Fouquet, *Histoire civile, politique et commerciale de Rouen,* vol. 1 (Rouen, 1876), pp. 905–7; Levainville, op. cit., pp. 224–26.

99. MR 1169, ''Mémoire sur la reconnaissance du Canal de la Haute-Deule, du Bac de Wavrin au Pont de Couteleux près de Lille'' (1846); Pierre Pierrard, *Lille et les Lillois* (Paris, 1967), pp. 620, 82, 95. The ''Mémoire'' noted the spread of the French language at the expense of Flemish.

100. MR 1169 (1846).

101. MR 1235, ''Mémoire sur la reconnaissance de la route de Nantes à Clisson'' (1827); Paul Bois, ed., *Histoire de Nantes* (Toulouse, 1977), pp. 339–40, noting that workers who were relatively well off, such as the sugar refiners, lived in the quarter of Richebourg, where the railroad station is today; Alfred Lescadieu and Auguste Laurant, *Histoire de la ville de Nantes* (Nantes, 1836).

102. François Dornic, ed., *Histoire du Mans* (Toulouse, 1975), pp. 195–97, 234–43, 269–70. Special note should be made of this excellent volume. Le Mans's population grew from 19,800 in 1831 to 23,000 in 1836, 25,000 in 1841, and 27,600 in 1846.

103. Roger Gauchat, ''L'Urbanisme dans les villes anciennes: les faubourgs de Dijon''; *Mémoires de la Commission des Antiquités du département de la Côte-d'or* 23 (1947–53), 342.

104. François Lebrun, ed., *Histoire d'Angers* (Toulouse, 1975), p. 214.

105. MR 1209 (1835).

106. A. D. Landes, 1M 39, prefect, November 9, 1832.

107. George Livet, ed., *Histoire de Colmar* (Toulouse, 1983), p. 161; MR 1188, "Mémoire" (1824).

108. Anne Meyering, "Industrialization and Population Change in Montluçon, 1815–1870" (Ph.D. diss., University of Michigan, 1979), pp. 36–37, 335, 343–52. Meyering notes the absence of signs of working-class solidarity and militancy: no unions and no strikes, at least until the 1870s.

109. See Lion Murard and Patrick Zylberman, *Le Petit Travailleur infatigable* ou le prolétaire régénéré (Fontenay-sous-Bois, 1976), pp. 24–29, 119–91.

110. See Donald Reid, *The Miners of Decazeville: A Genealogy of Deindustrialization* (Cambridge, Mass., 1985).

111. Christian Devilliers and Bernard Huet, *Le Creusot: naissance et développement d'une ville industrielle, 1782–1914* (Seyssel, n.d.), pp. 46–53, 112. "The Creusotins explain that they are born in a Schneider maternity ward and are buried in a Schneider cemetery after going to a Schneider school and being married in a town hall, the gift of, and almost always controlled by, Schneider, after having worked in the Schneider factory" (p. 112). See also Murard and Zylberman, op. cit., p. 27, quoting a contemporary writing in 1874: "the town and the factory are two sisters who have grown up with the same guardian."

112. MR 1266 (1846).

113. MR 1266 (1850); MR 1304 (1844).

114. MR 1266 (1846).

115. André Vant, *Imagerie et urbanisation: recherches sur l'exemple stéphanois* (Saint-Etienne, 1981), pp. 16ff.

116. Lequin, op. cit., vol. 1, pp. 31–32.

117. MR 1266 (1837).

118. Ibid.; Claude Chatelard, *Crime et criminalité dans l'arrondissement de St.-Etienne au XIXème siècle* (Saint-Etienne, 1981), p. 21. The armaments industry helped make up for the decline in the production of hardware. About 70 workers were involved in the production of each gun (the pistol price ranging from 4 to 4,000 francs, this last a fabulous sum, while rifles went for from 14 to 30 francs).

119. David M. Gordon, *Merchants and Capitalists: Industrialization and Provincial Politics in Nineteenth-Century France* (University, Ala., 1985), pp. 24–26. The virtual dependence of the miners and their families on the Compagnie became a political issue during the Second Republic, giving the left hope of winning their support. See C 956, in which workers describe the disappearance of the 2% of their wages withheld for a fund for widows and children of miners killed in accidents.

120. C 956. After the revolution of 1848, the production of hardware had declined, but still employed 2,860 people. Ribbonmaking employed almost 11,000 men, women, and children, and braidmaking 13,000; 8,500 were employed by the armaments manufacturers. Two years later the situation had improved. Exuded one officer in 1850: "all branches of industry seem flourishing, the population has increased since the last census, education and well-being seem to increase with every day, order, saving, and work continue to increase . . . a still more brilliant future is opening up for the capital of the Stéphanois" (MR 1266 [1850]).

121. Saint-Etienne absorbed a faubourg in 1822 and during the Second Empire took in Montaud, Outre-Furan, and Valbenoite, which had a combined population of 22,186 in 1851 (14,584 in 1836). With only 38 streets and 1,100 houses in 1790, the industrial center had 100 streets and 1,800 houses in 1826.

122. Counting the suburbs, the population of Saint-Etienne reached 70,000 in 1846, and 94,500 in 1856, with the incorporation of the surrounding communes. Etienne Fournial, ed., *Saint-Etienne: histoire de la ville et de ses habitants* (Roanne, 1977), p. 230; poster, March 15, 1828, exposition, A. D. Loire, 1984; MR 1266, 1826. Jacky Neaudre, "Les Débuts de l'aménagement urbain de St.-Etienne (1820–1871)," *Etudes foréziennes* 4 (1971), 77, suggests that the influence of the state and of municipal leaders was extremely limited in the growth of Saint-Etienne, and that the *urbanisme* of the eighteenth century, "having been conceived principally in the interest of satisfying an aesthetic order," was doomed to "crumble under the pressure of needs" that forced the town and its classes of population to follow trails blazed by speculation on property.

123. MR 1266 (1850); C 956. A military survey undertaken in 1837 (MR 1266) provides an interesting account of metal work: the *forgeurs* of razor blades put each blade 6 times into the flames, then each time hit it 12 times with a hammer. To make a dozen blades—and earn 5 centimes—the worker had to put each piece of the steel into the fire 72 times and apply the hammer 864 times. This process of maddening repetition would have to be multiplied 30 or 40 times per day to earn a living wage in 1837. Each worker had to pay for the coal, his tools, and the rent of the forge out of his salary.

124. Neaudre, op. cit.

125. Fournial, ed., op. cit., p. 234.

126. Ibid., pp. 86–87. The exceptions included the rues Royale, Foy, and Grand Moulin.

127. Ibid., pp. 234–35.

128. MR 1266 (1826).

129. Chatelard, op. cit., p. 15.

130. Vant, op. cit., pp. 26, 71; Fournial, op. cit., pp. 226–27, 235–37. Montaud was resented by its neighbor Valbenoite. Valbenoite grew from 4,106 inhabitants in 1801 to 6,040 in 1851; Outre-Furan, from 2,417 to 6,670; and Montaud, from 1,480 to 5,726.

131. Vant, op. cit., p. 89.

132. Ibid., pp. 82–84.

133. Vant, op. cit., pp. 157–58.

134. Ibid., p. 170.

135. Quoted from *Le Mercure ségusien*, October 29, 1831, by Fournial, ed., op. cit., p. 86.

136. MR 1266 (1850); MR 1304 (1844).

137. Fournial, ed., op. cit., p. 96.

138. Vant, op. cit., pp. 158–59.

139. MR 1266 (1850); MR 1304 (1844).

140. Vant, op. cit., p. 155.

141. MR 1266 (1826, 1850).

142. MR 1266 (1852): "agriculture is considerably neglected and discredited: the soil of the countryside is leased out to peasants called *grangers* who are without resources; whether they raise animals or provide manure, they let the earth waste away more and more . . . the spirit of the people of St.-Etienne is so much turned toward industry and commerce that this town has literally no rural element."

143. Vant, op. cit., p. 65.

144. Ibid., pp. 56, 67; Fournial, ed., op. cit., pp. 239–40, noting that 2,300 meters of the Furan lay within Saint-Etienne, but that only 200 were in the riverbed, the rest in sections (*biefs*) owned by nine or ten people, making the construction of small bridges or any other changes extremely complicated. Fournial cites municipal decrees attempting to limit the emptying of private latrines and textile dyes.

145. MR 1266 (1850).

146. MR 1266 (1850); MR 1304 (1844), including the unkind comment that nowhere else could one find "traits more ugly or coarse, manners more rude or common. Here a thick film of coal covers each face like a mask, and one notes with sadness signs of the most excessive filth on all people, men and women alike."

147. MR 1266 (1826). See James Lehning, *The Peasants of Marlhes* (Urbana, 1984).

148. Vant, op. cit., pp. 164–65, 171. Eight gendarmes kept order easily.

149. Fournial, ed., op. cit., p. 245.

150. 10M 21, speech of M. Royet-Carreaud.

151. As the events that followed the revolution of 1848 would demonstrate. But the Saint-Etienne workers lacked the organization of their Lyonnais counterparts.

Chapter 3

1. Louis Chevalier, *Labouring Classes and Dangerous Classes in Paris during the First Half of the Nineteenth Century* (London, 1973), p. 2.

2. Ibid., pp. 86, 102, the latter quoting Hugo's preoccupation with the "murder of the *barrière* of Fontainebleau," and the description in *Les Misérables* of the setting of the tenement of Gorbeau (p. 103) that had stood on the boulevard Saint-Jacques: "But at nightful, at the hour when the light has waned, especially in winter, at the hour when the chilly evening breeze is tearing the last rusty leaves from the elms; when the darkness is profound and starless, and when the moon and the wind make rents in the clouds, this boulevard became suddenly terrifying. The straight lines plunged into the gloom and were lost in it like sections of the infinite. The passerby could not refrain from thinking of the countless gallows traditions on the spot. This solitude in which so many crimes had been committed had something awful in it."

3. T. J. Clark, *The Painting of Modern Life: Paris in the Art of Manet and His Followers* (New York, 1985), p. 38.

4. Ibid., p. 238.

5. Ibid., p. 423.

6. Constant-Taillard, *Guide résumé du voyageur aux environs de Paris* (Paris, 1826).

7. Maurice Daumas, Jacques Payen, et al., *Evolution de la géographie industrielle de Paris et sa proche banlieue aux XIXᵉ siècle*, 2 vols. (Paris, 1976), p. 307.

8. Ibid., p. 106.

9. Bronislaw Geremek, *Les Marginaux parisiens aux XIVᵉ et XVᵉ siècles* (Paris, 1976), pp. 85, 89, adding (p. 95) that it is risky to speak of "veritable 'kingdoms' of misery."

10. Arlette Farge, "L'Espace parisien au XVIIIᵉ siècle d'après les ordonnances de police," *Ethnologie française* 12 (1982), 124.

11. David Garrioch, *Community and Neighborhood in Paris, 1740–90* (New York, 1985), p. 218; Arlette Farge, "Un espace urbain obsédant: le commissaire et la rue à Paris au XVIIIᵉ siècle," *Les Révoltes logiques* 6 (1977), 11–12. Garrioch has marshaled considerable evidence contradicting the image of anonymity of neighborhood life in Paris and its faubourgs, including the following telling description by Mercier of the faubourg Saint-Marcel: "There all private quarrels become public; and a woman displeased with her husband pleads her case in the streets, brings him before the tribunal of the populace, gathers the neighbors into a riotous assembly, and recites her man's scandalous confessions" (p. 16).

12. Steven Kaplan, "Les Corporations, les 'faux ouvriers' et le faubourg Saint-Antoine au XVIIIᵉ siècle," *Annales E.S.C.* 43:2 (March–April 1988), pp. 353–78; quote from p. 356.

13. Ibid., pp. 354, 356–57, 361–65, 369. In contrast, Kaplan notes that the "faubourg Saint-Antoine was thus according to its partisans a type of utopia, an enclave of freedom (but not of license) in a universe of obstacles, inquisition, and artificial doctrines" (p. 360); for "these very mobile, restless workers, the faubourg is a sheet anchor, a viable and reassuring alternative" (p. 362), for whom the markets of Paris and their customers should have been grateful. Thus Kaplan argues that, on the eve of the Revolution, "the faubourg unconsciously transforms itself into one of the stakes of political life, a fortuitous model of social ingenuity. It becomes despite itself a subversive space" (p. 370).

14. Steven L. Kaplan, "Social Classification and Representation in the Corporate World of Eighteenth-Century France: Turgot's 'Carnival,'" in Steven Laurence Kaplan and Cynthia J. Koepp, eds., *Work in France: Representations, Meaning, Organization, and Practice* (Ithaca, 1986), p. 191.

15. Ibid., p. 367.

16. Ibid., p. 374, taken from Levacher-Duplessis, *Réponse des délégués des marchands en détail et des maîtres artisans de la ville de Paris aux rapports et délibérations des conseils généraux de commerce et de manufactures* (Paris, 1817), p. 23.

17. Richard Cobb, *Paris and Its Provinces* (Oxford, 1975).

18. Line Teisseyre-Sallmann, "Urbanisme et société: l'exemple de Nîmes aux XVIIᵉ et XVIIIᵉ siècles," *Annales* 35:5 September–October (1980), 979.

19. Constant-Taillard, op. cit., entry for Bondy. They sang: "*Notre compagnie est de trente/ C'est la nuit qu'elle est diligente/ Le jour, nous rions, nous trinquons/ Et des gendarmes nous nous moquons./ Au maire, rien chez nous à rendre/ Quant au préfet, nul n'en veut rien entendre.*" The author of the guide reassured potential visitors by pointing out that most of the band "have for their (Mont)parnasse the King's galleys."

20. Clark, op. cit., p. 67, quoting Denis Poulot's classic, *Le Sublime*.

21. A point made by Clark, op. cit., pp. 58–59, quoting *L'Assommoir:* "Underneath the rising tide of luxury from Paris, there was the misery of the *faubourg*, spoiling and befouling this new city in the making, put up in such haste"; also p. 69.

22. MR 1176, "Environs de Sedan, route de Verdun" (1822), "Sedan" (1825), and "Note sur le camp retranché de Sedan" (1839); Pierre Congar, Jean Lecaillon, and Jacques Rousseau, *Sedan et le pays sedanais* (Paris, 1969), pp. 482–83.

23. Constant-Taillard, op. cit., Boulogne.

24. John M. Merriman, *The Red City; Limoges and the French Nineteenth Century* (New York, 1985), p. 96.

25. A. D. Côtes-du-Nord, 1M 326, sp Guingamp, January 15, 1819.

26. A. D. Haute-Saône, 35M 2, mayor of Vesoul, April 30, and cp April 29, 1821.

27. A. D. Eure, 4M 76, sp Bernay, November 1, 1815, and prefect, September 19, 1814.

28. A. D. Nord, M 201/2 prefect, n.d. [May 1824], August 11, 1825; mayor, February 2 and October 2, 1824, and January 15, 1825; police report, December 28, 1824; municipal decree, August 13, 1825.

29. M 201/3 cc, interrogation of Sylvie Descamps, November 25, 1844; M 201/1, letter of June 15, and prefect, July 3, 1848; M 201/3, mayor of Lille, November 25, 1842; cc November 28, 1844, and March 25, 1846. Yet in April 1849 a letter from a resident complained that for years prostitutes had continued to "run the streets and attract passersby by gestures and words that are more or less obscene"; some of them were seamstresses or young factory girls twelve to eighteen years of age, with venereal disease. In the case of the rue du Bois Saint-Etienne, the police did close down one house and tossed its *propriétaires* (quite illegally) into the street.

30. See Thomas Brennan, *Public Drinking and Popular Culture in Eighteenth-Century*

Paris (Princeton, 1988), pp. 82–85. Brennan quotes (note 15) a source suggesting that the word *guinguette* came from *guinguet,* or "small wine," sold in such places.

31. A. D. Bas-Rhin 3M 944, "Etat nominatif des débits de boissons, arrondissement de Strasbourg."

32. Maurice Agulhon, *Une ville ouvrière au temps du socialisme utopique: Toulon, 1815–51* (Paris, 1971), pp. 19–20, 53–54.

33. A. D. Rhône 4M 2, cp La Guillotière, October 11, 1822. Three years later the prefect noted that "it is not rare to see thousands of inhabitants [of Lyon] set out for Brotteaux" (August 31, 1825).

34. 4M 2, deputy mayor, August 21, and cp October 11, 1822.

35. 4 M 2, prefect, March 29, 1824; cp May 27 and October 20, 1822; mayor of La Guillotière, May 6, 1828. The mayor did not indicate whether crimes were increasing more rapidly than the population.

36. Ibid.

37. 4M 2, mayor of Lyon, September 28, 1825.

38. Ibid.

39. 4M 2, prefect, November 25, 1825.

40. MR 1166 (1824).

41. A. D. Aube, M 1257 bis, mayor of Troyes, November 28, 1831; M 1185, mayor, January 5, 1831. In 1787 the 400 households in Saint-Martin-ès-Vignes included 285 *manoeuvriers: Histoire de Saint-Martin-ès-Vignes, quartier et paroisse de Troyes* (Troyes, 1936).

42. A. D. Aube, M 1180, mayor, June 14, 1845.

43. M 1180, mayor of Troyes, November 10, and a letter from one of the people attacked, October 22, 1843.

44. A. D. Aube M 1259, report of prefect, March and August 8–10, 1847. There were many arrests of workers and several peasants from Rouilly-Saint-Loup.

45. A. D. Puy-de-Dôme M 098, mayor of Clermont, June 15, 1818, and August 17, 1819. The two were juridically joined, sharing the same court and justice of peace.

46. *Recherches clermontoises,* vol. 4: *Clermont sous le Second Empire* (Clermont-Ferrand, 1972), p. 70.

47. A. G. Manry, *Histoire de Clermont-Ferrand* (Clermont-Ferrand, 1975), p. 370. *Clermont sous le Second Empire,* pp.11–12, 70. For most of its history, Clermont had been only a center of commerce and the small-scale production of a candy (*pâtes de Gênes*); the rubber industry transformed the city and its region.

48. The population of Clermont and Ferrand stood at 29,912 in 1851.

49. BB18 1097, *procureur* of Privas, May 13, and pg Nîmes, July 6, 1823.

50. A. D. Hérault, 39M 80, sp Béziers, April 8, 17–18; int. May 13, deploring the hostility between faubourg and town; and prefect, May 15, 1817. Trouble followed when the national guard came to remove the body of the victim (he had been shot at such close range that his shirt was burned). An incident the previous month may have helped stir things up: two cultivators "had the nerve to come from the countryside to cross the faubourg du Pont and part of the town completely nude." They were arrested after going to the house of a widow on the rue de la Vache. Their hurried tour of Béziers won them the twelve francs they had bet on a dare, but got them arrested. Outside Montpellier, it took three warnings in 1818 to break up a dispute in the "faubourg" of Celleneuve, when some villagers argued that the person chosen to carry the flag in the *fête* was "unworthy" (A. D. Hérault, 39M 87, cp Montpellier, p.-v. May 3, 1818).

51. F7 9528, prefect of the Pyrénées-Orientales, date misplaced.

52. A. D. Eure-et-Loire, 4M 183, cp Chartres, August 7, 1826; MR 1260, "Recon-

naissance militaire des environs de Chartres'' [1841] and André Chedeville, ed., *Histoire de Chartres et du pays chartrain* (Toulouse 1985), pp. 260–61; A.G. E5 4, gendarmerie report, November 15, 1830; BB18 1335, pg Paris, May 1 and July 5, and int. May 7 and June 17, 1833. Lèves had a population of 1,118 in 1841 and 1,074 in 1858; many of its residents were farmers and *vignerons*. Of the 58 villagers tried, only one was convicted by a sympathetic jury.

53. A. D. Haute-Loire, 5M 43, prefect, March 19, 1817.

54. 5M 43, prefect, August 31, and cp August 16, 1821.

55. A. D. Haute-Loire, 5M 58, prefect, March 20 and 29, 1829. The faubourg de Breuil had itself been noted as a site for thefts (5M 43, prefect, January 13, 1816). 5M 65, cp June 20, 1833, noted a bloody brawl between *cultivateurs* in a cabaret in the faubourg Saint-Jean.

56. A. D. Haute-Loire, 5M 61, gendarmerie report, April 7 and 9, 1832.

57. A. D. Haute-Loire, 5M 62, procureur, April 22, 1833; subprefect of Yssingeaux, April 24, 1834; and int. October 22, 1830; 5M 61, mayor of Le Puy, May 8, 1835, and prefect, December 8, 1836.

58. 5M 62, prefect, December 29, 1843, January 3, 1844, April 4, 1846; *procureur,* May 10, 1845; prefect of the Rhône, September 4, 1845; int. February 16 and March 7, 1846; 5M 65 cp December 23, 1836, noting brawls and *tapage* in the cabaret of Thivel and the café of Chanal, faubourg de Breuil. The minister of the interior provided 400 extra francs in an attempt to catch Gros, ''légerement marqué de la petite vérole, en ayant une légère cicatrice sur le nez,'' last seen wearing a coat of blue cloth with yellow buttons, blue pants, a black cloth cap, whose brother took out a passport to visit him in Switzerland. He apparently was never caught. His lover was condemned to death, and his brother Augustin to ''travaux forcés à perpétuité.''

59. 5M 61, prefect, November 18, 1836.

60. 5M 62, *procureur,* November 28, 1838.

61. Copies of the minister of the interior's letter, December 14, 1844, can be found in many departmental archives, including A. D. Aube, M 1180.

62. Susanna Barrows quotes Emile Zola who, in response to the storm that followed the serial publication of *L'Assommoir* in 1876, wrote in *Le Bien public:* ''If I were forced to draw a conclusion, I would say close the cabarets, open the schools. . . . And I would add: clean up the faubourgs.'' Barrows, ''After the Commune: Alcoholism, Temperance, and Literature in the Early Third Republic,'' in John M. Merriman, ed., *Consciousness and Class Experience in Nineteenth- Century Europe* (New York, 1979), p. 215.

63. A. D. Puy-de-Dôme, 098, mayor, August 13, 1820.

64. A. D. Meuse, 71M 10, prefect, June 7, 1822.

65. A. D. Ain, 10M 4, prefect, October 23; gendarmerie report, October 27; prefect of the Isère, July 15, 1843.

66. A. D. Loire-Atlantique, 1M 504, April 6, 1822.

67. A. D. Nord, M 199/3, subprefect of Cambrai, April 16, 1817.

68. F7 6782, gendarmerie report, September 21, 1831.

69. MR 1252 (1824, 1833, 1838, 1840, 1844); A. D. Charente, M 642 (old classification), mayor of Angoulême, May 8, 1814; M 735 (old classification); F7 9640, prefect, September 9, 1820.

70. BB18 1104, reports of November and December 1823.

71. BB18 1187, pg Orléans, September 3 and 4; A.G. E5 2, gendarmerie report, September 6, 1830. On August 23 a crowd formed outside the cathedral, where a mission cross had been moved from a public promenade; in Orléans, such crosses seemed to many a ''monument to the triumph and power of the missionaries'' (pg Orléans, August 28 and

September 6, 1830). See R. D. Price, "Popular Disturbances in the French Provinces after the July Revolution of 1830." *European Studies Review* 1:4 (1971), 323–50.

72. F7 6780, gendarmerie report, October 22, 1832.

73. A. D. Jura, M 11, sp Poligny, September 30, and gendarmerie report, October 2, 1830; BB18 1188, pg Besançon, January 3, 10, 31, and February 8, 1831.

74. M 11, sp August 31, 1830.

75. A. D. Hérault, 39M 110, *procureur,* November 3, and sp December 9, 1831, where "troublemakers" took advantage of the proximity of the faubourg Sainte-Aphrodise to stir up trouble.

76. Jacques Michaud and André Cabanis, *Histoire de Narbonne* (Toulouse, 1981), pp. 262–64, 269–70. A. D. Aube 5M 23, prefect, September 7, 1831, and following.

77. Manry, op. cit., p. 354; A. D. Puy-de-Dôme M 0269; MR 1282 (1842).

78. A. D. Lot 1M 200, mayor of Cahors, October 23; prefect, October 24–25, 19; *juge d'instruction,* November 3; *directeur des impôts indirectes,* November 14; *procureur,* November 22, 1831; pg Agen, March 8, 1832, etc.

79. Philippe Wolfe, *Histoire de Toulouse* (Toulouse, 1958), pp. 360–61.

80. Charles Tilly, "The Changing Place of Collective Violence," in Melvin Richter, ed., *Essays in Theory and History* (Cambridge, Mass., 1970), and "How Protest Modernized in France, 1845–55," in William O. Aydelotte, Allan G. Bogue, and Robert William Fogel, eds., *The Dimensions of Quantitative Research in History* (Princeton, 1972).

81. A. D. Jura, M 25, gendarmerie report, April 3, and mayor of Lons, April 3, 1840.

82. Congar, Lecaillon, and Rousseau, op. cit., p. 490.

83. André Latreille, et al., *Histoire de Lyon et du Lyonnais* (Toulouse, 1975), p. 325. Girardin added, "Every manufacturer lives in his factory like the colonial planter in the midst of his slaves," reflecting the fear from within industrial cities as well.

84. Chevalier, op. cit., pp. 265–66.

85. François Lebrun, ed., *Histoire d'Angers* (Toulouse, 1975), p. 253.

86. A. D. Bas-Rhin 3M 48, cp June 11, 1832.

87. F7 6780, gendarmerie report, May 20, 1835.

88. A. D. Loire-et-Cher 1M 91, prefect, December 12, 1838.

89. A. D. Hautes-Pyrénées 1M 212, October 13, 1830.

90. F7 6779, gendarmerie report, Charente-Inférieure, February 1, 1832.

91. A. D. Maine-et-Loire, 1M 6/25, sp May 3, 1829.

92. William M. Sewell, Jr., *Work and Revolution in France* (New York, 1980).

93. A. D. Saône-et-Loire, M 111, prefect, September 7, 1840; A. D. Gard, 4M 48, cp April 20 and following.

94. MR 1209 (1841).

95. Quoted by William Langer, *Political and Social Upheaval, 1832–1852* (New York 1968), pp. 337, 345–46.

96. A. Corret, *Histoire de Belfort et de ses environs* (Belfort, 1855), p. 103.

97. Jacques Rancière, *La Nuit des prolétaires* (Paris, 1981), p. 312.

98. Gabriel Desert, ed., *Histoire de Caen* (Toulouse, 1981), pp. 218–19.

99. BB30 379, pg Lyon, October 26, 1850.

100. See Maurice Agulhon, *1848 ou l'apprentissage de la République* (Paris, 1974), and John M. Merriman, *The Agony of the Republic: The Repression of the Left in Revolutionary France, 1848–51* (New Haven, 1978).

101. Robert Balland, "Les Goguettes rurales autour de Paris au milieu du XIXe siècle," *Ethnologie française* 12:3 (1982), 247–60 (quotes from pp. 252 and 255). Among those dissolved in 1849 by the government, despite its generally good reputation, was the Goguette dite Société des Enfants d'Apollon of Argenteuil, founded in 1837.

102. François Dornic, ed., *Histoire du Mans* (Toulouse, 1975), p. 259.

103. See Pierre Lavedan, *Histoire de l'urbanisme (Epoque contemporaine)* (Paris, 1952).

104. Clark, op. cit., p. 46.

105. Jean Rougerie, quoted in Fernand Braudel and Ernest Labrousse, eds., *Histoire économique et sociale de la France*, vol. 3 (Paris, 1976), p. 799.

106. Gérard Jacquemet, "Belleville aux XIXᵉ et XXᵉ siècles: une méthode d'analyse de la croissance urbaine à Paris," *Annales E.S.C.* 30 (1975), p. 819, quoting Léon Beauvallet, *Les quatre âges de Paris* (Paris, n.d.), and T. Labourrieu, *Les Bandits de Montfaucon* (Paris, 1869), and p. 837.

107. Jacquemet, op. cit., p. 837; 445 Bellevillois were tried by court-martial in the wake of the June Days.

108. Alain Dalotel, Alain Faure, and Jean-Claude Freiermuth, *Aux origines de la Commune; le mouvement des réunions publiques à Paris, 1868–1870* (Paris, 1980), p. 72; Clark, op. cit., p. 45. "Belleville was not the worst; beyond it was a hinterland of exiles, half wilderness and half armed camp, peopled by those who knew—they were told so often—that they had lost their city, and might still try to take it back" (Jacquemet, op. cit., p. 838).

109. See Stewart Edwards, *The Paris Commune of 1871* (New York, 1971), and *The Communards of Paris, 1871* (Ithaca, N.Y., 1973); *Journal des débats*, April 18, 1832; Jacquemet, op. cit., p. 824.

110. Lion Murard and Patrick Zylberman, *Le Petit Travailleur infatigable ou le prolétaire régénéré* (Fontenay-sous-Bois, 1976), p. 35.

111. Michelle Perrot, "Dans la France de la Belle Epoque, les 'Apaches' premières bandes de jeunes," in Bernard Vincent et al., *Les Marginaux et les exclus dans l'histoire* (Paris, 1979), pp. 387–88.

112. Ibid., p. 388, quoting *Le Gaulois*, September 13, 1907.

113. Perrot, op. cit., pp. 392, 394. See Walter Benjamin, *Charles Baudelaire: A Lyric Poet in the Era of High Capitalism* (London, 1973), pp. 78–79: for Baudelaire, "the image of the hero . . . includes the apache. . . . The apache abjures virtue and laws; he terminates the *contrat social* forever."

114. Jean Maitron, ed., *Ravachol et les anarchistes* (Paris, 1964), pp. 110–11.

115. Henry Leyret, *En plein faubourg, moeurs ouvrières* (Paris, 1895), pp. 13–14, 17, 103, 113. Examples of argot included *afure* for *bénéfice; pognon* for *argent* (still common today); *y a pas plan* for *pas moyen;* and *empiter* for *tromper* (e.g., to leave without paying for one's drinks).

116. Quoted by Pierre Ayçoberry, "Au-delà des ramparts: 'vrais colonais' et banlieusards au milieu du XIXᵉ siècle," *Mouvement social* 118 (January–March 1982), p. 38.

117. A. D. Seine, 0 9 14, deputy mayor of Bercy, January 16, 1827.

118. Steven Kaplan, "Les Corporations," pp. 373–74.

Chapter 4

1. La Comtesse Dash (Anne-Latrelle de Cisterne de Coutiras de Poulloüe de Saint-Mars), *Mémoires des autres*, vol. 1, *souvenirs anecdotiques sur le Premier Empire et les Cent Jours* (Paris,1896), p. 5. She married Eugène de Saint-Mars, an officer posted in Poitiers. There were at least 130 nobles in Poitiers in 1788 according to Robert Favreau, ed., *Histoire de Poitiers* (Toulouse, 1985), p. 225.

2. Now the rue Théophraste Renaudot. In 1828 it was the site of the schools of the Pères de Picpus and the order of the Sacred Hearts of Jesus and Mary.

3. Comtesse Dash, op. cit., pp. 56–59. Irland de Bazoges, former lieutenant-general of the *sénéchaussée* of Poitiers, sat in the National Assembly beginning in August 1789; after emigrating, he returned to Poitiers following the Concordat and was mayor until 1813. See Robert Favreau, et al., *Histoire de Poitiers* (Toulouse, 1985), p. 298.

4. A. D. Vienne, M4 39, prefect, May 7, 1825. The family residence of the countess's family was in fact some distance from the two principal quarters of the nobles, farther than she may have remembered it.

5. Comtesse Dash, op. cit., pp. 12–14, 40–41, 56, 85.

6. Ibid., pp. 26–31, 65, 129. Public executions were held on the place du Pilori until 1829, and then moved to the place du Pont-Guillon.

7. Favreau, ed., op. cit., p. 207.

8. Ibid., pp. 146–56.

9. F19 5696, prefect, February 14, 1817.

10. M4 37, prefect, March 24, 1823; F19 5696, letter of the *grand aumônier,* December 14, 1815; parish council of Notre-Dame, n.d. [March 1816].

11. F 19 354, letter of *vicaires généraux,* April 11, 1817; letter of L. Cavayon, June 15, 1815, and June 28, 1818; F19 5696, prefect, February 5, 1817; M4 37, prefect, June 2, 1823. There were also incidents surrounding the so-called "ritual of Poitiers" in late 1816 or early 1817; issued in 1765, it was opposed by moderates within the clergy (prefect, February 5 and 18, 1817).

12. Comtesse Dash, op. cit., p. 125; F19 5696, prefect, February 14, 1817.

13. MR 1298, "Mémoire sur la feuille de Poitiers" (1841). That year the municipal council proposed a plan to construct a new quarter west of the place d'Armes, which would have helped reduce the relative isolation of the aristocratic rue des Hautes-Treilles, but the city lacked funds for such an enterprise. Gas lighting, introduced in 1845, seemed only to illuminate Poitiers's stagnation. Yet for others the construction of a hyraulic pump drawing from the Clain, resolving at least partially the problem of an inadequate water supply, suggested that a new era had begun.

14. Favreau, op. cit., p. 283.

15. Ibid., pp. 326–27.

16. H. Chemioux, *Oraison funèbre du vieux Poitiers* (Poitiers, 1861), lamenting the construction of the new prefecture on the bluff above the station. Both structures, in his opinion, exercised an unjustified domination over urban planning in Poitiers. He criticized the allocation of three million francs to the new quarters, and the construction of the rue Neuve, which linked, however indirectly, the pont Neuf to the prefecture. See also J. Tourneur-Among, *Les onze villes superposées de Poitiers* (Poitiers, 1925), noting that the municipality was unable to keep its promise to encourage expansion in the direction of the faubourgs Saint-Cyprien and Saint-Saturnin: "each town wanted, following the example of Paris, a quarter of the Etoile, a quarter of Europe, the *tabula rasa,* a geometric plan. Poitiers envied Napoléon-Vendée" (p. 6). The martyrdom of some of the town's historical monuments had followed.

17. F7 9710, January 24, 1817.

18. Favreau, ed., op. cit., pp. 224–28, citing one study of marriage contracts from the eighteenth century giving the percentage of rentiers at 7.5%, that of the agricultural sector at 21.3%, and commerce and artisanal production at 51.7%.

19. Ibid. Accusations of laziness against the residents of Poitiers went back at least to the sixteenth century. See Favreau, op. cit., p. 218: in 1754 the town's image was of a "depopulated town, without either commerce or manufactures, in which inhabitants were 'naturally lazy, addicted to pleasures, kind, and sociable.'"

20. Favreau, ed., op. cit., pp. 256, 270–73, 285–88.

21. Ibid., pp. 265–66, 279–85. Deserted by fleeing noble émigrés, as late as 1799 the town was swept by rumors of aristocratic plots—a veritable *psychose*—closely linked to the proximity of the counterrevolution in the Vendée.

22. Poitiers increased by only 191 people between 1806 and 1821, when its population was 21,315. It reached 23,128 in 1823, and 26,764 in 1846 (Favreau, ed., op. cit., pp. 291–92, 285–88). The decline of the population of Poitiers had begun in the eighteenth century (pp. 237–43).

23. MR 1298, Thiébault, 1841.

24. "If one judges the importance of a town by its walls, Poitiers would perhaps be the first town of the kingdom after Paris" (abbé Expilly, *Dictionnaire des Gaules,* quoted by Favreau, op. cit., p. 217).

25. The only exception was that of Saint-Lazare, so the people of the faubourgs, and the firemen as well, could come and go as necessary.

26. F19 731A, report to minister of ecclesiastical affairs, June 1825; bishop, February 6, 1823.

27. Comtesse Dash, op. cit., pp. 60, 124–25, 174–75, 246–47.

28. Ibid., pp. 132–39.

29. Ibid., pp. 132–41, 183–87; La Comtesse Dash (Anne-Latrelle de Cisterne de Coutiras de Poulloüe de Saint-Mars), *Mémoires des autres,* vol. 2, *Souvenirs anecdotiques sur la Restauration* (Paris, 1896), p. 66.

30. Ibid., pp. 184–186.

31. M4 36, cp November 2, 1822; M4 37, prefect, April 26, 1823; cp Lami, October 24, 1823; M4 38, prefect January 1 and May 22, 1824; cp Lami, October 22, 1824; M4 39, prefect, July 30, 1825, and Favreau, ed., op. cit., pp. 300–301; M4 41, gendarmerie report, February 2, 1820. The murder of a woman by a liberal only seconds after she had jilted him in May 1824 did not help their image.

32. Favreau, op. cit., pp. 303–5. In 1840 there were 1,120 municipal electors in Poitiers. It proved difficult to find a mayor, until Louis-Antoine Regnault, the son-in-law of Cochon de L'Apparent, accepted.

33. BB18 1187, pg Poitiers, September 8, 1830; BB18 1321, pg May 31 and June 4, 1831; BB18 1322, int. August 11, 1831.

34. MR 1298 (1841).

35. BB18 1193, pg Poitiers, January 28, 1831; BB18 1206, pg May 8 and 14, 1832; BB18 1247, pg July 16, 1837; BB18 1254, pg July 15 and 16, 1838; BB18 1262; M4 41, "Leproy," February 12, 1831; BB18 1193, pg January 28, 1831; BB18 1323, pg April 14 and November 7, 1831; M4 42, int. March 21, and prefect, August 29, 1832, reporting that the *Gazette* had 630 subscribers.

36. M4 42, prefect, March 15, May 16–17, and December 3; int. March 21 and May 18; mayor, February 29, March 22, and June 16; deputy mayor, May 18, 1832; M4 43, cp September 21, 1836; BB18 1214, pg March 31, 1832; BB18 1212, pg March 31, 1833. Republicans were led by David de Thiais, an indebted lawyer and editor of the anticlerical *L'Echo du peuple.*

37. BB18 1356, pg Poitiers, July 13, 1834; BB18 1368, pg Poitiers, May 31 and May 1, 1837; BB18 1399, pg Poitiers, March 9, 1841; BB18 1451, pg Poitiers, March 6, 1847. The seizure by the police of correspondence between David de Thiais and republicans in Paris and Niort followed the 1834 events. Incendiary posters in 1837, a brief attempt to circulate a petition for electoral reform in 1841, and the arrival of the utopian socialist newspaper *Le Prolétaire* in 1847 were the extent of organized republicanism in Poitiers.

38. BB18 1204, *avocat général,* January 9 and March 6, and int. March 12, 1832. Other tensions existed between the faubourgs and the town itself, of which we have only a

few fleeting images. In June 1825 there was a brawl between soldiers and the inhabitants of the faubourgs, in this case in the faubourg de la Cueille, known for its fidelity to Napoleon (F7 9710, prefect, May 10, 1816). The fight started after two cavalrymen refused to dance with local women who had asked them. Soon the soldiers had their hands full with fifty ''peasants'' (M4 39, prefect, June 4, 1825).

39. The club made Ledru-Rollin its official candidate in the presidential elections of December 1848.

40. M4 54, gendarmerie report, n.d. to prefect (probably July 1848): ''there are no more clubs meeting, but they say that they exist in all the faubourgs of Poitiers''; BB30 364, pg October 17, 1848.

41. M4 54, gendarmerie report, p.-v. March 27, 1848. The arrival of the news of the revolution was marked only by a brief revolt of students who barricaded themselves in the university to show support for their dean (p.-v. March 23).

42. M4 54 gendarmerie report n.d.; complaint of M. Petit Guéritault, 21 rue Saint-Paul, August 20, 1848.

43. See Austin Gough, ''The Conflict in Politics: Bishop Pie's Campaign against the Nineteenth Century,'' in Theodore Zeldin, ed., *Conflicts in French Society: Anticlericalism, Education and Morals in the Nineteenth Century* (London, 1970).

44. Ibid., p. 99.

45. BB30 385, pg Poitiers, December 31, 1849, and May 31, 1851. The papers included the legitimist *L'Abeille de la Vienne,* followed by the review *Amis de l'ordre,* the *Journal de la Vienne,* and *L'Echo de l'Ouest.* The democratic socialist Collard, who did portraits in daguerreotype and organized a banquet in honor of Garnier-Pagès in the spring of 1851, had many contacts with the students of the Cercle des Ecoles in the Café Duchesne on the rue des Basses-Treilles. Workers gathered with Collard first in his shop, and then in the Café des Trois Pilliers, on the same street; both cafés were closed down in September 1851 (M4 60, cc September 24–October 25 and October 25–November 29, 1851; BB30 385, pg Poitiers, September 9 and November 9, 1851).

46. Gough, op. cit., p. 100. Gough describes the ongoing battle of wills between the irascible and determined Pie and the *procureur général,* N. Damay.

47. BB30 385, pg August 8, September 9, and November 9, 1851; M4 54, cc May 4 and June 22; M4 59, int. September 12, 1850; prefect, March 6 and August 24, 1851; cc September 24 and October 25, 1851.

48. Gough, op. cit., p. 103. See particularly his amusing account of Pie's attempt to promote the ''miraculous discovery'' by a nun in Poitiers of the Sacred Prepuce, believed to be the only part of Christ left on earth (pp. 163–64). The Saint-Vincent de Paul Society became a front for legitimist activity. Gough suggests that the nobles continued to be hesitant about seeking middle-class support (pp. 111–12), in line with Countess Dash's recollections. Gough (p. 127) quotes Pie's funeral oration for the mother of the Vendean general La Rochejacquelin in 1857: ''There is no other province in France where the gentleman and the peasant have enjoyed more points of contact and agreement than in this country of the Gâtine and the Bocage. . . . From [religious faith] springs this phenomenon hardly known elsewhere: a friendly and honored nobility, supported by a proud and submissive people.''

49. M4 60, cc December 2–28, 1851. When news of the coup arrived, a crowd gathered at the town hall. It surrounded the policeman Saba, forcing him to free the mayor of the neighboring commune of Biard, who had insulted the name of Louis Napoleon. Saba was struck once with his own cane, and a delegation tried to persuade the newly appointed mayor, Grilliet, to sound the tocsin.

50. MR 1298, ''Mémoire sur les environs de Châtellerault,'' M. Thiébault (captain),

1841; F3II Vienne 5, report to the king received April 15, 1822; F7 9874, prefect, November 11, 1817. In 1848, over 1,100 workers were employed making weapons; C 968: 971 men, 30 women, and 138 children, of whom 673 were from the region. The captain gave the population in 1841 as 9,904. The survey provided no statistics on the cutlery workers, hard hit by the economic crisis; no one from the industry responded to the request for information for the survey. Only those cutlery workers who could find nothing else continued to work such long hours for an exceedingly minimal return during those hard times, "dominated, lacking their own resources, by several merchants who exploit this type of industry."

51. 8M 3/69, census of 1851, *feuille* 17: among heads of household, on the first three streets mentioned, there were 46 day laborers, male and female, 37 weavers, 33 armament workers, 18 cutlery workers, followed by 11 rentiers, 9 shoemakers, 7 merchants, 7 masons, 5 secondhand dealers, 5 embroiderers, 5 blacksmiths, 4 property owners, butchers, bakers, etc.

52. Ibid.

53. M4 37, mayor, July 9, 1823.

54. M4 311, sp January 11 and 30, and int. February 26, 1840, the mayor of Naintré retaining his communal jurisdiction.

55. Alfred Hérault, *Souvenirs, 1837–1870* (Châtellerault, 1971), pp. 25–27.

56. Ibid., pp. 22–23.

57. M4 35, prefect, January 30, 1822; F7 6701, statutes and prefect, May 9, 1828. At the time of its (re)authorization in 1818, members of the Société Littéraire included 13 *propriétaires* (possibly from outside town, but almost certainly bourgeois, such as those described by Hérault, who owned property in the countryside), 5 wholesale merchants, a notary, a retired officer, a pharmacist, a doctor, a clerk, and a lawyer.

58. M4 35, sp February 26, 1822, claiming that 8,000 of the town's approximately 10,000 people were driven by money. "The worker greets the bourgeois first and demonstrates his deference to him; but in this respect he is neither humble nor servile, speaking freely. The bourgeois, for his part, shows an interest in this man whom he has always known, who has grown old at his side, who, far from inspiring mistrust or apathy in him, has his esteem and often his affection. The rich man chats with the poor man, his neighbor, out of friendship [*de bonne amitié*], as a local expression puts it" (Hérault, op. cit., pp. 30–31).

59. M4 40, prefect, March 28, 1827.

60. F19 5696, *vicaire général,* December 14, 1816, and January 8, 1817; protest of the Martineau family, December 8, 1816.

61. BB18 992, pg Poitiers, June 8, 1819.

62. M4 27, sp August 16, 1818, M4 35, sp February 21, 1822; M4 40, sp March 28 and April 4, 1827, and June 3, 1828; M4 43, sp September 9, 1820, noting the great influence of the liberal deputy Voyer d'Argenson in the region.

63. BB18 1181, pg Poitiers, February 27, March 27, April 6, and May 25, 1830; *procureur,* March 29 and April 5, 1830.

64. M4 42, cp March 1, 1833.

65. Hérault, op. cit., p. 34.

66. M4 56, sp June 4, 1849; Evrard (a munitions employee elected to the municipal council), letter of March 3, 1849. The director was dismissed by the provisional government. Evrard was apparently sent to work with the artillery based in Rennes (sp September 9, 1849). See Maurice Agulhon, *Une ville ouvrière au temps du socialisme utopique: Toulon de 1815 à 1851* (Paris, 1970), on the role of the workers of the arsenal, particularly those who were migrants from Paris and other cities.

67. BB30 364, summary report, pg Poitiers (Damay), July 30, 1849.

68. M4 56, lists n.d. and February 1849; M4 57, sp July 30, and cp July 10, 1849. The *procureur général* put it this way: "One finds socialists in agglomerations of men whose existence depends on the vicissitudes of industrial work" (BB30 385, December 10, 1849).

69. M4 56, sp February 4, 1849.

70. M4 56, sp February 10 and 16, and July 2, and int. February 14, 1849. The workers of the arms manufacture could always be transferred or fired, which appears to have been the case, as int. February 15 noted that 5 workers would be sent away. Pierre Pleignard, born in Châtellerault in 1795, served as provisional *procureur* and was elected to the Constituent Assembly. Hilaire Lespinière (b. 1787), a doctor, became provisional mayor after the February Revolution. Clément Fradin (b. 1792), a lawyer was named provisional subprefect, and was described by the subprefect in his report of December 3, 1851 (before receiving word of the coup d'état), as an "orateur de la rue et des clubs" (M4 60). Hérault's comment that Pleignard was not terribly interested in the social question is consistent with the separate direction democratic socialism took in the faubourg (Hérault, op. cit., pp. 38–40).

71. M4 58, sp February 2, 1850. Petitions against the elctoral law of May 31, 1850, circulated in town.

72. BB30 385, pg Poitiers, April 21, June 1, and August 15, 1850, and August 8, 1851; M4 59, sp May 2 and 3, 1851. In August it was reported that the "demagogues" hoped to form an association to bid for the right to operate the arms manufacture, headed by a former cutlery manufacturer with some experience working with canons (sp August 24, 1851). A list provided in July 1851 (M4 59, int. July 7, 1851) of those denounced as *démoc-soc* militants covered a wide range of professions, with by far the strongest concentration in the arms manufacture (35), including several Belgians (noted in M4 60, sp report of December 3, 1851). Only a single cutlery worker, from the faubourg Châteauneuf was listed, reflecting the devastating decline in the industry.

73. BB30 385, pg Poitiers, August 8, 1851; M4 59, sp May 1 and 5; prefect, May 6; prefect to sp July 28; and prefect, June 21 and August 4, 1851; mayor, October 1, 1851; Hérault, op. cit., pp. 40–43; M4 59, sp May 14, 1851, and BB30 402, extracts of deliberation of the mixed commission. Fradin was expelled from France; Pleignard, Lespinière, and others were placed under surveillance. Hérault noted that the 31 names added to the second list drawn up by the mixed commission were all workers, most of them from the arms manufacture.

74. See Ted W. Margadant, *Urban Rivalries during the French Revolution* (Princeton, 1992).

75. D IV bis 18.

76. In fact, the death rate exceeded the birth rate, 33/00 to 28/00, according to "Mémoire sur la ville de la Roche-sur-Yon" (MR 1234, 1826).

77. D IV bis 18.

78. Ibid.

79. See Charles Tilly, *The Vendée* (Cambridge, Mass., 1964); Donald Sutherland, *The Chouans: The Social Origins of Popular Counterrevolution in Upper Brittany* (Oxford, 1982); and Paul Bois, *Les Paysans de l'ouest* (Paris, 1971).

80. MR 1234, 'Quelques réflexions sur la feuille de Bourbon-Vendée," A. Goguel (1840); Marcel Faucheux, *L'Enfance difficile de la Roche-sur-Yon (1804–1854)* (La Roche-sur-Yone, 1954), pp. 14–15, citing the report of 9 Floréal, year II: "The inhabitants, deprived of commerce by the lack of main roads in the bocage and without communications in the marshlands, have not arrived at the degree of civilization that one would expect; they see outsiders so rarely that they eagerly seized upon the most absurd tales." See also Emile

Gabory, *Napoléon et la Vendée* (Paris, 1914), pp. 203–31, who indicates that a loyal priest, Hébert of Aizenay, recommended the construction of a new town to Gouvion. See Baron Prosper de Barante, *Notice sur la ville de La Roche-sur-Yon* (La Roche-sur-Yon, 1954), pp. 6, 18. Napoleon rejected a proposal that a new department be created to encompass the territory that had seen the most impassioned royalist uprisings, with Cholet as the capital.

81. Lewis Mumford, *The City in History* (New York, 1961).

82. Faucheux, op. cit., pp. 24–25. Pierre Lavedan, *Histoire de l'urbanisme (époque contemporaine)* (Paris, 1952), notes (p. 34) that the town was at first known as Napoléon-Ville or Napoléon-Vendée.

83. Ibid., pp. 44–47.

84. F1cIII Vendée 5, prefect report of 4 Nivôse, year XIII; ibid., p. 55.

85. Gabory, op. cit., p. 247. It also proved difficult to set the value of the property which the commune now owned, in order to indemnify the owners; F2II Vendée 3, decree of 9 Pluvôse, year XIII, cited by report to int., January 19, 1809. The value of the land was set before the prefecture had moved; this was disadvantageous to the commune, which received less money for the more valuable land. The minister of the interior retained the right to set the value of the land, after an assessment by experts chosen by the prefect, the mayor, and the primary concessionnaire (prefect, January 19, 1809). F2II Vendée 3 contains an extract of the municipal council meeting of July 19, 1809, listing 69 concessionnaires who received land from the commune.

86. Faucheux, op. cit., pp. 58–59.

87. Barante, op. cit., pp. 9–12; Gabory, op. cit., pp. 252–53; [L.R.] "En marge de l'histoire (La Roche-sur-Yon/Napoléon-Vendée/Bourbon-Vendée)," *Société d'émulation de la Vendée,* 1924, pp. 140–43, noting that the mayor told Napoleon, sensing his displeasure, "We fear that dissatisfaction may be the reason for your departure. We have done little to welcome you because we have little." Two years later, the municipal cashbox could barely afford the forty-three francs owed a man who transported a marble bust of the emperor.

88. Lavedan, op. cit., pp. 34–37.

89. F1cIII Vendée 5, prefect report of 4 Nivôse, year XIII. In 1820 there were 26 eligible voters in the town: 14 property owners, 9 officials, 1 attorney, 1 geometer, and 1 tanner (3M 25).

90. Faucheux, op. cit., p. 68.

91. Gabory, op. cit., pp. 256–58. In 1815 the population by one measure stood at 2,566. By 1826 it had crept to 2,792, less than Fontenay (6,245), Sables (4,698), or Luçon (3,739) (4M 29).

92. F3II Vendée 3, prefect, November 16, 1815, citing the plight of M. Esgonnière, president of the tribunal, when M. Onfroy, the *inspecteur des eaux et des fôrets,* tried to keep too much of one house for himself. Prefect Savary de Lepinerays was among those buying land. In 1811 there were 45 houses with two floors, 87 with but one (Faucheux, op. cit., pp. 63–65).

93. MR 1234, "Mémoire sur la reconnaissance de la route de Bourbon-Vendée à St. Sulpice-le-Vernon," M. Auguste de Laporte.

94. F1cIII Vendée 8, Prefect Urbain de Kerespertz, November 12, 1817.

95. F1cIII Vendée 5, n.d. [1814].

96. F7 9710, Acting Prefect and Mayor Savary de Lepinerays, March 28, 1815.

97. Ibid., p. 77. The town was briefly called "Bonneville" before "Bourbon-Vendée" was chosen; F1cIII Vendée 8, int. to Mayor Tortat, January 10, 1816.

98. BB18 1038, May 5, 1828; [Antoine Tortat] *Extraits des mémoires d'Antoine*

Tortat, 1775–1847 (Paris, 1911), pp. 89–94. The delegation returned to find the population "drunk with joy" at the news.

99. Tortat, op. cit., pp. 84–87. The lodge had been approved by the prefect in 1819, in the hope that it might be "useful" in healing wounds in a department with so many bitter memories (F7 6701, letter requesting authorization, December 26, 1818; prefect, January 15, July 26, 1820, and pg Poitiers, May 25, 1821).

100. 1M 372/3 and F1cIII Vendée 5, report of the prefect, November 1814–January 1815; 4M 29. The road to Challans was finally finished, as were the departmental sections of the road from Caen to Les Sables d'Olonne; several others were improved, and new roads were constructed from Bourbon-Vendée to Sainte-Hermine and from Belleville to Montaigne.

101. Faucheux, op. cit., p. 83; this action was a stern warning.

102. MR 1234; there were 300 houses in the nucleated settlement and 60 dispersed residences in the commune. The completed church cost 814,319 francs, three times the original estimate. At the time, Bourbon had an agricultural population of 1,500.

103. F19 654, bishop of Luçon, August 28, 1829; F21 428; F7 6772, prefect, February 1 and April 3, 1829; Tortat, op. cit., p. 107.

104. Tortat, op. cit., p. 66.

105. MR 1234, "Mémoire sur les environs de Bourbon-Vendée," M. Leclerc, captain (1842).

106. F7 9710, prefect June 11, 1815; F19 481 (1-3), commander of the 12th Military Division, April 29, 1815; 1M 394, prefect, March 13 and 17, 1815. Tortat, op. cit., p. 68.

107. Tortat, op. cit., p. 73.

108. F7 9710, September 23, 1816.

109. F7 9710, October 16, 1815.

110. BB18 1038, *procureur,* May 6, 1818.

111. F7 9710, letter of Savary de Lepinerays, July 12, 1815.

112. 1M 372/3, subprefect, February 28, 1815; F1cIII Vendée 8, Tortat, April 17, 1816; F7 9710, mj September 12, 1817. In 1825 the old Chouan chiefs gathered in Bourbon-Vendée to draw up a new legion that they hoped—in vain—would be incorporated as such into the army.

113. F1cIII Vendée 8, Prefect de Kerespertz, September 9, 1817.

114. F7 9710, pg Poitiers, October 26, 1820.

115. F7 6701, int. report of March, and May 26, 1829; F7 6772, prefect, August 25, 1829, and March 3 and 15, 1830. In 1836 there were two reading clubs (4M 112).

116. 1M 372/3, prefect, March 9, 1815, and subprefect, February 28, 1815.

117. Tortat, op. cit., pp. 83–84. Poiré-près-Bourbon and Beaulieu-sous-Bourbon lost their markets; p.-v. November 19, 1812; a Thursday market for calves and sheep was added in 1813. In March 1815, just before the Hundred Days, the prefect renewed the suggestion that some of the remaining fairs and markets in the region be eliminated, claiming that most were "only a pretext for the most shameful debauchery."

118. Tortat, op. cit., p. 117. Tortat became *procureur,* refusing, he claimed in his memoirs, a higher post in the ministry of finance because he liked his town and especially his *maison charmante.* Anticlerical incidents are recounted in 1M 401, prefect, August 31, 1830, and F19 5734, prefect, November 8, and bishop, November 29, 1830.

119. F19 5734, prefect, December 3; F19 5683, June 20, 1832; BB18 1211, int. October 10, 1832. See F7 6784, gendarmerie reports of February 19, May 21, 1832; etc.; BB18 1228, 1M 426, and especially series E5 in the Archives of the Ministry of War, Vincennes. In February 1832 a band of seven armed men held up a cattle merchant in the commune of Poiré-sous-Bourbon on the edge of Bourbon-Vendée. Armed bands continued

to appear through the end of 1832, particularly in the nearby canton of Les Herbiers. The first signs of republicanism appeared in 1835—no more than several placards posted at night (F7 6784, gendarmerie report, May 3 and 28, 1835).

120. 1M 528. Rural communes scrupulously ignored the 1833 festival celebrating the anniversary of the July Revolution.

121. 3M 43. In 1839 the three leading taxpayers were bankers, the fourth an entrepreneur in transport, and the eighth a tanner who turned a profit on the town's first fledgling industry (3M 43). Of the first 150 eligible to vote in the municipal elections, 27 were innkeepers or café owners, 16 were property owners, 15 were merchants, plus 8 functionaries, 7 businessmen, and only a handful of men from the liberal professions.

122. Faucheux, op. cit., pp. 84–87; F3II Vendée 3, December 10, 1831. The municipality claimed that "no government more than the July Monarchy had profited from its creation." The mayor's request that Bourbon-Vendée receive state funds had not even been answered; while Fontenay had been sent 20,000 francs and Les Sables d'Olonne 10,000 (F3II Vendée 3, Mayor Guitton, who resigned in March 1831).

123. F3II Vendée 3, construction authorized by the king on August 26, 1831; p.-v. of municipal council meeting, July 23, 1831. The municipality had contributed 120,000 francs to a barracks for 800 soldiers, finally completed in 1836.

124. F2II Vendée 3, p.-v. of municipal council, February 15, 1842, and May 8, 1845; int. March 10, 1845, authorization of August 7, 1845; prefect, January 28, 1845.

125. F2II Vendée 3, authorization of January 9, 1844.

126. 1M 127, *procureur*, June 30, 1848; MR 1234; another survey completed two years later emphasized the continuing hold of superstition in the *bocage*, "after the devil and the priest, a sorcerer is most respected and feared by the peasant" ("Mémoire sur les environs de Bourbon-Vendée, by M. Leclerc, captain" [1842]).

127. F19 5683, bishop of Luçon, April 4 and June 27, 1848; BB30 364, pg Poitiers, March 11, 1848.

128. 1M 427, prefect, April 5, 1848. Forty-five national guardsmen were among the contingent of 241 from the department who traveled to the capital to fight the June insurgents (1M 427, prefect, July 1, 4, and 6, 1848).

129. 1M 427, prefect, October 23, 1850; the *Publicateur vendéen* was legitimist, until taken over by moderate republicans in October 1850.

130. BB30 385, pg Poitiers, December 31, 1849, and March 17, 1851; 1M 427, prefect, July 7 and December 7, 1849, and March 26, 1851. The 1848 survey claimed that conditions for workers in Napoléon-Vendée were better than in many other places, that they benefited from relatively new houses and wider streets offering more air (C 967B). The mixed commission of the Vendée sentenced Napoléon Gallois to expulsion from the department; Paul Clémenceau, a lawyer and radical republican living in Nantes, who tried to win converts in the Vendée, was allowed to remain in Nantes with his family, which included his infant son, Georges, since "one could have great confidence in his most honorable family" (BB30 402 and 4M 390).

131. Faucheux, op. cit., pp. 89–93. The claim was for 1,920,789 francs, part of 12 million francs allocated between 1804 and 1813.

132. MR 1234, "Mémoire descriptif et militaire de Napoléon-Vendée," Feraud (1853); C 967B. The census of 1851 listed 351 people in the clothing trades, 466 in the production of food, 380 in the building industry, 91 in transportation, 548 in the liberal professions, 7 clergy, 17 domestics (a very small number for a town of 6,000), 44 beggars, 26 prostitutes, 27 prisoners, and 21 intellectuals. The 1,701 households lived in 996 houses (itself a very unusual ratio, far more typical of a faubourg than a city) on 58 streets. The population included 14 Protestants and 30 "foreigners."

133. Bernadette Wirtz-Daviau, 'La Statue de Napoléon I à La Roche-sur-Yon et son sculpteur, le comte de Nieuwerkerke,'' *Société d'émulation de la Vendée, Annuaire*, 1954, p. 88. Today one can still see ''Napoléon-Vendée'' inscribed on the station, but over an entrance that no longer exists, now virtually buried beneath a pedestrian overpass that stretches over the railroad yards.

Chapter 5

1. See Peter Sahlins, *Boundaries* (Berkeley, 1989).

2. Peter McPhee, '' A Case-Study of Internal Colonization: The *Francisation* of Northern Catalonia,'' *Review* 3:3 (Winter 1980), 403. McPhee notes that the measure on sermons had to be abandoned, with the exception of the cathedral, because too few priests could speak French.

3. Ibid., quoted on pp. 403–4.

4. Michel Brunet, *Une société contre l'état, 1780–1820* (Toulouse, n.d. [1986]), p. 535. See Peter McPhee, *Collioure et la Révolution française* (Perpignan, 1989).

5. The *généralité* of Roussillon had also included the Comté de Foix. Part of Occitan Fenouillèdes that should have been tacked on to the Aude was added to the Pyrénées-Orientales.

6. MR 1222; Abel Hugo, *France pittoresque. Département des Pyrénées-Orientales* (Paris, 1833), pp. 25–26.

7. MR 1222, ''Mémoire pour servir à l'intelligence de la reconnaissance de Perpignan à Peyrestortes'' (1824).

8. McPhee, ''A Case-Study'' p. 404, quoting the recollection of the noble Jaubert de Passa: ''at the time [before the Revolution] I was completely ignorant of the French language and I confess that I even felt a lively enough revulsion toward it.''

9. Prosper Mérimée, *Notes de voyages* (Paris, 1835), pp. 399–400.

10. Peter Sahlins, ''Before France and Spain: Territory and Identity in a Pyrenean Valley, 1659–1868'' (Ph.D. diss., Princeton University, 1987), pp. 114–15: ''the origins of the term are uncertain, but can be linked to the name of the Gevaudan region in France, from where many poorer immigrants to Spain originated.'' Sahlins argues that the term emerged in the early modern period to refer to the French from beyond the Corbières. In the nineteenth century the Spanish used it with reference to French Catalans; however, the French Catalans themselves, considering themselves ethnically distinct from the French, used it to refer to the French.

11. MR 1222; McPhee, ''A Case-Study'': ''The Revolution accelerated the process whereby institutional and linguistic unity had begun to be imposed by the monarchy before 1789'' (p. 406). He notes that ''the leading political club in Perpignan, dominated by Girondin-oriented bourgeois, was publicly committed to the idea of spreading knowledge of French'' (p. 405, n. 14) and quotes Barère's speech before the Convention: ''among a free people, language must be one and the same for all'' (p. 407).

12. Brunet, op. cit., pp. 413, and 519–21ff., 536. Brunet cities Jaubert de Passa, subprefect and author of a number of studies of local agriculture: ''One pays taxes in French, one sings the charms of one's love, celebrates the arrival of spring, and prays for the protection of the saints in Catalan'' (p. 531).

13. Brunet, op. cit., pp. 416–19, 438ff. Carcassonne had become the bishopric during the Revolution.

14. MR 1222, ''Mémoire sur la reconnaissance de la route de Perpignan à Salses, 1824.'' This point is made by F. Jalabert in his *Géographie du département de Pyrénées-Orientales* (Perpignan, 1819), and was perhaps taken directly from him by the officer for the

purposes of his report. Brunet, op. cit., p. 299. See also Laurent Grau, "Le Milieu de la notabilité politique dans les Pyrénées-Orientales sous la monarchie de juillet (1830–1848)," in *Le Roussillon dans la première moitié du XIXᵉ siècle* (Perpignan, 1985).

15. McPhee, "A Case-Study," passim.

16. Philippe Wolfe, ed., *Histoire de Perpignan* (Toulouse, 1985), pp. 178–81. The number of people dependent upon viticulture increased from 2,000 to 3,000 between 1789 and the year IX (A. D. Pyrénees-Orientales, Mnc 872/3), reflecting the gradual transformation of the regional economy.

17. Tableau statistique, MR 1222, 1824: 2,500 hectares producing grain, 1,608 in vineyards, 289 in olive trees, 168 in gardens in the commune, and 100 producing corn, 500 oats, 150 rye, and 200 barley, plus 177 of meadows, 166 of woods, 87 of pasture lands, and 451 of wasteland.

18. Marcel Durliat, *Histoire du Roussillon* (Paris, 1962), pp. 103–4. Durand's family had come to Perpignan from Montpellier in 1720 to undertake the commerce of wine.

19. Mnc 858/2, 872/3. The hospital of the Miséricorde employed, however, a good many patients and inmates to spin wool for miserable wages. The 1824 survey stated the population as 14,864, packed into 1,210 houses, with only 62 dispersed elsewhere within the communal limits. A number of small-scale forges were located in Perpignan, but none of the so-called "Catalan forges" of the department.

20. Wolfe, ed. op. cit., pp. 177–78; Geneviève Gavignaud, "Le Rapport foncier villes-campagnes en Roussillon au début du XIXᵉ siècle—le cas de Perpignan," *Société languedocienne de géographie,* July–December 1982, pp. 9–10: "the domination by the town over the country, measured as part of a network of landholding based in the city, was thus in place at the beginning of the nineteenth century." See also Geneviève Gavignaud, *Propriétaires-viticulteurs en Roussillon,* 2 vols. (Paris, 1983).

21. 2M5 20. Lazarme paid 27 francs *patente* in Elne. 121 of the 400 wealthiest taxpayers in 1835 were listed as *propriétaires* (as well as 195 of the 766 who qualified to vote by virtue of taxes paid). Only 3 *cultivateurs* and 1 *jardinier* were to be found among the 400 leading taxpayers; but toward the bottom of the scale, another 15 *cultivateurs* and 13 *jardiniers* were listed, along with 1 *agriculteur*. Only 15 paid taxes only on property owned in Perpignan.

22. Gavignaud, *Propriétaires-viticulteurs,* vol. 1, pp. 187–99.

23. Ibid., p. 549.

24. A. M. Perpignan, census of 1820.

25. Gavignaud, *Propriétaires-viticulteurs,* vol. 1, p. 509.

26. A. M. Perpignan, census of 1820.

27. Wolfe, ed., op. cit., pp. 177–78, counting 377 gardeners and 430 day laborers; in 1856, of about 300 of the former, only "26 or 28" owned the land they worked.

28. Gavignaud, *Propriétaires-viticulteurs,* p. 513, citing an unfinished *maîtrise* by N. Tixador. Few among the agricultural population, with the exception of gardeners, owned their own land. Thus, as Peter McPhee points out, "peasants" is probably less accurate a description than agricultural population, since most were rural day laborers or market gardeners.

29. McPhee, "A Case-Study," p. 408.

30. Wolfe, ed., op. cit., p. 178.

31. Brunet, op. cit., pp. 33–49, 60–61; quote from pp. 46 and 59. Brunet noted the description of Perpignan in the *cahiers* at the time of the estates-general as "rich, privileged, parasitical, living from the toils of the poor inhabitants of the countryside, themselves overwhelmed by taxes and debts, rustic people of little education but, nevertheless, the 'useful class of society'" (p. 33).

32. Ibid.

33. Wolfe, ed., op. cit., p. 181.

34. 3M 1 51, cp July 3, 1820 (among many others that year); BB18 1336, *procureur* report, May 27 and June 18, 1833; A. M. Perpignan, I 152. See Henry Aragon, *La Vie civile et militaire de Perpignan sous le général de Castellane* (Perpignan, 1926). The 1833 incident began with a fight between two *paysans et ouvriers* in a cabaret and then moved outside into the open space in front of the barracks. Periodic municipal decrees promulgated at the beginning of carnival banned "offensive" carnival disguises and masks, specifying military uniforms (for example, the decree of January 25, 1833).

35. Wolfe, ed., op. cit., pp. 176–77: "Even the gardens were tributaries of the cavalry regiments which furnished them fine manure."

36. F3II Pyrénées-Orientales 5, int. July 6, 1809, and municipal council deliberation, May 4, 1824; prefect, December 18, 1810; int. to minister of war, February 28, 1822.

37. D. M. J. Henry, *Le Guide en Roussillon ou itinéraire du voyageur dans le département des Pyrénées-Orientales* (Perpignan, 1842), pp. 115–16.

38. Brunet, op. cit., pp. 31–32, 59, 60–61, 73–171.

39. F7 9528, letter of the colonel commanding the fortifications, September 19 and October 17, 1828. Although insisting on the ultimate authority of the army, the new commander was willing to substitute lighter penalties than those prescribed by a law of July 10, 1791, and the regulations of 22 Germinal, year XI (F7 9527, prefect, August 27, 1824). One can only guess as to popular reaction in 1825 to the execution of a soldier who had insulted two officers while drunk, ripping the uniform of one and tearing off his epaulets; he was executed within twenty-four hours.

40. A. M. Perpignan, municipal council summaries of May 2, 5, and 22, 1830. This dispute may explain the resignation of three council members and their replacement in early March, after a commission had been appointed to "defend the interests of the town."

41. Municipal council deliberations, February 1830, and prefect, November 30, 1829; *Journal de Perpignan et des Pyrénées-Orientales,* February 17, 1827.

42. A. M. Perpignan, census of 1820; Claude-Paul Vincensini, "Une société urbaine: la paroisse Saint-Jean à Perpignan au XVIIIᵉ siècle" (mémoire de maîtrise, Université Paul Valéry, Montpellier, 1974). Saint-Jean had 47 *coronels* (La Réal 25, Saint-Jacques 64, and Saint-Mathieu 40)—a Catalan word for a circle or a ring (*couronne*) of houses bordered by a street, "a block of houses sometimes ventilated by an alley or small street," sometimes closed at night by a barrier. One entered the *coronels* by narrow streets or alleys, which were often closed tightly at night. Most of the manual laborers in the quarter of Saint-Jean lived on the rue Saint-Dominique: 8 day laborers and 6 gardeners in 1820; this street bordered the quarter of Saint-Jacques.

43. G. Galtier, *Le Vignoble du Languedoc méditerranéen et du Roussillon: Etude comparative d'un vignoble de masse* (Montpellier, n.d. [1960]), vol. 2, p. 125, quoted by Peter McPhee, "The Seed-Time of the Republic: Society and Polities in the Pyrénées-Orientales, 1842–52" (Ph.D. diss. University of Melbourne, 1977), p. 384.

44. A. M. censuses of 1820 and 1846; Wolfe, op. cit., p. 183; 2V 16, n.n., report to prefect, received 6 Fructidor, Year IX. Another report from 13 Pluviôse, year XII, responded to what appears to have been a request by "five or six" families of La Réal that their parish be promoted, noting that the other parishes all lay in only one-fourth of the town, while Saint-Mathieu had to take responsibility for five to six thousand parishioners who needed religious instruction (n.d., prefect and 2V 15, *conseiller d'état,* 28 Germinal year XI).

45. Wolfe, ed., op. cit., p. 183.

46. Ibid., pp. 178, 183. In 1855 the first commission gathering statistics on truck

farming reported that there were about 300 gardeners living in Perpignan, of whom only 20 or 30 could read and write (A. Siau, ''Rapport sur l'industrie maraîchère des les Pyrénées-Orientales,'' *Bulletin de la Société agricole, littéraire et scientifique des Pyrénées-Orientales* [1855], p. 199).

47. Censuses of 1820 and 1846, A. M. Perpignan; the latter figure—41.2%—comes from Wolfe, op. cit., p. 183. A perusal of the *cadastre* drawn up in 1810 (W 143 and 144) confirms the concentration of the ownership of the gardens—ranging in size from 48 square meters to 2.34 arpents—by residents of Saint-Jacques (including André Furès, Barthélémy Coll, and Portaries, gardeners, and Joseph Pomès *dit* Bongade), but also Jaubert de Passa, Jalabert, who owned considerable property, and the merchant Delmas, among others. There were certainly exceptions to the dichotomy between Saint-Jacques and Saint-Mathieu, including gardeners who owned property in Saint-Mathieu, and those living outside Saint-Jacques. Joseph Delhorte, gardener, owned considerable property beyond the walls of Saint-Jacques. In the Pré le Mas Belande, among other places, one found residents of Saint-Jacques and Saint-Mathieu owning land, including vineyards; in some rural territory beyond the walls, residents of one quarter or another were to be found in greater numbers, such as people of Saint-Mathieu in La Miséricorde. The day laborers of Saint-Mathieu were also less likely to own their own houses.

48. Gavignaud, ''Le Rapport foncier,'' p. 12, notes that by 1855 only about 26 of the 300 gardeners owned land, a pattern maintained by the high price of land for garden farming. At the beginning of the century, sharecropping had predominated in the gardens beyond the ramparts, but now ''renting (*fermage*) established itself as the type of land tenure characteristic of garden farming, perhaps because of the property owner's inability to predict the value of successive harvests produced by a rapid rotation of crops.''

49. Sahlins ''Before France and Spain,'' p. 168. He also notes the enjoyment of traditional collective rights to wood or water, and of pasture.

50. Henry, op. cit., pp. 63, 96–100; Brunet, op. cit., 418–20.

51. 3M1 51, cp October 7, 1824; 2V 5; F19 933B, bishop, April 19, 1825, and 2V 10, report of April 5, 1825; 3M1 47, cp June 1, 1818, relates the attempt of a priest under interdiction to exorcise the devil from a *malheureux paysan* of Perpignan.

52. Brunet, op. cit., p. 529. See Marie-Jeanne Trogno, ''Histoire de la confrèrie du Très Précieux Sang de Jésus-Christ'' in Joseph Deloncle, ed., *La Procession de la Sanch* (Perpignan, 1984), pp. 38ff. Trogno discusses Spanish influence on the cermeonies (such as the representations of the ''Misteris'' in polychrome sculpture on wood, and such touches as ''a heart pierced by seven knives that one finds on the chest of virgins at the foot of the cross'' [pp. 46, 58]).

53. François Carrère, quoting J. B. F. Carrère, ''L'Ancienne Procession du jeudi saint au XVIIIᵉ siècle,'' in Deloncle, op. cit., pp. 15–17.

54. Ibid.; Charles Bauby, ''La Procession du jeudi saint à Perpignan des origines à nos jours,'' in Deloncle, op. cit., pp. 23–27; Trogno, op. cit.; ''Jacques-Gaspard Deloncle, '''Misteris I Goigs' de la Procession de la Sanch,'' in Deloncle, op. cit., pp. 63–70, quoted on page 67; Henri Aragon, *Les Monuments et les rues de Perpignan* (Perpignan, 1928), p. 119, citing D. M. J. Henry on the Flagellants.

55. McPhee, ''Seed-Time of the Republic,'' p. 207. There ''the cadres of the left were inspired by itinerant day labourers from winegrowing areas who came to the Salanque for the grain harvest.''

56. Ibid., pp. 207–8. For example, in April 1851 *brassiers* from Saint-Mathieu went with workers from the communes of Saint-Estève and Corneilla-la-Rivière—about two hundred in all—to tend the fields of political friends in Saint-Estève who were in jail.

57. F7 9527, cp April 6, 1826.

58. Brunet, op. cit., pp. 420, 460–62, 467.

59. 3M1 48, cp January 12 and May 29, 1817.

60. F7 9692, prefect, April 23, 1819; 3M1 49, police report, March 8 and 31, 1818, April 23, 1819. The wearing of masks had been banned in the countryside; F7 9691, prefect report, March 3, 1816.

61. Hugo, op. cit., p. 26.

62. Wolfe, ed., op. cit., p. 188..

63. 3M1 49, prefect, August 18, 1818. In 1823 the clergy complained that the "entrepreneur" or contractor for the public dances held in Saint-Jean began the festivities before Mass had ended (3M1 51, report of September 2, 1823). The incident reflects some of the tensions between the poor and the elite of Saint-Jean.

64. Henry, op. cit., pp. 164–65, citing Jalabert's description; the dances "consist of the dancers turning in a circle and then backing up, while a couple does a round; each round ends with the man catapulting the woman high in the air, and sometimes she lands on his shoulders" (p. 103).

65. In 1829 the prefect forbade Martin *dit* Fouques from putting on other dances, including one on the Grande Rue Saint-Jacques. Martin protested—he needed his "petite industrie, ce faible gagne-pain de sa famille"—and claimed that the police and 25 neighbors could attest that his dances had never caused any problems (A.M. I 1 53, prefect, July 4 and August 1, 1829).

66. Wolff, ed., op. cit., pp. 188–89. Michel Brunet describes attempts by imperial prefects to ban "nighttime processions, disguises during Holy Week and the representations of the mysteries on public places" (op. cit., pp. 430–31).

67. Brunet, op. cit., p. 431; 2V 16, report n.d., year X; decree of 10 Fructidor, year XII.

68. F. Balledent, "Une mascarade anti-cléricale à Perpignan en 1827," in *Bulletin de la Société agricole, scientifique et littéraire des Pyrénées-Orientales* 91 (1983), 51–64.

69. *Journal de Perpignan et des Pyrénées-Orientales,* February 18, 1827; F7 9528, prefect, January 23, 25, February 7, 1827, and bishop's decree of January 17; F7 9528, January 17, 1827; 2V 15, int. July 11, 1826.

70. F1c III Pyrénées-Orientales 5, prefect, February 1819.

71. 3M1 48, report of October 3, 1817.

72. 3M1 48, December 6, 1817.

73. F7 9692, prefect, January 1, 1819; 3M1 51, report of June 11, 1824.

74. BB18 1136, pg Montpellier, May 1, 1816, and int. April 25, 1826; U 3255, cp p.-v., April 5, 1830.

75. As by a decree of the mayor in 1838 (I1 118, decree of April 21, 1838); I1 119, March 17, 1832, and March 14, 1838 (3M1 34, police report, March 2, 1817).

76. 3M1 48, report of October 25, 1817. In the arrondissement of Perpignan in 1816, there were approximately 150 "fallen women in the profession of prostitution . . . most of these are miserable Spaniards, without a residence, who come and go in this region, wandering from one commune to the next" (3M1 43, cs November 7, 1816).

77. 3M1 47, cp November 23 and December 7, 1816.

78. This despite the fact that "what is important about this political commitment [allegiance to democratic socialism during the Second Republic] for the fate of 'Catalanism' is, first, that it was made within the framework of French national politics; and, second, that it was made to an ideology which, haunted by the Great Revolution, had at best been equivocal, at worst hostile, toward minorities in France." McPhee, "A Case-Study," p. 411.

79. Ibid., pp. 412–14: "They [the Montagnards] were unwilling or unable to develop a

dynamic relationship between their political radicalism and their 'Catalanism.'" McPhee cites the example of Pierre Lefranc, a Montagnard leader from the Jura, whose advice in 1846 to Catalans in Spain had been to stop thinking of themselves as Catalans, but rather as Spaniards (p. 413), and who had complained that same year that the town crier shouted out his announcements in Catalan. On social structure, see Wolfe, ed., op. cit., p. 181.

80. Brunet, op. cit., p. 532. For Brunet, "Catalan is neither right nor left, it is the language of opposition." In sharp contrast, McPhee writes: "Their 'Catalanism' can be reduced to a strong but vague pride in their ethnocultural distinctiveness. Their embracing of the attractive radical and revolutionary tradition in French politics obscured the consequences that *francisation* would have for local culture and language" ("A Case Study," p. 415).

81. McPhee, "Popular Culture, Symbolism and Rural Radicalism in Nineteenth-century France," *The Journal of Peasant Studies* 5:2 (January 1978), p. 247.

82. Ibid., p. 246.

83. Wolfe, ed., op. cit., pp. 161–64. The consuls—whose number included one noble, one "bourgeois" noble or a lawyer, two members chosen among the merchants or other wealthy commoners, and a fifth one from the artisans—could ennoble up to two men a year, a power that the old nobility resisted.

84. Brunet, op. cit., p. 290. Outnumbered, the Club de la Paix did not meet after December 1790.

85. Abbé Philippe Torreilles, *Perpignan pendant la Révolution (1789–1800)*, 3 vols. (Perpignan, 1896–97), vol. 1, pp. 64, 94, 105, 200–210. Torreilles claimed that the Revolution had considerably altered "religious habits" in Perpignan. National guard companies were recruited by quarter, intensifying the rivalry. The churches of Saint-Mathieu and Saint-Jacques opened their door again after the Terror only in 1796 (pp. 411–68).

86. Brunet, op. cit., pp. 537–40. "They exchanged a monarchical state that demanded little and did not offer much for a state that asked much and offered practically nothing" (p. 540). The Revolution and the Empire "thus had a powerful destabilizing effect. They could not complete the integration of the Roussillonais to the rest of France, but they contributed by sweeping away the very basis of the old society" (p. 546).

87. Wolfe, ed., op. cit., pp. 161–70.

88. The prefect estimated the number of purchasers at 40,000, reporting that "almost all the rich, distinguished families lost their rank and fortune"; he had first written *la plupart* then crossed it out (3M1 26, 1818 annual report). The same figure was given by the prefect Villeneuve-Bargemon in his report of May 17, 1816 (F7 9691). See also F1cIII Pyrénées-Orientales 5, May 17, 1816, and February 10, 1820. The imperial prefect Louis Joseph Duhamel had placed the number of émigrés at 6,000, claiming that 30,000 people purchased property valued at 20 million francs (F1cIII Pyrénées-Orientales 5, "Situation du département des Pyrénées-Orientales pendant l'année 1814"). The population of the city declined during these troubled years, from 13,365 in 1774 to 10,066 in 1799. Brunet, op. cit., p. 244, sets the number of émigrés at 3,854. He notes that of 450 people who left Perpignan, almost half "belonged to the privileged orders: 150 priests, 80 or 90 nobles and bourgeois nobles" (p. 253).

89. Gavignaud, *Propriétaires-viticulteurs,* vol. 1, pp. 187–99.

90. Wolfe, ed., op. cit., pp. 161–70.

91. Torreilles, op. cit., vol. 1, pp. 185, 194. Of the 60 wealthiest men in Perpignan during the Empire, only 15 were *gentilshommes* or "bourgeois nobles" of the last decades of the ancien régime.

92. BB18 946, *procureur,* July 29 and October 22, 1814; F7 9691, prefect, March 15 and April 21, 1815; F1cIII Pyrénées-Ortientales 5, 1814 annual report, which complained

that the administration was no longer listened to and spoke of "bad people of all nations and of both sexes" who had been washed through the gates of Perpignan by the tides and misfortunes of war.

93. F7 9691, reports of June 30, July 18–19, August 24, 1815; Paul Masnou, *Le Département des Pyrénées-Orientales pendant les cent jours* (Perpignan, 1899); 3M 143, *commissaire spécial,* November 7, 1816; F19 5695, prefect, n.d., 1815; Charles-Olivier Carbonnel, "Les Députés des Pyrénées-Orientales de 1815 à 1870," *Cerca,* 13–14 (1961), pp. 24–25. Ten people were banished from the department and 146 imprisoned, most briefly. La Tour d'Auvergne, the department's only noble of importance, was elected to the Chamber of Deputies as an Ultra in 1815.

94. F7 9691, prefect, September 15, 1815; 3M1 47, especially reports of July 15, August 4, September 5, October 11 and 13, and December 26, 1815.

95. F1bII Pyrénées-Orientales 3, prefect, December 9, 1814, and February 13, 1815; F7 9691, prefect, April 10, October 4, and November 3, 1815; and 3M1 26, annual report, 1818.

96. F7 6771, prefect, March 8, 1822.

97. F7 6771, prefect, March 12, 1823, and June 2, 1828.

98. F7 6771, prefect, May 2, 1828. Other anticlerical incidents are reported in F7 6705, prefect, April 12 and May 10, and F7 9527, prefect, July 30, 1824, and May 25, 1825.

99. F1cIII Pyrénées-Orientales 5, prefect reports of February 1819 and February 10, 1820.

100. F7 6771, prefect, May 2, 1828: "we must not lose sight of the fact that the men who have for their whole lives professed the most entire devotion to the noble heritage of their fathers are disappearing each day. Another generation is succeeding them."

101. BB18 1183, *procureur,* April 22, 24, and May 2, 1830. Charles Tilly, "Charivaris, Repertoires and Urban Politics," in John M. Merriman, ed., *French Cities in the Nineteenth Century* (London, 1981), pp. 79–81. "In short, the charivari had become a means of conducting politics as usual in Perpignan" (p. 81). A rumor that "the class of agricultural day laborers have planned to pillage the houses of the rich and especially the army warehouses" may reflect an increase in social tension that accompanied the difficult winter of 1829–30 (F7 9528, *secrétaire général* of the prefecture, February 8, 1830).

102. F7 6771, prefect, March 8, 1822, September 13, 1825, March 12, 1827, and March 10, 1828.

103. BB18 1192, pg Montpellier, December 14, 1830. In the first incident, shots were allegedly fired from the crowd in response to use of bayonets by the soldiers; eight were arrested (U 3434, letter of *procureur,* n.d.; p.-v. December 10, 1830, and testimony of witnesses).

104. BB18 1320, commander of military division, February 20, 1830; pg Montpellier, December 28, 1831. The bishop had been absent at the time of the revolution. His return on August 19 brought more than a thousand people to the gates of his controversial palace, singing "patriotic" songs and shouting against him. Powdered and well-dressed, he was detested for "ostentation and conceit that contrast unfavorably with the simplicity that generally reigns in this part of France," he did not return for almost three years. 1V 7, prefect, July 27, 1831, and prefect of the Lot-et-Garonne, July 23, 1831; Philippe Rosset, "L'Agitation anticléricale dans le diocèse de Perpignan au début de la Monarchie de Juillet," *Revue historique,* July–September 1982, p. 190; F19 5747, October 15, 1830; F19 5747, prefect, October 14 and 15, 1830, int. November 8, 20, and 29, 1830, May 21, 1833; prefect, December 30, 1830, April 18 and October 10, 1831, June 6 and 7, 1832; bishop, December 22, 1830, and February 15, 1831; F7 6779, gendarmerie report, April 6, 1833.

105. The council voted to close a new school run by the Brothers of Christian Doctrine, abrogated a contract with the Sisters of Sacré-Coeur for another school, and reduced several subventions (A. M. Perpignan, meeting of August 31, September 18 and 30, 1830).

106. See McPhee, "A Case Study." The municipality's inauguration of a new fountain in 1831 on the place de la Liberté might be considered a symbolic victory over the army.

107. A. M. Perpignan, council meeting of November 2; F1II Pyrénées-Orientales 2, "Observations sur les noms de quelques rues de la ville de Perpignan, proposés par le conseil municipal, dans sa délibération du 2 novembre 1830."

108. 3M1 56, March 26, 1831.

109. 3M1 61, prefect, September 9; gendarmerie report, March 21, 1831.

110. A.M. I1 52, mayor, January 25, 1833.

111. The names of the town's republican leaders surfaced in correspondence seized in Toulouse in 1835, in 1839 (the case of Alibaud), and again in 1843, at the time of the investigation of "communists" living there. 3M1 57, int. January 26, 1843; 3M1 55, prefect, July 8, 15, and August 3, 1836; int. July 8, 1836; and letter, n.d., of the curé of Saint-Jacques; F19 5747, int. August 9; 3M1 54, int. January 9, 1838; gendarmerie report, April 27, 1839.

112. F7 6782, ct. gendarmerie, August 8, 1833; 3M1 54, int. July 17 and 23, 1833, and February 23, April 20, and June 19, 1834; J. Calmette and P. Vidal, *Histoire du Roussillon* (Paris, 1975), p. 248.

113. Tilly, op. cit.

114. 2V 16, bishop, May 23, 1833, and prefect, May 24, 1833. On May 16, 1832, people from Le Faubourg and from the countryside, armed with sticks and rocks, refused to pay the tax on animals brought to the market (3M1 61, prefect, February 10 and May 16, 1832).

115. 3M1 61, ct. gendarmerie, August 25, and prefect, August 26, 1833.

116. Improvements in the departmental road system contributed to a modest growth in the local economy, including small-scale industries. Between 1825 and 1850, the wine-growing land in the department increased by 50% (Mnc 2506, prefect, November 22, 1835.)

117. BB18 1386, pg Montpellier, September 30, 1840. The 230 people attending the reform banquet in 1840 included "several young republicans without a following or clientele, a small number of master artisans, and some day laborers."

118. Peter MacPhee [*sic*], "Les Semailles de la république dans les Pyrénées-Orientales (1830–1851): François Arago, semeur . . . ou moissonneur?", in *François Arago: Actes du Colloque National des 20, 21, & 22 octobre 1986,* University of Perpignan, pp. 205–6.

119. McPhee, "Seed-Time of the Republic," p. 435; McPhee, "Les Semailles," pp. 203–8, disputing Maurice Agulhon's characterization of Arago as one of the rare bourgeois republicans "who is naturally elected in his region, and who determines local opinion more than follows it," and the assertion that the success of the radicals in the department depended upon the Arago family. See Horace Chauvet, *Histoire du parti républicain dans les Pyrénées-Orientales* (Perpignan, 1909), pp. 26–37; and Georges Weill, *Histoire du parti républicain en France (1814–1870)* (Paris, 1928), p. 263.

120. Peter McPhee, "On Rural Politics in Nineteenth-Century France: The Example of Rodès, 1789–1851," *Comparative Studies in Society and History* 23:2 (April 1981), 256.

121. F7 6771, prefect, June 2, 1828.

122. F7 6771, prefect, June 2, 1828.

123. Wolfe, ed., op. cit., p. 189. See Peter McPhee, "Popular Culture, Symbolism

and Rural Radicalism in Nineteenth-century France,'' *The Journal of Peasant Studies* 5:2 (January 1978), 238–53 (quotation from pp. 240–41).

124. McPhee, "Popular Culture," pp. 242–43.

125. 3M 1 47, for example, cp May 3, 1816.

126. 3M1 56, int. May 5, 1831; F19 5747, prefect, February 21 and June 2, 1831; int. May 5, 1831; BB18 1320, pg Montpellier, February 20, 1831; 3M1 61, int. March 6, and prefect, March 11, 1831; BB18 1192, report of May 14, 1831; BB 1202, int. December 11, 1831.

127. McPhee, "Popular Culture": "The symbols with which peasants in southern France communicated have to do with voice and body movements, shapes and colours, rather than with the printed word: hence the importance of shouted slogans, processions, and . . . provocative songs and the color of flowers and clothing" (p. 244).

128. 3M1 47, cp May 18, 1816: "for some time nocturnal songs have become à la mode in town."

129. 3M1 34/4, cp May 13, 1816, prefect of the Hérault, September 3, 1817.

130. 3M1 49, cp March 31, 1818; 3M1 36, letter of the tailor Bruyas, January 12, 1819; 3M1 34/4 *procureur* and cp, September 14, 1817, and Bruyas, October 2, 1817); 3M 1 50, prefect, December 13, 1819; 3M1 34/4, *procureur,* September 14, 1817; 3M1 36, int. August 3, 1819. The lyrics of several Catalan songs may be found in 3M1 36.

131. U 3448, police p.-v. of July 20 and report of July 21, 1818; 3M1 49, March 22 and July 20, 1818; 2M1 49, April 30, 1818.

132. 3M1 49, cp April 30 and September 23, 1818.

133. 3M1 61, report of February 11 and 13, 1832, ct. gendarmerie, May 16, 1832.

134. 3M1 61, cp April 14, 1831.

135. 3M1 61, cp April 16 and 18, 1831. In May 1832 legitimists started a brawl in a cabaret in Saint-Jacques, wounding several people with swords (3M1 54, int. May 23, 1832, and 3M1 61, prefect, May 15, 1832).

136. 3M1 56, prefect, March 26, 1831.

137. 3M1 49, March 31, 1818. The victim was Boubal, an employee of the *octroi;* his tormentors were all agricultural laborers, one of whom was from Saint-Jacques (testimony in U 3448, p.-v. of cp February 20, 1817, report to prefect, February 22, etc.).

138. 3M1 36, letter of the tailor Bruyas, January 12, 1819, who had briefly fallen under police suspicion in 1817 when he received copies of royalist songs, that he claimed had been sent anonymously (3M1 34/4 *procureur* and cp September 14, 1817, and Bruyas, October 2, 1817).

139. 3M1 49, report of July 20, 1818.

140. 3M1 50, cp, February 20, April 12 and 19, 1819.

141. 3M1 50, cp January 3, 4, 6, and 18, and February 15 and 20, March 27, November 2 and 30, 1819. Cp March 27: "We presume that it is again Cami, a *brassier* of this quarter, who is the composer," suggesting that he had also written "La Guinée"; U 3448–50, cp January 19, 1819.

142. U 3448–50, p.-v. February 3, and cp reports of February 5, 6, and 8, 1817.

143. 3M1 40, cp March 5 and 10, 1817.

144. F7 9692, February 26, 1819; 3M1 48, report of May 26, 1817.

145. 3M 48, report of February 17, 1817.

146. Differences in class behavior may be seen in an incident in 1841 at the theater, when workers "wearing small caps, and who never go to the theater," came to applaud a controversial tenor who was hooted down by the bourgeoisie.

147. Chauvet, op. cit., p. 37; McPhee, "Seed-Time of the Republic," pp. 32–33; Aragon, op. cit., pp. 233–43. When Mayor Giraud de St. Marsal and the municipal council

refused to pass any motions except for some assistance for the unemployed, he was dismissed. Resentment of the army helped unite bourgeois liberals, moderates, and republicans.

148. McPhee, "Seed-Time of the Republic." See also Ted W. Margadant, *French Peasants in Revolt: The Insurrection of 1851* (Princeton, 1979).

149. 3M1 70, cp October 26, 1849.

150. Ibid., April 11, 1849.

151. For example, 3M1 70, cp report of January 15, 1850, noting that five *exaltés* went out of town to meet their "political friends" from Rivesaltes, Baixas, and Estagel.

152. 3M1 70, cp January 18, 1850.

153. 3M1 74, prefect February 4, 1848, describing Perpignan as calm, although "several workers have lent their ears to communist doctrines." The police reported on meetings of the masons, shoemakers, gardeners, and rural daylaborers, the latter being the largest in number and meeting once a month.

154. McPhee, "Popular Culture," p. 246.

155. 3M1 72, *commissaire,* February 27–March 6, 1848; BB30 333, *procureur,* September 15.

156. 3M1 73, p.-v., April 30, 1848; McPhee, "Seed-Time of the Republic," chapter 3. In the presidential elections of December 10, 1848, Ledru-Rollin received 29% of the vote.

157. 3M1 74, telegrams of the *commissaire* (Hippolyte Picas), June 5, 6, and 9, and gendarmerie report, June 6; BB30 362, pg Montpellier, June 7, July 17, and September 9, 1848; *procureur,* June 10, 1848; *avocat général,* June 10, 1848; U191, trial.

158. U191, trial record; nine workers were tried, four receiving stiff sentences. One of the workers battling legitimists at the place de la Loge at the time of the June Days lashed out: "I want to play boules with the heads of those responsible for my finding no work." A group of *ouvriers et agriculteurs* asked that everything possible be done to "conciliate the interests of the working class with the prescriptions of the law" (3M1 70, cp June 23 and 28; 3M1 76, letter of June 26; 3M1 48, gendarmerie report, June 16; 3M1 74, *procureur,* August 24, 1848, and petition of June 22, 1848; Mayor, September 18, 1848).

159. 3M1 70, October 26, 1849.

160. McPhee, "Seed-Time of the Republic," pp. 152–53.

161. 3M1 70, cp June 29, July 5, 12, and 17, 1849, U 195.

162. 3M1 70, cp March 12, 1850.

163. Ibid., November 25.

164. 3M1 70, cp December 17, 1849. Teachers may have provided a link between French songs and Catalan Montagnards. Four out of eleven teachers did "not merit the confidence" of the regime; one, in particular, "never misses the street gatherings . . . on Sunday he offers his hand to the workers' leaders who are as dangerous as he is and at night he goes to inns in the same company."

165. 3M1 70, May 2 and 5, 1850.

166. Only the *président* of a gathering welcoming a released political prisoner was not a worker (3M1 70, cs November 15, 1850).

167. 3M1 70, cp June 12, 1850; McPhee, "Seed-Time of the Republic," pp. 184–85.

168. 3M1 70, cp April 14–25; BB18 1488, pg Montpellier, August 25 and December 28, 1850, and March 11, 1851; 3M1 70, cp April 29 and September 1, 1850. See McPhee, "The Seed-Time of the Republic," p. 185. The legitimists won the municipal elections in 1850, in which the members of the Société Saint-Michel distributed ballots. The electoral law of May 31, 1850, had eliminated at least half of the *démoc-socs* from the electoral rolls (40% in the department). This left only about 600 to 700 "democrats" eligible to vote in

Perpignan compared to 1,200 to 1,300 legitimists and 400 to 500 Orleanists and others willing to support the "party of order," among the 2,536 eligible voters. In protest, the Montagnards abstained in the elections (BB30 380, pg Montpellier, August 24 and November 29, 1850; 3M1 70, October 21–28, 1850).

169. 3M1 70, cp August 24, 1850.

170. 3M1 70, cp September 29 and 30, 1850; this latter event occurred in Saint-Jacques.

171. 3M1 70, cs October 31, 1850.

172. BB30 362, pg Montpellier, April 25 and May 7, 1849; BB18 1477, *procureur,* April 24 and May 5, 1849; 3M1 71, gendarmerie report, June 14 and 26, 1849; BB18 1475, minister of justice, March 13, 1849.

173. 3M1 70, cp February 13, 1850. The goddess apparently received two francs for her part in the procession.

174. 3M1 70, cs September 2, 1850.

175. 3M1 70, September 16, 1850.

176. 3M1 70, cp September 23, 1850; BB18 1450, pg Montpellier, September 26. Thérèse Lafon received a fine of six francs and court costs (3M1 70, cs November 14, 1850). See also McPhee, "Seed-Time of the Republic," p. 190.

177. 3M1 70, cp May 15, 16, 21, 22, 25, and 27, July 7, and November 11, 1850.

178. 3M1 70, cp June 29, 1850.

179. 3M1 70, cp June 30, 1850. 775 out of 1,200 approved the statutes.

180. 3M1 70, cp June 25, 1850.

181. 3M1 70, cp May 27 and June 4, 1850.

182. 3M1 70, cp July 8, 1850.

183. 3M1 70, cp June 17, and 24, 1850.

184. Like that in 1830, when twenty *vignerons* from the commune of Palau-del-Vidre carrying a red and white flag crossed the territory of Saint-André as they returned from work. Their rivals took this to be a provocation. The mayor, wearing his scarf of authority, managed to end the brawl, but not before there had been "a good number of wounded and blood shed through and through" (*Journal de Perpignan et des Pyrénées-Orientales,* April 10, 1830).

185. BB30 391, pg Montpellier, December 17, 18, and 21, 1850; 3M1 74, cp December 16 and 17, 1850; the other wounded were Michel Massel, match seller, who had been walking by, and François Copié, a royalist "lodged among the reds." The latter had been drinking in a cabaret owned by Illa's brother-in-law, and heard Dapère yell, "Get out of here of I'll make tripes of you!"

186. BB30 391, pg Montpellier, December 21, 1850.

187. 3M1 70, cp November 30 and December 1, 8, and 10, 1849; by this time, a secret agent was at work for the police.

188. 3M1 70, cp September 29 and October 20, 1850. The police confiscated more than 4,000 cartridges, some sold by an employee of the garrison.

189. 3M1 70, April 8, at a time when a rumor of a movement in Paris on April 4, called the "coup d'Alibaud," was circulating, and April 25, 1850.

190. BB30 391, pg Montpellier, September 23 and October 14, 1850. The mayor's decrees of July 31 and August 4 also banned the promenades known as *"passe-ville";* A. M. Perpignan, I1 53.

191. 3M1 70, December 23 and 30, 1850; McPhee, "Seed-Time of the Republic," p. 209.

192. BB30 380, pg Montpellier, March 9, 1850.

193. 3M1 70, cp May 21, 1850.

194. 3M1 70, June 6 and 8 and July 22, 1850, cs October 30, 1850; 3M1 73, cp February 19, 1851; BB30 391, pg Montpellier, December 21, 1850; McPhee, "Seed-Time of the Republic," p. 192. The *gardes de nuit* had been denounced in an anonymous letter received March 6 (3M1 72).

195. 3M1 75, prefect, November 2, 1850.

196. 3M1 70, cp July 17, 1850.

197. 3M1 70, report of January 8, 1850.

198. 3M1 70, November 18, 1850. For example, Paivi, who worked at the hospice, abandoned his old political friends after the ill-fated Parisian insurrection of June 13, 1849, fearful of losing his job; now living "very withdrawn, he stays away from the café" (3M1 70, January 17, 1850).

199. 3M1 70, February 11, 1851. The policeman was nonetheless thorough in gathering information on the legitimists: for example, he was able to learn that Grosset, first clerk at the post office, gambled for moderate stakes in the cafés; of higher stakes were his relations with the ravishing daughter of a wealthy holder of the legion of honor. The young woman, "recherchée par les lions de la ville," had a "secret life of scandal," visiting other men besides Grosset. The latter paid dearly for his lover's expensive tastes. But Grosset too had a secret life, carrying on a two-year affair with the lover of the postal inspector. One day an indiscreet letter accidentally fell into the hands of the *amant titulaire*. Thereafter, Grosset received bad marks of his work, being relegated to the ranks of those officially deemed "incapable"—the kiss of bureaucratic death, a terrible revenge. All this left little time for royalist activities.

200. 3IM1 74. Cf. Peter McPhee: "in outlawing *'bonnets rouges'* or red caps, masquerades, Catalan songs and dances, the wearing of red sashes and flowers, amongst other things, the authorities were attacking the very texture of Catalan communal life" ("Seed-Time of the Republic," pp. 198–99). In 1850 dances were banned in Saint-Mathieu.

201. 3M1 70, cp August 19, 1851.

202. 3M1 74, prefect, September 27, 1850.

203. 3M1 70, cp August 24, 1850.

204. 3M1 70, cp February 25, 1850. Military and civil authorities feared contacts between civilians and soldiers, sending away the 44th infantry regiment for that reason in March 1850 (3M1 70, March 21 and 28, and April 2, 1850).

205. 3M1 70, February 20, 1850.

206. 3M1 74, prefect, March 8; 3M1 70, February 26–27, 1850. The arrest of a porter called Ventre de Chou for having insulted a man of means brought out a crowd of 300 to protest.

207. 3M1 70, cp June 1, 30, and August 4, 1850; 3M1 74, cp April 17, July 5, and October 2, 1851.

208. 3M1 70, June 26, 1851.

209. 3M1 70, cp April 7 and 13, 1851.

210. 3M1 70, cp April 19 and August 22; BB30 380, pg Montpellier, February 19 and June 7, 1851.

211. Mata-Pouillets was tried in Nîmes in June, with a crowd in Perpignan showing up in support; he received a relatively light sentence in view of "extenuating circumstances" (BB30 380, pg Montpellier, September 3, 1851).

212. BB30 380, May 7, 1851.

213. 3M1 73, February 19, 1851. The Cercle de Laborie, with 55 members, was purely social and seemed to be above suspicion, as did the clubs of the rue de L'Aloës, the rue des Potiers, and several others, each with between 12 and 25 members. See BB30 391, pg

Montpellier, March 10, 1851. The informal workers' gatherings called *parterres,* were the equivalent of Provençal *chambrées.*

214. 3M1 70, May 8 and June 15, 1851. Early in the summer of 1851, Montagnard leaders began to reappear cautiously at the place de la Loge and in the socialist gatherings above the Café Desarnaud.

215. 3M1 70, cp September 16 and 22, 1851.

216. 3M1 70, cp August 28 and October 29, 1851.

217. 3M1 70, cp November 16, 1851.

218. 3M 81–82. Most of the 75 men convicted by the court-martial (*commissions mixtes*) were drawn from a variety of artisanal trades. That shoemakers and cabinetmakers were the two largest categories of artisans is not surprising, since they were the two most organized trades. That only two day laborers were convicted suggests that the authorities in the Pyrénées-Orientales as elsewhere went after the traditionally militant and organized trades with a vengeance, considering the *travailleurs de terre* to have been mere foot-soldiers.

219. C. M. Lesaulnier, ed., *Biographie des neuf cents députés à l'Assemblée nationale* (Paris, 1848), quoted by McPhee, ''A Case-Study,'' pp. 421–22.

220. Horace Chauvet, *Histoire du Parti républicain dans les Pyrénées-Orientales* (Perpignan, 1909), pp. 198–99.

Chapter 6

1. MR 1217 (1837); D. Nisard, *Nîmes* (Nîmes, 1835), p. 165.

2. Brian Fitzpatrick, *Catholic Royalism in the Department of the Gard, 1814–1852* (Cambridge, Eng., 1983), p. 15.

3. See Raymond Huard et. al., *Histoire de Nîmes* (Aix-en-Provence, 1982), pp. 220–21.

4. See Gwynne Lewis, *The Second Vendée: The Continuity of Counter-revolution in the Department of the Gard, 1789–1815* (Oxford, 1978), pp. 10–11, 167–68, and chapter 6. Lewis writes: ''There is some evidence to suggest that the process of industrialization which . . . had brought the craftsman into collision with the merchant manufacturer long before the Revolution, was, by 1815, tending towards the elimination of the smaller independent merchant or *fabricant,* many of whom were Catholics'' (p. 225). He also puts the counterrevolution into the context of regional resistance to increasing centralization.

5. A. D. Gard, 6M 273, prefect, December 27, and gendarmerie report, December 30, 1830; BB18 1048, prefect, December 30, 1830; Lewis, op. cit., p. 229. Lewis is incorrect, however, in claiming that the ''White Terror of 1815 represented the last violent manifestation of Catholic-Protestant antagonism'' (p. 231).

6. BB18 1048.

7. F7 9658, prefect, September 21, 1820. In his eagerness to describe the evolution of class antagonisms in the Gard, Raymond Huard underplays religious and neighborhood solidarities. In his unpublished thesis (''La Préhistoire des partis: le parti républicain et l'opinion républicaine dans le Gard de 1848 à 1881,'' 5 vols. University of Paris IV, 1977) he writes: ''it is not religious proselytism that arouses confessional hatreds; the latter are the ideological form that clothes political and social antagonisms, and they retain their vigor, not from religious faith, but from the antagonisms themselves'' (p. 57). He then goes on to cite Flora Tristan on the Nîmois: ''their only life was the hatred that Catholics and Protestants had for each other'' (p. 58). To explain the fact that most workers continued to follow the leadership of legitimist notables, Huard asserts that ''their social conscience remained very confused'' (p. 64).

8. F7 9658, prefect, April 3 and May 30, 1820; BB18 1048, pg Nîmes, December 30, 1830.

9. F7 9658, prefect reports of April, June, and August 1820; August 1, 1821.

10. BB18 1136, pg Nîmes, March 23, 1826.

11. F7 9658, prefect, February 11, 1826.

12. BB 18 1137, pg Nîmes, April 24 and 26, May 23, cp April 22, and pg Nîmes, June 16, 1826.

13. BB18 1161, pg Nîmes, May 16, June 12 and 17, 1828.

14. Emilien Frossard, *Tableau pittoresque, scientifique et moral de Nîmes et de ses environs* (Paris, 1846), p. 88. Frossard lumped artisans and the poor into one class, "because they are separated or brought together, depending on circumstances." The Catholics of the Enclos Rey had even reacted violently against the missions of 1833, responding with "cannibal yells" when the mission priests arrived.

15. MR 1218 (1827); Huard, "La Préhistoire des parties," p. 85.

16. Frossard, op. cit., p. 90.

17. M. de Jouy, *L'Hermite en Province ou observations sur les moeurs et les usages français au commencement du XIXe siècle*, vol. 2 (Paris, 1819), p. 404.

18. BB18 1237, pg Nîmes, February 22 and 23, 1836. This arrangement had been worked out by the bishop and the mayor and had in fact been suggested by the clergy, for whom the city's growth had entailed more frequent treks to the cemetery.

19. M. de Jouy, op. cit., pp. 384–85.

20. Ibid., p. 399; Huard et al., *Histoire de Nîmes*, pp. 292–93, noting that there were 613 *masets* near Nîmes in 1832 and perhaps 4,000 a hundred years later. In 1827 an officer described Provençal as having been "relegated to the people" (MR 1218).

21. MR 1218 (1827).

22. Ibid.: "There are few towns where charity is undertaken with such munificence and delicateness as Nîmes; the diversity of religions, often so fatal, in this respect established a noble rivalry among inhabitants.

23. De Jouy, op. cit., p. 401; Huard et al., *Histoire de Nîmes*, p. 329. De Jouy describes the modern *taurocatapsies,* during which participants armed with long sticks called *bédiganes* attacked the bulls.

24. MR 1218 (1837); Armand Cosson, "Industrie de la soie et population ouvrière à Nîmes de 1815 à 1848," in Gérard Cholvy, ed., *Economie et société en Languedoc-Roussillon de 1789 à nos jours* (Montpellier, 1978), p. 211. This parish had 46% of the population in 1790, but less and less thereafter.

25. Ibid., p. 210.

26. Line Teisseyre-Sallmann, "Urbanisme et société: l'exemple de Nîmes aux XVIIe et XVIIIe siècles," *Annales E.S.C.* 35:5 (September–October 1980), p. 971 (376 people per hectare, compared with 400 in Paris in 1789).

27. De Jouy, op. cit., p. 403, who made an exception of a small number of houses rebuilt within the past fifty years, "two or three of which would not do injustice to the chaussée d'Antin, offering at least some symmetry and architectural form."

28. Huard et al., *Histoire de Nîmes*, p. 250.

29. 6M 227, decree of June 12, 1822; MR 1217 (1837).

30. Cosson, op. cit., p. 211.

31. MR 1217 (1837).

32. De Jouy, op. cit., pp. 383–84: "the hate for liberal institutions is, with very few exceptions, the distinctive character of the nobility."

33. Ibid., p. 396.

34. Huard et al., *Histoire de Nîmes*, pp. 209–13, noting the attempt to create "one of

the beautiful corners of Europe,'' despite the fact that "aristocrats and bourgeois ignore these too recent neighborhoods, preferring their old town houses of the center.''

35. F7 6769, prefect, March 29, 1829: "They don't see each other any more . . . barely saying hello in the streets, and avoid going to houses where they might run into someone [from the other camp].'' A new prefect arriving in 1829 congratulated himself for having, for the first time, managed to attract both Catholic notables and Protestants, as the latter had routinely refused all invitations "with disdain.''

36. Frossard, op. cit., pp. 84–85. For example, a decision in 1821 forbidding the posting of Protestant banns of marriage could not itself even be posted for fear it would spark brawls.

37. F7 6696, prefect, June 20, 1820, and note, June 18, 1823; F7 6769, prefect, March 5, 1827; 6M 227; Huard et al., *Histoire de Nîmes,* p. 327. De Jouy, op. cit., pp. 394–400, discusses the *cercles,* cafés, and theater.

38. MR 1218 (1827); Frossard, op. cit. pp. 88–96, complaining of the difficulty of finding devoted servants. On the bourgeoisie of the *monarchie censitaire,* see Huard, "La Préhistoire des partis," pp. 34–37.

39. Nisard, op. cit., pp. 182–85. The author praised the Protestant bourgeoisie for its moderation following the revolution of 1830.

40. MR 1217 (1837).

41. See David Garrioch, *Community and Neighborhood in Paris, 1740–70* (New York, 1986).

42. Teisseyre-Sallmann, op. cit., pp. 966–71. Huard, *Histoire de Nîmes,* p. 246, notes that 25.5% of the population in 1810 was composed of "agricultural laborers, day laborers, and farmhands working by the day,'' making it difficult to determine the percentage of those actually living from working the land. Rural laborers probably contributed mightily to Froment's forces during the Revolution and the White Terror of 1815. MR 1218 (1827): agricultural population, 6,325; artisans, 15,043; commerce, 5,320; property owners, 735; rentiers, 192; outside residents, 2,158 (the garrison, for the most part).

43. See Huard et al., *Histoire de Nîmes,* pp. 244–51, noting that the heads of household who were "artisans of all kinds, living from the products of their work,'' in 1811 represented 21.4% of the population, a low figure explained by the economic crisis of the Empire.

Year	Textile Workers	Population
1810	7,100	38,000
1820	7,000	40,000
1834	17,640	42,243
1841	11,250	42,720
1846	10,600	47,215
1856	7,194	49,291

Source: Armand Cosson, "Industrie de la soie et population ouvrière à Nîmes de 1815 à 1848," in Gérald Cholvy, ed., *Economie et société en Languedoc-Roussillon de 1789 à nos jours* (Montpellier, 1978), p. 198.

44. Cosson, op. cit., pp. 198ff. There were few strikes by workers in Nîmes during the July Monarchy: printers in 1833, *taffetassiers* in 1834, tailors and other silk workers in 1835, although Huard, "La Préhistoire des partis," asserts that these served to "shake traditional political and religious solidarities'' (p. 72).

45. MR 1218 (1827).

46. BB18 1357, pg Nîmes, October 20 and November 3, 1834. See also Huard, "La Préhistoire des partis," pp. 22–23.

47. Cosson, op. cit., p. 212.

48. Huard et al., *Histoire de Nîmes*, p. 270: a forge, a manufacture of steam engines, two flour mills, and a manufacture of faience.

49. Xavier Gutherz, Michel Py, et al., *Histoire de Nîmes* (Aix-en-Provence, 1982), p. 203.

50. Ibid., p. 979.

51. Frossard, op. cit., p. 79.

52. Ibid., pp. 75–76.

53. Op. cit., p. 387. Teisseyre-Sallmann, op. cit.: "The essential given in the evolution of the urban fabric of Nîmes in the modern period lies in the existence of its faubourgs and the reversal during the eighteenth century of the harmony of forces and relations that ties the city to its immediate surroundings" (p. 974).

54. Teisseyre-Sallmann, op. cit., pp. 967ff; quotations from pp. 972, 974, and 978–79.

55. Fitzpatrick, op. cit., pp. 22–23, Adolphe Pieyre, *Histoire de la ville de Nîmes* (Nîmes, 1886), p. 220, gives the population figure of 47,215 in 1846. This increase depended upon migration, as the city's death rate was greater than its birth rate during the period. In 1845, the year after the great railway viaduct was completed, the population stood at 44,000.

56. See Teisseyre-Sallmann, op. cit., pp. 965–80; Cosson, op. cit., especially pp. 209–11; Fitzpatrick, op. cit., pp. 19–27; Huard, "La Préhistoire des partis," p. 53; Huard et al., *Histoire de Nîmes*, pp. 247–51.

57. F7 9658, prefect, September 11, 1823.

58. De Jouy, op. cit., pp. 387–89. He titled his description, with the White Terror in mind, *Moeurs nîmoises*.

59. Frossard, op. cit., p. 96.

60. Pieyre, p. 106. "The artisans are generally lodged economically in the least pleasant, badly located, badly ventilated, and unhealthiest places. . . . Some are stuck in humid, somber basements." Quoted from Jean-César Vincens and Baumes, *Topographie de la ville de Nîmes et de sa banlieue* (Nîmes, 1802), by Huard et al., *Histoire de Nîmes*, p. 247.

61. MR 1217 (1837).

62. Frossard, op. cit., p. 75, described the faubourgs as "wide and well-ventilated; they stretch out from the exterior boulevards and take up a large area" (cf. de Jouy, op. cit., pp. 405–6), C 953: the survey of 1848 reported that working men earned 2 to 3 francs, women 1 to 1.25, and children 50 to 60 centimes a day, when work was available. It estimated that only 20% of the men and 10% of the women retained the ability to read and write at the age of 20.

63. Cosson, op. cit., pp. 210–12.

64. Ibid., p. 212.

65. Huard et al., *Histoire de Nîmes*, pp. 290, 295. A gradual decline in the percentage of Protestants, who had a lower birth rate, followed—from more than a third in 1818 to 26% in 1846, 25% in 1872, and 23.9% in 1901. There were 415 Jews in Nîmes in 1840.

66. Cosson, op. cit., p. 208. Over 94% of the *taffetassiers* had been born in the two most predominantly working-class sections, while only 18.3% of the *ouvriers en étoffes* were born outside the city (half of them in the Cevennes), in contrast to seamstresses, of whom 47.2% came from outside.

67. Frossard, op. cit., p. 93.

68. The fastest growing sections were the 9th and 12th, toward the railroad station; the 5th, between the chemin d'Uzès and the chemin d'Avignon; and the 4th beyond the Petit Cours. Three of the sections in the old city—the 7th, 8th, and 11th—as well as the 3rd in the Bourgades—were already saturated and hemmed in by hills.

69. Cosson, p. 210.

70. Ibid., p. 210.

71. MR 1218 (1827); Huard, "La Préhistoire des partis," p. 81.

72. F7 9658, gendarmerie report, December 8, 1820; prefect, December 9, 1822, and February 10, 1823.

73. 4M 47, cp February 28, 1830; 4M 48, cc May 29, 1839, involving 33 *compagnons,* and December 27, 1839, when *dévorants* and *gavots* brawled on the place de la Bouquerie, On November 18, 1839, another brawl was reported between several workers and 15 porters in a café; on December 27, 1840, a fight between *compagnons* and "bourgeois," which here means local workers; and others from 1843–45 (4M 48, cp May 28–29, 1844; 6M 288, cp May 27–29, 1844).

74. During carnival of 1837, one of the friends of the mayor was attacked by a masked reveler on the boulevard des Calquières.

75. BB30 217, pg Nîmes, September 14, 1823, and following. One brawl began when the imposing champion of one side announced that he had come to defend those of his religion.

76. F7 6769, prefect, July 19, 1828. Two Protestants were later convicted of assault.

77. Fitzpatrick, op. cit., pp. 60–96; see also F7 9658.

78. F7 6769, prefect, March 6, 1822.

79. F7 6769, prefect, January 6, 1830. The violence of both the Ultras and popular royalism had waned by the last years of the Restoration.

80. F7 6769, prefect, March 5, 1827, June 19, 1828, and following.

81. Emilien Frossard, *Evénémens de Nîmes depuis le 27 juillet jusqu'au 2 septembre 1830* (Nîmes, 1830), p. 82. 6M 243, mayor, August 3; prefect, August 3–4, and following, 1830.

82. 4M 47, police reports for August 9, 11, and following. The first reported incident was an attack on someone wearing a tricolor by a street porter; 4M 47, cp August 9, 1830.

83. 4M 47, police reports, October 5, 11, 27, and November 2 and 5, 1830; 6M 243, cp November 27, 1830. On November 2 a rumor quickly spread that someone had been murdered on the chemin d'Uzès; an old man had been attacked but not killed by unknowns, presumably Catholics.

84. BB18 1319 pg Nîmes, March 6, 1841. See Fitzpatrick, op. cit., and Huard, "La Préhistoire des partis," for a full discussion of the subject.

85. Pieyre, op. cit., p. 14. Carnival masks were permitted in 1833 for the first time since 1829 (p. 46).

86. F7 7680, gendarmerie report, March 13 and 14, June 16, October 10 and 24, 1831, March 12, May 2, June 9, and December 18, 1832; F19 5742, prefect, March 16, 1831, gendarmerie report, February 21, 1831, and bishop of Nîmes, February 22, 1831. On February 21, 1831, a crowd in rags searched "with decency" the seminary for a rumored bust of Charles X. An estimated 800 people watched a rock fight, one of the most traditional forms of sectarian fighting, but also probably of amusement, in December 1832. The Catholics had responded with songs in Provençal (*chansons patoises*). See Pieyre, op. cit., pp. 14–15.

87. BB18 1211, pg Nîmes, November 5, 1832.

88. BB18 1217, *procureur,* July 23, pg Nîmes, July 16 and 23, and int. July 20, 1833;

F7 6780, prefect, June 16, July 23, and October 30; BB18 1220, pg Nîmes, December 31, 1833.

89. BB18 1454, pg Nîmes, July 31, 1847, and following; five were eventually tried for the disturbances. See Pieyre, op. cit., p. 224.

90. Huard, "La Préhistoire des partis," p. 197. In March 1848 the republicans began a newspaper, *Le Républicain du Gard.*

91. Ibid.

92. Ibid., pp. 88–89: "In the milieu of workers, social conscience is born obscurely." Flora Tristan remarked in contrast: "these unfortunate workers are of such ignorance that they know absolutely nothing, not about politics, not about anything. They read nothing, leading the lives of stupid beasts" (Flora Tristan, *Le Tour de France, Journal, 1843–1844*, vol. 2 [Paris, 1980], p. 112). Ledru-Rollin did well in the December presidential election in the first canton (24.4%, compared to 56.8% for Louis Napoleon and 17% for Cavaignac). A police informant claimed that Nîmois radicals had no real faith in socialism, but rather "had coarse revolutionary instincts. Their goal is to change the form of government; what they detest is the priest, the aristocrat, and by the latter they mean anyone they believe is above them by virtue of education or social position" (6M 303, cc October 30, 1850).

93. Huard, ibid., pp. 185–95, 432–35, 1192, 1199. Two shoemakers and two tailors were among the leaders, along with the bookseller Encontre. Huard notes protests by dyers against a longer workday and reduced wages in December 1849; a strike in May 1850 by glovemakers and stocking makers; and a protest by shoemakers against competition from inmates in the Maison Centrale. There had been little artisanal militance during the July Monarchy. Exceptions include a mobilization of tailors in May 1836 (BB18 1239, pg Nîmes, May 25, 1836); attempts by silk workers to force the manufacturers to duplicate raises given by some of their colleagues (400 to 500 workers met in a *guinguette*, the Près aux Clercs, in one of several meetings [BB18 1239, pg Nîmes, September 21ff]); a strike in April 1845 of bakers' workers (6M 288 cp April 20 and following, 1845) who met at the tour de l'Evêque, leading to 39 arrests and 15 convictions when troops broke up the meeting.

94. Huard et al., *Histoire de Nîmes,* p. 287.

95. BB30 333, *juge d'instruction,* April 11, 1848 (the person writing the alleged threat warned that he had "two thousand attack dogs; if I sic them on you, their teeth will tear out pieces of you"); BB30 382, pg Nîmes, January 3, 1849.

96. Fitzpatrick, op. cit., p. 152; Huard, "La Préhistoire des partis," pp. 154–55.

97. Fitzpatrick, op. cit., pp. 154–55; Huard et al., *Histoire de Nîmes,* p. 303. Adding to the tension was the struggle for control of the national guard, where a third of the officer posts were reserved for Protestants, and the municipal elections, in which the Orleanist system of district representation, intended to ensure representation of the Protestants, had been abandoned, which obviously favored the Catholics (Fitzpatrick, op. cit., pp. 155–57).

98. BB30 333, pg Nîmes, August 29, 1848. Legitimists continued to control the municipal council and the departmental general council.

99. 6M 303, cc September 14/15 and following, especially October 19 and 20, 1848. Encontre's club became indistinguishable from that of Martin Cadet, the café in which it met.

100. Raymond Huard, *Le Mouvement républicain en Bas-Languedoc, 1848–1881* (Paris, 1982), pp. 79–80; 6M 303, prefect, February 1, 1850; cc June 26 and July 2, 1850, cp n.d.

101. 6M 303, cp September 21/22, 1848, and following. There were several brawls between the workers of a Protestant cloth printer and those of his Catholic rival.

102. 6M 303, int. October 20, 1848; p.-v. of gendarmerie, October 19, 1848; 6M 304

reports on October 29 and 30, 1848. See also Huard, "La Préhistoire des partis," pp. 185–95, 215–16. A second banquet followed a week later, again outside of town, in a former hermitage, sponsored by the seven republican clubs: 136 tables were set; each seating 14 people who shared sausages, bread, and wine. The postbanquet procession was disbanded before it could reach the place de la Bouquerie (6M 303, cp November 6, and cc note, October 31, 1848). The prefect's account varies sharply from that of the *commissaire;* the former claimed that only 200 attended, and that there were no red caps or allusions to "1793," and only one red flag. On December 3 an electoral meeting in support of Ledru-Rollin of 300 to 600 workers "of all ranks and all professions" took place in the courtyard of a small faience factory on the chemin d'Arles.

103. Huard, "La Préhistoire des partis," p. 500. He notes that only 3 or 4 of the 36 legitimist candidates for the municipal council were workers, and that only by maintaining electoral sections could the legitimists be kept from controlling the municipality (Huard et al., *Histoire de Nîmes,* p. 314). Legitimists used the Café Guibal on the boulevard du Petit Cours as a headquarters; there about 400 royalists met in October 1850, to try to patch up their differences.

104. Huard et al., *Histoire de Nîmes,* p. 302, noting Associations of Redoute, Etoile, Laurier, Pigeonnier, and Immortelle; Fitzpatrick, op. cit., pp. 148–82. The legitimist newspapers were the *Gazette du Bas-Languedoc* and Lourdoueix's more militant *Etoile du Gard.* Fitzpatrick has described the division between intransigents and moderate royalists well into 1850; the former attempted to impose their candidates for the May 1849 elections on another electoral committee, marching down the boulevard des Carmes, before the mayor arrived to break up the show of force (6M 304, Mayor Eyrette, April 29, 1849). Among the legitimist intransigents was Barbresse, a poacher, condemned to death in the Drôme for the murder of a Protestant. He was living in the Catholic environs of Nîmes, protected as Quatre-Taillons had been before him (BB30 382, pg Nîmes, August 16, 1850).

105. Huard, *Le Mouvement républicain,* pp. 441–42, 1189; Huard et al., *Histoire de Nîmes,* pp. 302–3, 318. See also Fitzpatrick, op. cit., pp. 167ff.

106. 6M 304, cc May 14, 1849.

107. 6M 303, cc July 14/15 and October 20, 1850.

108. 6M 303, report to prefect, probably by a spy, February 15, 1850; June 9/10, 1851. On the Esplanade, an eighteen-year-old apprentice butcher "walked boldly through the crowd with a cravat of white silk with fleurs-de-lis and ornamented with the arms of France, capped by a crown, all surrounded by flags, wearing a garland of green laurels on a white background." He was arrested.

109. 6M 303, cc September 19/20, 1848.

110. Huard, "La Préhistoire des partis," pp. 235–39; "the Montagnard organization successfully utilized the forms of traditional sociability, inserting the militant in his daily life and leisure" (p. 459).

111. 6M 303, statutes, which were confiscated. The café was at the corner of the rues Neuve and Saint-Paul.

112. Huard, "La Préhistoire des partis," pp. 235–36, 276, 300–305, 325–53; "The *cercle* is a privileged place where indirect democracy takes place" (p. 1192). See also Huard, *Le Mouvement républicain,* p. 870.

113. In October 1851 police estimated that there were about 200 active Montagnards in the city, far fewer than those who considered themselves fervent legitimists (6M 303, cc October 30, 1851).

114. 6M 303, cc November 16/17, 1850. When Favart, the representative of the people, arrived in Nîmes in February 1850, 500 to 600 people had gathered there to hear him; most were workers.

115. 6M 303, decree of November 19, 1850; cc October 30, 1850, and January 3, 1851.

116. 6M 303, report of January 21–22, 1851.

117. BB30 391, pg Nîmes, February 3, 1851; 6M 303, cc July 26, 1851: list of 210 members, including 17 property owners, 6 taffeta makers, 6 stonecutters, 6 masons, 6 plasterers, 5 wholesale merchants, 4 employees, locksmiths, bakers, 3 merchants, cultivators, clerks, cabinetmakers, etc., including many in the Enclos Rey. In February 1851, of the more than 30 popular associations remaining in Nîmes, 20 were legitimist, 9 "mixed," 2 "radical republican," and none socialist.

118. 6M 303, cc February 23–24, 1851.

119. 6M 303, cc March 21–22 and n.d., 1851.

120. 6M 303, cc May 5–6, 1851.

121. BB30 382, pg Nîmes, August 29, 1851.

122. Huard et al., *Histoire de Nîmes*, p. 307.

123. Huard, "La Préhistoire des partis," pp. 553–61, 1183–85; 6M 303, cc October 30, 1850.

124. Leslie Page Moch, "Migrants to the City: Newcomers to Nîmes, France, at the Turn of the Century," (Ph.D. diss., University of Michigan, 1979), pp. 55–56. Moch notes that, in 1906 as in 1836, the hymn of the Enclos Rey was: *"Si Henry V vienne demain/ Ah, quelle fête/ Ah, quelle fête/ . . . Ah, quelle fête, mes enfants!"* (p. 56).

Chapter 7

1. A. D. Marne 33M 4, April 12, 1825; and "Etat des condamnés grâciés le 28 mai 1825 à Rheims par sa majesté Charles X."

2. G. Crouvezier, *La Vie d'une cité: Reims au cours des siècles* (Paris, 1970), p. 122; Georges Boussinesq and Gustave Laurent, *Histoire de Reims depuis les origines jusqu'à nos jours,* vol. 2, pp. 565, 577–78. Croutelle, a member of the municipal council, was accused of saying "that the wages of the workers could be reduced to 60 centimes a day . . . that a pound of potatoes is all they need . . . and that with 400 men from the garrison, he could ensure peace in the town"—accusations similar to those made against the wallpaper manufacturer Reveillon, whose factory was pillaged in the faubourg Saint-Antoine in Paris in April 1789. Croutelle subsequently sued the city for damages, winning 430,000 francs, by virtue of the law of 10 Vendémiaire, year IV, which made the commune responsible for such damages (194M 9, municipal council meeting, July 14, 1849).

3. C.-J.-Ch. Siret, *Précis historique du sacre de S. M. Charles X* (Reims, 1825). See Marc Bloch, *Les Rois thaumaturges* (Paris, 1924).

4. Crouvezier, op. cit., p. 73.

5. Lynn Avery Hunt, *Revolution and Urban Politics in Provincial France* (Stanford, 1978), pp. 141–43. The line between merchant-manufacturers, buying products turned out by homeworkers to whom they provide raw materials, and manufacturers per se is sometimes difficult to draw; in Reims, the implosion of work into the city and into factories marked the victory of the manufacturers.

6. BB18 1080, mj June 4, 1822.

7. Maurice Hollande, *Essai sur la topographie de Reims* (Reims, 1976), p. 23. See also Pierre Desportes, ed., *Histoire de Reims* (Toulouse, 1983), pp. 257–79.

8. F1c III Marne 9, mayor, September 18, 1821.

9. Crouvezier, op. cit., pp. 73–75; Desportes, op. cit., p. 294. The cross stood at a site known as the place de la Mission, to the right of the Monument aux Morts today.

10. Boussinesq and Laurent, op. cit., vol. 2, pp. 443–44. The worker was sent to prison for six months and fined 500 francs.

11. 47M 21.

12. Desportes, op. cit., p. 296. See also Boussinesq and Laurent, op. cit., pp. 462–73); P. A. Dérodé-Géruzez, *Observations sur les monuments et établissements publics de la ville de Reims* (Reims, 1827), p. 107.

13. Hunt, op. cit., p. x; Desportes, op. cit., pp. 267, 282, 292.

14. A. D. Marne, 51M 11, sp Reims, February 1, 1821; MR 1184, "Mémoire sur la reconnaissance de la route des Petites Loges à Reims," M. Lefebvre, 1828; Desportes, op. cit., pp. 289–90. The arrondissement of Reims had 11,584 hectares of vineyards in 1828, worth an average of 30 francs an acre, an amount that would be somewhat greater today; its ordinary red wines, far more of which were produced then than today, were consumed locally or sold in the North of France or in Belgium and Holland.

15. MR 1184, "Mémoire sur la reconnaissance de la route des Petites Loges à Reims." In 1820 the mayor noted that Reims imported most of its grain from the Soissonais, though enough rye was grown inside the limits of the commune that the city could survive for two months without additional grain supplies, if besieged (51M 11, January 20, 1821).

16. Boussinesq and Laurent, op. cit., vol. 2, p. 403, quoting P. A. Dérodé-Géruzez, op. cit.: The manufacturer "wanted to gather, as much as possible, under one vast roof, all of the objects necessary for the manufacture of a piece of cloth. He brought in weavers, shearers, preparers, and dyers."

17. William M. Reddy, *The Rise of Market Culture: The Textile Trade and French Society, 1750–1900* (New York, 1984), pp. 94–95; David M. Gordon, *Merchants and Capitalists: Industrialization and Provincial Politics in Mid-Nineteenth-Century* (University, Ala., 1985), p. 17.

18. 51M 11, prefect, February 1, 1821; Gordon, op. cit., pp. 17–18; Desportes, op. cit., pp. 297–98.

19. Gordon, op. cit., p. 17. One spinning mill employed 250 workers.

20. Boussinesq and Laurent, op. cit., vol. 2, p. 521. The Société Industrielle was founded as a *société en commandite* in December 1834 and took up the feasibility of mechanical looms in 1837, although the first mechanical looms had already been experimented with in 1835 in another factory.

21. Marc Vincent, "La Situation économique et la condition des travailleurs dans le département de la Marne," in *Le Département de la Marne et la Révolution de 1848, ed.*, Comité Départemental Marnais de Célébration du Centenaire de la Révolution de 1848 (Châlons-sur-Marne, 1948), pp. 92–93.

22. Boussinesq and Laurent, op. cit., vol. 2, pp. 516, 522–23.

23. Desportes, op. cit., p. 291.

24. Boussinesq and Laurent, op. cit., vol. 2, pp. 554–56. The northern branch of the canal, from Berry-au-Bac to Reims, was finished in 1848, the southern branch only in 1861.

25. These were quarters with a considerable transient population as well. See 82M 11, for example: complaints against innkeepers for keeping improper registers of guests or ignoring this police requirement completely, on the rue de Barbatre (May 3, 1822) and the rue Fléchambault (July 3, 1822).

26. 122M 22, census of 1841.

27. From the census of 1841 (122M 22): the impasse Chénia: 20 weavers among 26 textile workers of 30 heads of families; rue and cour des Quatre Chats Grignants: 19 textile workers among 27 heads of family; rue des Crénaux: 21 weavers; rue Perdue: 11 weavers, 1 comber, 1 spinner, and 2 day laborers among 22 heads of household; rue des Salines: 46 weavers, 5 combers, 5 spinners, 5 bobbin girls, and 5 day laborers among 84 heads of

household; rue Bailla: 10 weavers, 6 combers, 2 spinners, and 5 other textile workers among 31 heads of household; the rue and impasse Saint-Julien; 34 weavers, 11 combers, 4 winders, 4 wefters, and 3 seamstresses among 101 heads of household, with a single rentier of whatever means, 1 employee, and 1 clerk; the rue du Grand Cerf: 56 weavers; the rue de l'Esquerre: 10 spinners, 11 weavers, 6 day laborers, 5 combers, and 7 other textile workers among 55 heads of household; the rue Neuve: 53 weavers, 33 spinners, 24 day laborers, 15 combers, 16 threaders; the rue Saint-Jean Césaré: 31 weavers, 6 combers, 10 wefters among 84 heads of household; the rue Tournebonneaux: 46 weavers, 8 day laborers, and only 3 heads of household who were not textile workers; and the place Saint-Nicaise: 65 textile workers, including 42 weavers, among 93 heads of household.

28. 51M 11, prefect, January 20, 1821.

29. 72M, cp May 22 and sp May 23, 1822; and his letter, n.d., dictated to someone who knew French (but who spelled the city's name "Rainse").

30. 51M 11, January 20, 1821, "mairie de Rheims, rapport détaillé . . . sur l'administration publique de la ville de Rheims, pendant l'exercise de 1820."

31. Boussinesq and Laurent, op. cit., vol. 2, p. 533.

32. The money was raised by a charity drive and an annual ball, with another 9,000 francs from private donations.

33. 51M 11, sp February 1, 1821. In 1820 there were 374 children in Saint-Louis at the beginning of the year, and 414 at the end; of the 199 who entered that year, 36 had been placed in homes, including their own, and 123 had died.

34. 51M 11, sp February 1, 1821. Between 1780 and 1820, 5,547 foundlings were cared for by the institution of Saint-Louis. The subprefect noted, just four years before the coronation of Charles X in Reims, that *scrofuleux* were almost never cured: cures were only apparent, the disease reappearing after several years.

35. See also Boussinesq and Laurent, op. cit., vol. 2, pp. 534–35. The first, the Société d'Ouvriers Serruriers de Saint-Eloi, had been established in 1833. The association included seven mutual aid societies for woolens workers; associations for carpenters and saw-pit workers, shearers, shoemakers, and construction workers; and another for workers of various trades. Five were named after saints.

36. 72M 2–3. In 1832 the Bureau de Bienfaisance had spent 170,000 francs obtained from municipal council allocations, gifts, and charity balls on assistance—an average of almost 16 francs per indigent and 71 francs for the 250 workers assisted.

Year	Number of Indigents	Sums Allocated	Workers Assisted	Sums Allocated
1830	7,323	51,895	500	25,183
1832	9,591	152,285	250	17,826
1834	5,428	34,759	260	18,506
1836	4,800	15,758	450	20,236
1838	4,963	53,248	190	15,391

Source: 72M 2–3, report of mayor, n.d. [1840]

37. 81M 12, laws of August 16 and 24, 1790, decree of 5 Brumaire, year IX, and law of July 19 and 22, 1791.

38. 81M 12, sp October 3 and 31, 1826; cp 1st arrondissement, August 12, 1814, condemning the behavior of several prostitutes, including among others Fifette Huart, who insulted the gendarmerie; Nicolle Chammond *dite* la Bordeaux, whose *cris affreux* could be heard at the Hôtel-Dieu; and Marie-Jeanne Adam *dite* la Planche, condemned for theft.

39. 81M 12, sp October 2, 1845 (the ward held 30 beds); decree of November 12, 1837; 10U 634, cp December 20, 1826. A municipal decree followed on December 12, 1837.

40. 72M 2–3, reprint of mayor, n.d. [1840].

41. 72M 2–3, brochure published by the prefect, 1847.

42. 47M 21, excluding January and April, for which there are no records. In 1821 police citations averaged only 32.2 per month, peaking at 55 in August and 43 in September, with as few as 19 in May. There were 45, 31, and 50 police citations in January, March, and April 1829, 40 in April 1830, and 19 for August and a peak of 70 for September 1830, after the revolution.

43. 30M 14, report of sp July 28, 1825. In July 1830 there were 130 ex-convicts living among a population of over 30,000, most of whom had served time for very minor crimes, not necessarily in Reims. Rural areas may have been more subject to thefts because of the lack of policing and the vulnerability of property owners to petty extortion for fear of fire or violence.

44. BB18 1014, gendarmerie report, February 3, 1817. The writer and moralist Louis René Villermé blamed ''several Belgians and freed convicts'' for disorders (Boussinesq and Laurent, op. cit., vol. 2, p. 535).

45. Boussinesq and Laurent, op. cit., vol. 2, pp. 474–75.

46. In April 1825 eleven workers were arrested for resisting the guard, perhaps during a walkout or the incident at the time of the missions.

47. F7 6770, prefect, July 11 and August 10, 1827.

48. 30M 14, sp March 28, 1822, and April 8, 1826.

49. Boussinesq and Laurent, op. cit., vol. 2, p. 477. Mayor Ruinart de Brimont, though a wholesale merchant, represented ''the conservative landed element, royalist and even ultra royalist, of high society, relying—though himself descended from the ennobled bourgeoisie—on the old nobility and the clergy.''

50. Ibid.; BB18 1008, pg Paris, October 20, 1821; 30M 14, int. November 6, 1829, and prefect, May 13; sp March 28, June 19 and 28, and September 17, 1848; p.-v., October 30, 1822; ''liste des établissements''; Boussinesq and Laurent, op. cit., vol. 2, p. 482; Desportes, op. cit., p. 298. Jobert-Lucas had defeated François Ruinart in 1821 and had in turn been defeated in 1824.

51. 30M 14, sp, July 29; *conseiller de préfecture* Poisson, n.d., August 12 and following, 1830; Boussinesq and Laurent, op. cit., vol. 2, pp. 483–84, 496. Gordon, op. cit., p. 28, counts the most established woolens manufacturers, with wine producers, as among the losers in 1830 to ''an Orleanist manufacturing group supported by anticlerical workers.''

52. 30 M 14, Poisson, August 4, 1830; Boussinesq and Laurent, op. cit., vol. 2, p. 490. Allegations that the ''Jesuit party'' still dominated Reims reached the floor of the Chamber of Deputies. Said a placard of June 1832: ''The public is advised that Carlists with a certificate of liberalism can find a lucrative position in the administration.''

53. 30M 14, prefect, August 16, 18, and 19; sp August 19, and gendarmerie report, August 18, 1830; BB18 1186, pg Paris, August 19. Placards had, it was thought, ''convoked'' the crowds to the convent. Boussinesq and Laurent, op. cit., vol. 2, p. 496. Among those manufacturers ruined by the economic crisis was Jobert-Lucas, who, thus disgraced, resigned as deputy in December 1830.

54. Gordon, op. cit., pp. 15–17. In 1848 they constituted 41% of the wealthiest notables in the city, 28.6% of the ''enfranchised bourgeoisie as a whole,'' and 4.7% of those who paid 500 francs in taxes per year, and included two of the four paying over 1,000 francs. Gordon demonstrates that the woolens manufacturers preferred investment in their own businesses to the purchase of land.

55. Four years later, Léon Faucher succeeded Houzeau-Muiron as the deputy of "movement," though he was far—as his future activities would confirm—from republicanism (Gordon, op. cit., pp. 15, 29). In 1834 there still seemed to be more legitimists than republicans among the political elite.

56. Crouvezier, op. cit., p. 120; Desportes, op. cit., pp. 298–300. A succession of mayors followed Andrieux's resignation in 1832. As an example of the apathy, in 1836, only 14 of 36 councilmen appeared for a meeting. The following year, the minister of interior was unable to find anyone to serve as mayor to replace Saint-Marceaux who served between resignations from 1835 to 1845, despite being bitterly opposed by the legitimists (Boussinesq and Laurent, op. cit., vol. 2, p. 492). Perhaps the only municipal revolution in Reims was the replacement of relatively devoted local leaders loyal to the Restoration with a series of indifferent men interested in making money, and who were more easily tempted by the prestige of national political prominence.

57. Boussinesq and Laurent, op. cit., vol. 2, pp. 508–9.

58. Ibid., p. 499.

59. 30M 15, sp December 7, 1833.

60. Tailors too suffered, undercut by ready-made clothes, and cabinetmakers faced stiff competition and lower prices from Sainte-Ménéhould, as well as from Paris (13M 1, report of deputy mayor, December 29, 1847). Male spinners earned 2.50 francs a day in 1831, 3 in 1836–37, and 2 in 1847; female spinners' wages rose from 1.25 to 1.50 before falling to 1.10 over the same period. *Nouveauté* workers earned 4 francs in 1837, 2.25 in 1842, and 1.60 in 1847.

61. Boussinesq and Laurent, op. cit., vol. 2, p. 531.

62. C 958.

63. It loaned almost 275,700 francs in 1831, and 289,200 in 1832 (30M 15, prefect, November 15, 1832).

64. Boussinesq and Laurent, op. cit., vol. 2, pp. 527–28, 531. See Reddy, op. cit., pp. 180–82, 229–33, etc. Reddy principally objects to his conclusion that a market for labor existed. See also C 958, which counted 4,850 men, 4,900 women, and 1,150 children in the industry. Yet the *fabricants* agreed that only more mechanization, particularly the production of merinos, flannels, and neopolitans, could protect the industry from competition from Alsace and the Nord.

65. 30M 15, sp November 12, 1832.

66. 31X 1, sp Reims, October 17, 1853, the law being that of April 13, 1850. According to the subprefect, nothing had been done to fulfill the requirements of the law, although some improvement was noted in the quarter of Saint-Nicaise (sp Reims, October 4, 1850, and August 1, 1851). Early in the Empire, twenty small houses of two floors were to be built in the clos Saint-Remi and the faubourg de Cérès, but nothing ever came of the plan (sp October 26, 1852).

67. Boussinesq and Laurent, op. cit., vol. 2, p. 535.

68. F7 6781, prefect, April 24, 1834.

69. 194M 9, prefect, May 31 and following; sp June 4; BB18 1224, *procureur,* May 31 and June 3, 1834. The subprefect decided to send Belgian workers away, so that there would be fewer needy workers, and offered *secours de route* and a passport to all workers not from Reims, if they would leave. On this strike, see Reddy, op. cit., pp. 130–31, who notes that the fact that spinning mills had introduced "mules" that were mechanically powered, accounts for the term "mechanical spinning mills" in authorities' reports and in the workers' shouts as well. Reddy insists that the workers had, as yet, no sense of withholding their labor, and that the term "strike" is inappropriate to this movement.

70. Jean-Pierre Aguet, *Les Grèves sous la monarchie de juillet* (Geneva, 1954), p. 150.

71. 194M 9; Boussinesq and Laurent, op. cit., vol. 2, p. 496. The first manufacturer struck had apparently given in to his workers' demands during the first strike.

72. BB18 1296, pg Paris, August 29; 194M 9, reports of sp and gendarmerie, August 25 and following, int. September 5, and sp September 2 and November 16, 1834.

73. See Reddy, op cit., particularly his excellent chapter 9, pp. 253–88.

74. BB18 1375, *procureur*, December 13 and 15, 1838; Boussinesq and Laurent, op. cit., vol. 2, pp. 549–50; 51M 18, extract of charivari, December 24, 1838. The sermon described the suffering of the Pope at the hands of Napoleon. A brief, unsuccessful strike of fifty woolens workers in April 1837 followed a reduction in wages and was accompanied by threats of machine-breaking (194M 9, sp April 10 and following). Another strike in 1841 followed the workers' attempts to force a raise in wages (gendarmerie report, February 13, 1841).

75. Boussinesq and Laurent, op. cit., vol. 2, p. 516; 194M 9 (sp August, 16, 17, 21, int. September 11, 1840). Reddy, op. cit., p. 202, admits that the first of these strikes "was perhaps the earliest . . . that in every way satisfies the modern notion of a strike," and that the second was "the first of its kind in the records on textile laborers of the northern centers," because the workers "initiated the demand and then backed it up with a refusal to work (rather than responding to a mill owner's announcement of a cut)."

76. 194M 9, sp January 24, 1844. There had also been rumors of machine-breaking in 1837, and during a strike of spinners in 1841 that followed wage reductions.

77. 51M 21 sp March 5 and 6, 1847, and gendarmerie report, March 7, 1847.

78. Boussinesq and Laurent, op. cit., vol. 2, pp. 547. Cabet also presided over a banquet in the town where he had a good many supporters (p. 548): Christopher Johnson, *Utopian Communism in France: Cabet and the Icarians, 1839–1851* (Ithaca, N.Y., 1975). See 30M 15, cp Reims east, February 19, and 51M 21, sp February 23, 1847, on the crisis.

79. Gordon, op. cit., p. 37, notes that in 1843 seventeen mutual aid societies had "first joined together," led by a master weaver, and that in 1848 twenty-one such groups belonged to this loose association.

80. Boussinesq and Laurent, op. cit., vol. 2, p. 515, n. 3, quote Eugène Courmelle, a leading *quarante-huitard,* as saying that his "socialist conceptions" began with the visit by Victor Considérant to Reims. The worker-poet Jean-Louis Gonzalle indicated that the *communistes,* despite their influence on the workers of Reims, numbered no more than a hundred (ibid., p. 515).

81. See Gordon, op. cit., pp. 34–42, 47–53, and Boussinesq and Laurent, op. cit., vol. 2, pp. 617–88, on the politics of the Second Republic. Reddy, op. cit., writes: "Nowhere in 1848 did the working class seem more self-conscious, more well organized, or more successful than in Reims" in the wake of the February Revolution (p. 220).

82. The work of Maurice Agulhon on this subject remains fundamental, particularly *La République au village* (Paris, 1970) and *La Vie sociale en Provence intérieure au lendemain de la Révolution* (Paris, 1970).

83. "Genin" and "Armand Moret" in Jean Maitron, ed., *Dictionnaire biographique du mouvement ouvrier français,* vol. 1 (Paris, 1964); Boussinesq and Laurent, op. cit., vol. 2, pp. 606–7ff.

84. Boussinesq and Laurent, op. cit., vol. 2, pp. 565–66, 577–78, 583–84, 598–99, and 624; "Agathon Bressy" and "Théodore Courmeaux" in *Dictionnaire biographique,* op. cit.

85. 47M 22, cp south, November 23, 1849.

86. In April 1848, in the midst of a social fear compounded by the presence of several workers on the municipal council, the subprefect requested troops (194M 9, sp April 11, 1848). It would be interesting to know whether Belgian workers were included in the sense

of community within the *haute ville*. The first reflex of French workers in the Nord was to try to expel them after the February Revolution.

87. *Dictionnaire biographique,* op. cit., gives some sketchy information on Icarians like Caze, *musicien et ménestrel,* who harangued the crowd demanding the replacement of the municipality on February 26, 1848.

88. Bressy was born in Arpajon (Seine-et-Oise), outside Paris. A member of the Society for the Rights of Man (and possibly a correspondent of Marx's), after the February Revolution he served as a surgeon with the Garde Républicaine until May 16, when he was let go with the departure of Caussedière (30M 46, interrogation of Bressy, and "Agathon Bressy," *Dictionnaire biographique,* op. cit.). See also John M. Merriman, *The Agony of the Republic* (New Haven, 1978), pp. 70–77.

89. 47M 22, cp April 8, 1850. Description from 30M 46, testimony of J. B. Lefranc.

90. "Bressy," *Dictionnaire biographique,* op. cit.; 47M 22, cp April 8, 1850. The Montagnards certainly benefited as well from the unpopularity of the tax on drink (30M 16, mayor, October 11, 1849). Bressy lived on the rue Talleyrand just to the northwest of Reims's old center.

91. "Bressy," "Louis Lecamp," and "Courmeaux" in *Dictionnaire biographique,* op. cit. Théodore Eugène Courmeaux (1817–1902) was the son of a *vigneron* from the commune of Faverolles (canton of Ville-en-Tardenois).

92. 194M 9, gendarmerie report, November 11, 1850; BB30 383, pg Paris, February 6 and June 19, 1850; 47M 22, sp March 23, 1850.

93. Boussinesq and Laurent, op. cit., vol. 2, p. 642.

94. 47M 22, cp February 20, 1850; BB30 383, pg Paris, February 6, 1850; "Bressy," *Dictionnaire biographique,* op. cit. A banquet in 1850 commemorating the anniversary of the February Revolution moved to Pontfaverger after being banned in Reims.

95. 47M 22, cp east, October 31, 1849; "Jules Bienfait" in the *Dictionnaire biographique,* op. cit.

96. 47M 22, cp south, October 23 and November 23, 1849, and February 23, 1850; cp east, December 19, 1849, and January 16, 1850; cp January 16 and February 20, 1850; BB30 383, pg Paris, November 23, 1850. The strike followed in early December.

97. 47M 22, cp south, October 23, 1849, and January 8, 1850.

98. 47M 22, cp west, December 18, 1849; cp south, December 8, 1849, February 23 and March 23, 1850; cp east, January 16, 1850; cp March 23 and April 8, 1850; cc April 23, 1850; BB30 383, pg Paris, June 19, 1850; 82M 19, list of cafés. Given rich archival documentation to the contrary in the National Archives and the Departmental Archives of the Marne, it is difficult to see how Reddy, op. cit., could have come to the conclusion that "Reims authorities felt no anxiety about the actions that the Association sponsored" (p. 220).

99. 47M 22, cp March 2, 1850.

100. 47M 22, cp south and cp March 23, 1850.

101. 47M 22, cp January 1, 1850.

102. 40M 6, decree of April 26, and mayor, April 11, 1850.

103. BB30 383, pg Paris, June 19, 1850; 47M 22, sp east, January 20 and February 3, 1850.

104. 30M 46, interrogation of Bressy. BB30 383, pg Paris, February 15 and August 21, 1851. Bressy had also quarreled with his associate Lecamp. In 1850 Bressy and his friends began selling shares in the hope of launching the *Association de la Marne, journal des travailleurs.*

105. BB30 383, pg Paris, November 23, 1850. Wages fell further, as manufacturers combined to impose unified rates in the industry.

106. In November 1849, for example, even beggers were "happily not numerous"; there were "no crimes" (47M 22, cp November 1, 1849); the subprefect noted on March 8, 1850, that there were practically no crimes or misdemeanors in Reims.

107. BB30 382, pg Paris, August 21, 1851.

108. BB30 382, October 25, 1851. The *procureur général*'s unsubstantiated claim in a report of November 29 was that emissaries of secret societies, sent from Paris or Epernay, were active in the countryside.

109. Boussinesq and Laurent, op. cit., vol. 2, p. 667.

110. 30M 46. Lecamp been in Bressy's café, where it was decided to inform the municipal council that they would recognize only its authority.

111. 30M 46, interrogation of Bressy; testimony of Jean-Laurent Cap; Jules Courtois, a fifteen-year-old café waiter; Aline Waffland, Bressy's cleaning lady; Ferdinand Leflanc; and J. B. Louis Lefranc. Etienne Carquin, *charbonnier,* testified to a rumor that protesters would set fire to the scaffolding around the cathedral to "frighten the town."

112. Several emissaries had gone out to the surrounding communes, including Saint-Brice and Witry-les-Reims; a socialist sent by the faubourg de Cérès arrived in the latter (30M 46, testimony of Savin and Augustin Cellier, and of Jean-Nicolas Pierlot and Thierry Muiron of Witry-les-Reims). A *tisseur* living on the rue Saint-Nicaise claimed that no workers from the quarter were among the crowd of 300 *en blouse,* but rather "people from the lower town" who gathered on the square, but he contradicted himself by also saying that many were from the streets adjacent to the place Saint-Nicaise, especially the rues Saint-Jean Césare, du Réservoir, and des Cloîtres.

113. BB30 382, pg Paris, February 25, 1852.

114. Boussinesq and Laurent, op. cit., vol. 2, p. 670. Of 7,810 voting in the plebiscite, there were 1,398 votes of no, 195 left blank, 34 invalidated, and 4,136 abstentions (p. 676).

Chapter 8

1. A.D. Yvelines IV M1 18, prefect, Seine-et Oise, n.d. [1817]. An earlier and shorter version of this chapter appeared as "Le Maintien de l'ordre à la périphérie des villes (1815–1851)" in *Cahiers du Centre de recherches historiques* 2 (October 1988), 51–70.

2. Arlette Farge, "Un espace urbain obsédant: le commissaire et la rue à Paris au XVIIIᵉ siècle," *Les Révoltes logiques* 6 (1977), p. 11.

3. Ibid., p. 9. "One has to . . . disperse the populace, control these immoderate gestures of a violence that is only the mirror image of their own daily life . . . yet to prevent a crowd from forming is not sufficient. . . . One has to go further: make hygienic, cleanse [and] enlighten these obscure masses who represent the faubourgs. . . . There follows a determined volition to construct a productive and pacified space" (p. 17).

4. A.D. Yvelines 4M 2/128, sp Corbeil, September 19, 1816, citing "the large establishments employing many workers, the mills of the hospitals and the manufactures of M. Oberkampf."

5. 4M 2/128; 4M 1 18, subprefect of Corbeil, January 1, 1820, and first trimester reports of 1822, 1823, and 1824; 3M 1 18, subprefect, first trimester, 1826. Among his suggestions in the latter report for struggling against "debauchery" was an increase in the tax on billiard halls, "the plague of our countryside," where "young men go to be corrupted." He also advocated forcing women to announce their pregnancy, and banning unauthorized books in reading associations.

6. 4M 2/128, prefect of the Seine-et-Oise, January 1, 1835. The mayor had asked for a *commissariat* "both because of the increase in population and because of the nature of the people who form its base." The first policeman had served in the army and as a tax

employee in Essonnes and Corbeil for 17 years; in other words, he had perfect qualifications.

7. 4M 2/128, sp Corbeil, May 6, 1840, and municipal council meeting of February 10, 1840.

8. F7 9868, letter of the Marquis d'Alon, n.d.; A.D. Seine D. 0⁹ 8, census summary; MR 1291, "Mémoire sur la reconnaissance de la route de Neuilly à partir de l'arc de Triomphe jusqu'au pont de Neuilly" (1842).

9. D. 0⁹ 36, sp Sceaux, February 5, 1822; prefect of police, February 13, 1822.

10. D. 0⁹ 36, mayor of Vaugirard, May 4, 1820; MR 1292 (1842).

11. D. 0⁹ 36, cp Vaugirard, January 30, 1826. On August 25, 1825, the municipal council asked for the appointment of a *commissaire de police,* the commune's population having reached 6,526. It was in Vaugirard that, in 1832, two people who stopped in one of the many cabarets at about 2 P.M. near the *barrière* were accused of selling rotting or poisoned food (it was the time of the cholera). Both were "massacred," one by a band of Parisians, another apparently by residents, before the door of a policeman (mayor of Vaugirard, April 6, 1832).

12. D. 0⁹ 14, mayor, February 4, 1832.

13. D. 0⁹ 13, report, n.d.; decree, mayor of Bercy, June 9, 1841; Bercy added a *sergent de ville* in 1847.

14. 4M 2/128, petition, n.d. [1839]; Saint-Gratien municipal council deliberation of April 7, 1839. The former petition stated that, if a measure for "order" were necessary in the resort, the hamlet could be joined to Saint-Gratien, although the latter did not want a policeman either for the same reasons.

15. 4M 2/128, mayor of Deuil, n.d. [1843]. The new *commissaire* had jurisdiction over Saint-Gratien, Deuil, and Soisy.

16. 4M 2/128, mayor of Meudon, October 14, 1837, and May 16, 1838; municipal council, August 16, 1830; prefect of police, February 4, 1838; prefect, October 27, 1837. Sèvres, with approximately the same population, had earlier received a *commissariat* because of the frequent presence of the king.

17. 4M 2/128, subprefect, January 16, 1826.

18. A.D. Indre-et-Loire, 4M 71, cp September 7, 1824. In August 1825 a man was attacked in the commune of Saint-Etienne in the cabaret of Pipard, "a bad place, the continual site of scandalous scenes caused by prostitutes." Gendarmes had not drawn up a complaint (ibid., August 17, 1825).

19. 4M 71, cp April 16, May 11, August 14, 1825, and June 3, 1826; October 11, 1831, etc. Among the alleged *marginaux* was a carpenter who refused to join the *compagnonnage;* he left town in August 1825 after being confronted by François Danay, known as "Crushed Fox," who had a reputation for backing up his threats.

20. 4M 71, deputy mayor of La Riche, August 29, 1822.

21. In the year X, Tours had been divided into three arrondissements, center, north, and south, the latter two including the rural communes where "there are many rooming houses beyond these barriers, not far away, to which those who should be watched retreat every day" (note, *chef de bureau* of the prefecture, year X). But by the Restoration police authority was limited to Tours itself; 4M 2, *procureur,* April 19, 1832.

22. 4M 2, mayor of Tours, April 8; prefect, April 14, 16, 24, and 26; cp Cazeaux père, April 13, 1832.

23. 4M 2, mayor of Saint-Symphorien, April 28, and mayor of Saint-Cyr, May 5, 1832.

24. 4M 2, prefect, November 11, 1843, and February 28, June 20, and August 3, and mayor of Saint-Cyr, March 18, 1844. A decree of August 20, 1828, authorized that

proposals for the extension of police authority could be submitted to the *conseil d'état;* mayor of Saint-Cyr, March 18, 1844.

25. A.D. Saône-et-Loire M 109, prefect, December 6, 1838.

26. For an earlier perspective on this rivalry, see A.N. D IV bis.

27. M. 109, prefect, August 20, 1834. For example, when the butchers of Mâcon stocked only chicken in an 1840 protest, a woman, referred to as an idiot in the police report, shouted from an angry crowd of four hundred that the meat for sale was not fit "for the dogs of Saint-Laurent" (M 111, cp January 3, 1840).

28. D IV bis 16, "Résumé des observations faites par les députés du Mâconnais sur le chef-lieu de département"; "Mémoire"; and "Aperçu des motifs de réunion du fauxbourg St. Laurent à la ville de Mâcon."

29. A.D. Saône-et-Loire M 109, gendarmerie report, August 12; national guard report, August 11–13; prefect, August 20 and 31; mayor of Saint-Laurent, August 12; int. September 28; and municipal council of Mâcon, September 11, 1835.

30. A.D. Indre, M 3874 bis, prefect, March 17; municipal council, June 21; *procureur,* March 12, 1843.

31. A.D. Deux-Sèvres, 4M 4.1, mayor of Niort, March 26, 1823.

32. A.D. Vosges, 8 bis M 58, int. June 6, 1847.

33. A.D. Vendée, 1M 337, cp July 1847; mayor, February 2, 1845, and int. January 7, 1846; 2 of the 6 leading taxpayers in Bourg-sous-Bourbon (population 2,092 in 1847) lived in Bourbon-Vendée. In 1847 there were 7 brothels in Bourbon-Vendée, and at least 34 prostitutes.

34. Jean Legoy, *Le Peuple du Havre et son histoire* (n.p, n.d.), vol. 2:2, pp. 48, 50.

35. Legoy, op. cit., vol. 2:2, pp. 50–51, 54–55, 93, quoting Joseph Morlent, writing in 1825, on p. 50.

36. See the print "Le Roy sur le haut d'Ingouville," Musée du Vieux Havre.

37. Legoy, op. cit., vol. 2:2, pp. 48–49. A comparative table in the Musée du Vieux Havre notes that the port city had 460 people per hectare in 1723, and 600 in 1787, while Rouen had 350 and 401 for the same dates.

38. André Corvisier, ed., *Histoire du Havre et de l'estuaire de la Seine* (Toulouse, 1983), pp. 156–57.

39. Ibid., pp. 154–56; MR 1245 (1839); Legoy, op. cit., vol. 2:2, 183, 287, 289, 300, and 303. Legoy gives the surface of the basins as 13.54 hectares in 1815, 28.88 in 1845, and 63.53 in 1855.

40. Legoy, op. cit., vol. 2:2, p. 144, and description from the Musée du Vieux Havre.

Year	Le Havre	Le Havre/Ingouville/ Graville/Leure
1800	17,644	24,610
1815	16,231	21,204
1818	21,108	26,620
1828	24,562	29,235
1836	25,618	37,173
1841	27,154	43,065
1846	31,325	54,377
1851	28,954	56,126

Source: Jean Legoy, *Le Peuple du Havre et son histoire* (n.p., n.d.), vol. 2: 2, p. 84

41. *Perreys* are *"criques d'échouage . . . utilisés initialement en fonction de leurs conditions nautiques"* (Corvisier, op. cit., p. 19).

42. Jacob Venedeys, *Excursions in Normandy,* vol. 1 (London, 1842), p. 178 (Robert Herbert first called my attention to Venedeys's book.) After 1852 the old bourg and part of the coast remained the domain of *beau commerce;* Legoy, op. cit., vol. 2:2, p. 160. Legoy (p. 95) quotes Joseph Morlent writing in 1825: "Among the population of Ingouville are found many English. They live there as if they were in their own country."

43. Richard Cobb, *The Police and the People* (Oxford, 1970), p. 28, argues that "the police will endeavor to prove their own thesis about the origins, motivations, and leadership of a riot by the type of people they arrest. . . . One reason, in the eighteenth century, would be the desire to see their powers extended to include the anarchical communes on the fringe of Paris, le Havre, Rouen, Lyon and so on."

44. Corvisier, ed., op. cit., p. 10: "What a contrast indeed, when one looks at the hinterland of Le Havre!" Itself bounded by the Seine, "traditionally limited, the zone of influence of the town barely extends toward the Caux beyond the road from Fécamp to Lillebonne. . . . Le Havre for a long time had only an insignificant role as a point of attraction for the rural world." 55.8% of the population of Le Havre, Ingouville, Graville, and Leure in 1810 (a total of 24,610 inhabitants) were unmarried, reflecting the attraction of the port to a very geographically mobile population (Legoy, op. cit., vol. 2:2, p. 10).

45. Legoy, op. cit., vol. 2:2, p. 30; Corvisier, ed., op. cit., p. 138.

46. Legoy, op. cit., p. 139.

47. Venedeys, op. cit., pp. 159–62.

48. A.D. Seine-Maritime, 6M 28, census of 1841. Sanvic had a population of 2,810. Sainte-Adresse's population of 789 included proletarians living on the edge of Le Havre, Sainte-Adresse having 69 day laborers among its 208 households, as well as many fishermen and laundresses. Families of means, decidedly a minority in Ingouville, lived on the rue de Montvilliers and the Grande Rue. The rue d'Etretat, rue de la Mer, rue Traversière, the rue de Perrey along the sea, and the Chemin Militaire housed some of the proletarians whose presence gave Ingouville its reputation. At least 46 taverns and inns welcomed the thirsty to Ingouville in 1841.

49. 4M 3, jp, September 26, 1822, and n.d.; prefect, March 13 and May 15, 1823; sp April 5 and 10, 1823; sp September 18, 1818; gendarmerie report, April 8, 1822; jp February 22, 1822, proposing new communal limits to facilitate policing. 4M 116, sp n.d. [February 1822]: "It is a fact that prostitution has reached the point that one cannot even walk at night, and often during the day as well, without being beckoned or stopped by indecent approaches and suggestions, such that several property owners cannot rent their buildings because they are completely at the mercy of the houses that lodge prostitutes."

50. 4M 3, sp April 5, 1823. The agent, or *appariteur,* was paid 1,000 francs a year by the municipality of Ingouville; the population of Ingouville fell short of the 5,000 required for a police *commissariat,* but if the inhabitants of Sanvic, Graville, Leure, and Sainte-Adresse were added to that of Ingouville, the population was more than enough.

51. 4M 3, jp, n.d.; 4M 116, prefect (date obliterated, but probably February 12, 1822). Both the mayor and subprefect requested funds for a secret police.

52. 4M 3, jp, n.d., sp April 5, 1823, and December 1 and 15, and prefect, December 12, 1826.

53. 4M 117, subprefect, September 24, 1834.

54. 4M 3, prefect, March 13, 1823; sp April 5 and 10, and prefect, May 15, 1823. The general council and the arrondissement council both supported this request; see the latter's report from 1823 and int. September 17, 1823. It appears that the justice of the peace first requested the establishment of a *commissariat* in Ingouville on September 26, 1822.

55. 4M 116, jp February 22, 1822; 4M 3, sp April 5, 1823.

56. In March 1848 workers in Le Havre, Graville, and Ingouville petitioned the

authorities, complaining of competition from "foreign workers," by which they meant Germans and Alsatians. The wave of Breton migration to Le Havre did not begin until after 1850. In the legislative elections of April 1848, only 46% of the registered voters in Ingouville and Graville participated, in contrast to 82% in Le Havre.

57. 4M 3, commissioner of the Republic, April 26, 1848; "Projet d'organisation d'un Commissaire Général de Police," April 26, 1848, probably inspired by the bloody insurrection of Rouen and Elbeuf after the legislative elections.

58. Legoy, op. cit., vol. 2:2, p. 42.

59. 4M 3, sp November 14, 1850. But the workers opposed the lowering of the piece rate.

60. Ibid.; *Revue du Havre,* December 12, 1850, and sp December 12 and 14, 1850. There were then five *appariteurs* assisting the *commissaire* of Ingouville. Now there were public baths and *cafés-concerts* to watch as well. The previous year the jurisdiction of Ingouville had been extended to Sanvic and Sainte-Adresse.

61. A.D. Sarthe, M sup 389, 396.

62. A.D. Jura, M 121, prefect of Jura, March 24, October 3 and 11; mayor of Lons, February 25, 1851. The mayor of Montmorot had requested such a measure himself. Perrigny, 3 kilometers away, had 861 inhabitants; Macornay, 4 kilometers away, had 690; Montaigu, 3 kilometers, 783; Courbouzon, 3 kilometers, 425; and Montmorot, 2 kilometers, 1,946.

63. 4M 2/128, mayor of Argenteuil, April 9, and minister of general police, June 26, 1851. See also Paul Hayes Tucker, *Monet at Argenteuil* (New Haven, 1982).

64. 4M1 46, sp Corbeil, July 5, 1849, and n.d. [1850]. See Sanford Elwitt, *The Making of the Third Republic: Class and Politics in France, 1868–1884* (Baton Rouge, 1978).

65. Ted W. Margadant, *French Peasants in Revolt: The Insurrection of 1851* (Princeton, 1979).

66. 4M1 46, subprefect, July 17, 1849; 4M 2/128, prefect, January 8, 1849, and gendarmerie report, December 29, 1849.

67. 4M1 46, sp Corbeil, July 17, 1849. The subprefect of Pontoise reported on October 21, 1849, that there had been fires set in a number of communes in his district, including Valmondois and Frouville; 4M 2/128, prefect of the Seine-et-Oise, January 3, 1850, asking also for secret police to be used to obtain information from convicts in jail.

68. 4M1 46, gendarmerie report, November 30, 1851; 4M 2/128, int. correspondence, January 14, 1851, and sp Corbeil, February 14, 1850. Thus on November 27, 1851, a gathering of about fifteen socialists of Corbeil and Essonnes drew police attention.

69. 4M1 46, sp Pontoise, October 31, 1849.

70. 4M1 46, sp Pontoise, April 14, 1851, and prefect of the Seine-et-Oise, June 3, 1851.

71. 4M1 46, sp Pontoise, May 6, 1850.

72. 4M1 46, jp Sèvres, October 29, 1851.

73. 4M1 46, sp Pontoise, November 30; mayor of Maisons-sur-Seine, December 1; and cp Meudon, December 1, 1851.

74. A.G. D3 127, military report, August 15, 1829, and E5 1, commander of 15th military division, August 14–16, 1830. See John M. Merriman, "The 'Demoiselles' of the Ariège, 1829–31," in Merriman, ed., *1830 in France* (New York, 1975).

75. 4M3, municipal council, November 7, 1839, and February 10 and 18, 1840.

76. John M. Merriman, *The Agony of the Republic* (New Haven, 1978), pp. 13–20.

77. André Vant, *Imagerie et urbanisation: recherches sur l'exemple stéphanois* (Saint-Etienne, 1981), pp. 73–77, quoting "Observations pour les quatres communes de Beaubrun, Valbenoîte, Outre-Furan et Montaud sur l'exposé des motifs du projet de loi portant la

suppression de ces quatres communes et leur réunion à la ville de Saint-Etienne.'' In 1829 the municipality resisted a plan to place a permanent garrison in Saint-Etienne, claiming that the fear of riots or even insurrections ''does not exist in Saint-Etienne, where the mass of the population is peaceful and hard-working.'' Saint-Etienne requested a further extension of its territory in 1827 and again in 1832.

78. Ibid., p. 77. The concern for social control in Saint-Etienne of course dated back to the ancien régime. Ted Margadant called to my attention its merchants' complaint that the royal judges at the *bailliage* court of Montbrison were ignoring the needs of Saint-Etienne.

79. Ibid., p. 92.

80. A.D. Rhône 4M 2–3. La Guillotière received a second *commissaire* in 1841, a third in 1848 (mayor, October 3, 1851). It had asked to remain independent of Lyon.

81. See ''L'Organisation de la police du département du Rhône de l'an viii à 1940,'' in *Répertoire numérique de la sous-série 4M,* A.D. Rhône. From the Hundred Days to January 16, 1822, policing in the Lyon region was placed under the direction of a *lieutenant de police;* his authority, however, was limited to Lyon and its faubourgs. With authority over the *haute police* (concerned with politics and conspiracy) and the municipal police, he remained under the command of the prefect.

82. Ibid., *conseiller d'état* in charge of police, first arrondissement, November 22, 1813. The municipality had apparently several times already requested the absorption of the surrounding communes.

83. A.D. Rhône, 4M 1, deputy mayor of Lyon, September 3, 1813; mayor of La Guillotière, September 17, 1813, indignantly pointing out that the mayor of Lyon had no administrative authority over the police of his commune.

84. Ibid., mayor of Lyon, May 9, 1815.

85. Ibid.

86. Ibid., secretary of state for the department of general police, December 20, 1817.

87. Ibid., letter of the lieutenant of police, July 12 and 27, 1820. There had been 88 *procès-verbaux* since July 1 in La Guillotière, but they were for false weights, insulting the police, and, in one case, emptying a latrine while the anniversary of the execution of Louis XVI was being solemnly observed.

88. Ibid., prefect of the Isère, August 29, 1820. See chapter 3.

89. ''L'Organisation de la police,'' op. cit. The number of *commissaires* for the suburbs did, however, increase with their population. There were two for La Guillotière in 1841, and a third added in 1848 (4M 3, mayor of La Guillotière, October 3, 1851). In 1851 there were twenty-two commissaires serving in the Lyon region, including two each in the Croix-Rousse and Caluire, and one in Oullins, Sainte-Foy, and so on, and one charged with ''l'exploration de la banlieue et des communes limitrophes des départements de Ain et Isère,'' by virtue of the state of siege (4M 3, law of June 19, 1851). In 1852 Villeurbanne, Bron, Vénissieux and Vaux-en-Velin, which had been in the Isère were added to the Rhône.

90. André Latreille, *Histoire de Lyon et du lyonnais* (Toulouse, 1975), p. 317. Twice before, the municipality of Lyon had, in contrast to the Napoleonic period, opposed such a measure; this time it had no choice.

91. See Margadant, op. cit., passim.

Conclusion

1. On Haussmann, see the thoughtful, nuanced analysis of Maurice Agulhon et al., *Histoire de la France urbaine,* vol. 4, *La Ville de l'âge industriel* (Paris, 1983).

2. Cited by T. J. Clark, *The Painting of Modern Life: Paris in the Art of Manet and His Followers* (New York, 1985), p. 39. See also David H. Pinkney, *Napoleon III and the*

Rebuilding of Paris (Princeton, 1958), and Anthony Sutcliffe, *The Autumn of Central Paris* (London, 1970). Clark writes (p. 40) that "Napoleon [III] intervened directly in 1857 to prevent the encirclement of the Faubourg Saint-Antoine from being spoiled by a mere architect's whim: 'the construction of arcades on the Boulevard Mazas,' he wrote, 'would seriously damage the strategic system of Paris.' The arcades were quietly dropped from the designs."

3. David Harvey, *Consciousness and the Urban Experience: Studies in the History and Theory of Capitalist Urbanization* (Baltimore, 1985); T. J. Clark, op. cit., p. 54. Clark quotes a character from Victorien Sardou's *Maison neuve* (1866): "I applaud [Haussman-nization] heartily—and beg leave to think it fortunate that God himself was ignorant of this marvelous municipal system, and did not choose to arrange the trees in the forest in rows . . . with all the stars above in two straight lines" (p. 42). He also quotes *Paris Guide,* vol. 2 (1867): "The straight line has killed the picturesque, the unexpected. The Rue de Rivoli is a symbol; a new street, long, wide, cold, frequented by men as well dressed, affected, and cold as the street itself."

4. Alain Dalotel, Alain Faure, and Jean-Claude Freiermuth, *Aux origines de la Commune: le mouvement des réunions publiques à Paris, 1868–1870* (Paris, 1980), especially pp. 54–144; "La réunion quitta les beaux quartiers pour les faubourgs" (p. 55).

5. Clark, op. cit., p. 53.

6. Marilyn R. Brown, *Gypsies and Other Bohemians: The Myth of the Artist in Nineteenth-Century France* (Ann Arbor, Mich., 1985), p. 96.

7. Michel Foucault, *Madness and Civilization* (New York, 1965). See Brown, op. cit., p. 37.

8. Henry Leyret, *En plein faubourg, moeurs ouvrières* (Paris, 1895), pp. 219–29.

9. Particularly the *descente de la Courtille,* which began at the *guinguette* that Favié purchased; an illustration of this festive occasion can be found in Jacques Hillairet, ed., *Dictionaire historique des rues de Paris,* 7th ed. (Paris, n.d.), vol. 1, p. 173.

10. Hillairet, ed., op. cit., notes only that it became a *palais du travail* and then a concert hall in 1910. The Salle Favié is mentioned by Dalotel, Faure, and Freiermuth, op. cit., pp. 49 and 67.

BIBLIOGRAPHY

Primary Sources

National Archives

Series BB18:

946,	1136–37,	1212,	1247,	1368,
992,	1161,	1214,	1254,	1375,
1008,	1181,	1217,	1262,	1386,
1014,	1183,	1220,	1292,	1399,
1038,	1186–88,	1224,	1296,	1451,
1048,	1193,	1228,	1319–20,	1454,
1080,	1204,	1237,	1322–23,	1474
1097–98,	1206,	1239,	1335–36,	
1103–4,	1211,	1241,	1356–57,	

Series BB30:

217, 333, 359–60, 362, 364, 373, 379–80, 382–83, 385, 391, 402

C 945, 953–58, 960, 962–64, 967B, 968

DIV bis 14, 16, 18

F1a 438

F1bII Pyrénées-Orientales 3, 4

F1c III Gard 5, 7, 13

F1c III Marne 6, 9

F1c III Pyrénées-Orientales 5

F1c III Vendée 5 and 8

F2II Eure-et-Loire 3

F2II Pyrénées-Orientales 2

F2II Vendée 3

F3II Pyrénées-Orientales 5

F3II Vendée 3, 5, 8

F7

6696, 6701, 6767–72, 6779–82, 9527–28, 9640, 9658, 9691–92, 9710, 9874

F19

341, 481(1–3), 354, 654, 731(A), 933(B), 5683, 5696, 5734, 5742, 5747

F21 428

Departmental Archives

Ain:
8M 10 bis; 10M 4

Hautes-Alpes:
4M 19, 157–59

Aube:
M 1180, 185, 1257 bis, 1259

Aude:
5M 24

Calvados:
M 2847–49, 2852

Charente:
M 642–43, 735

Côtes-du-Nord
1M unclassified; 1M 326

Drôme:
M 1558

295

Eure:
4M 76

Eure-et-Loire:
4M 183

Gard:
I 34 + (Archives municipales), 4M 47–
48, 77, 6M 227, 243, 264, 273, 288,
301, 303–5, 309

Hérault:
39M 80, 86–87, 90, 110, 115M 32(1)

Indre:
1M 117; 4M 21

Indre-et-Loire:
4M 2, 6, 7, 71–72, 134, 136, 342–43

Jura:
M 12

Landes:
1M 39

Loir-et-Cher:
1M 79, 91; 4M 466

Loire:
10M 21, 30–31, 8M 27, 10M 21, 20M
10, 21M 20, 92M 2, 94M 1

Haute-Loire:
5M 43, 58, 61–65

Loire-Atlantique:
1M 504

Lot:
1M 200, 4M 15, 6M 30

Maine-et-Loire:
31M 15

Marne:
4M 6–8; 30M 13–17, 46, 86; 31M 5;
33M 4; 39M 1; 47M 21–22; 51M 11,
18, 21; 72M 2–3; 81M 1, 12; 82M
11, 19; 87M 4; 122M 22; 194M 9;
195M 1; 31X 1

Haute-Marne:
61M 14–16, 63M 3, 69M 4

Meuse:
71M 9–12

Nord:
201/1–3

Puy-de-Dôme:
M 090, 098, 0269

Hautes-Pyrénées:
1M 212

Pyrénées-Orientales:
Mnc 820/4, 858/1, 858/2, 872/1, 872/3,
Mnc 2506, M 2525
2M1 31/1; 2M5 20; 3M1 26–27, 34/4,
36–37, 47–51, 54, 56–57, 59, 61, 70–
76, 81–82, 4M unclassified
4R 210, 212
U 191, 195, 3434, 3448–55
IV 7, 2V 5, 10, 15–17, 62, 4V 35, 5V 6
1025 W 143–44

Bas-Rhin:
3M 47–52, 348, 944

Rhône:
4M 1–3

Haute-Saône:
14M 10, 35M 2

Saône-et-Loire:
M 108–9, 111, 115–16, 131

Sarthe:
M sup 389, 396

Seine:
0 9 8, 13, 14, 36

Seine-Maritime:
4M 1, 3, 116–17, 162, 180, 6M 28

Deux-Sèvres:
4M 4.1, 5.5, 6.6, 6.7

Vendée:
1M 394, 142, 337, 371–73, 395, 402–3,
424, 426–29, 528; 3M 25, 37, 43; 4M
23–24, 112, 127, 142, 390–91, 6M
298–99

Vienne:
M4 27, 35–43, 56–60; 8M 3/69

Vosges:
8 bis M 58

Yvelines:
4M 1 18, 46; 4M 2/128

Municipal Archives

Narbonne:
Census of 1820

Perpignan:
I1, 33–34, 52–53, 55, 118, 119, 135
Censuses of 1820 and 1846
Deliberations of the municipal council

Archives of the War Ministry

D3 127

E5 1–4

Series MR (*Reconnaissances militaires*):

1165–69,	1208–9,	1237–39,	1252,	1282,
1176–77,	1217–20,	1243,	1260–61,	1287–94,
1184,	1222–24,	1243 bis,	1266,	1298,
1186–88,	1226,	1245,	1269,	1300,
1201–3,	1233–35,	1249–50,	1272–74,	1302–4

Secondary Sources

Aguet, J.-P. *Les Grèves sous la monarchie de juillet*. Geneva, 1954.

Agulhon, Maurice. *Une ville ouvrière au temps du socialisme utopique: Toulon de 1815 à 1851*. Paris, 1971.

———, ed. *Histoire de Toulon*. Toulouse, 1976.

Aminzade, Ronald. *Class, Politics, and Early Industrial Capitalism: A Study of Mid-Nineteenth-Century Toulouse, France*. Albany, 1981.

Aragon, Henry. *Les Monuments et les rues de Perpignan*. Perpignan, 1928.

———. *Perpignan et la Cerdagne en 1822 d'après A. Thiers*. Perpignan, 1921.

———. *La Vie civile et militaire de Perpignan sous le général de Castellane*. Perpignan, 1926.

Ayçoberry, Pierre. "Au-delà des ramparts: 'vrais colonais' et banlieusards au milieu du XIX siècle." *Le Mouvement social* 118 (January–March 1982).

Bailly, Antoine S. "L'Emergence du concept de marginalité: sa pertinence géographique." In André Vant, ed., *Marginalité sociale, marginalité spatiale*. Paris, 1976.

Balland, Robert. "Les Goguettes rurales autour de Paris au milieu du XIXe siècle." *Ethnologie française* 12:3 (1982), 47–60.

Balledent, F. "Une mascarade anti-cléricale à Perpignan en 1827." In *Bulletin de la Société agricole, scientifique et littéraire des Pyrénées-Orientales* 91 (1983), 51–64.

Barante, Baron Prosper de. *Notice sur la ville de La Roche-sur-Yon*. La Roche-sur-Yon, 1954.

Baratier, Edouard, ed. *Histoire de Marseille*. Toulouse, 1973.

Bastié, Jean. *La Croissance de la banlieue parisienne*. Paris, 1964.

Benjamin, Walter. *Charles Baudelaire: A Lyric Poet in the Era of High Capitalism*. London, 1973.

Berlindis, Eliette, Maryse Boudet, and M. Rose Coromina. "Contribution à l'étude démographique, économique, et sociale—la ville de Narbonne de 1851 à 1871." Unpublished paper, 1975.

Bernadac, Yannick. "Perpignan, fin 1795–99." Mémoire de maîtrise d'histoire, University of Montpellier, 1975.

Bernard, Réjean. "Croissance d'une commune suburbaine de Paris: le cas de La Villette, première moitié du XIXᵉ siècle." Paper presented to the Western Society for the Study of French History, Las Cruces, N. Mex., November 1987.

Bezucha, Robert. *The Lyon Insurrection of 1834.* Cambridge, Mass., 1974.

Biget, Jean-Louis, ed. *Histoire d'Albi.* Toulouse, 1983.

Blanchard, Raoul. *Grenoble: étude de géographie urbaine.* Grenoble, 1911.

Bois, Paul, ed. *Histoire de Nantes.* Toulouse, 1977.

Bordes, Maurice, ed. *Histoire d'Auch et du pays d'Auch.* Roanne, n.d.

Bourderon, Roger, and Pierre de Peretti, eds. *Histoire de Saint-Denis.* Toulouse, 1988.

Boussinesq, Georges, and Gustave Laurent. *Histoire de Reims depuis les origines jusqu'à nos jours,* vol. 1 and 2. Reims, 1933.

Brennan, Thomas. *Public Drinking and Popular Culture in Eighteenth-Century Paris.* Princeton, 1988.

Brown, Marilyn R. *Gypsies and Other Bohemians: The Myth of the Artist in Nineteenth-Century France.* Ann Arbor, Mich. 1985.

Brunet, Jean-Paul. *La Ville rouge, Saint-Denis.* Paris, 1980.

Brunet, Michel. *Une société contre l'état, 1780–1820.* Toulouse, n.d. [1986].

Cabantous, Alain. *Histoire de Dunkerque.* Toulouse, 1983.

Calmette, J., and P. Vidal. *Histoire du Roussillon.* Paris, 1975.

Canini, Gérard. "Verdun sous la monarchie constitutionnelle: aspects économiques et sociaux." In *Verdun: la société verdunoise du XIIIᵉ au XIXᵉ siècle.* Nancy, 1975.

Carbonnell, Charles-Olivier. "Les Députés des Pyrénées-Orientales de 1815 à 1870," *Cerca* 13–14 (1961).

Castells, Manuel, "Structures sociales et processus d'urbanisation." *Annales E.S.C.* 25 (1970), 1155–99.

Chabot, Georges. *Les Villes.* Paris, 1978.

Chartier, Roger, "Les Elites et les gueux: quelques représentations (XVIᵉ–XVIIᵉ siècles)." *Revue d'histoire moderne et contemporaine* 21 (July–September 1974), 376–88.

———. "La 'Monarchie d'Argot' entre le mythe et l'histoire." In Bernard Vincent, ed. *Les Marginaux et les exclus dans l'histoire.* Paris, 1979.

Chatelard, Claude. *Crime et criminalité dans l'arrondissement de Saint-Etienne au XIXᵉᵐᵉ siècle.* Saint-Etienne, 1981.

Chauvet, Horace. *Histoire du parti républicain dans les Pyrénées-Orientales.* Perpignan, 1909.

Chedeville, André, ed. *Histoire de Chartres et du pays chartrain.* Toulouse, 1983.

Chemioux, H. *Oraison funèbre du vieux Poitiers.* Poitiers, 1861.

Chevalier, Louis. *La Formation de la population parisienne au XIXᵉ siècle.* Paris, 1950.

———. *Laboring Classes and Dangerous Classes in Paris during the First Half of the Nineteenth Century.* London, 1973.

Cholvy, Gérard. "Indifférence religieuse et anti-cléricalisme à Narbonne et en Narbonnais au XIXᵉ siècle." *Narbonne, archéologie, histoire* 43 (1973), 73–93.

Chomel, Vital, ed. *Histoire de Grenoble.* Toulouse, 1976.

Clark, T. J. *The Painting of Modern Life: Paris in the Art of Manet and His Followers.* New York, 1985.

Cobb, Richard. *Paris and Its Provinces.* London, 1975.

———. *The Police and the People.* London, 1970.

———. *Promenades.* Oxford, 1980.

Congar, Pierre, Jean Lecaillon, and Jacques Rousseau. *Sedan et le pays sedanais*. Paris, 1969.

Constant-Taillard. *Guide résumé du voyageur aux environs de Paris*. Paris, 1826.

Corret, A. *Histoire de Belfort et de ses environs*. Belfort, 1855.

Corvisier, André. *Histoire du Havre et de l'estuaire de la Seine*. Toulouse, 1983.

Cosson, Armand. "Industrie de la soie et population ouvrière à Nîmes de 1815 à 1848." In Gérard Cholvy, ed., *Economie et société en Languedoc-Roussillon de 1789 à nos jours*. Montpellier, 1978.

Coulon, J. B. *Epoques saumuroises*. Marseilles, 1977.

Crouvezier, G. *La Vie d'une cité: Reims au cours des siècles*. Paris, 1970.

Dalotel, Alain, Alain Faure, and Jean-Claude Freiermuth. *Aux origines de la Commune: le mouvement des réunions publiques à Paris, 1868–1870*. Paris, 1980.

Dash, La Comtesse (Anne-Latrelle de Cisterne de Coutiras de Poullöüe de Saint-Mars). *Mémoires des autres*. Vol. 1, *Souvenirs anecdotiques sur le Premier Empire et les Cent Jours*. Vol. 2, *Souvenirs anecdotiques sur la Restauration*. Paris, 1896.

Daumas, Maurice, Jacques Payen et al. *Evolution de la géographie industrielle de Paris et sa proche banlieue aux XIXᵉ siècle*. 2 vols. Paris, 1976.

Deloncle, Joseph, ed. *La Procession de la Sanch*. Perpignan, 1984.

Demangeon, Albert. *Paris, la ville et sa banlieue*. Paris, 1938.

Depaux, Jacques, "Pauvres, pauvres mendiants, mendiants valides ou vagabonds? Les hésitations de la Législation Royale." *Revue d'histoire moderne et contemporaine* 21 (July–September 1974), 401–18.

Dérodé-Géruzez, P. A. *Observations sur les monuments et établissements publics de la ville de Reims*. Reims, 1827.

Desert, Gabriel, ed. *Histoire de Caen*. Toulouse, 1981.

Desportes, Pierre, ed. *Histoire de Reims*. Toulouse, 1983.

Devilliers, Christian, and Bernard Huet. *Le Creusot: naissance et développement d'une ville industrielle, 1782–1914*. Seyssel, n.d.

Dornic, François, ed. *Histoire du Mans*. Toulouse, 1975.

Douglas, Mary. *Purity and Danger: An Analysis of Concepts of Pollution and Taboo*. London and Henley, 1966.

Dugrand, Raymond. *Villes et campagnes en Bas-Languedoc*. Paris, 1963.

Dupeux, Georges. *Aspects de l'histoire sociale et politique du Loir-et-Cher, 1848–1914*. Paris, 1962.

Durliat, Marcel. *Histoire du Roussillon*. Paris, 1962.

Edwards, Stewart. *The Paris Commune of 1871*. New York, 1971.

Enjalbert, Henri, ed. *Histoire de Rodez*. Toulouse, 1981.

[L.R.] "En marge de l'histoire (La Roche-sur-Yon/Napoléon-Vendée/Bourbon-Vendée)." *Société d'émulation de la Vendée*, 1924.

Farge, Arlette. "L'Espace parisien au XVIIIᵉ siècle d'après les ordonnances de police." *Ethnologie française* 2 (1982).

———. "Un espace urbain obsédant: le commissaire et la rue à Paris au XVIIIᵉ siècle." *Les Révoltes logiques* 6 (1977).

———. "Le Mendiant, un marginal? (Les Résistances aux archers de l'hôpital dans le Paris du XVIIIᵉ siècle)." In Bernard Vincent, ed., *Les Marginaux et les exclus dans l'histoire*. Paris, 1979.

Faucheux, Marcel. *L'Enfance difficile de la Roche-sur-Yon (1804–54)*. La Roche-sur-Yon, 1954.

Faure, Alain. "Classe malpropre, classe dangereuse? Quelques remarques à propos des

chiffonniers parisiens au XIXᵉ siècle et de leurs cités.'' In Lion Murard and Patrick
    Zylberman, *L'Haleine des faubourgs.* Fontenay-sous-Bois, 1978.
Faure, Petrus. *Histoire du mouvement ouvrier dans le département de la Loire.* Saint-
    Etienne, 1956.
Favreau, Robert, ed. *Histoire de Poitiers.* Toulouse, 1985.
Fitzpatrick, Brian. *Catholic Royalism in the Department of the Gard, 1814–1852.*
    Cambridge, 1983.
Fouquet, Henri. *Histoire civile, politique et commerciale de Rouen,* vol. 1. Rouen, 1876.
Fourcaut, Annie. *Bobigny, banlieue rouge.* Paris, 1986.
Fournial, Etienne, ed. *Saint-Etienne: histoire de la ville et de ses habitants.* Roanne, 1977.
Frémont, Armand. "Marginalité et espace vécu." In *Identités collectives et travail social.*
    Toulouse, 1979.
Friedmann, Georges, ed. *Villes et campagnes: civilisation urbaine et civilisation rurale en
    France.* Paris, 1953.
Frossard, Emilien. *Evénémens de Nîmes depuis le 27 juillet jusqu'au 2 septembre 1830.*
    Nîmes, 1830.
———. *Tableau pittoresque, scientifique et moral de Nîmes et de ses environs.* Paris,
    1846.
Gabory, Emile. *Napoléon et la Vendée.* Paris, 1914.
Gagnière, Sylvain, and Jacky Granier, eds. *Histoire d'Avignon.* Aix-en-Provence, 1979.
Gaillard, Jeanne. "Assistance et urbanisme dans le Paris du Second Empire." In Lion
    Murard and Patrick Zylberman, *L'Haleine des faubourgs.* Fontenay-sous-Bois,
    1978.
———. *Paris, la ville, 1852–70.* Paris, 1979.
Garrioch, David. *Community and Neighborhood in Paris, 1740–90.* New York, 1986.
Gauchat, Roger. "L'Urbanisme dans les villes anciennes: les faubourgs de Dijon."
    Mémoires de la Commission des Antiquités du département de la Côte-d'or 23
    (1947–53), 280–343.
Gavignaud, Geneviève. *Propriétaires-viticulteurs en Roussillon.* 2 vols. Paris, 1983.
———. "Le Rapport foncier villes-campagnes en Roussillon au début du XIXᵉ siècle—le
    cas de Perpignan." *Société languedocienne de géographie,* July–December 1982.
Gay, Peter. *The Bourgeois Experience.* 2 vols. New York, 1984, 1986.
George, Pierre. *Précis de géographie urbaine.* Paris, 1969.
Geremek, Bronislaw. "Criminalité, vagabondage, paupérisme: la marginalité à l'aube des
    temps modernes." *Revue d'histoire moderne et contemporaine* 21 (July–September
    1974), 337–75.
———. *Les Marginaux parisiens aux XIVᵉ et XVᵉ siècles.* Paris, 1976.
German, Dr. Paul. *Histoire de Falaise.* Alençon, 1966.
Girardot, Alain, ed. *Histoire de Verdun.* Toulouse, 1982.
Gordon, David M. *Merchants and Capitalists: Industrialization and Provincial Politics in
    Mid-Nineteenth-Century France.* University, Ala., 1985.
Gough, Austin, "The Conflict in Politics: Bishop Pie's Campaign against the Nineteenth
    Century." In Theodore Zeldin, ed., *Conflicts in French Society: Anticlericalism,
    Education and Morals in the Nineteenth Century.* London, 1970.
Gras, Pierre, ed. *Histoire de Dijon.* Toulouse, 1981.
Grau, Laurent. "Le Milieu de la notabilité politique dans les Pyrénées-Orientales sous la
    monarchie de juillet (1830–1848). In *Le Roussillon dans la première moitié du
    XIXᵉ.* Perpignan, 1985.
Guilaine, Jean, and Daniel Fabre. *Histoire de Carcassonne.* Toulouse, 1984.

Harvey, David. *Consciousness and the Urban Experience: Studies in the History and Theory of Capitalist Urbanization.* Baltimore, 1985.

———. *The Urbanization of Capital: Studies in the History and Theory of Capitalist Urbanization.* Baltimore, 1985.

Henry, D. M. J. *Le Guide en Roussillon ou itinéraire du voyageur dans le département des Pyrénées-Orientales.* Perpignan, 1842.

Hérault, Alfred. *Souvenirs, 1837–1870.* Châtellerault, 1971.

Herbert, Robert. *Impressionism: Art, Leisure and Parisian Society.* London, 1988.

Histoire de Saint-Martin-ès-Vignes, quartier et paroisse de Troyes. Troyes, 1936.

Hollande, Maurice. *Essai sur la topographie de Reims.* Reims, 1976.

Huard, Raymond, et al. *Histoire de Nîmes.* Aix-en-Provence, 1982.

———. *Le Mouvement républicain en Bas-Languedoc, 1848–1881.* Paris, 1982.

———. "La Préhistoire des partis: le parti républicain et l'opinion républicaine dans le Gard de 1848 à 1881." 5 vols. Unpublished thesis, University of Paris IV, 1977.

Hubert, Jean. *Histoire de Charleville.* Marseilles, 1977.

Hunt, Lynn Avery. *Revolution and Urban Politics in Provincial France: Troyes and Reims, 1786–1790.* Stanford, 1978.

Hugo, Abel. *France pittoresque. Département des Pyrénées-Orientales.* Paris, 1833.

Jacquemet, Gérard, "Belleville aux XIXᵉ et XXᵉ siècles: une méthode d'analyse de la croissance urbaine à Paris." *Annales E.S.C.* 30 (1975), 819–43.

Jalabert, F. *Géographie du département des Pyrénées-Orientales.* Perpignan, 1819.

Jolibois, Emile. *Histoire de Chaumont.* Chaumont, 1856.

Kaplan, Steven. "Les Corporations, les 'faux ouvriers' et le faubourg Saint-Antoine au XVIIIᵉ siècle." *Annales E.S.C.* 43:2 (March–April 1988), 353–78.

Latreille, André. *Histoire de Lyon et du Lyonnais.* Toulouse, 1975.

Lavedan, Pierre. *Histoire de l'urbanisme (Epoque contemporaine).* Paris, 1952.

Lebrun, François, ed. *Histoire d'Angers.* Toulouse, 1975.

Lees, Andrew. *Cities Perceived: Urban Society in European and American Thought, 1820–1940.* Manchester, 1985.

Legoy, Jean. *Le Peuple du Havre et son histoire.* 2 vols. N.p., n.d.

Lequin, Yves. *Les Ouvriers de la région lyonnaise.* 2 vols. Lyon, n.d. [1977].

Lescadieu, Alfred, and Auguste Laurant. *Histoire de Nantes.* Nantes, 1836.

Levainville, Jacques. *Rouen: étude d'une agglomération urbaine.* Paris, 1913.

Lewis, Gwynne. *The Second Vendée: The Continuity of Counter-revolution in the Department of the Gard, 1789–1815.* Oxford, 1978.

Leyret, Henry. *En plein faubourg, moeurs ouvrières.* Paris, 1895.

Ligou, Daniel, ed. *Histoire de Montauban.* Toulouse, 1984.

Livet, Georges, ed. *Histoire de Colmar.* Toulouse, 1983.

Longat, Pierre, Jean Lecaillon, and Jacques Rousseau. *Sedan et le pays sedanais.* Paris, 1969.

MacPhee [*sic*], Peter. "Les Semailles de la république dans les Pyrénées-Orientales (1830–1851): François Arago, semeur . . . ou moissonneur?" *François Arago: actes du Colloque National des 20, 21 & 22 octobre 1986,* University of Perpignan, pp. 201–13.

McPhee, Peter. "A Case-Study of Internal Colonization: The *Francisation* of Northern Catalonia." *Review* 3:3 (Winter 1980).

———. "On Rural Politics in Nineteenth-Century France: The Example of Rodès, 1789–1851." *Comparative Studies in Society and History* 23:2 (April, 1981).

————. "Popular Culture, Symbolism and Rural Radicalism in Nineteenth-Century France." *The Journal of Peasant Studies* 5:2 (January 1978), 238–53.

————. "The Seed-Time of the Republic: Society and Politics in the Pyrénées-Orientales, 1846–1852." Ph.D. diss., University of Melbourne, 1977.

————. "The Seed-Time of the Republic: Society and Politics in the Pyrénées-Orientales, 1848–51." *Australian Journal of Politics and History* 22:2 (August 1976).

————. "Social Change and Political Conflict in Mediterranean France: Canet in the Nineteenth Century." *French Historical Studies* 12:1 (Spring 1981).

Manry, A. G. *Histoire de Clermont-Ferrand.* Clermont-Ferrand, 1975.

Margadant, Ted W. *French Peasants in Revolt: The Insurrection of 1851.* Princeton, 1979.

————. *Urban Rivalries during the French Revolution.* Princeton, 1992.

Martourey, Albert. "Formation et gestion d'une agglomération industrielle au XIXᵉ siècle: Saint-Etienne de 1815 à 1870." *Bulletin du Centre d'histoire économique et sociale de la région lyonnaise,* 1985.

Masnou, Paul. *Le Département des Pyrénées-Orientales pendant les cent jours.* Perpignan, 1899.

Mérimée, Prosper. *Notes d'un voyage dans le midi de la France.* Paris, 1835.

Merriman, John M. *The Agony of the Republic: The Repression of the Left in Revolutionary France, 1848–51.* New Haven, 1978.

————. "Le Maintien de l'ordre à la périphérie des villes (1815–1851)." *Cahiers du Centre de recherches historiques* 2 (October 1988), 51–70.

————. *The Red City: Limoges and the French Nineteenth Century.* New York, 1985.

————, ed. *French Cities in the Nineteenth Century.* London, 1981.

Meyer, Jean, ed. *Histoire de Rennes.* Toulouse, 1972.

Meyering, Anne. "Industrialization and Population Change in Montluçon, 1815–1870." Ph.D. diss., University of Michigan, 1979.

Michaud, Jacques, and André Cabanis. *Histoire de Narbonne.* Toulouse, 1981.

Morandière, Charles de la. *Histoire de Granville.* Paris, 1966.

Mumford, Lewis. *The City in History.* New York, 1961.

Murard, Lion, and Patrick Zylberman. *Le Petit Travailleur infatigable ou le prolétaire régénéré.* Fontenay-sous-Bois, 1976.

Neaudre, Jacky. "Les Débuts de l'aménagement urbain de Saint-Etienne (1820–1871)." *Etudes foréziennes* 4 (1971).

Nisard, D. *Nîmes.* Paris, 1835.

Perrot, Michelle, "Dans la France de la Belle Epoque: les 'Apaches,' premières bandes de jeunes." In Bernard Vincent et al., *Les Marginaux et les exclus daus l'histoire* (Paris, 1979).

————. "On the Formation of the French Working Class." In Ira Katznelson and Aristide R. Zolberg, *Working-Class Formation: Nineteenth-Century Patterns in Western Europe and the United States.* Princeton, 1986.

Pierrard, Pierre. *Lille et les Lillois.* Paris, 1967.

Pieyre, Adolphe. *Histoire de la ville de Nîmes.* Nîmes, 1886.

Pinkney, David H. "The Crowd in the French Revolution of 1830." *American Historical Review* 70:1 (October 1964), 1–17.

————. *Napoleon III and the Rebuilding of Paris.* Princeton, 1958.

Pufferey, E., ed. *Histoire de Dole.* Marseille, 1977.

Rancière, Jacques. *La Nuit des prolétaires.* Paris, 1981.

Recherches clermontoises. Vol. 4, *Clermont sous le Second Empire.* Clermont-Ferrand, 1972.

Rochefort, Renée. "La Marginalité de l'extérieur et de l'intérieur." In André Vant, ed., *Marginalité sociale, marginalité spatiale*. Paris, 1986.

Rosset, Philippe. "L'Agitation anticléricale dans le diocèse de Perpignan au début de la Monarchie de Juillet." *Revue historique*, July–September 1982.

Rougerie, Jacques. *Paris libre 1871*. Paris, 1971.

Rouillard, Dominique. *Le Site balnéaire*. Liège, 1984.

Rouleau, Bernard. *Villages et faubourgs de l'ancien Paris*. Paris, 1985.

Rudé, George. *The Crowd in the French Revolution*. New York, 1959.

Sahlins, Peter. "Between France and Spain: Territory and Identity in a Pyrenean Valley, 1659–1868." Ph.D. diss. Princeton University, 1987.

———. *Boundaries: The Making of France and Spain in the Pyrenees*. Berkeley, 1989.

Schnetzler, Jacques. "Saint-Etienne et ses problèmes urbains." In *La Vie urbaine dans le département de la Loire et ses abords*. Saint-Etienne, 1969.

Shils, Edward. *Center and Periphery: Essays in Microsociology*. Chicago, 1975.

Siau, A. "Rapport sur l'industrie maraîchère des les Pyrénées-Orientales." *Bulletin de la Société agricole, littéraire et scientifique des Pyrénées-Orientales*, 1855.

Siret, S.-J.-Ch. *Précis historique du sacre de S. M. Charles X*. Reims, 1825.

Taveneaux, René, ed. *Histoire de Nancy*. Toulouse, 1978.

Teisseyre-Sallmann, Line. "Urbanisme et société: l'exemple de Nîmes aux XVIIe et XVIIIe siècles." *Annales E.S.C* 35:5 (September–October 1980), 965–80.

Tilly, Charles, "The Chaos of the Living City." In Tilly, ed., *An Urban World*. Boston, 1974.

———. "Charivaris, Repertoires and Urban Politics." In John M. Merriman, ed., *French Cities in the Nineteenth Century*. London, 1982.

———. "The People of June, 1848." In Roger Price, ed., *Revolution and Reaction: 1848 and the Second French Republic*. London, 1975.

Torreilles, Philippe. *Perpignan pendant la Révolution*. 3 vols. Perpignan, 1896–97.

[Tortat, Antoine]. *Extraits des mémoires d'Antoine Tortat, 1775–1847*. Paris, 1911.

Tourneur-Among, J. *Les onze villes superposées de Poitiers*. Poitiers, 1925.

Trenard, Jean, ed. *Histoire de Cambrai*. Lille, n.d.

Tucker Paul Hayes. *Monet at Argenteuil*. New Haven, 1982.

Turner, Victor. *Dramas, Fields, and Metaphors: Symbolic Action in Human Society*. Ithaca, N.Y., 1974.

———. *The Ritual Process*. Ithaca, N.Y., 1969.

Vant, André. *Imagerie et urbanisation: recherches sur l'exemple stéphanois*. Saint-Etienne, 1981.

———. "Géographie sociale et marginalité." In Vant, ed., *Marginalité sociale, marginalité spatiale*. Paris, 1986.

Venedeys, Jacob. *Excursions in Normandy*, vol. 1. London, 1842.

Vigouroux, Michel. "Quelques aspects de la croissance de Perpignan." *Société languedocienne de géographie* 6:2 (April–June 1972), 179–97.

Villermé, Prosper-Réné. *Tableau de l'état physique et moral des ouvriers employés dans les manufactures de coton, de laine et de soie*. 2 vols. Paris, 1840.

Vincensini, Claude-Paul. "Une société urbaine: la paroisse Saint-Jean à Perpignan au XVIIIème siècle." Mémoire de maîtrise, Paul Valéry University, Montpellier, 1974.

Vincent, Bernard, ed. *Les Marginaux et les exclus dans l'histoire*. Paris, 1979.

Vincent, Marc. "La Situation économique et la condition des travailleurs dans le département de la Marne." In *Le Département de la Marne et la Révolution de 1848*. Ed.

Comité Départemental Marnais de Célébration du Centenaire de la Révolution de 1848. Chalons-sur-Marne, 1948.

Vovelle, Michel. *Ville et campagne au 18ᵉ siècle (Chartres et la Beauce)*. Paris, 1980.

Weber, Eugen. *Peasants into Frenchmen: The Modernization of Rural France, 1870–1914*. Stanford, 1978.

Wirtz-Daviau, Bernadette. "La Statue de Napoléon I à La Roche-sur-Yon et son sculpteur, le comte de Nieuwerkerke." *Société d'émulation de la Vendée, Annuaire*, 1954.

Wolfe Philippe. *Histoire de Perpignan*. Toulouse, 1985.

———. *Histoire de Toulouse*. Toulouse, 1958.

Index